The Marriage Plot

STANFORD STUDIES IN JEWISH HISTORY AND CULTURE

Edited by David Biale and Sarah Abrevaya Stein

The Marriage Plot

OR, HOW JEWS FELL
IN LOVE WITH LOVE,
AND WITH LITERATURE

Naomi Seidman

STANFORD UNIVERSITY PRESS
STANFORD, CALIFORNIA

Stanford University Press
Stanford, California

Printed in the United States of America on acid-free, archival-quality paper

Library of Congress Cataloging-in-Publication Data

Names: Seidman, Naomi, author.
Title: The marriage plot : or, how Jews fell in love with love, and with literature
  / Naomi Seidman.
Other titles: Stanford studies in Jewish history and culture.
Description: Stanford, California : Stanford University Press, 2016. |
  Series: Stanford studies in Jewish history and culture | Includes
  bibliographical references and index.
Identifiers: LCCN 2015043515 (print) | LCCN 2015044293 (ebook) |
  ISBN 9780804798433 (cloth : alk. paper) | ISBN 9780804799676 (pbk. : alk. paper) |
  ISBN 9780804799621 (e-book)
Subjects: LCSH: Jewish literature—19th century—History and criticism. |
  Jewish literature—20th century—History and criticism. | Jewish marriage
  customs and rites—History. | Marriage customs and rites in literature. |
  Love in literature. | Sex in literature.
Classification: LCC PN842 .S45 2016 (print) | LCC PN842 (ebook) |
  DDC 809/.88924—dc23
LC record available at http://lccn.loc.gov/2015043515

Typeset by Bruce Lundquist in 11/14 Adobe Garamond Pro

Contents

Acknowledgments

I explore the intersection between pedigree and fiction, lineage and writing in Chapter 3; but a solitary signature on an academic book is also a kind of fiction, more so in this case than most. This book shifted in its configuration and even its authorship over the many years of its writing and has multiple origins and lines of descent. One way it began is through a 2006 grant from the Posen Foundation to develop a course on secular Jewish culture, "Secularization and Sexuality in Haskalah Literature," that was certainly a major impetus for this book. I thank Felix Posen and the foundation for that encouragement and the students from the Graduate Theological Union (GTU) and University of California, Berkeley (UCB), who taught me so much in various iterations of that class. A 2009 conference on "Sex and the Shtetl" emerged from that course (ChaeRan Freeze generously allowed us to steal that title and gave a riveting talk). Zehavit Stern brought a Yiddish film series and live performance to Berkeley for the occasion, making this the best conference any of us had ever experienced.

If it were not already clear that this book has multiple "parents," at one point it was a collaborative project: A Hadassah-Brandeis Institute grant in 2007 supported Zehavit Stern and me as we began research for the book, and Zehavit's fingerprints (that is to say, her academic rigor, broad knowledge, and intellectual creativity) are throughout the finished product. While our work together did not outlive Zehavit's graduation, our friendship did, and I was grateful to be invited last year to deliver the David Patterson lecture at Oxford University, "Tevye's Dream," and even more so, to spend time with Zehavit, her partner, Riki Ophir (another brilliant graduate of the Joint Doctoral Program at GTU and UCB), and their sweet family.

In 2008–9, I spent a sabbatical year working on the book with the generous support of an American Council of Learned Societies sabbatical grant.

Shaina Hammerman and I were awarded a Newhall Research Grant from the GTU in 2012 to work on the "aunt-niece" relationship within the fiction of Grace Paley. The resulting essay, published in *Prooftexts* in 2012, is now the third section of Chapter 5; I thank *Prooftexts* for the permission to republish and Shaina Hammerman for being my coauthor, friend, and, if not quite "niece," so much more.

Several other parts of the book have already appeared in earlier versions. A section of the Introduction first appeared in *The Routledge Handbook of Contemporary Jewish Cultures*, edited by Laurence Roth and Nadia Valman (Routledge); a different section was part of an article that was published in a special issue on Jewish performance, edited by Jill Dolan and Stacy Wolf, of *TDR* (*The Drama Review*). A section of Chapter 2 first appeared in *Queer Studies and the Jewish Question*, edited by Daniel Boyarin, Daniel Itzkovitz, and Ann Pellegrini (Columbia University Press). A section of Chapter 6 appeared in an earlier version in *The Passionate Torah: Sex and Judaism*, edited by Danya Ruttenberg (New York University Press), and *Keep Your Wives Away from Them: Orthodox Women, Unorthodox Desires*, edited by Miryam Kabakov (North Atlantic). Another section of that chapter appeared in a special issue of *Journal of Jewish Identities* dedicated to Chana Kronfeld and "The Berkeley School of Jewish Literature," edited by David Shneer and Robert Adler-Peckerar; a third section appeared in *Sholem Asch Reconsidered*, edited by Nanette Stahl (Beinecke Rare Book and Manuscript Library). A final section of Chapter 6 appeared in *The Shtetl: New Evaluations*, edited by Steven T. Katz (New York University Press). A section of the Afterword was part of my review of Josh Lambert's *Unclean Lips: Obscenity, Jews, and American Culture* for the *Chronicle of Higher Education: Review*; another section appeared in *Dibur Literary Journal*, in the special issue edited by Vered Karti Shemtov, Anat Weisman, and Amir Eshel. I thank these editors, journals, and presses for permission to reprint this work.

Many other lines and relationships extend from these pages: Ken Frieden and I spent two years in weekly SKYPE havruta, and these deadlines, along with his generous and astute comments, helped bring this book into the light of day. Rachel Biale and Marcia Freedman were my writing buddies for many years, heard much of the book spoken aloud, and shared their insights about how to improve it. The two years Yahil Zaban spent in Berkeley, during which he regularly fed me Haskalah sources, brilliant insights, and delicious food, were much too short. Alan Mintz, whose fascinating work on Hebrew autobiography first got me hooked on Haskalah writing, read an early draft and said such nice things that they shot me to the finish line. Zohar Weiman-Kelman, whom I trust with my life, read through a draft in the last few months, saving me from some embarrassing blunders.

Invitations from Dartmouth College, Brandeis University, Carleton College, and Stanford University to lecture on the subject of secularization and sexuality were other jumping-off points of this book, and dear colleagues at these institutions—Susannah Heschel at Dartmouth; ChaeRan Freeze and Sylvia Fuks Fried at Brandeis; Shana Sippy at Carleton; Charlotte Fonrobert, Ari Kelman, Gabriella Safran, Vered Shemtov, and Steven Zipperstein at Stanford—make the academic world feel like home. My 2013 semester as the Shoshana Shier Visiting Professor at the University of Toronto gave me time to write and introduced me to such new friends and intellectual partners as Doris Bergen, Sol Goldberg, Jeffrey Kopstein, Andrea Most, Ato Quayson, and Karen Weisman, and an excellent research assistant, Noam Sienna. My office neighbor, writing buddy, and instant best friend, Anna Shternshis, who was working on a project about love and work among Soviet Jews, warmed my months in Toronto even as fall turned to winter. In Berkeley, it gives me particular pleasure that my first Hebrew and Yiddish teachers are now longtime colleagues and dear friends: Robert Alter, Bluma Goldstein, and Chana Kronfeld. I have been blessed with more exceptional students than I can count or name and other colleagues and friends, whose support I treasure and generosity and brilliance I rely on: Eliyahu Arnon, Daniel Boyarin, Nathaniel Deutsch, Ofer Dynes, Rena Fischer, Michael Gluzman, Erich Gruen, Paul Hamburg, Susannah Heschel, Laura Levitt, Anita Norich, Mantra Plonsey, Miryam Sas, Jeffrey Shandler, Eleanor Shapiro, Susan Shapiro, Vered Shemtov, Dina Stein, and Anat Weisman. On Holy Hill, I have the best colleague anyone can ask for, the amazing Deena Aranoff. At the GTU, along with Deena, Arthur Holder, Munir Jiwa, Christopher Moreland, and Shana Penn always have my back.

The comments of the anonymous readers of the manuscript for Stanford University Press filled in some gaps in my work; Kate Wahl at the press came up with the title in the eleventh hour (replacing my much drier, more academic one); Friederike Sundaram, Cynthia Lindlof, and Anne Fuzellier Jain ably prepared the manuscript for publication. David Biale, co-editor with Sarah Abrevaya Stein of the series in which this book appears, is the person who opened my eyes to the subject of "Eros and Enlightenment," who always tells it to me like it is, and whose unflagging support I regularly lean on. My sister-in-law Sara Brown created a writing colony in her Seattle home one summer just for me, and my father-in-law, Ernest Schott, plunged into Yiddish literature to see where I was spending my time. My mother, Sara Seidman, stuck by me with ferocious love through my own secularization; the solidity of our bond and my own love for and gratitude to her owe everything to her patience, openness, and generosity.

It has not escaped me that the acknowledgment page is perhaps the last refuge for the conventional and sentimental rhetoric of marriage and that even the overthrow of these conventions is by now itself conventional. But surely it must mean something good that my twenty-odd (some of them very odd) years with the estimable John Schott have produced not one but two books with the word *marriage* in the title (not to mention the recording he made with his band "Dream Kitchen"). The life we made together now includes not only our dear son, Ezra, but also two housemates who are much more than that, Krash (a.k.a. Scott Novins) and Driftwood (a.k.a. David Laskin). If modern marriage is in many regards a disaster, we have nevertheless managed to build something rather wonderful in the ruins. It is to John that I dedicate this book.

The Marriage Plot

Introduction

Plotting Jewish Marriage

> A long chain of equivalences links all the lovers in the world. In the theory of literature, "projection" (of the reader into the character) no longer has any currency: yet it is the appropriate tonality of imaginative readings: reading a love story, it is scarcely adequate to say I project myself; I cling to the image of the lover, shut up with his image in the very enclosure of the book (everyone knows that such stories are read in a state of secession, of retirement, of voluptuous absence: in the toilet).
>
> —Roland Barthes, *A Lover's Discourse: Fragments*

> Falling in love with love is falling for make believe.
> Falling in love with love is playing the fool.
>
> —Richard Rogers and Lorenz Hart, *The Boys from Syracuse*

Eastern European Jews seem to have fallen in love with love not gradually but suddenly, "virtually overnight."[1] The moment, fortunately for us, was captured by a few acute observers. For Pauline Wengeroff, the dramatic and traumatic transformation between traditional marriage and modern love came between her sister Eva's 1848 engagement and her own engagement in 1849:

> I was fifteen years old when my sister, who was two years older than I, was betrothed. Yes, she was betrothed and not (as girls today call it) got engaged herself. Our parents and those of the bridegroom dealt with each other through the marriage broker, the *shadkhen*, and agreed how much dowry,

clothing, and jewelry from both sides of the marriage party was to be given. My sister did not see the face of her bridegroom, her life's companion, at all, and she was not able to satisfy herself about whether she would be able to love him, and whether he suited her fancy and met the ideals that a girl privately formed about her intended.[2]

Alive to the subtle as well as broadest workings of modernization, Wengeroff makes a fine distinction in this description between her sister *becoming* betrothed (*sie wurde verlobt*) and her sister and the bridegroom *getting* engaged (*sie haben sich verlobt*). For all the similarity between these German phrases, they express a world of difference: in the first instance, the bride is the passive object of a betrothal arranged for her by others; in the second, the young people are the active agents of mutual betrothal. Indeed, Eva's engagement was entirely the doing of her parents and the groom's parents. Despite her tearful attempts to persuade her mother to allow her to meet the young man in question, Eva was not permitted to lay eyes on him until the very hour of the wedding. Eva was nervous and unhappy in the weeks before her wedding, but Wengeroff assures us that most such marriages "contracted in the old way" turned out well and "such a marriage my sister also was allotted by dear God." Wengeroff ends her detailed description of Eva's wedding by looking ahead to her own very different experience: "Only this sister was still engaged and married in the manner described here. My engagement, two years later, already had a different character. Indeed, the reform under the regime of Nicholas I had powerfully affected the Jewish way of life."[3]

In comparison with her older sister, in 1849 the sixteen-year-old Pauline was permitted to meet the young man her parents had chosen for her, and Wengeroff implies that the betrothal was contingent on the young people finding each other appealing. After initial discussions with a marriage broker, the two extended families met in a town midway between their homes to become acquainted and hammer out the terms of the betrothal; while the older people negotiated the financial arrangements,

> little by little, the younger people withdrew to the neighboring room. My intended followed also and finally my sister Kathy invited me to follow the others. Here, etiquette was set aside. We sat down freely next to one another, I, of course, near my bridegroom. Scarcely had we sat for a moment near one another when the room emptied—everyone left in order to leave the two of us undisturbed. This behavior irritated me so much that I was unable to utter a word, and kept silent, embarrassed. But then my intended began to speak.

Trembling from emotion, he spoke to me of his feelings, of love, of loyalty, of undying happiness. Far more than his words, his eyes spoke.[4]

Pauline's engagement, unlike her sister's, thus commenced with both a financial agreement and an emotional coming-to-terms. Wengeroff ascribes the differences between her engagement and her sister's to the political climate of the period, which was influenced by "the reform under the government of Nicholas I."[5] But these liberalizing political reforms are in the background of the memoir: the sections of the memoir that intervene between the descriptions of the two engagements are more directly taken up with the intellectual and cultural changes in her immediate environment, in particular with the effect of the nascent Russian Haskalah (Jewish Enlightenment) on her two brothers-in-law (including Eva's new husband): these "intellectually curious" young men were eager for knowledge, members of the elite of the city of Brest, "where the circle of the enlightened was already quite large."[6] As Wengeroff describes this fervid atmosphere, the young people in Brest could finally dare to study "alien books" (*fremden Bücher*). They organized meetings to read German classics, scientific works, and, in particular, the ancient Greeks. "Gradually they even admitted women to these meetings."[7]

Wengeroff also relates in this chapter that she spent her precious final years of formal education in a private girls' school where she was introduced to Russian and German literature. She had always been a great reader, enjoying Yiddish tales in her childhood, but now she turned to *Robinson Crusoe* (probably in German translation), the Swiss-German reformer and author Heinrich Zschokke, and especially Friedrich Schiller, "whose poetry blew like a breath of spring into the depressed, dark atmosphere of the ghetto." In those days, Wengeroff writes, many Hebrew translations appeared by Jewish writers, "who all tried their hand at Schiller."[8]

Wengeroff's memories of the dramatic events of 1848 and 1849—the moment, it could be said, when Jews fell in love with love—can serve to introduce the two intertwined themes of this book: the secularization and modernization of Jewish marriage and the role of literature in that transformation. In the two years that separated the engagements of sisters, the marriage practices in one Russian Jewish family were significantly and fatefully transformed; with the waves of modernization that washed over traditional Jewish societies, such experiences and their variants were repeated throughout Jewish Eastern Europe. What interests me in this book is the literary dimension of Jewish modernization. That new reading habits propelled transformations in marriage practices is evident from Wengeroff's narration, which places in a single chapter ("Meine Verlobung," or "My Engagement") the twin topics of changes in literary taste and in romantic practices; the memoirs are otherwise careful to separate disparate themes under distinct headings. For Wengeroff, as for many others, these two phenomena are clearly part of the same sea change in Jewish society.

Wengeroff does not explain how alien books led to new romantic ideas, perhaps because this process seems obvious to her. Nevertheless, the relationship between reading and the modernization of Jewish marriage is a complex and multivalent phenomenon. Reading alien books may in fact not have caused the shift (although so it seemed to many) as much as signaled a more general openness to "alien practices," including those that governed the making of a marriage. But literature itself also created new social practices, including the mingling of men and women; unlike Talmud study, which occurred in entirely male spaces, European literature seemed to invite the innovations instituted in the circles of the young men of Brest. These undoubtedly imitated situations found within this literature, just as nineteenth-century Talmud study mimicked the largely male discourse recorded on the pages under discussion. As Wengeroff also points out, the study of modern literature by young men with traditional upbringings inevitably led to syncretic cultural practices, in which Schiller was parsed for shades of meaning in Talmudic singsong within a collective oral environment native to traditional rabbinic text study and foreign to the private reading practices of European modernity.

The pedagogical workings of literature may also explain the ability of a young man—at first meeting his irritated and speechless prospective bride—to find ready poetic expression for his hopes regarding "Liebe, Treue, unvergänglichen Seligkeit" (love, loyalty, undying happiness) to the young woman before him.[9] And something like an invisible cultural hand seems to have guided their young friends and relatives to orchestrate a separate gathering away from their elders and then the gradual withdrawal from this space that provided the young couple with some time alone. Wengeroff suggests that, unlike the more formal seating and conversational arrangements that accompanied the parents' negotiations in the next room, "Hier wurde der Etikette beiseiten geschoben," and in this neighboring room, "where etiquette was set aside," it seemed entirely natural for the prospective bride and groom to find themselves seated side by side. Surely, however, there was another etiquette at play in this wordless, collective choreography. Although Wengeroff remembers experiencing it as the (carefully calibrated) *loosening* of the restrictions that had kept her sister from setting eyes on her groom before the wedding, what she describes is also a culture in formation, in which it is understood that romantic conversation is conducted "in private"—precisely what tradition forbids between an unmarried man and woman. That these conventions were still untested may account for the "ritual misfire," in which Pauline seems to have experienced her solitude with her young fiancé not as romantic opportunity but as manipulation by her sisters and friends (if I understand her irritation correctly). The propagation of these new cultural practices in such a short period no doubt required multiple agents and derived from a variety of sources, but Wengeroff's intuition that they were also tightly connected with emerging reading practices is the path I will travel here.

There is a final point to be made about the role of literature in the modernization of Jewish marriage: Wengeroff's memoir is of course itself a *literary* description of this transformation, governed by the conventions of both autobiography and the literary treatment of young love. As an autobiography written fifty years after the events it describes, it constructs as it remembers childhood experiences, expressing the "grandmotherly" writing self of 1898 as surely as the sixteen-year-old of 1849. It is thus a retrospective description of Jewish modernization like the other autobiographies described here, reading Jewish tradition from the ideological perspective of what succeeded it and with the hindsight accorded by the passage of time. Wengeroff's memoir is distinct from many of the other nineteenth-century autobiographies in consistently mourning the lost traditional world; even so, the memoir's critique of modernization is itself "modern."

Wengeroff's memoir indeed invites us to view both engagement chapters not as premodern "chronicle" but already as "literature" in the events that unfold within it but also in its writing: the epigraph to the chapter mentions the date of its writing (July 1898) and sets the scene—"Written under an oak tree on a small bench in the woods." The chapter begins:

As chance would have it, just today I bumped up against the strong box in which my husband's and my letters from the time of our engagement lay stored. I opened it, leafed pensively through the yellowed pages, deep in thought, and before I realized it I was enveloped by that entire happy past. . . . I am once again the sixteen-year-old Pessele in her beloved home, surrounded by parents and siblings. And one picture after another arises.[10]

Something of the fairy tale inheres in this setting, in the tree that canopies the writing bench, in the locked box holding the love letters, in the power these letters have to produce in the writer—and, ideally, in the reader—fully formed pictures of a cozy past. In an analysis of modern literature, Talal Asad argues that secularization, so often seen as rationalizing and utilitarian in its drive, is accompanied and tempered by its associated reading practices, by "the growing habit of reading imaginative literature—being enclosed within it and by it—so that images of a 'pre-modern' past acquire in retrospect a quality of enchantment." If modernity provides "a direct access to reality, a stripping away of myth, magic, and the sacred,"[11] this stripping away of myth is itself accompanied by another myth, the myth of what tradition had been, of what it was that modernity had stripped away. Secularization is thus *simultaneously* an ideology of the present and a myth about the past, a myth constructed, in Asad's view, most powerfully and magically by secular narrative. Wengeroff's memoir, then, provides an ethnographic description of the influence of modern European literature on nineteenth-century Russian Jews even as it itself is already caught up entirely in the perspectives and atmosphere provided by European literature. Wengeroff's nostalgia for the past is itself part of the process of modernization that produces as it "charms" tradition. Once one recognizes the seductive power of literature and its production of an enchanted past (as well as a future governed by the laws of romantic love), the effects of romance are more widely distributed than a simple narrative of "progress" from arranged marriage to romantic courtship might lead us to expect.

This book explores the intersection between literature and romantic practices, studying the effects of European literary and sexual conventions on Jewish sexual structures, analyzing the literary character of Jewish sexual modernity, and tracing the distinctively literary (that is, erotic) views of Jewish tradition that emerge in modern Jewish literature. Jewish secularization is a broad field and complex historical phenomenon, and I should make clear what I mean by secularization in this context. The pioneering proponents of what is generally called "the secularization thesis" focused their attention on secularization as a gradual transformation of traditional metaphysical worldviews. Peter Berger, borrowing Max Weber's famous phrase, describes secularization as "the disenchantment of the world," emblematized by an "immense shrinkage in the scope of the sacred." As Weber had argued, this "shrinkage" begins in the early modern world, in particular in Protestant revisions of Catholic worldviews. The Reformation left a channel between "fallen" humanity and transcendent divinity in its conception of God's grace, but this channel was so ethereal and narrow that it was easily severed. "A sky empty of angels," Berger writes, "becomes open to the intervention of the astronomer and, eventually, of the astronaut."[12]

In recent years, the Protestant biases of what has been called "the secularization thesis" have been revised to account for the secularizing experiences of other groups, from post-Catholic European societies to Europe's former colonies throughout the world. It is now clear to most critics that no single "secularism" exists (including in the Jewish world), despite the universalist claims and aspirations of some varieties of secularism. Under the influence of postcolonialism, the philosophical understandings of an earlier era of scholarship have given way to new political, economic, and cultural perspectives on the secularization process. With these resources, critics have called into question the empirical truth and underlying value judgments of the secularization thesis: It no longer seems obvious that the exemplary feature of modernity is the narrowing, privatizing, or "subtraction" of the religious sphere under the salutary pressure of rational thought and religious tolerance. Many observers, including some who earlier asserted the inevitability of global secularization, also recognize that we are now living in a "desecularized" or "post-secular" age.[13]

While it is evident that Jewish secularization emerged from the larger context of European trends of secularization, it is nevertheless distinct from it. The progression traced by Weber from Renaissance humanism to the Protestant Reformation and post-Calvinist capitalism, for instance, only very partly correlates with the historical and cultural conditions that gave rise to Jewish secularization.[14]

Although Berger and others aim to draw a gradual line between traditional beliefs and secular rationalism, it seems that the story of Jewish secularization is more persuasively told as one that involves practice at least as much as belief, culture at least as much as Reason. In *The Origins of Jewish Secularization in Eighteenth-Century Europe*, Shmuel Feiner provides an analysis of Jewish secularization not as the organic, dialectical ripening of a metaphysical tradition but as the abrupt abandonment of Jewish practice, beginning primarily in eighteenth-century Central and Western Europe; that Jewish secularization should be defined less as a rejection of a set of beliefs than as the cessation of halakhic observance is particularly apt, given the centrality to Judaism of what Feiner calls "religious discipline." Feiner argues that the cultural rupture involved in the cessation of religious observance has been neglected in favor of intellectual history, particularly of the Haskalah, a movement associated with Jewish secularization in its textual and conservative mode, which, in Feiner's view, "simultaneously represented a reaction to secularization and a secular revolution."[15] The abandonment of Jewish practice invites cultural rather than philosophical analysis, drawing our attention to new patterns of (ambivalent, paradoxical, and partial) integration in the context of public debate on "the Jewish question," political gestures toward the amelioration of Jewish civil status, and the popularization of Enlightenment ideas. Jewish secularization was not, as for Protestantism, the snip of a theological thread but the opening of social, political and—I would add—literary possibilities. Secularization, in this view, expresses the project and challenges of connecting Jews and Gentiles and only incidentally the recalibration of human and divine realms. My own argument in this book is that it also expressed the project and challenge of connecting Jews with one another, through new patterns of courtship, marriage, kinship, and community.

The effect of postcolonial analyses of secularization as the imposition of European norms on Jewish practice has sometimes been to cast religion as the primary site of cultural resistance to the colonial demands of secularization. It is certainly possible to view contemporary movements of Jewish religious "return" in the light of both post-secularization and postcolonialism, as skepticism about the liberating powers of "the rational" and as challenges to the leveling forces of cultural homogenization. But the resistance to Europeanization, as I claim throughout this book, also took shape *within* secularist Jewish practices and secular Jewish culture. Jacob Katz long ago argued that the limits of Jewish social integration into Christian society were the result of ambivalence on both the Jewish and Gentile sides of the cultural divide, which expressed itself, for Jews, in such forms as persistent occupational patterns and cultural allegiances. Katz writes, "The definition of the Jewish community as a purely religious unit was, of course, a sham from the time of its conception. It was contradicted by social reality and much of Jewish activity."[16] Jews, that is, both did and did not capitulate to demands for the dissolution of Jewish collectivity and cultural particularity, enthusiastically embracing some aspects of the Europeanization project (the separation of church and state, the abandonment of Jewish religious ritual) and rejecting others (the "normalization" of Jewish occupations, the disaggregation of Jewish local and global networks).

Homi Bhabha's now-ubiquitous notion of hybridity, the "interstitial space between fixed identifications," may illuminate the complexity and multiple paradoxes of Jewish secularization,which should not be simply read as adherence to European "internal colonialism" or (to put it in more old-fashioned terms) "assimilation."[17] The notion of assimilation rests on the outdated conception of a purely Jewish realm, free from colonial contagion—but where might one discover such cultural purity? It also views cultural influence as working in only one direction, from the majority to minority culture. It is possible to argue, though, that secularization should be read simultaneously as the Westernization of Jews and as the Judaization of the West, if one grants Spinoza a pioneering role and recognizes Jewish political impulses as primary support for such emblematically secularist values as *Bildung* and the separation of church and state. That there is also a Jewish counter-discourse to the dominant Western one on sexuality and marriage, and that it has been enormously influential, is part of the argument I make in this book.

The study of Jewish secularization, once the notion that it simply represents Europeanization has been qualified (or disqualified), invites the question of what constitutes the Jewishness of Jewish secularity. Such an inquiry might benefit from Asad's insight that secularity, not only religion, is amenable to anthropological analysis, as a network of embodied practices, modes of being, "cultivated sensibilities and passions, an orchestration of the senses" that emerges from the cultural "shift in grammar" that is secularization."[18] Secularization may have led to the widespread abandonment of halakhah, but Jewish practice was never simply identical with Jewish law.

A concrete and relevant example of the persistence of Jewish practice within secular Jewish culture is that the Eastern European Haskalah, so often identified with Europeanization, adopted a series of European reading practices while developing new "hybrid" cultural patterns. These shifts represented both Jewish continuity and difference, both the adoption of

European models and the forging of new hybrid varieties. On the one hand, the traditional Jewish, modern European, and Haskalah worldviews all accorded books, whether secular or religious, a value that could border on the fetishistic; against this shared valuation one might pose the different cultural practices of (traditional Jewish) collective text study versus (modern European) private reading. The Haskalah, moreover, despite its explicit embrace of European cultural models, developed entirely new hybrid models of reading in the shared text study of German poetry Wengeroff records, in which young men studied Talmud and Schiller "with the same method. Each important verse was dissected individually and debated loudly; questions and possible answers followed one another [and] were discussed until a satisfying solution and the profound meaning that was said to lie behind the words was found."[19] As I have argued elsewhere, "the maskilic *bukh* [secular book] did not evacuate the complex canonical, textual, ritual, and bodily practices that accompanied the traditional *sefer* (sacred book) but rather transformed them, accruing a distinctive and stylized set of body practices and sensibilities that were neither traditionally Jewish nor entirely European." The same holds true for secular Jewish culture in general. "Jewish secularity might be conceptualized, then, neither as an expression of Jewish acculturation nor as the triumph of Jewish cultural continuity but rather as the very site of their negotiation."[20]

.   .   .

My path through Jewish secular culture travels through three particularly rich and charged intersections: the first flourishing of modern Hebrew and Yiddish literature in nineteenth-century Eastern Europe and the attempts to forge new romantic models of Jewish romance in these works; the erotic recovery of Jewish tradition in Hebrew and Yiddish modernist texts of the early twentieth century, reversing earlier modernizing critiques of traditional practices; and the surprising reemergence of aspects of the traditional Ashkenazic sexual practices in contemporary Jewish American literature, beginning with the renewed interest in the 1950s in Yiddish culture and the Eastern European Jewish past. This is not meant as an exhaustive genealogy of the line that connects Jewish sexual secularization and Jewish literature; clearly, another story could be (and has been) told that accounts for developments in modern Hebrew and Israeli literature.[21] Although I maintain a focus on Eastern European cultural formations and their later expressions in the Ashkenazic diaspora, there is no doubt that the processes I describe have their echoes elsewhere in the Jewish world, as well as in the larger global movements of secularization and post-secularization. The international popularity of *Fiddler on the Roof*, the best-known cultural expression of the history I am tracing here, is evidence enough that this is not solely a Jewish story.

Because I am drawing on a wide range of texts to make an argument about literature and the transformation of Jewish marriage practices, I have also attempted to narrow the argument by exploring Jewish marriage in only a very limited sense, discussing literary representations of the period that immediately precedes marriage—which in traditional arrangements involves matchmaking and family negotiations and in modern formations is shaped by the rhythms of courtship. This period is limited only in a sociological sense; in the novel, it often expands to fill the space available—beginning with "boy meets girl" and ending with a wedding. Chapter 1 traces the nineteenth-century beginnings of modern Hebrew and Yiddish romantic literature and its connection with emerging trends in organizing marriage and sexuality in nineteenth-century Eastern Europe. I also discuss the debates that arose toward the end of the nineteenth century around the mismatch between European literary conventions and Jewish social realities. This sets the stage for the following chapters, each of which more closely follows a particular dimension of Jewish sexual secularization in the three historical moments that structure this study.

Chapter 2 analyzes the role of arranged marriage in Jewish literature through the figure of the marriage broker, first as the enemy of true love and then, in later works, as its enabler or even mystical embodiment. Nineteenth-century memoirs decry the intrusions and deceptions of matchmakers and urge the replacement of arranged marriage with romantic choice. While Jewish literature in some sense served as this replacement—with the author "arranging" matches between characters—literary works also rescued and even invented the matchmaker. In Sholem Aleichem's *Menachem Mendl*, the matchmaker is given Yiddish literary voice, while in Bernard Malamud's *The Magic Barrel*, the matchmaker finds a place in modern America, and Jewish American literature, as a recognizable "type" and a figure of erotic fascination in his own right.

Chapter 3 presents a genealogy of lineage in Jewish marriage, another aspect of traditional marital negotiations derided in Haskalah polemic. Like the matchmaker, pedigree finds a surprising afterlife even in those literary works that champion erotic attraction in the construction of a marriage partnership. At first performing the conservative-bourgeois function of maintaining class boundaries in a post-traditional society that ostensibly espouses the class-neutral ideology of romantic love, pedigree takes on a far wider range of meanings in modern Jewish literature. Along with the mystical eroticism that links romance with intergenerational ties, lineage has a long afterlife in the realist novel, in which the narrative condensed and encapsulated in the *yikhes brif* (genealogical document) is expanded and transformed into family saga; this saga, which adds a "vertical" dimension to the more "horizontal" horizons of the marriage plot, both narrates the generational disruptions of modernity and serves as narrative cure. In the late twentieth century, the literary tracing of lineage reemerges in Tony Kushner's *Angels in America*, finding genealogical expression for even the post-genealogical phenomenon of queer kinship in the era of AIDS.

Chapter 4 describes the role of literature in constructing a modern Jewish ideology of heterosexual romance through its articulation of new notions of romantic time, on the one hand, and gender complementarity, on the other. While traditional marriages had collapsed the time between puberty and marriage, attraction and consummation (while expanding the historical perspective of a match by including ancestors in the arrangements), the novel introduced new romantic temporalities in the rhythms of sexual maturation, attraction, and (deliciously delayed) consummation. These new models of romance depended on strictly delineated gender roles, which the novel served to map and inculcate. Twentieth-century Jewish cultural productions, particularly on the stage and screen, form a counter-discourse to the gender complementarity on which European romance rested, featuring cross-dressed, antiromantic heroines who resist and denaturalize European gender conventions. And in Erica Jong, readers encountered a full-fledged (Jewish) argument against the erotic tempos set out in literary romance.

Chapter 5 follows the process of "nuclearization," in which the move to romantic, companionate marriage reduced the role of parents and extended family in the construction of modern family. Reading Sholem Aleichem's *Tevye the Dairyman* not through its usual focus—the move from arranged marriage to romantic love—but through what this move entails—the end of the system whereby marriage is produced by and produces broad kinship networks—I argue that the stories nevertheless reproduce in submerged form the traditional practices whereby a young girl's father chooses a young bridegroom for his daughter. In the final section of the chapter, I explore the "aunt-niece" relationship in Grace Paley's inaugural story "Goodbye and Good Luck," which presents the persistence and cultural productivity of alternative models of kinship at the margins of Jewish American literature and society.

Chapter 6 explores the structure of sexual segregation through its literary expressions. Among the evils of traditional Jewish society denounced by the Haskalah was the strictness of its sexual segregation, which left no room for social interaction or erotic discovery between the sexes. In the twentieth century, however, writers discovered erotic pleasures in what earlier generations had seen as repressive social structures. S. Y. Agnon in "The Tale of the Scribe," Sholem Asch in *God of Vengeance*, and Dvora Baron in "Fedke" stage love affairs within sexually segregated spaces, while Singer's "Yentl the Yeshiva Boy" makes an implicit case for the superiority of romances that proceed through the (homosocial and agonistic) camaraderie of Torah learning over those conducted according to Western conventions.[22]

The Afterword, which touches on the work of Freud, Philip Roth, and Erica Jong, argues that Jewish writers played a crucial role in the twentieth-century desublimation of Eros, stripping the "erotic sublime" of its mystification and grounding sexuality in the "natural" bodily realities that characterize many varieties of Jewish sexual discourse. For the sublime notion of the "soul mate," Freud, Roth, and Jong suggest that sexual partners are easily interchanged—an ideology that, in its "conservative" form, also underpins arranged marriage. While Jewish sexual modernity begins with the adoption of European literary conventions, by the end of the twentieth century, modern Jewish culture had come to play a critical role (in both senses) in European sexual discourse. In the sexual ideologies expressed in twentieth-century Hebrew, Yiddish, and Jewish American literature, the modern religion of romantic love met first its most profound challenge and ultimately its heretical overthrow.

· · ·

A word on the title: It occurred to me, rather late in the process of writing this book, that the title of Jeffrey Eugenides's 2011 novel was the perfect one for my own book; I borrowed it for my own work-in-progress (grateful that titles are not subject to copyright) before I read his novel. I was amazed to discover, after I bought the book and began to read it, that the protagonist of the novel is a Brown University student who is writing a senior honors thesis on the topic of changing models of marriage in literature, having taken an inspiring course called "The Marriage Plot: Selected Novels of Austen, Eliot, and James." Madeleine's plan was to begin with Austen:

> After a brief examination of *Pride and Prejudice*, *Persuasion*, and *Sense and Sensibility*, all comedies, essentially, that ended with weddings, Madeleine was going to move on to the Victorian novel, where things got considerably darker. *Middlemarch* and *Portrait of a Lady* didn't end with weddings. They began with the traditional moves of the wedding plot—the suitors, the proposals, the misunderstandings—but after the wedding ceremony they kept on going. . . . For a conclusion, Madeleine thought she might cite the wife-swapping in Updike. That was the last vestige of the marriage plot: the persistence in calling it "wife-swapping" instead of husband-swapping. As if the woman were still a piece of property to be passed around.[23]

As the reader will see, neither Jane Austen nor George Eliot appears in this book (although the titles of Austen's novels find a distant echo in a few of my chapter titles), and my own ending calls on Philip Roth and Erica Jong to do some of the work that Madeleine entrusts to John Updike. Nevertheless, it should be clear that my project has a very similar trajectory to that of Madeleine's thesis, with the difference that she is working her way through the nineteenth- and twentieth-century English and American novel while my examples are drawn from Hebrew, Yiddish, and Jewish American literature of the same periods. The discovery in a just-published novel of a close double of my own project, which itself is often concerned with the question of literature as a mirror of social reality, was peculiar and, I'll admit, a little disconcerting. On reflection, it was less of a coincidence than at first it seemed: Among the greatest debts I owe (aside from the considerable one to Eugenides I have just acknowledged) is to Ian Watt, whose pioneering 1957 work, *The Rise of the Novel*, includes a brilliant reading of the connection between the emergence of modern bourgeois marriage and of the eighteenth-century English marriage novel.[24] This book must have been on the syllabus of the course Madeleine took at Brown that inspired her thesis, just as my own reading of Watt was one impetus for this book. Simply put, I am analyzing the beginnings of modern Jewish literature using many of the tools Watt developed for the eighteenth-century English novel; like Madeleine, I also push forward to see what happened next.

There is yet another curious overlap between my experiences writing this book and Madeleine's anxieties about the topic she has chosen, which come to a head when her roommate's boyfriend "materialized at their kitchen table, reading something called *Of Grammatology*."[25] Watt's approach was extraordinarily promising in relation to Jewish literature, but it came from an earlier era than mine or Madeleine's. To write about marriage, after Derrida, post-structuralism, and queer studies, relying on a book first published in 1957? *Really?* But as this book testifies, I stayed the course. There is something in Watt's wider lens and interdisciplinary approach that can expand a conversation that has been shaped for the past few decades by other concerns and approaches. How, then, is this work related to the post-colonial and queer studies analyses of Jewish gender and modernization published in the 1990s? These approaches all had an enormously productive impact on Jewish studies, producing an explosion of new insights and a host of fresh readings. If these new readings had a broad range, encompassing the Talmud as easily as they did Yiddish cinema, they also had a strong center, clustering most thickly around the couch in Freud's Viennese study.[26] It is not hard to understand the magnetism of that focus. In fin-de-siècle Vienna, the broadest currents of sociological and historical-political transformation met the deepest recesses of psychosexual subjectivity. With Freud, theorists found a range of flexible methodological tools, a paradigmatic case study, and a clear path through the charged intersection of secularization and sexuality.

From this vantage point, Jewish modernization, Europeanization, and *embourgeoisement* emerge as an encounter between two radically asymmetrical sex-gender systems: on the one hand stood the traditional Ashkenazic structure, with roots in rabbinic-Talmudic culture and rich embodiment among the Eastern European Jewish masses; on the other hand appeared the bourgeois European sexual system, with roots in Greco-Roman, Christian, and heroic-chivalric cultural formations, in which modernizing Jews aspired to participate. As I discuss elsewhere, the Jewish romance with Europe was notoriously unreciprocated: In the judgment of the dominant European cultures into which Jews were (imperfectly) integrating—a perspective thoroughly internalized by aspiring Jewish citizens of Europe—Jewish men were unmanly cowards and effete hysterics, while Jewish women were hypersexual, coarse, and unfeminine. Jewish "queerness," then, is a symptom of Jewish modernity as cultural mismatch, category crisis, incomplete integration, and colonial mimicry.[27] It is no coincidence, as Sander Gilman and others noted, that "the invention of homosexuality" coincided with the entry of Jews into the Central European bourgeoisie, an entry productive of and complicated by the sexual stigmatization of Jewish men.[28] Psychoanalysis, in a variety of related readings, was a primary effect of this stigma while also providing tools for its diagnosis and "cure," but it was not the only such effect. Among the other significant reverberations of this sociosexual crisis was Zionism, as both the collective internalization of Jewish sexual stigma and treatment for the wounds of modern Jewish masculinity.

There is no doubt that these insights can profoundly illuminate Jewish modernization in Eastern Europe, and I draw on them often in this book. Nevertheless, I take Watt as my steadier guide and follow a somewhat different route through my material. The queer studies approach I have just outlined seems by now to have reached something of an impasse, of which the predictability and repetitiveness of new readings is symptomatic. Various difficulties apparent at the outset remain unresolved: Ann Pellegrini long ago called attention to the near-obsessive focus on Jewish masculinity, even when the subject being addressed is ostensibly cross-dressed *women*; "in the implicit equation of Jews and women . . . the Jewish female body goes missing."[29] Because the queer studies and postcolonial approaches have been so centered on Central rather than Eastern European Jewry, they focus almost entirely on what could be called "comparative masculinity," returning again and again to the trope of the Jewish man who is feminized in relation to his non-Jewish counterpart. (Boyarin's *Unheroic Conduct* is an important exception to this rule in many regards, including analyses both of the effects of Jewish masculine religious practices on Jewish women and of the resistance to *embourgeoisement* on the part of such women as Bertha Pappenheim.) Such an approach neglects not only women and Eastern Europe but also the question of how the Jewish sex-gender system, either in its traditional or modern forms, worked as a whole, internally rather than in its external and comparative mode.

What seems to be required is a "thick" description, from "inside" Ashkenaz rather than through the pathologizing lens of Central European sexual stigmatization. It is within this thick Jewish context that Jewish masculinity might be calibrated with Jewish gender roles more generally, as well as with sexual practices, marital structures, kinship systems, varieties of heteronormativity, and shifting modes of patriarchy. That many of these other concerns are slighted or absent in the queer studies literature perhaps reflects the methodological problems associated with the interarticulation of "race" and gender, that is, with translating a set of terms developed in the realm of individual psychology and sexual minority discourse (sexual orientation, gender performance) into the tools necessary to understand the modernization of a collective. Jewish "queerness" has meaning primarily in comparison with European gender ideals, and critics who rely heavily on the associated terms end up adopting, intentionally or not, a colonial perspective even if they also transvalue sexual stigma into countercultural difference and subversion. In contrast to this view from outside, I prefer the self-analysis of Eastern European Jewish culture: Wengeroff's close reading of the marital shifts in her own family is ample evidence that many Jews were capable of such analysis; and as Wengeroff's defense of the traditional ways indicates, they were not entirely blinded by the prevailing ideological winds of modernization.

There is a related problem with postcolonialist approaches to Jewish gender systems. That the traditional Ashkenazic gender order represents a coherent cultural system that is not merely different from normative Christian-Roman-European models but intentionally subversive of them is the argument brilliantly put forward in Daniel Boyarin's *Unheroic Conduct*. But for Boyarin, this countercultural subversion ends with the Haskalah, which he reads as a wholesale capitulation of Jews to European norms, with unfortunate effects for Jewish culture and Jewish women:

> For some three hundred years now, Jews have been the target of the civilizing mission in Europe. The civilizing mission, and its Jewish agents among "the Enlighteners," considered the fact that Jewish women behaved in ways interpreted as masculine by European bourgeois society to be simply monstrous. Modern Jewish culture, liberal and bourgeois in its aspiration and its preferred patterns of gendered life, has been the result of this civilizing mission. . . . The richness of Jewish life and difference has been largely lost, and the gains for Jewish women were largely illusory.[30]

Jewish cultural productivity in its modernizing moment is thus an effect of what Boyarin calls "colonial mimicry."[31] But it was never the case, as I intend to show in this book, that Jews imitated Western models *tout court*, and of course, not even the most traditional culture is pure of foreign influence. If *Unheroic Conduct* makes the claim that Jews have a different way of organizing gender, my own argument is that this difference persists after and even within the apparently sincere embrace of European norms.

Secular Ashkenazic culture provides plentiful resources and methodologies for understanding what constitutes Jewish difference in its larger and more collective dimension. S. An-sky's 1919 play *The Dybbuk*, for instance, can be read as an alternative to Freud's couch in the therapeutic interventions performed by the Hasidic Rebbe (and by the playwright who imagines him) in the case of Leah, who has been possessed by the soul of her dead lover; what distinguishes this theater-as-therapy and therapy-as-theater from the psychoanalytic treatment of hysteria is that it involves not only the afflicted girl but also her father, her dead lover, his dead father, and the community called in to witness the exorcism and the "trial" between the living and dead fathers who betrothed their unborn children to each other when they were young men. An-sky thus stages the trauma that is demonic possession as a *collective* rather than individual psychosexual crisis, just as Wengeroff is careful to put her own romantic awakening in the context of a larger social transformation. This collectivity is not the *context* for the shifting sexual systems, gender roles, and marital practices I am analyzing but intricately bound up with them. Marriage was an important part of this cultural system, not in the modern bourgeois understanding of the union of two individuals but as part of a larger economy that united families and friends and that reached back into the past as well as forward into the future.

Jewish "queerness" shows up in this larger system not only in the differences by which traditional Jewish masculinity and femininity were constructed and performed but also in the ways that such erotically charged homosocial spheres as the yeshiva and the Hasidic court were sites for the construction of heterosexual marriages. That is, Jewish homosociality contributed to and was often the affective basis for the formation of Jewish kinship bonds. In retaining a focus on the psychosexual individual, "proper" or "improper" gender performance and the sexual couple, queer studies has followed rather than overturned the bourgeois individualism and romantic ideologies of modernity. The traditional Ashkenazic distribution of sexual energies between the two connected spheres of a partially eroticized homosociality and a partially deeroticized heteronormativity is both too queer and not queer enough for what has been the Jewish queer studies template. The model Watt provides, with its triple focus on transformations in marriage practices and kinship structures, the emergence of new literary genres and conventions, and the broad economic and social conditions that led to and emerged from these shifts, is thus an appropriate one for my own subject; and, in the end, I was pleased to see that Eugenides's Madeleine had undertaken—if only in fiction—to follow it as well.

CHAPTER ONE

A Sentimental Education

> Over all the quiet sea-shore
> Shadowing falls the hour of Hesper,
> Through the clouds the moon is breaking,
> And I hear the billows whisper.
>
> "Can that man who wanders yonder
> Be a lover or a dunce?
> For he seems so sad and merry,
> Sad and merry both at once."
>
> But the laughing moon looks downward,
> And she speaks, for she doth know it:
> "Yes, he is both fool and lover,
> And, to cap it all, a poet!"
>
> —Heinrich Heine, *Songs to Seraphine*, II

Loving The Love of Zion

In the summer of 1869, shortly before leaving his Lithuanian hometown of Vilkomir (Polish, Wilkomierz; Lithuanian, Ukmergė) in pursuit of secular education, the twenty-six-year-old Moshe Leib Lilienblum met a young woman who was finding herself in similar conflict with the traditional world. As Lilienblum recounts in his 1876 Hebrew autobiography, many of his friends had already left town "in fear of the fanatics," and Lilienblum felt lonely, persecuted, and confused. His wife, to whom he was married when he was fifteen and she thirteen, provided no intellectual companionship. But "N," as Lilienblum referred to his new friend, was a woman who shared

Lilienblum's literary tastes. What would otherwise have been a difficult summer thus passed with the young people meeting almost daily. Lilienblum writes that "N. did well when she asked me to read to her *The Love of Zion* [Ahavat Tsiyon], since it gave us something to talk about when we met each evening."[1] The book Lilienblum was referring to was Abraham Mapu's 1853 biblical romance, which is generally considered the first Hebrew novel and which Lilienblum had fallen in love with at the very beginning of his move away from tradition.

Between 1853 and 1928, *The Love of Zion* appeared in fifteen editions (there were another eleven editions of Mapu's collected works) and was translated into Yiddish at least three times, as well as into Judeo-Arabic, Judeo-Persian, Ladino, Arabic, German, Italian, French, English, and other languages.[2] The novel had an impact in many spheres, but its influence was particularly strong in Eastern Europe: Joseph Klausner vividly describes the potent impression Mapu's book made on its first readers:

> Before the eyes of the young reader arose new-old Jews, with no resemblance to the Jews living in the small Jewish towns of Poland and Lithuania, but who nevertheless were connected with them through a powerful bond: this bond was—the Bible, the greatest and holiest of all Jewish books. These Jews of those days were living free lives, blossoming young lives, overflowing with physical strength and powerful emotions at the same time. And yet these lives were the lives of true Hebrews, since among them also lived Isaiah the Prophet and King Hezekiah, sacred figures even to the young children in the *heder* or to the boys in the yeshiva. The Jewish life described in *The Love of Zion*, then, was both ours and not ours: ours—because it was the life of our ancestors in the Land of Israel, and not ours—because it was a million miles away from the contemporary life in the dark corners of Lithuania and Poland.[3]

Klausner's description of the effect of *The Love of Zion* is corroborated and lent nuance by a variety of nineteenth-century accounts (even if was undoubtedly also colored by the Zionist context in which his words were written). In a passage of her memoir that echoes her description of the effect Schiller produced on the Jewish "ghetto," Pauline Wengeroff recalled the otherworldly impression made by Mapu, whom she met when he tutored her eldest son in German and Russian in Kovno in the 1850s: "From the narrow, crooked little streets of the Pale of Settlement with all its misery and poverty, out of the stifling, oppressive atmosphere of ghetto life, his imagination carried him to the great, brilliant past of his people. . . . He gave the youth new ideas, showed them new directions, opened new horizons and life possibilities for them."[4]

We know from a host of Jewish autobiographies besides Lilienblum's that the novel shook the Jewish world to the core. In a memoir describing growing up in the 1860s and 1870s, Buki ben Yogli (the pseudonym of the writer Yehudah Leib Katzenelson) blamed Mapu's novel for his reluctance to marry the daughter of the head of the yeshiva he was attending:

> I had never dreamed of such a suitable match; in fact, in my dreams I had seen an entirely different picture, one that remained with me in waking life— that was the picture of Tamar, Amnon's beloved, as Mapu had described her in *The Love of Zion*. Oh, Mapu, Mapu, if you had only known what you were doing to me. For whenever I gazed at the face of the girl who was supposed to be my bride, the exalted figure of Tamar rose up before the eyes of my spirit with all the sublime glory that Mapu had granted her; and when I measured this image against the short round girl with the small eyes and thick lips and nose, "a great terror seized me" and in my heart I cursed her handsome, tall father, and refused to forgive him for knowing how to give birth only to beautiful Talmudic ideas, taking no care also to produce just one beautiful daughter for a son-in-law.[5]

The ethnographer and playwright S. An-sky (born Shloyme Zaynvil Rapoport) remembered leaving his hometown of Vitebsk in 1881 in search of enlightenment with four books in his satchel, one of them Mapu's romance (Lilienblum's autobiography was another).[6] In 1895, at the age of fourteen, the future poet and literary critic Ya'akov Fichman ran away from home with just a change of clothes, some food, and his copy of *The Love of Zion*.[7] In his autobiographical novel *From the Fair* (1914–16), Sholem Aleichem relates that Sholem, the protagonist, first realized he wanted to be a writer after "he devoured" *The Love of Zion*, reading it from beginning to end in one Sabbath, lying on the floor "tingling with excitement." As the narrator describes it,

> He wept and shed bitter tears over the fate of the unfortunate Amnon. And like the hero of the novel, he fell madly in love with the beautiful, divine Tamar, perhaps even more than Amnon. He saw her in his dreams and talked to her in the language of the Song of Songs, hugging and embracing and kissing her.
>
> The next day the infatuated Sholem walked around all day like a shadow. He had a splitting headache; his appetite was gone.[8]

Along with a headache and loss of appetite, Sholem's reading of *The Love of Zion* resulted in his decision to write a novel "à la Mapu." However, "Sholem called his book *Daughter of Zion*, and his heroes Solomon and Shulamis."[9] Both this infatuation with Mapu's novel and the desire to mimic its language are echoed in the autobiography of Eliezer Ben-Yehuda, the "Father of the Hebrew Revival," who recounts that after reading Mapu, his friends "went out to a field so as not to be overheard, and tried to speak exactly like Amnon and Tamar, with all that artificial flowery Biblicism that Mapu put in the mouths of his characters."[10] In 1900, the Hebrew writer Reuven Brainin recorded the extent to which Mapu's novel "became a model for real people, who attempted to imitate it. Male and female lovers on the Jewish street now called each other 'Amnon' and 'Tamar.'"[11]

The impact of the novel lasted well into the twentieth century. Writing in the 1930s, Klausner claimed that "the names Amnon and Tamar were beloved among *maskilim* [Jewish Enlighteners], who from the first days of national awakening [*Hibbat Tsiyon*] and onward called their sons Amnon and daughters Tamar—popular names in the Land of Israel until this very day."[12] The effects of Mapu's novel were not lost on traditionalists: One Orthodox pamphlet declared in 1870 that, with the publication of *The Love of Zion*, "new benches were added in the brothels."[13] According to Klausner (who claims to have heard these calumnies with his own ears), traditionalists referred to Mapu as "Mapke, may-his-name-be-blotted-out."[14]

Scenes recounting the intense impression made by *The Love of Zion* appear not only in traditionalist screeds, Hebrew autobiographies, and literary criticism but also in novels of the period. David in S. Y. Abramovitsh's first novel, *Learn to Do Well* (1862), advises his writer friend to transfer his energies from writing Bible commentary to the novel:

> I am sure, Nahum, that if you wrote a story instead of your exegesis "On the daughters of Lot and the daughters of Zelophehad" you would be rewarded for your labor and it would prove useful, for there are many readers in Israel. Evidence is *The Mysteries of Paris*, translated into our own language. . . . Many have read that book multiple times, and the book *The Love of Zion* is sought out like a great treasure and its price is driven up.[15]

Fictional references to *The Love of Zion* were made even in Mapu's own later work: Mapu may be doing some self-promotion when he repeatedly mentions *The Love of Zion* in *The Hypocrite*, but in sharing and discussing the biblical romance and in comparing their own lives to the ones depicted in *The Love of Zion*, the characters of *The Hypocrite* are also enacting social practices abundantly attested among Mapu's real-life readers. Thus, the hero Na'aman (whose name is a near-anagram of Amnon's) thanks his friend in a letter for sending him the wondrous *Love of Zion* and adds that he has found his own Tamar in Elisheva and duly passed along the book for her to enjoy. "The situation described in *The Love of Zion* and my own with Elisheva are one and the same," Na'aman writes to his friend. "And who knows, perhaps Elisheva will say to me, as Tamar said to Amnon: 'Hope, Amnon! Because hope is stronger than life.'"[16] In the course of the novel, Elisheva indeed has the opportunity to fulfill Na'aman's prediction by quoting these very words from Mapu's debut novel. Such adoring references and self-references inevitably gave way to satirical echoes, as in the 1887 novel by A. S. Rabinowitz, *At the Crossroads* (Al ha-perek), in which the hero gives a copy of *The Love of Zion* to his pious wife in the hopes of arousing amorous feelings in her, to no avail.[17]

These varied texts all suggest the power of secular literature and, more particularly, a single novel, to transform both consciousness and social practice. According to these accounts, Mapu's novel supplied conversational material for the budding romance between Lilienblum and "N," provided Wengeroff with a glimpse of the exalted biblical past, played a role in the adolescent break with their families for An-sky and Fichman, erotically awakened Sholem Aleichem's autobiographical protagonist and led him to take his first steps as a writer, helped instigate Ben-Yehuda's famous linguistic revolution, soured the young Katzenelson on an otherwise distinguished match, and inspired generations of readers to name their children not after a dead relative—as is the norm among Ashkenazic Jews—but after a fictional character.

Because these accounts are so similar that they seem to form a collective meta-narrative, it is easy to miss the complexity of the novel's effects, which resonate in at least four distinct spheres. The first and perhaps most obvious is the linguistic dimension of the novel, its resurrection of biblical Hebrew to write detailed pastoral descriptions and create believable dialogue; it was this aspect of the novel that laid the groundwork for Ben Yehuda's revolutionary language project. The second influential aspect of the novel is its unique literary character and status, as a modern novel set against the backdrop of biblical Israel, combining biblical and invented characters and plots; it was this aspect that excited admiration by Wengeroff, imitation by Sholem Aleichem and others, and has been credited, as well, with founding modern Hebrew literature (and providing a literary vision of Zionist return *avant la lettre*). The third dimension, which makes itself apparent especially in Hebrew autobiographies, was its role in encouraging at least some of its readers to break with their traditional families and religious practices; the presence of Mapu's book in the satchels of runaway teenage boys is testimony to this power. Finally, the novel exerted erotic and romantic power, which sexually awakened a generation of young readers, drove a nail in the old system of arranging marriage, and provided a template for modern courtship, marriage, and family practices. In what follows, my interest is primarily in this last dimension, in the complex interconnections between literary genre and sexual experience that both expressed and propelled the erotic transformation and sexual secularization of Eastern European Jews.

The role of Mapu's novel in literary history has often been discussed in the context of its astonishing mobilization of biblical Hebrew for the construction of a modern novel in the European mode, a crucial exercise that rendered possible modern Hebrew literature—even if that literature had to expand Mapu's linguistic palette before it could become truly flexible as a literary medium. That Mapu provided a template not only for the revival of Hebrew as a vernacular and for the construction of a Jewish homeland in Palestine but also for the destruction of traditional families in Eastern Europe is evident from at least four of the autobiographies just cited. Mapu exercised both the constructive and destructive power of secularization by reviving, through intertextual citation, the "profane" love affair of the Song of Songs obscured by rabbinic allegoresis and by rendering such characters as the biblical prophet Isaiah, through the conventions of the novel, as a man of flesh and blood. Secularization, in this analysis, proceeds not through direct philosophical or metaphysical (or antimetaphysical) argument but through indirect literary-erotic means. Works such as Mapu's *Love of Zion* thus played an important role in the sexual modernization and Europeanization of traditional Jews; as in Sholem Aleichem's autobiographical account, Mapu's romance awakened Jews to the intoxicating and headache-inducing power of literature and sexuality simultaneously. Demonstrating this thesis requires an interdisciplinary approach, bringing together the study of Jewish sexual secularization as a historical phenomenon with Jewish literary history and criticism. While historians of Jewish secularization have long mined literary texts—particularly autobiography and memoir—for historical and sociological evidence, my own research takes a different approach, focusing on the co-emergence of sexual secularization and modern Jewish literature.

Despite the intensely personal way in which Mapu's novel was received by its readers, it is evident that one can draw only an indirect connection between its themes and plot and the transformations in the world of its readers. No character in *The Love of Zion* experiences anything resembling the break with tradition described by Wengeroff, Lilienblum, An-sky, and Fichman; the novel, given its ancient setting, could hardly make a direct case for the modernization of Jewish life, marital or otherwise. Mapu himself was and remained in most respects a traditional Jew, if one committed to the enlightened reform of Jewish life. Nevertheless, the novel does indirectly refer to a few of the controversies of Mapu's own time, insisting, for instance, on the right of young people to choose their own mates: Tamar's high-born parents, concerned that their daughter has fallen in love with the penniless shepherd Amnon while resisting the affections of the man to whom they have betrothed her, discuss the winds of change that have caught up their daughter. It is Tirzah, more inclined to sympathize with her daughter, who reminds her husband of what the prophet Isaiah had recent prophesied: "In that day, seven women shall take hold of one man, saying, 'We will eat our own bread and wear our own clothes; only let us be called by your name.'" As Tirzah comments, "These days are approaching, and a new era is coming to the land, when women seek the men."[18]

Selectively quoting Isaiah 4:1 to placate her husband, Tirzah takes the prophecy out of its biblical context, in which Isaiah laments the calamitous wartime shortage of marriageable men; she manages to avoid Isaiah's tone by omitting the final words of the verse, "esof herpatenu" (take away our disgrace). Tirzah instead draws on the authority of the prophet to put their rebellious daughter's scandalous pursuit of a man into the larger social and religious context of cultural change. Her husband, Yedidiah, disinclined to take Tamar's rebelliousness in stride, revives the prophetic tone of lament even as he accepts that his daughter's actions reflect the new era in which she is maturing: "'Woe for such days!' groaned Yedidiah—'woe that they have come to our palace and turned our daughter's heart against her parents, to lead her astray after her own desires.'"[19] Just as Tirzah finds prophetic perspective for Tamar's overthrow of traditional gender roles, Yedidiah reverses

Malachi 3:24 ("And he shall turn the heart of the parents to the children, and the heart of the children to their parents") to lament the "generation gap" wracking his family.[20] These multiple citations and displacements of Isaiah and Malachi reach beyond the biblical context (and its prophesied near future) to express the worries of the parents of newly assertive girls in the Pale of Settlement in the very late 1840s and the 1850s. As did Wengeroff, ChaeRan Y. Freeze describes this period as one of rapid change, in which the political and cultural liberalization of Russian attitudes toward the Jewish population and, especially, the advent of the Era of Great Reforms (1855–81) under Alexander II had profound ramifications for a host of Jewish practices and ideologies:

> Despite all the vagaries, contradictions, and partial retractions of later decades, the new order created immense new opportunities for mobility, education, litigation, and careers for men and women. All this inevitably had far-reaching repercussions on the institution of the family, marriage, and gender relations and expectations. The new order enhanced intellectual and economic independence, fostering not only a greater sense of individuality but also a more critical view of traditional Jewish values and customs. Contemporary intellectual movements in Russia shifted the emphasis from "economic and social considerations in marriage" to the importance of "individual emotions, feelings, and self-fulfillment," a shift in values that inescapably affected spousal expectations and relationships. Whereas couples once tolerated certain forms of behavior and lower levels of affection, they now insisted that marriages embody the ideals of mutual love and respect being promoted by educated society.[21]

David Biale, analyzing sources from the same period, calls attention to the "new possibilities for boys and girls to meet unchaperoned," adding that nature played a role in these new social practices and ideologies: "In particular, walks in the fields and forests, beyond the boundaries of the shtetl, became increasingly popular and provided an unsupervised opportunity for intercourse (of all kinds) between the sexes."[22] The modernization of gender relations should be understood against the background of traditional marriage. Mining the traditional marriage system for its implicit rationale and justifications, Jacob Katz argues that the practice of arranging marriages among very young boys and girls, as he claims was typical of Jewish life in Central and Eastern Europe until the modern era, combines a clear-eyed assessment of the power and danger of sexual desire with a range of other concerns. Early arranged marriage sprang "from the parents' desire to settle their children's future while they, the parents, were still alive," as well as from the influence of "the traditional religious and ethical norms regarding sexual activity," which emphasizes that "he who is without a wife has almost no hope of withstanding the temptations of the flesh."[23] Such a reading accords with Lilienblum's description of how he overcame his reluctance to marry; as a young adolescent beset by nocturnal emissions, which he understood as seductive attacks by female demons, he agreed to be wed "in order not to help along Lilith and her crew."[24]

Alongside the importance of marriage as a bulwark against prohibited sexual activity (which was accompanied by a frank appreciation for mutual satisfaction in marital sex and a resistance to masculine ascetic impulses), Katz argues that traditional Ashkenazic Jewish marriages served the social need of securing class boundaries in a society that in theory allowed for all Jewish marriages.[25] The ideology of traditional marriage, according to Katz, fully acknowledged the power of sexual desire while ruling out erotic attraction as legitimate grounds for constructing a marriage, not only because erotic attraction might lead to "unsuitable" matches—especially those that transgressed class boundaries—but also because traditional Jewish attitudes resisted "the deliberate cultivation of erotic life." In the absence of such motivating factors, marriages were determined by a range of other, ostensibly more significant considerations. A desirable feature was "a good lineage, that is, descent from prominent scholars and other famous personages," while, more negatively, "a familial blemish—sexual licentiousness or apostasy occurring among the proposed spouse's relatives—was a negative value that had to be balanced out by other, positive assets." Other considerations could more directly involve the prospective bride or groom, for instance, "a prospective groom's learning or the bride-to-be's efficiency." Katz continues, "Beauty and good appearance were also considered, although they were not as important as they would be in a society that based its marital system on free choice." In summary, "The outstanding characteristic of this society's approach to marriage was the extreme rationalism with which it calculated the chances of that 'proper match' to which each aspired in his own way. Such criteria as personal compatibility, not to speak of romantic attachment, were not considered at all." Sexual attraction did sometimes play a role in traditional marriage, but when it did, "a matchmaker would still be used for appearance' sake."[26]

Katz describes the modern bourgeois marriages that increasingly became the norm among Jews beginning in late-eighteenth-century Central Europe as essentially the reverse of the traditional model, raising romantic attraction to the status of a cultural norm in contracting marriages and indeed as a supreme value in human existence. Such an ideological transformation is manifest not only in the modes by which each ideology is practiced and embodied but also—perhaps especially—in the ways that the ideology of romantic love camouflaged aspects of marriage that contradicted its tenets. Thus, where traditional parents might have rendered "love matches" legitimate by the retroactive employment of a marriage broker, modern couples disguised any "practical" considerations behind their marital decisions through a required discourse of sublime mutual love.[27]

In Katz's view traditional Jewish marriage stands in stark contrast with its modern counterpart, particularly when one takes into account the relative weight paid in each system to sentimental attachment or erotic attraction rather than more practical considerations. It is striking, then, that Katz suggests that the dramatic contrast in erotic ideologies may be less clear-cut than at first appears, since what constitutes the dominant ideology in each instance may function as a mask for realities that deviate from the approved model. Traditional marriages conceal the workings of attraction in contracting a match, while modern bourgeois marriages obscure the practical or externally arranged aspects of what must publicly be presented as a product of spontaneous mutual love and attraction. Katz's qualifications imply that traditional and modern marriage ideologies may function in consort with significantly more complex and concealed social and psychological realities, signifying a practice in which multiple ideologies and strategies work together to negotiate and maximize social and individual benefits.[28] These complexities further suggest that, as dramatic as the transformations from traditional to modern Jewish marriage practices might appear, there are undoubtedly also submerged continuities between them. Given that secularization was a long process, with multiple "waves" that moved gradually eastward, uneven application, and traditionalizing countermovements, the presence of overlapping models should not surprise us. And since traditional marriages were typically contracted at an early age and modern marriages later, the nineteenth century saw many complex marital histories in which an older sister's marriage was arranged, while a younger sister had considerably more freedom in choosing—or at least approving her parents' choice of—her own mate (Wengeroff's memoirs are particularly revealing in this regard); or in which an arranged first marriage gave way to a romance or "modern" second marriage; or for such unlucky and, as he saw it, permanently encumbered and psychologically damaged men as Lilienblum, a modern romance arose after the young man was already married and could never be consummated.

Recent scholarship has revised Katz's description of traditional marriage and its evolution in modernity in a number of significant ways. While Katz readily acknowledges that his account of traditional marriage does not apply to poorer, less educated, or more rural Jews, the emphasis of his work leaves the impression that it constituted the practice of a Jewish majority; this impression is certainly bolstered by the ubiquity of descriptions in memoirs, rabbinic responsa, and other textual records that conform to Katz's model. With the research of David Biale, Immanuel Etkes, Shaul Stampfer, and others, it is now abundantly clear that these records reflect the experience of the educated class of *Lomdim* (those who "learn" the Talmud) and that early arranged marriage and *kest* (called in Hebrew *mezonot*; parental room and board for the young couple) were practiced only among a small minority of Jews in the period preceding the introduction of bourgeois marriage models, which similarly had the most direct effect on Jewish elites.[29] Moreover, Biale reminds us, the marital age of the traditional elite rose in the course of the nineteenth century "independent of Haskalah polemics," alongside other changes within traditional marriage.[30] Thus, the practice of early arranged marriage, universally decried by modernizing reformers, was itself far from universal.

As Stampfer summarizes Eastern European Jewish marriage practices in the eighteenth and nineteenth centuries, "Most Jews did not marry in their early teens and many did so only in their twenties," given that commercial, property, and lineage considerations had little relevance for those without means or pedigree. Poorer and less learned Jews married later, more locally, and without the "benefit" of matchmakers or intricate arrangements for dowry and *kest*. Reflecting on the nonelite marriages that constituted the majority in this period, Stampfer supposes that they were often propelled by the romantic considerations that Katz views as arising only as part of the modern bourgeois "erotic ideology." In the eighteenth century, Stampfer writes, it was in the circles of the poor that there was room for romance and love and from which came the popular Yiddish folk songs that began to emerge in that era, if not earlier.[31]

I would add to these critical interventions that Katz's description of the modern marriage as underwritten by an erotic ideology must also be reread in the light of the finer sociological distinctions made in recent histories of the European family between the role of "sentiment" and "sex" in modern marriage.[32] This distinction actually points to two successive revolutions in conceiving of the proper grounds for marriage, which can also be mapped onto the romantic styles of Haskalah literature and the more sexually direct literary trends that followed. The distinctions and overlaps between the sentimental and the sexual revolutions that characterize Jewish sexual modernity (along with other varieties) are thus significant not only for evaluating the sociological transformations documented by Katz and the historians that followed; they may also illuminate the development of Jewish literature from the Haskalah to late nineteenth- and early twentieth-century Jewish modernisms. The Haskalah, it is now clear, promoted a sentimental revolution that concealed powerful, conflicted, and transgressive sexual impulses. The more explicit recognition of sexuality that characterized the fin-de-siècle Hebrew writers recently analyzed by Shachar Pinsker signaled both a radicalization of the Haskalah sentimental revolution and, in some way, a dialectical return to the frank recognition of "the temptations of the flesh" that, in Katz's view, was a feature of traditional views of sex and marriage but was obscured by the sentimental rhetoric of bourgeois marriage.[33]

Despite these critical interventions, many of Katz's insights have held up and been further substantiated. Marion Kaplan, for instance, takes the full measure of Katz's view that the erotic ideology of love matches sometimes masked more practical considerations, discovering that, in nineteenth-century German Jewish bourgeois households, matches arranged by parents or others were often made to appear as if they were an outcome of the free choice of the young couple. Kaplan describes "the fine art of coincidence" by which Jewish families camouflaged their matchmaking maneuvers: "Conscious of the growing contradictions between social ideology and social reality, some [Jewish] parents 'covered up' traditional, arranged marriages. Others arranged circumstances where certain young people could meet each other." When an engagement resulted, it was declared a "real love match."[34] ChaeRan Y. Freeze documents that the opposite was the case, too; as in more traditional eras, modern love matches were sometimes accompanied by "traditional formalities to lend respectability to the betrothal."

Thus, "Golda Meir's grandparents summoned a *shadkhan* to negotiate the technical arrangements after their daughter had already met and become engaged to a young army recruit on her own."[35] Children also learned to play a double game. In an early twentieth-century letter from a *brivnshteler* (model letter collection) that Nathan Hurvitz cites, a prospective bridegroom presents the young woman he is courting with a choice: "I will approach your good parents and ask for your hand myself as soon as you let me know that this is agreeable to you; or I will send a matchmaker to your family in the name of my parents."[36] Traditional forms and new romantic models coexisted for many decades, with parents and children strategically mobilizing multiple ideologies and conventions for maximum erotic, social, and economic gain.

This historical research clearly has ramifications for literary history. While Katz implicitly encourages us to view the transformation of Jewish marriage alongside the adoption of European literary and cultural models, Biale reminds us that such turn-of-the-twentieth-century Hebrew writers as Micha Yosef Berdichevsky "found vitality and eroticism" in Jewish folklore as well.[37] There is evidence that even nineteenth-century Jewish writers who identified with the modernizing avant-garde and the European bourgeoisie were well aware of the "indigenous" Jewish experiences with love Stampfer mentions, recognizing that romance could be found not only in the European novel, in faraway capitals, or in ancient Israel (where Mapu discovered his lovers) but also in the lower classes and social margins of Eastern European Jewish society: Shloyme Ettinger's 1861 closet drama *Serkele* stages three parallel love stories, with the most "natural" and believable one arising between a maid and manservant, with no assistance from parents or matchmakers. As Dan Miron points out, Sholem Yankev Abramovitsh set the only persuasive love story he wrote among a traveling band of beggars in his 1869 novel *Fishke the Lame*.[38] And in the 1888 novella *Stempenyu* (subtitled *A Jewish Romance*), Sholem Aleichem found a romantic Jewish hero in the wandering klezmer musician who gives the novella its title.

Modern literature thus emerges not only from the broad revolution in sex and marriage described by Katz and others but also from the ambivalent social formations that complicated this revolution. Indeed, modern Jewish marriage continues to be troubled by the dangers that, in Katz's analysis, traditional marriage was designed to combat: the contraction of "unsuitable" matches. While some modernizers of the Eastern European Haskalah, particularly those influenced by Russian radicalism in the 1860s and 1870s, championed free love, more moderate or conservative Jewish social reformers were compelled to resolve, contain, or circumvent the explosive powers of sexual desire, even if what they considered an unsuitable match was different from those an older generation might have ruled out. Sholem Aleichem's *Tevye the Dairyman* stories (the first of which appeared in 1894) take the breakdown of the old system of arranged marriage as primary focus and quickly move from the question of whether young people have the right to choose their own mate to the more vexing issue of intermarriage. With these anxieties, the question of the ideal method of organizing Jewish marriages comes full circle. What seemed to modernizers an obvious benefit, the elimination of a system that negated the erotic freedoms and suppressed the healthy development of young people, only gradually and dialectically revealed its underlying justifications.

· · ·

The Love of Zion was written and read within the environment Biale and Freeze describe, and it seems clear that the novel provided a model of romantic love drawn from the new practices of finding a mate without the participation of family and new ideals of mutual love for which Tamar's pursuit of a poor shepherd provided exemplary cultural expression. Nevertheless, Mapu constructed this model not by directly mobilizing the Russian rhetoric of companionate marriage but by discovering ancient Jewish support—in the prophecies of Isaiah himself!—for new modern ideals (if not realities). *The Love of Zion* turned back the clock to an era of Jewish history earlier than the rabbinic, finding models for Jewish modernity in the amorous atmosphere it discovered in the Bible. As in other spheres of Haskalah cultural production, the Bible functioned as a potentially modernizing alternative to the Talmud, the mainstay of the traditional male curriculum associated with diasporic Jewish insularity; the Bible, however, was known to and esteemed by Christians so could provide Jews a royal road into European culture. The novel is thus primary evidence for what Tova Cohen calls the model of "double influence" in the new Jewish literature, of both European literature and the classical Jewish sources. The literature of the Haskalah, according to Cohen, "wanted and intended to weave together European and Jewish culture in order to create—nearly *ex nihilo*—a literature that was simultaneously both Hebrew and European."[39]

As an alternative to traditional rabbinic texts, the novel functioned both as an expression of new approaches to Jewish marriage and the basis for a new form of Jewish reading, with its own pleasures and practices; thus, the novel was not a wholesale escape from Jewish textual culture but a translation of this textual identity into another sphere, one as saturated with passionate devotion—and practical instruction—as the religious literature it came to replace. While the modern novel is often associated with silent private reading, in the case of Lilienblum and "N" *The Love of Zion* provided the material for shared or partner reading, instituting a hybrid practice that partook in equal measures of the partner study that is the hallmark of Talmud study and the rituals of modern heterosexual courtship (adulterous and unconsummated as it was in this case). The literature of Jewish modernization was thus not a simple reflection of modern European reading or social practices, much less the wholesale imitation that later critics sometimes saw and see in it. The modern Jewish novel, in exposing young readers to the rituals of heterosexual courtship and serving as a nexus for new forms of reading, simultaneously inherited, transformed, and replaced some of the more distinctive cultural practices associated with traditional marriage and traditional learning.

The connection between Jewish sexual modernization and the emergence of secular Jewish literature is thus a rich and ambivalent one, as even my brief reading of the cultural reception of Mapu's novel can illustrate. At the simplest level, what I am exploring in this study is the emergence of what could be called, in awkward shorthand, a "sexual-literary form," in which literary romance and heterosexual practices are simultaneously propagated. Jews adopted European gender models alongside and through European genre conventions, learning the choreography of modern courtship and its attendant gender roles from the characters, plot, pacing, and conventions of romantic novels; one common term for the novel in mid-nineteenth-century Eastern Europe was "love story" (*sippur ahavim*), while another was "romance" (*roman*).[40] As this terminological and cultural knot indicates, narrative literature embodied the erotic hopes and ideals of modernizing Jews. The example of *The Love of Zion* should caution us, however, that neither the secularization of Eastern European Jews nor the literature of this community should be understood as cultural mimicry, a straightforward appropriation of values and cultural forms alien to traditional Jewish culture. Rather, Jewish literature and Jewish modernity took on distinctive shapes even in their literary and cultural borrowing.

The role of mimesis in the double process of sexual modernization and the formation of a modern Jewish literature is thus a crucial but complex one, and the ideological reduction of mimesis to the pejorative terms "imitation" and "assimilation" among generations of critiques from the earliest post-Haskalah nationalists to contemporary postcolonialist and queer theorists has only served to muddy the critical understanding of the multiple valences and literary character of this cultural operation. This is not to deny the role of imitation as part of the cultural and literary effects of such works as *The Love of Zion*: Ben Yehuda's circle of friends and Sholem Aleichem's protagonist vacillated between extraordinary attraction to and identification with the characters of Mapu's novel, attempting to speak their language, falling in ecstatic love with them, taking on their very names, or bestowing them on their lovers and children.

This literary effect is already evident within the workings of the novel itself. Despite the efforts Mapu took to depict his characters' passions as "natural," they insistently present themselves as also textual (and thus both "traditionally Jewish" and in keeping with the European role of literature as sexual stimulant). The characters of Amnon and Tamar participate in this imitative and self-reflective game, falling in love with each other not directly but through a kind of visual and textual hall of mirrors: Tamar is drawn to Amnon not (only) because of his beauty and song but also because of his resemblance to the young man of whom her grandfather dreamed, described to her in a letter from him. When she encounters Amnon at the riverbank the day after her dream, "like doves by the river, so did their eyes drink in the reflection on the face of the water, which filled them with pleasant feelings, for the vision of their desire faithfully appeared in the water, since they were embarrassed to gaze at each other's face directly."[41] Despite the ideological associations of sexual desire with the individual in his or her most primal essence, Amnon and Tamar fully demonstrate the workings of textual mediation, the imagination, and self-reflexivity in the construction of romantic love. The "natural" location in which their love unfolds, described by Dan Miron as "the pleasant place" (*locus amoenus*) outside the constraints of the social order, has been understood by Yahil Zaban as the place of literature, or more specifically of the Haskalah novel. The pleasant place is a fictional site in which the intimate double encounter of the hero and his beloved and the maskilic reader and the Haskalah novel takes place, demonstrating how closely intertwined love in the Haskalah novel is with the love of reading.[42] Not nature but its textual production and cultural idealization become the site of modern love, just as this love is less the natural love of young people for one another than the cultural love of reading itself.

The self-reflexivity, indirection, and vicarious erotic experience that Zaban sees as characteristic of the Haskalah novel may in fact attest to more widespread connections between literature and Eros than be a special case deriving from the uniquely "artificial" or "colonial" conditions of Jewish modernization. René Girard, in *Deceit, Desire and the Novel*, argues for the ubiquity of "triangular desire," the concept he later and more famously termed "mimetic desire." As he writes, "Emma Bovary would not have taken Rudoph for a Prince Charming had she not been imitating romantic heroines." We love not others but our own image of these others and their image of us, which in turn propels us to construct an image of ourselves as lovers. We love what others love, and we love them in the way that characters in the novels love, which is to say that we love because we love novels. For Girard, the novel embodies "the spiritual wedding without which the virgin imagination could not give birth to fantasies," since "the printed word has a magical power of suggestion."[43] It is evident enough that, for Jews, the printed word has always had a magical power of suggestion; the manifold effects of *The Love of Zion* suggest that this power did not diminish but perhaps even increased with the "disenchanting" advent of modernization and secularization.

It is already clear that, for all the evident distance between Mapu's fiction and the realities of his readers, the effect of the introduction of Mapu's pastoral romance into the Jewish world complicated the ostensibly clear distinctions between fiction and reality. As Wolfgang Iser points out, the opposition between fiction and nonfiction always dissolves under closer scrutiny: "Are fictional texts truly fictions, and are nonfiction texts truly without fictions? . . . How can something exist that, although actual and present, does not partake of the character of reality?" Iser's interests are directed not only to the relations between fiction and nonfiction but also to "literary anthropology," to the function of fictions in "the repatterning of the culturally conditioned shapes human beings have assumed." Iser argues, "If literature permits limitless patternings of human plasticity, it indicates the inveterate urge of human beings to become present to themselves; this urge, however, will never issue into a definitive shape, because self-grasping arises out of overstepping limitations."⁴⁴ His primary case for thinking through the relationship between fiction and reality is the pastoral romance:

> Pastoralism held sway in the West as a literary device for over fifteen hundred years. Its basic pattern features two worlds that are distinctly marked from one another by a boundary, the crossing of which can be effected only by donning a mask. The disguise allows those who have veiled their identity to act out either what they are denied in the socio-historical world out of which they have come, or what seems impossible even in the pastoral realm of artifice that they have penetrated. Thus duality is maintained, unfolding the distinguished positions into a changing multiplicity of their possible relationships, which issue into proliferating iterations between the two worlds as well as between the characters and their disguises.⁴⁵

Among the reasons that pastoralism is so persistent in literary history is that it "thematizes the act of fictionalizing, thereby enabling literary fictionality to be vividly perceived." Fictionality, Iser stresses, has political effects less in reflecting "the socio-historical world" than precisely in standing outside it as a "counterimage" or double of it: "Being outside does not mean transcending oneself; it means staging oneself." In Iser's method, reading involves the reciprocal relationship between fiction and the sociohistorical world, as a means of reintroducing "into what is present whatever the present has excluded."⁴⁶

Iser's approach to literary anthropology allows us to conceptualize the effects of Haskalah literature beyond the "problem" of its betrayal of the rules of mimetic realism (as many post-Haskalah critics charged). The "doubling" effect of make-believe—pastoral romance above all—influences readers not because these fictions accurately reflect the nineteenth-century Jewish sociohistorical world but precisely because they do not. Haskalah novels should not be read only as aspirational models to guide the efforts of Jewish reformers or as satirical jabs designed to provide a critical distance from traditional habits. As in the pastorals Iser analyzes, Mapu's *Love of Zion* presents double worlds, that of the Jerusalem nobility and of the pastoral hills, as well as double characters, shepherds masquerading as princes and princes masquerading as shepherds. It is this doubling, which also thematizes the workings of fiction, that communicates and embodies new possibilities of human experience. Klausner saw this clearly: "The Jewish life described in *The Love of Zion*, then, was both ours and not ours."⁴⁷ Fiction is thus real and has absolutely real effects in staging the self "ecstatically" (as Iser puts it), which prior Jewish genres had failed to accomplish. Iser considers the effects of the pastoral romance over a millennium, but in the case of Jewish Ashkenaz, these effects were largely accomplished over a few decades in which the challenges of rapidly shifting social norms were serendipitously met with a fictional work in which the "plasticity" of social selves could be opened and explored.

Iser suggests that among the paradoxes mobilized by fiction is the simultaneous accessibility and impermeability of experiences and selves, the impossibility of distinguishing experience from appearance; this paradox explains why love "is the most central topic of literary staging." We are "within" this experience, but it also approaches us "almost like an assault" from the outside, which in turn "awakens in us a desire to look at what has happened to us, and this is when the evidence explodes into alternatives."[48] If Iser is correct, then the romantic fictions explored here are not simply a "theme" or series of conventions (literary and social both) but also a fundamental site for exploring what it means to be human beyond what is evident and real. It is on just such an anthropological level that the phenomenon of Mapu's fiction must be understood.

Lust in Translation: The Problem with the Jewish Novel

The novel was a late development in the literature of the Haskalah, which had gravitated, at the late eighteenth-century Berlin-based outset of the movement, to other, more "serious" genres—Bible translation and commentary, treatises on pedagogy and philosophy, travel narratives, even zoology and other sciences.[49] But the novel quickly demonstrated its appeal, and by the 1860s and 1870s it had become the dominant literary form of the Eastern European Haskalah, aided by the evident usefulness of the novel in spreading Haskalah ideology beyond the narrow circle of its adherents.[50] Nevertheless, the Hebrew or Yiddish novel was not universally embraced even by maskilim in the first decades of its emergence. Along with the fierce opposition of traditionalists, some maskilim with more conservative inclinations considered the novel, and the very notion of reading for pleasure, antithetical to Jewish Enlightenment values. Such a stance was already evident in the Berlin Haskalah: Alexander Altmann records Moses Mendelssohn's response to the transgressions of a thirteen-year-old girl, the daughter of a friend, who was caught by her father reading and discussing *The Sorrows of*

Young Werther with a "handsome young man." In a letter to Goethe written much later, the now-grown woman, Sara von Grotthus (née Meyer),
recounted the episode: "I was punished by confinement to my room, and
Mendelssohn, my mentor, appeared: he bitterly reproached me. Could I
have forgotten God and religion, he asked, and amid foolish reproofs of this
sort he took the dear W[*erther*], the innocent corpus delicti, and threw it
out of the window."[51]

For Mendelssohn, the danger Goethe's novel posed to the young Sara no
doubt extended beyond the act and content of her reading to the romantic
friendship (with a non-Jew) in which the book played a role; it was perhaps
this friendship that posed the most immediate threat to "God and religion."
The "Werther fever" driving young German readers to imitate not merely
Werther's passion but also his suicide may have contributed to the perception that the girl was courting danger. Sara's "innocent" book thus embodied a complex set of transgressions from the perspective of Jewish religion,
patriarchal control, and philosophical rationalism.

Similar ethical, national, and philosophical concerns about pleasure
reading rose to the surface of the Eastern European Haskalah along with
the publication of the first Hebrew novels. In 1858, the Hebrew poet Adam
Hacohen Lebensohn signaled his disapproval of romantic narrative; he preferred the philosophical, lyrical, scientific, and exegetical writings prized
by the maskilim of the period and at which he himself excelled.[52] Another
Haskalah poet and critic, Eliezer Tzvi Zweifel, was more ostensibly neutral in dividing secular reading into two arenas: on the one hand, such
fields as mathematics, measurement, and the rules of proper comportment
"that reason alone derives pleasure from"; on the other, "love stories and
romances" in which "the heart delights because of the pleasantness of the
subject matter and the beauty of speech."[53] This cool taxonomy, however,
failed to conceal Zweifel's disdain for these love stories; referring to the
recent craze for novels, and echoing Mendelssohn's reproach of Sara's abandonment of "God and religion," Zweifel continued: "It is not appropriate
for men of the covenant of Moses immersed in love of his Torah to con-
tinually chase after empty pleasures and clasp the bosom of a daughter of
the void [*u-lehabek hek bat tohu*], reading passionate love stories abhorrent
to the heart of a wise man."[54]

Zweifel's objections to the novel, which may also reflect the envy of a less
successful poet for best-selling novelists, express a double complaint. On the

one hand, these stories are irrational flights of erotic fancy, stimulating the lowly imagination to the detriment of exalted reason; on the other, they are foreign to Jewish (male) sensibilities and endanger the integrity of Jewish identity. These dangers have a long-intertwined double genealogy: Zweifel's rhetoric draws on the ubiquitous biblical link between foreign women and alien religions, associating the pleasures of fiction with the sexual encounters decried in Proverbs 5:20: "Why be infatuated, my son, with a forbidden woman? Why clasp the bosom of an alien woman?" The associations between the erotic and the foreign are overdetermined in the case of the novel, for which forbidden love is such a staple. Nevertheless, the very longevity of the associations between foreign women and borrowed cultural practices undermines the contemporary force of Zweifel's rhetoric by suggesting that chasing after alien pleasures is itself a long-standing, and in this sense perfectly traditional, characteristic of Jewish experience.

If Dan Miron is correct in supposing Zweifel's 1858 attack to have been directed primarily against Mapu's *Love of Zion*, then Zweifel's rhetorical mobilization of Proverbs' alien woman is particularly striking, since the attraction to foreign women plays no role in Mapu's novel (which, on the contrary, according to Zaban, is secretly obsessed with incestuous desires, as suggested by the names of the protagonists, Tamar and Amnon, who in the book of Samuel are half siblings).[55] Zweifel's metaphorical figure points not to any fictional foreign woman in *The Love of Zion* but to the foreignness of the love Mapu describes and the genre conventions with which he describes it. It might be argued, in fact, that Mapu's choice of setting makes a claim for the indigenousness of his Jewish love story precisely as a prophylactic against such attacks as Zweifel's. *The Love of Zion* is clearly a love story along the lines Zweifel lays out, motivated by "the pleasantness of the [romantic] subject matter and the beauty of the [neo-biblical Hebrew] speech"; nevertheless, the very title of the novel declares its native Jewish roots, announcing itself as a story of love *of Zion* (in the multiple meanings of the genitive form), arising in a time and place in which robust Jewish heroes and beautiful Jewish heroines fell in love not in imitation of European manners but presumably from autochthonous impulses. Zweifel's excoriation, then, aims to expose the buried contours of the European pastoral under the rolling hills of Mapu's Galilee, while Mapu plays the opposite game of discovering a Jewish *Ursprache* and native Hebrew soil for the (ostensibly foreign) workings of young love.

Despite these objections to Jewish romance, the decades that followed saw a host of novels in Hebrew and Yiddish, a great portion of which took Jewish love as their primary concern.[56] Nevertheless, the notion that romance (as both experience and literary form) was foreign to Jewish culture did not disappear, even as this discourse shifted both its assumptions and its primary targets. For Zweifel, the novel represented both foolishness and Gentile pleasures, a betrayal of Enlightenment rationality and Jewish integrity. The first of these objections had much less currency for the writers who emerged later in the nineteenth century, for whom the stern supremacy of sober Reason had ceded ground to the enchantments of Romanticism, leavened by a new adherence to literary realism. Scholars of Jewish Eastern Europe sometimes mark 1881 (or the decade preceding) as a watershed moment in which the universalist and rationalist Enlightenment ideals of the earlier decades of the century gave way, under the pressure of rising anti-Semitism and diminishing hopes of integration, to an explosion of radical and nationalist Jewish ideologies and discourses. As did the Enlightenment itself, this new literary-intellectual climate had its counterparts in other regions of Europe. But for all the pan-European character of the movement, romantic nationalism encouraged reflections precisely on what distinguished "the national character," just as realism supported the construction of characters that were "true to type."

Absorbing and countering the nationalisms in the larger environment, these Jewish discourses came to include reflections on the "spirit" and even "folk genius" of the Jewish people; Jewish cultural modes viewed with disgust by the reformers and modernizers of the Haskalah could now be transvalued as evidence of Jewish distinctiveness and the charm of Jewish "folkways." In this cultural environment, Jewish novels were sometimes perceived as foreign to the Jewish spirit, but not—as for Zweifel—because they trafficked in erotic intoxications that were, in their very nature, foreign. Eros was a part of Jewish as of other human experience, but the form it took had to be shown to be distinctly Jewish. While Jewish writers who merely imitated the love stories of other nations, borrowing alien forms and failing to conform to Jewish realities, were subject to harsh criticism, the discovery of distinctively Jewish approaches to Eros became, in the post-1881 era, a central feature of the Jewish national-literary enterprise.

What nevertheless links the Enlightenment moralism of Mendelssohn and Zweifel with the romantic nationalism of generations of Jewish writers that followed is the persistent association between three apparently distinct issues: the uniqueness and continued viability of the Jewish collective, the character of Jewish erotic ideals and experience, and the form and content of the (Jewish) novel. The long associations between "alien" erotic experience and threats to the integrity of the Jewish collective formed an underpinning for this rhetoric; more recent connections between European literary forms and erotic practices created a modern framework for an old problem, contributing to keeping the problem of Eros at the center of the project of forging a national literature. In this way, even as Jewish literature drew from modern European notions of the erotic as the private domain of the individual and the couple, writers continued to mobilize the capacity of the novel to describe—or even constitute—a larger collective. Among the other modern genres, it was the novel, with its attention to interiority as well as its broad social sweep, that was best suited for "imagining the community," representing the larger world of Eastern European Jews as it described, imagined, and gave birth to the Jewish (sexual) individual.[57]

For writers, the project of accounting for Jewish Eros at the individual and national levels was sometimes experienced as a literary conundrum: If Jews had unique erotic practices and ideologies, what were these characteristics, and how might they express themselves in a literature shaped by very different European sexual-literary models? This question came to a head in the late 1880s, when a number of established and emerging writers weighed in on the problem. Sholem Aleichem's literary compilation, *Di Yidishe folks-bibliothek* (Jewish people's library), the first volume of which appeared in 1888, was, as its name attests, a product of the new folkist-national mood (although Zweifel also made an appearance in the volume) and thus an appropriate forum for testing the question of the relationship between a national literature and Jewish Eros, of what constituted the different strokes of Jewish folks.[58]

The compilation, edited and financially supported by Sholem Aleichem, featured in the inaugural volume one of his very first novellas, *Stempenyu*. In an extended foreword that was also included in the compilation, Sholem Aleichem explains that he is dedicating the work to his literary "grandfather" Mendele Moykher Sforim (S. Y. Abramovitsh) "not only because I wrote it in your honor, but also because you aroused in me the desire to write such a novel."[59] The idea for his novel, Sholem Aleichem continues, was suggested in a letter he received from Abramovitsh, which he goes on to quote: "I advise you not to write novels [*romanen*]. Your tastes, and your genre, lie elsewhere. And I doubt if there are romances [*romanen*] among our people. They are so different from the rest of the world that one must understand them perfectly, before attempting to write about them!"[60] Abramovitsh begins here by recommending that the younger writer avoid a literary genre Abramovitsh saw as uncongenial to his particular talents, but he goes on to raise the more general question of whether Jews have romantic experiences, a question that, despite its ostensibly sociological character, turns out also to be related to the problem of literary genre. Romance, Abramovitsh suggests, may not be a universal characteristic of human life but an experience with specific cultural or even racial-ethnic dimensions. If, as Abramovitsh believes, Jews have romances that are "different from other peoples'," this difference must affect the participation of Jewish writers in literary genres developed under the influence of foreign models of romantic experience.

In what Ken Frieden calls a "willful misreading" of Abramovitsh's counsel, Sholem Aleichem responded to the older writer's warning by transforming a recommendation that Sholem Aleichem avoid the novel into an invitation to write a novel about Jewish romance. Sholem Aleichem thus cleared the way for his own project of producing *Stempenyu*, a novella that faithfully follows the conventions of the European genre in its presentation of a handsome man and beautiful woman whose mutual and forbidden attraction provides the impetus for the plot, while nevertheless remaining true to what its author saw as the particulars of Jewish love.[61] Sholem Aleichem writes that Abramovitsh provided him with the recognition that

> a Jewish [or Yiddish] novel must differ from all the other novels. The truth is that the circumstances under which a Jew falls in love, and declares his passion, are altogether different from the circumstances which control the lives of other men. Besides, the Jewish nation has its own peculiarities—its own Jewish spirit [*gayst*] with its own habits, and manners, and customs. And, our national symbols have remained unchanged despite everything. And these, too, must have their place in the Jewish novel if it is to bear a true resemblance to Jewish life.[62]

The letter exchange and dedication shed light on the multiple valences of the novel's full (and untranslatable) title, *Stempenyu: A yidisher roman*. *Stempenyu*, Sholem Aleichem seems to be signaling, is not only a Yiddish novel but also, more interestingly, "a Jewish romance," that is, not just a

romantic novel that happens to involve Jewish characters but also a characteristically *Jewish* romance. (*Stempenyu* thus stands in contrast with Sholem
Aleichem's just-published novella *Sender Blank and His Clan*, subtitled in
Yiddish *A roman on a roman*—which could be translated as "a novel *without* a romance.") In the dedication of *Stempenyu*, Sholem Aleichem provides no details of what he views as the characteristically Jewish approach
to love—these are left to be gleaned from the novella—but he makes it
clear that this approach should be read within the context of the romantic
discourse on national character and spirit. Jewish Eros is thus a positive national trait, an expression of the Jewish life force rather than, as many earlier
maskilim would have it, a conglomeration of oppressive cultural practices
that deny young people fundamental rights and corrupt their natural sexuality. And while maskilim often saw Jewish erotic practices as evidence of
Jewish "backwardness," Sholem Aleichem is persuaded that the distinctiveness of Jewish love (alongside other "authentically Jewish" national symbols)
is a long-standing aspect of Jewish life that continues and should continue
even today, that is, despite the effects of modernization, secularization, and
acculturation.

It is striking that this exploration of the nature of Jewish Eros should
arise not within the context of ethnography or religious reform but around
the question of the nature of Jewish secular literature and, in particular,
of the Jewish novel. The subtitles of Sholem Aleichem's two 1888 novellas, Abramovitsh's advice to the younger writer, and *Stempenyu's* dedication
circle the issue of Jewish love specifically in relation to the problem of genre.
That these are, in some sense, one and the same question is evident from the
way this discourse plays on and vacillates between the multiple meanings of
the words *yidish* (as Yiddish and Jewish) and *roman* (as novel, romance, and
love affair), suggesting the overlap between the novel and romance (in both
senses of the word) while pointing to the distinctiveness of both the Yiddish
novel and Jewish romantic experience. The strategy Sholem Aleichem takes
in pretending to accept Abramovitsh's advice is enabled by the slipperiness
of these terms, which resist English translation even as they open vistas onto
the continuities between literary and romantic experience and the tensions
between its Jewish and non-Jewish expressions.

That the attitudes expressed in this exchange were not limited to these
two writers, or indeed to the genre of the novel, is evident elsewhere in
the inaugural issue of *Di Yidishe folksbibliothek*. Y. L. Peretz's satirical ballad

Monish, which marked his Yiddish literary debut, describes the romance between the title character, a pious and gifted yeshiva student, and the lovely, and German, Maria; at the very height of Monish's tormented passion, the narrator interrupts his story to turn to the audience in mock lament or apology for the unsuitability of Yiddish for his literary purpose:

> My song would sound very different,
> If I sang it for *goyim* in *goyish*,
> And not for Jews, in *zhargon*.
> No proper sound, no proper tone
> Not one word and no style
> Do I have for "love," for "feeling." . . .
>
> Pay a compliment in Yiddish—
> It comes out with no hands or feet:
> "My life, soul, oy, my treasure!"
> Has a taste like a licorice pretzel.
> It has no spirit, it has no salt—
> And it smells of goose *shmaltz*![63]

The problem of expressing passion in Yiddish is not only described but also metapoetically embodied in these stanzas, with the narrator's radical slide from the "sublime" poetry that presumably closely mimics Monish's exalted state in the previous stanzas of the poem to a "novelized" and prosaic rhyming that reflects the coarse, down-to-earth quality of Monish's linguistic and cultural environment. (That the more passionate discourse is *also* expressed in Yiddish partly gives the lie to Peretz's complaint about the impossibility of Yiddish Eros.) This downshift in register accords as well with the contrast often drawn between the erotic/aesthetic sublime associated with Christian-European romantic-literary conventions and the traditional Jewish approach to sexuality, which, as Biale notes, maskilim considered coarse and carnal in its attention to the body and its operations rather than the heart and its sentiments.[64] In Peretz's view, while European romance is taken up entirely with beauty and emotion, the Yiddish language can give birth only to a misshapen body "with no hands or feet"; even in attempting to capture the high sentiment of "love" and "soul," Yiddish gravitates to the materiality and carnality of eating and food. Dan Miron aptly describes the nineteenth-century sense of Yiddish as "the language of Caliban," a deformed linguistic medium appropriate only for expressing the ugliness of the life of its Jewish speakers.[65]

This ugliness sometimes has a specifically sexual dimension: Peretz's pinpointing of what might be called the "sexual style" of Yiddish accords with Katz's characterization of traditional Jewish approaches to marriage as mercenary and practical, joining together "good families" rather than uniting "true soul mates," as well as with the halakhic discourse that openly discusses the details of menstrual stains and prescribes the frequency of marital intercourse for husbands in different occupations, in contrast with the spiritualized eroticism of European romantic convention. It is certainly true that the Jewish textual tradition also holds within its multiple genres sublime erotic poetry, mystical images of divine sexual union, and beautifully simple statements of human love (see, for instance, Genesis 24:67: "Isaac then brought her into the tent of his mother Sarah, and he took Rebekah as his wife. Isaac loved her, and thus found comfort after his mother's death"). Nor were such exalted or ordinary sentiments foreign to traditional Ashkenaz: Stampfer cites the evidence of Yiddish love ballads, and the literature of Hasidism is replete with the erotic imagery of *devekut* (cleaving) for divine-human and Rebbe-Hasid relations. Twentieth-century Hebrew literature, Ilana Pardes shows, found in the Song of Songs ample Jewish warrant for infusing secular Eros with religious content.[66] Nevertheless, Jewish culture in many of its formations followed a different path than the process scholars have traced for post-Christian European culture, whereby Christian Mariolatry and "the choice of suffering or difficulty in preference to gratification" were translated into chivalric adoration for an unattainable noblewoman and then "democratized" to both characterize women as a group and grant to romantic love the status of sublime quasi-religious experience.[67]

Support for Peretz's diagnosis of Jewish sexual culture in *Monish* might be found in one of the memoirs quoted by Iris Parush: Shlomo Saltzman, writing on the twinned emergence in his childhood circles of novel reading and the love match, recalls that his grandmother was mystified by both new phenomena, wondering, "What is there to 'love'? One could love stuffed dumplings or fried goose fat, but a maiden's love of a boy—what could it possibly mean?"[68] Both the language play of *Monish* and the skepticism of Saltzman's grandmother emerge from a pivotal moment in Jewish culture: on the one hand, a sexual "awakening" to the sublimity of love under the influence of European sexual-literary models; on the other, the accompanying recognition (painful or ironic) of the absence of such sublimity in everyday

Jewish discourse, a perspective on love that reduces it to appetite and flesh. Saltzman's memoir presents this pivot through the voices of a grandmother and the grandson who remembers her confusion, while Peretz's poem expresses the presence of twin sexual and cultural perspectives in its "plot" and language, recasting the problem of Jewish sexual modernity not in Katz's rhetoric of social progress but as sexual-linguistic duality, ambivalence, and incoherence.

Such concerns about the mismatch between modern Jewish literary production and modern Jewish experience arose in the context of Hebrew literature as well. Moshe Leib Lilienblum's scathing essay on the subject, which also first appeared in 1888, lamented "the recent 'epidemic' of love poetry" and suggests that these poems can be reduced to one simple formula: "*Her* deep blue eyes, *his* mournful sighs." To this poetic redundancy, Lilienblum poses a rabbinic question: "What new point is each of these statements teaching us?" (*may ka mashma lon*).[69] Lilienblum does not deny that human beings experience love or that the poetic among them might wish to express their experiences; what arouses his skepticism is the formulaic quality of these expressions of passion and their unrelenting obsession with one and only one variety of love:

> Love is a natural human emotion, and it expresses itself in many forms, the simplest and most common of which are the love between a man and a woman and the love of parents for children. And while these are not the same—the first burns like fire and boils the blood, while the second is as calm as a mild breeze; the second is generally long lasting, the first is changeable—they are both strong and natural emotions. Nevertheless, it never occurs to our writers to write poetry about the love parents feel for their children.

Given that these repetitious and predictable love poems cannot be assumed to reflect the actual experiences of their writers, their literary fascination with male erotic anguish must derive from another source. Lilienblum is clear about the nature of that source: "Most of [our poets] are not actually giving voice to the pangs of their own love but rather expressing their desire to write poetry. . . . If these poets were to honestly account for their subject matter, they would acknowledge that they write as they do because that is what they found in world literature." Lilienblum's response to this literary mimicry is that "it is true that nothing human is foreign to us [Jews], and we must examine and learn from it all, but from that it does not follow that we must do as others do." Launching into a summary of the development of French romantic poetry from its origins in the chivalric romance, with its near-religious worship of the inaccessible woman, Lilienblum concludes:

> Among us there never was a cult of women, and we never had knights or noblemen. As for love, although it also is a natural feeling, we never valued it more than any of the other human feelings, including the feeling of hunger and so on, or the feeling of love for children. That is why those poems about simple love, about blue eyes, about sighs, are no more than private issues that might affect an individual but have no place in general literature.[70]

Relegating erotic experience to the (apparently nonliterary) realm of the individual, Lilienblum also denies that the modern era is one that has discovered the power of love. Quoting Heine as saying that love is "an old story," Lilienblum argues that "the new times have brought a reduction in innocence, and once modern calculations are brought to marriage, the role of love is diminished from what it was in previous times. . . . Not many young men these days would work for fourteen years for the sake of love as Jacob worked for Rachel, and there are not many courageous young women now who fight to marry the man they love against the wishes of parents as powerful as King Saul." The proliferation of contemporary love poetry does not augur a new age of love but is symptomatic of its irreversible modern decline. What is signaled in the new love poetry is less the power of love than "the desire to poetize and rhyme."[71] Let no one bring up the Song of Songs, Lilienblum continues, as evidence of the Jewish propensity for love; those lovers were simple shepherds, not modern Jews. What is required from modern Jewish writers is not empty expressions of love but the thoughtful exploration of national problems and communal challenges.

Lilienblum concludes his essay with a note on the Hebrew romantic novel, which he believes began (presumably with Mapu) in the right spirit, using love as "a spice and salt on the main meal," which involved social critique rather than mere love. It is only more recently that novelists began to take love as sufficient sustenance in itself, "absolving themselves of the responsibility to express any matter other than love, as if it itself, love alone, is the most significant activity of the human species. Forget ethical thought, forget common opinions, there is nothing to be explored but love and love alone."[72] That Lilienblum falls under the spell that reduces all varieties of love to its romantic heterosexual expression is evident from the turn in his own language, which begins by using the term "love" to describe a range of human emotions and ends by assuming, along with those he criticizes, that "love" may be used without loss as a synonym for romantic love.

The question of Jewish love, and its relation to Jewish literature, was obviously in the air in 1888, even if these writers are not in full agreement about the nature of what could be called "the problem of Jewish sexual modernity." Abramovitsh seems to suggest that Jews simply lack anything that resembles European romance, either as literature or as real experience. Sholem Aleichem implies that Jews have, and have always had, romantic experiences alongside other humans, although these are as markedly Jewish as other Jewish customs and habits and form part of a national *Geist* that calls for Yiddish literary expression. For Peretz the problem is not so much Jews as their vernacular and discourse: Monish appreciates the sight of a beautiful woman and has the same responses to her as any other red-blooded literary character; but the Yiddish in which his story is told (to us, but presumably also to himself), the Jewish culture through which his love must necessarily be mediated, destroys romantic feeling, bringing it down to the level of food and thus rendering it unlovely and carnal. Lilienblum provides the sharpest explanation for how and why Jewish love diverges from that of Christian-European discourse, with its roots in chivalric love and the overestimation of (unobtainable) women. While the love for women is given sacred and cultic status in Christian-European culture, clear-eyed Jews recognize that romantic love is just one emotion among others and unworthy of literary exaltation or communal attention. Only a blind imitation of European literary formulas accounts for the love poetry "epidemic" Lilienblum diagnoses. For all of these writers, the sublime erotic discourse or even ordinary sexual experience available to their neighbors throughout Europe is held up at the Jewish border. Decades into the modernization process and the experiment of writing secular literature in Jewish tongues, the conventions of European literary genres and romantic life and those of the Jewish social-erotic sphere remain mutually untranslatable.

Writers embarking on the project of forging an authentically Jewish modern literature were thus confronted with a double task: to fight against the urge to allow foreign genres and literary conventions to set the stamp on the Jewish novel and to translate the lineaments of an authentically Jewish Eros into coherent literary form. As Lilienblum did with the formulaic Hebrew-speaking "lovers, poets, and fools," Sholem Aleichem expressed his

disgust at the flights of fancy, melodramatic plots, and implausible characters of the sentimental popular Yiddish literature of his day. Dramatically
staging his indictment of these "crimes," Sholem Aleichem "convicted" the
best-selling author Shomer (the pen name of Nokhem Meyer Sheykevitch)
of unthinking adherence to the romantic conventions of the European pot-
boiler and a lack of faithfulness to the realities of Jewish life in a fictional
"trial," "The Judgment of Shomer" (1888, the writer's *annus mirabilis*). As
the "indictment" charged, Shomer borrowed wholesale from Eugène Sue's
novels, but since he published these novels as his own, "we are obliged to
discuss the merits of *The Poor Millionaire* as a Jewish work, as a novel by
Shomer." Sholem Aleichem continues:

> Unfortunately, there is not a single Jewish type, not a single Jewish scene,
> not a grain of Jewishness in the entire novel. The author conducts himself
> like a performer: he parades before us an entire series of mannequins, arti-
> ficial characters who wander about, run, sit, speak. This one loves that one;
> that one is in love with this one. . . . Shomer orders this or that hero to fall
> on his knees and declare: "I love you, my angel!" So he falls on his knees and
> declares: "I love you, my angel!" . . . Wherever he goes, he finds a rich bride
> with a substantial dowry and piles of money. According to Shomer, money is
> as common as garbage—millions pile up in every corner![73]

Lilienblum's and Sholem Aleichem's judgments of the Hebrew and Yiddish literature of their time are echoed in many twentieth-century critiques.
David Patterson, writing about the Hebrew novel written in Czarist Russia
between the years 1868 and 1888, describes these novels as "hybrid" texts,
with an "awkward jostling of fantasy and realism" and incongruous plots
and settings:

> The violence which so many of the plots contain in the shape of theft, ab-
> duction, arson, suicide and·murder stands out in striking contrast to the
> values and patterns of behavior of the society which they purport to de-
> scribe. This strange paradox stems from the attempt to superimpose the
> flamboyant themes of the western European romantic novel upon a back-
> ground of Jewish life in Eastern Europe which was characterized by sobriety,
> timidity and—in the case of the emotional and passionate instincts—a rigid
> self-control and discipline.[74]

While Patterson and Lilienblum confine their projects to literary criticism, "The Judgment of Shomer" functions as both a devastating attack on

the derivativeness and artificiality of the "highly interesting" works of the writer under indictment and as a manifesto of Sholem Aleichem's more Jewish realism (this realism was, of course, *also* of European provenance as a literary trend). Sholem Aleichem's *Stempenyu*, which first appeared the same year as "The Judgment of Shomer," is populated with a host of unmistakably Jewish types and discovers a distinctive setting for Jewish romance— the attraction of a pious young Jewish matron to the figure of the wandering klezmer fiddler—as well as a distinctively Jewish set of languages, most memorably, the Yiddish lingo Stempenyu speaks with his fellow musicians. Even money is far more realistically rendered: rather than piling up "in every corner," Sholem Aleichem presents it as scarce, an object of constant worry and negotiation.

For all Sholem Aleichem's fidelity to the details and languages of Jewish life and the ultimate faithfulness of his heroine to her husband, the romance that plays itself out between Stempenyu and Rokhele is not entirely divorced from the "low" romantic conventions Sholem Aleichem excoriates in "The Judgment of Shomer"; popular potboilers, it turns out, haunt the emerging Jewish realist novel (and perhaps also Jewish social realities) just as, in Ian Watt's view, the chivalric romance and courtly love have never been fully exorcised from the realist bourgeois novel.[75] *Stempenyu*, described by the author as an attempt to write a love story drawn from Jewish life, also alludes to, parodies, and satirizes as it resists sentimental European romantic conventions. Ultimately, the distinction between "highly interesting romances" and the new Jewish novel rests not in the external world of the emerging Yiddish literary canon but *within* the Jewish novella—and Jewish psyche. Interrupting the rendezvous on Monastery Road between Stempenyu and Rokhele just before it can take place (as Peretz interrupts the fateful encounter of Monish and Maria), the narrator writes:

> The reader, who has probably been accustomed to highly interesting romances, has surely been tortured enough in reading this romance down to this particular point in the narrative, for it contains neither stirring scenes nor extraordinary happenings. No one was shot, and no one was poisoned. And neither dukes nor earls have come upon the stage, so to speak. All the characters are the most ordinary, commonplace folks of everyday life— commonplace men, ordinary musicians, and plain women of rather coarse grain. And the reader is probably waiting for the Sabbath evening to come around, when will be enacted the great melodramatic scene—the romantic

meeting between the hero and the heroine on Monastery Road. But, I must say in advance that the expectation is in vain. There will be no dramatic scene; because our Rokhele did not come here after the fashion of an abandoned woman—not at all like one of those wicked women of highly spiced romances who runs to kiss her lover in every dark corner. No such thing. Rokhele only wanted to see Stempenyu in order to ask him how he—a mere musician—had the audacity to write her, the daughter-in-law of Reb Isaac-Naphtali and the wife of Moshe-Mendel, a letter. And what a letter!![76]

The distinction Sholem Aleichem makes between "highly interesting romances" and his own brand of literary realism is not, of course, limited to Jewish literature. Sholem Aleichem's rueful acknowledgment that his work will present to the reader no dukes or earls echoes as well, Justin Cammy has shown, in American literature; such writers as Hawthorne similarly considered themselves "bereft of a romantic past," since writers from their background "could not draw on the same sources that European literature took for granted—royal families, high society, world-class universities, the Church, architecturally distinguished cities, and so forth."[77] But such distinctions between the world's "proper" arenas for literature and its gritty backwaters were not only of geography but also of genre, in which the melodrama and sepia tones of romance contrasted with the more sophisticated techniques of literary realism rather than with reality; it is just this juxtaposition that characterizes the "antiliterary manifesto" that is part of the prelude of Charlotte Brontë's 1849 *Shirley*:

> If you think from this prelude that anything like a romance is preparing for you, reader, you never were more mistaken. Do you anticipate sentiment, and poetry, and reverie? Do you expect passion and stimulus, and melodrama? Calm your expectations: reduce them to a lowly standard. Something real, cool, and solid lies before you; something as unromantic as a Monday morning.[78]

Sholem Aleichem's discussion of the differences between romance and reality (or realism) draws these issues into the more specific question of Jewish romance, thus commenting not only on generic convention but also on Jewish character. The passage both poses and subverts the apparently straightforward distinction the narrator makes between popular romances and his own Jewish novel by staging it as a difference between the romantic heroine who eagerly runs "to kiss her lover in dark corners" and his own more pious heroine, who is merely meeting her would-be, not-quite lover to express her disgust at his importunities. But in Sholem Aleichem's portrayal of Rokhele's "Jewish" response to Stempenyu's love letter as the transparently manufactured outrage of a good daughter-in-law and loyal wife at the advances of a lowly if fascinating musician, what might constitute its Jewish character? Her piety or her "piety," which is to say, her pious self-deception? Rokhele's desire to meet Stempenyu only in order to tell him off for his audacity both assures the reader of her Jewish "purity" and leaves open the tantalizing possibility that her high dudgeon might be transformed, under the influence of moonlight and Stempenyu's fiery gaze (if not the spell of sentimental literature), into the stolen kisses Sholem Aleichem warns us not to expect. Sholem Aleichem thus both delineates and collapses the distinction between conventional romance and its Jewish varieties, maintaining and even heightening the sexual tension within a scene that claims only to wish to foreclose it in advance. The "highly interesting romances" so foreign to Jewish life, in this passage from a novel that apparently embodies Sholem Aleichem's creed of Jewish erotic realism, thus return to haunt a scene that is staged as their exorcism.

During this same period, Abramovitsh similarly reflected on the problematic lack of fit between European romantic conventions ("princes and marquises") and Jewish life ("ordinary people") in the 1894 introduction to his fictionalized autobiography *Of Bygone Days*. Describing the difficulties that troubled his beginnings as a writer, Abramovitsh pseudo-laments the profound mismatch between the experiences accorded by the Eastern European Jewish social milieu and the stuff of European literature. As the narrator puts it, traditional Jewish life fails to provide opportunities for the adventures—romantic, heroic, martial, courtly—that are, in his view, the very underpinnings of the European novel:

> None of us ever did anything to set the world on fire. Dukes, governors, generals, and soldiers we were not; we had no romantic attachments with lovely princesses; we didn't fight duels, nor did we even serve as witnesses, watching other men spill their blood; we didn't dance the quadrille at balls; we didn't hunt wild animals in the fields and forests; we didn't make voyages of discovery to the ends of the earth; we carried on with no actresses or prima donnas; we didn't celebrate in a lavish way. In short, we were completely lacking in all those colorful details that grace a story and whet the reader's appetite. In place of these we had the *cheder*, the *cheder*-teacher, and

the *cheder*-teacher's assistant; marriage brokers, grooms, and brides; abandoned women, widows with orphans and widows without orphans. . . . This was our life, if you call it a life.[79]

Thus, while Peretz had supposed that pious yeshiva boys were perfectly capable of falling madly in love with beautiful German maidens (even if Yiddish deflated the pathos and sublimity of this experience), the narrator of Abramovitsh's *Of Bygone Days* suggests that such experiences were simply lacking in Jewish life, which conspired in all its particulars to keep yeshiva boys away from girls, especially girls named Maria. Abramovitsh nevertheless makes it clear that although the inhabitants of the *shtetl* were neither dukes nor likely to meet one in life, the narrator of his autobiography certainly had dukes on the brain—and this immersion in popular romance must be counted as itself a significant feature of his erotic life. The complaint here is rendered in terms of both the limited horizons of Jewish adolescent boys and the problem posed to the would-be writers among them, who in being deprived of direct romantic experiences (if not feelings) must also be woefully ignorant of those aspects of life necessary to construct an exciting story.

Taking Abramovitsh's letter to Sholem Aleichem and his own literary oeuvre as more direct evidence of his position on the possibilities of Jewish writing than that provided by this satirical passage, it is clear that Abramovitsh chose the imperatives of realism (which of course were also of European provenance) over the demands of the romantic conventions of European popular literature; indeed, after some initial forays Abramovitsh avoided romantic themes almost entirely in his fiction, presumably in acknowledgment of the foreignness of romance to Jewish life.[80] Sholem Aleichem took a different route out of the same problem, allowing Jewish attitudes to marriage, sex, and romance to shape his 1888 novella, even if he thereby sinned against the conventions of European (or, more particularly, French) romance; the handsome and musically gifted Stempenyu and the lovely and passionate Rokhele come perilously close to adultery but (presumably in keeping with their Jewish character and spirit) are stopped at the last moment by Rokhele's loyalty to her husband. Peretz, however, neither decries nor celebrates the foreignness of romance to Jewish life—Monish finds both the opportunity and emotional wherewithal to fall madly, passionately, and conventionally in love with the beautiful Maria despite being a sheltered yeshiva boy. What the narrator of this love affair discovers is that such passion cannot be faithfully rendered in Yiddish, which coarsens erotic feeling and renders it inappropriately carnal for describing the love Monish feels for such an angelic girl.

The discourse I have been tracing here is almost uniformly ironic, in keeping with the gap these writers perceived between their reach and their grasp, the European genres in which they hoped to participate, and the circumstances from which they could draw as writers. But the irony is not entirely directed at Jewish conditions: Peretz's impossible "translation" of Monish's passion into Yiddish provides an opportunity for comic reflection on both Jewish sexual inadequacies and the flimsy fantasies of the European romance. In Peretz's poem, the shift in register from "my treasure" to "licorice pretzel" demonstrates the erotic "failings" of Yiddish discourse, but it also punctures the conventionality and inflated sentiment of European love. Abramovitsh's depiction of the conventions of the European romance similarly has multiple targets: the Jewish readers whose lives are so small and insignificant in contrast with these romances, the romances whose depictions bear so flimsy a relationship to ordinary life, and perhaps also the ideological values embodied in these romances. After all, fighting duels or even just watching "other men spill their blood" should probably be considered, and not only from the Jewish perspective, foolhardy or immoral behavior.

For all the differences in nuance among the double-edged comedy of Peretz's translation of high-German love into low-Yiddish farce, the Jewish pseudo-distance of Sholem Aleichem's novella from the high-flown conventions of erotic temptation, the satirical cleverness of Abramovitsh's pretend infatuation with European romantic fantasy, Lilienblum's reminders that Jews have no share in European chivalric traditions, and even the humorless moralism of Zweifel's defense of Jewish erotic and national integrity, these texts all participate in a discourse that locates Jewish Eros in a contested border zone between the emerging Jewish national literature and the European context in which it arose. The notion that European romantic conventions are foreign to Jewish experience is common to all these writers, but it is Zweifel who is both the harshest critic of the Jewish trafficking in romance and the most direct in his suggestion that the very foreignness of romance to Jewish sensibilities is an important source of its seductive—its romantic—attractions.

The project of "Judaizing" the romance, for Abramovitsh, Sholem Aleichem, and Peretz, indeed necessarily involves acknowledging the temptations of the foreign. Even in *Stempenyu*, which discovers a romantic hero at the Jewish margins of proper Jewish society, the lovers not coincidentally arrange to meet for their post-Sabbath assignation on Monastery Road, evading Jewish eyes as they indulge in presumably Christian experiences.[81] It is not accidental that the problem of Jewish romance in *Monish* is expressed through Monish's admiration for and adoration of both the beauteous Maria and the songs she sings in a foreign tongue, or that Tevye's daughter Chava and her Cossack husband-to-be, Fyedka, meet over a Russian novel. When Chava tells her father about her new friend, and Tevye asks to know a little bit more about the new man in his daughter's life, Chava proudly tells her father that Fyedka is a second Gorky. Of course, Tevye has no idea who the first Gorky was, so Chava produces a photo of the Russian novelist. Looking at the photo, Tevye asks, "This tsaddik is your Rabbi Gorky"? (*Un dos iz er, der tsaddik deyner, Rav Gorky?*)[82] Tevye's irony precisely captures Watt's point, that the novel both displaces and inherits the functions of sacred texts, serving as catechism and manual—we might say, the *Shulhan Arukh* or *In Praise of the Baal Shem Tov*—of the new religion of love Chava is learning to embrace. At the very moment these writers were beginning to construct a literature faithful to what they considered Jewish distinctiveness, the romantic plot exposed the seductive and inextricable relation between the Jewish and the "foreign." Eros, the necessary building block of Jewish family and community, was also—always and inevitably—the crack in the national edifice, the weakest link in the long chain of Jewish continuity.

The Jewish novel, then, is irremediably divided against itself in its attempt to describe the folk spirit and Jewish Eros. But European literature, and Eros itself, should be read as similarly split. Abramovitsh's complaint that he lacked the opportunity to fight a duel is a statement of how Jewish literature and experience differed from its European counterparts, but it could also be read as a belated Jewish echo of that most characteristic of European novels, Miguel de Cervantes's *Don Quixote* (1605, 1616), which also captures the dissatisfaction of its hero with the lack of opportunities to fight a duel. The novel, in a range of cases throughout its history, incorporates both romance and its absence, the lure of the erotic as a feature of its impossibility. Critics generally distinguish between the older romance and the newer (as the English term suggests) novel, even while demonstrating the persistence of the tropes and structures of the romance within the novel. As Vera Lee writes, the romance is "relatively unbelievable, contains high-flown heroics, unusual adventures and/or a sentimental, idealized love story," while the novel "portrays the real world and is far more prosaic than the romance, is sometimes even a parody of it." Nevertheless, Lee continues, citing *Don Quixote* as prime example, these "two basic trends cohabit in the great literatures at almost any given moment."[83] Indeed, such an interpenetration of novel and romance becomes clearer if one takes *Don Quixote* as early exemplar of the genre: Cervantes's novel is a romance as well as a parody of and commentary on the romance, opposing its own flights of fancy while ultimately transposing them to a different register. As latecomers to the scene (but so was Quixote!), Jewish writers could hardly escape either the lure of romance or the pleasure of its deflation; Jewish literary history is the record of the distinctive modes these writers found of mocking both European romantic fantasies and those Jews (including themselves) who persisted in chasing them.[84]

The Novel and the Rise of the "Sex Religion"

That the novel was fundamentally and from its birth concerned with sexual experience, and played a role in the construction of modern notions of marital love, is most brilliantly demonstrated in Ian Watt's classic study of eighteenth-century English fiction, *The Rise of the Novel* (1957). In Watt's understanding, such English "novels of love" as *Pamela*, *Clarissa*, and *Tom Jones* reflect the new socioeconomic conditions of the eighteenth century, which gave rise to a middle-class urban readership for popular literature. The middle-class culture of these readers was a product of the consolidation of commercial capitalism; the emergence of the individual as an autonomous economic, political, and philosophical unit; and the expansion of the private domestic sphere and modern modes of leisure. Among the most important dimensions of this culture was the ideology of gender complementarity that developed in support of the modern division of labor and other socioeconomic characteristics of the new commercial class. This ideology was economic in its origins and (submerged) logic, but as a set of assumptions about masculine and feminine "nature," it served the important cultural role of underpinning and shaping both reading practices and modern notions of romance.

While the modern middle class was built on the eclipse of feudal, aristocratic, and traditional social and economic structures, these social forms were not entirely effaced. Watt argues that the novel is both a progressive phenomenon, with its bourgeois readership and association with urban modernity, and a conservative phenomenon, in preserving, transforming, democratizing, and thus revivifying such older literary models as the chivalric romance. In Watt's view, both the literary persistence of premodern conceptions of love and emerging eighteenth-century socioeconomic developments contributed to modern bourgeois ideologies of romance, which generalized and universalized the sublime beauty and chastity of the beloved noblewoman to the class of women in general.

Central to the sexual ideology of the new middle class, and to the novel as the most direct expression of this sexual ideology, is the valuation of erotic love as a primary, even defining feature of both modern life and modern literature. In Watt's understanding, this valuation obscures the economic structures of modern marriage, while absorbing and redirecting some of the religious impulses vacated by the secularization process:

> The idea that love between the sexes is to be regarded as the supreme value of life on earth is generally agreed to have its origin in the rise of *amour courtois* in eleventh-century Provence. Courtly love is in essence the result of the transfer of an attitude of religious adoration from a divine to a secular object—from the Virgin Mary to the lady worshipped by the troubadour. Like modern individualism, therefore, the rise of romantic love has deep roots in the Christian tradition, and so it is very appropriate that it should be the basis of the ideal pattern of sexual behavior in our society.

Watt's insights about the role of a secularized chivalric-Christian bourgeois sexual ideology in the emergence of the novel are not limited to the eighteenth-century English novel or indeed to the realm of literary production. Watt continues, "The most universal religion of the West . . . is the sex religion; the novel supplies it with its doctrine and its rituals, just as the mediaeval romance had done for courtly love."[85]

Despite the persistence of courtly ideals in the novel, this genre is nevertheless modern, depending for its structure on developments that arose only in the eighteenth century. As Watt argues, "The values of courtly love could not be combined with those of marriage until marriage was primarily the result of a free choice by the individuals concerned."[86] The freedom to choose one's own marriage partner was neither a possibility nor a value, according to Watt, until the eighteenth century in England (this freedom was achieved significantly later in France, Germany, and elsewhere in Europe), at which point the basic family unit was reduced to "an entity formed by the voluntary union of two individuals." Watt writes, "The characteristics of this [new] family are correspondingly different from those that preceded it. On marriage the couple immediately sets up as a new family, wholly separate from their own parents and often far away from them." In this "reduced" family, "extended kinship ties in general, to grandparents, aunts and uncles, cousins, etc. have no compelling significance." The erosion of extensive kinship networks was accompanied, in eighteenth-century England, by a new imbalance between the necessity and benefits of marriage for men and for women, which in turn led to a dearth of men who wished to marry (in a startling echo of Isaiah's ancient prophecy). With these changes, Watt argues, "marriage was both much more important to women, and much more difficult to achieve."[87]

Watt's description of modern marriage as arising from the free choice of two individuals to construct a "voluntary union" has attracted pointed scholarly critique, given the constraints of eighteenth-century class and gender hierarchies and postmodern skepticism of such optimistic Enlightenment notions as the autonomous individual and the notion of marriage as a "contract" between "consenting adults."[88] So, too, is it important to distinguish, as Watt is not always careful to do, between sentimental and sexual ideologies. Nevertheless, Watt's insights form the basis of many feminist readings of the novel; Nancy Armstrong, for instance, argues that the production of gender binaries is fundamental to the work of the novel and that "the novel exercised tremendous power by producing oppositions that translated the complex and competing ways of representing human identity into a single binary opposition represented by male versus female."[89] Watt's view of the fictionality and internal contradictions of eighteenth-century gender ideologies remains particularly illuminating. Thus, Watt suggests that criticism of Samuel Richardson's 1740 novel *Pamela; Or, Virtue Rewarded* for the calculated and showy "modesty" of its protagonist—the mutual workings of Pamela's prudishness and coquetry (pretentions that Henry Fielding's 1741 parody *Shamela* mocks to devastating effect)—misses the point: these attitudes should be ascribed neither to the slipperiness of the writer nor to the hypocrisy of his female protagonist but to Richardson's exposure of a characteristic double bind of eighteenth-century gender norms, which demanded from literary heroines both passion and temperance, rejection of sexual advances as a strategic form of flirtatious communication, and erotic energy constrained (we might say, after Foucault, constructed and energized) by a host of "manners" and romantic rules:

> The opposite qualities in Richardson's outlook, his Puritanism and his pruri-ence, are the result of the same forces, and this no doubt explains why their effects are so intricately connected. . . . If the latent ambiguities of the sexual code helped Richardson to produce the first true novel, they at the same time conspired to create something new and prophetic in quite another sense: a work that could be praised from the pulpit and yet attacked as pornography, a work that gratified the reading public with the combined attractions of a sermon and a striptease.[90]

Watt's analysis of the ambiguities of the eighteenth-century sexual ethic and their expression in the novel is echoed in a recent sociological study of marriage by Stephanie Coontz, which explores the fundamental ten-sion between the emergent ideal in the eighteenth century of companion-ate marriage and the accompanying ideology of absolute gender difference; bourgeois ideology cast men as essentially carnal, while seeing women as the more spiritual sex, essentially reversing premodern ideologies that con-sidered women, in Watt's words, "a species characterized by an insatiate fleshly cupidity," by democratizing and generalizing the courtly idealization of the angelic heroine who was the object of chivalric love.[91] In the new bourgeois romantic ideology, women and men were seen as inherently dif-ferent in their sexual natures and deepest motivations even as they were encouraged to settle for nothing short of perfect companionship and sub-lime harmony in choosing a mate. Coontz demonstrates that the very doc-trine of sex differences rendered marriage ideologies unstable: "While the doctrine of difference made men and women complementary figures who could be completed only by marriage, it also drove a wedge between them. Many people felt much closer to their own sex than to what was seen as the literally 'opposite'—and alien—sex."[92]

For Watt as for the critics who followed, the novel presented both the ideal of a marriage for love (aided in this idealization by the archetypal end-ing at the wedding altar) and a wide range of difficulties in achieving an appropriate and satisfying match, among which we might count the one pinpointed by Coontz. These difficulties may have frustrated eighteenth-century young men and (especially) women, but the plot of the novel could hardly do without them, generated as it was by both the promise of erotic fulfillment and the need to delay sexual satisfaction in exciting and satisfying ways, to spin out a story and maximize the sexual tension that drove it. For a culture in which marriage was both increasingly important (especially for women) and increasingly difficult (especially for women), the novel was the supreme genre because it staged both the fantasy of ideal marriage and the obstacles to its achievement.

.   .   .

The relevance of Watt's discoveries for the emergence of the Hebrew and Yiddish novel in mid-nineteenth-century Eastern Europe should already be clear. Cultural historians have amply demonstrated that this era, like Watt's eighteenth-century England, was one of significant changes in Jewish marital practices and gender roles, changes that find expression in such novels as *The Love of Zion*. Nineteenth- and twentieth-century Hebrew and Yiddish literature emerged from the same social and cultural conditions that propelled transformations in sex and marriage and played a role in shaping these new cultural realities, each in its distinct way. Beyond Hebrew and Yiddish, a wide range of literary texts, translated into Jewish languages or in foreign languages, participated in populating the reading worlds of modernizing Jews. Zeev Gries suggests that Yiddish translations of European literature had a particularly powerful effect in opening "tantalizing new worlds" before an eighteenth-century Jewish reading public:

> For centuries, the only reading material available to the vast majority of Jews who knew no language other than Hebrew or Yiddish was the traditional religious literature and the commentaries and homiletic texts that derived from it. The literature circulating among the non-Jewish public by the seventeenth and eighteenth centuries, in contrast, bore the whiff of tantalizing new worlds: scientific discoveries, folk tales, and chivalric romances, as well as travel narratives and picaresque novels of an almost mythological character, such as *Don Quixote* and *Robinson Crusoe*. . . . When these roving heroes eventually found their way into the Jewish literary repertoire in the eighteenth century through Yiddish translations, they were eagerly devoured by a ravenous public that included but was not limited to children and young people.[93]

Gries may be overstating the novelty of these translated genres in Jewish languages, since we know that such early modern Yiddish romances, storybooks, and epics as *Bovo Bukh*, *King Arturs Court*, and *Maysebukh*, which also "bore the whiff of tantalizing new worlds," were read in Eastern Europe in numerous editions from their first publication through the nineteenth century.[94] Nevertheless, the late eighteenth and early nineteenth centuries saw a remarkable broadening of available books for interested readers, among them varieties of romantic literature that conveyed new ideologies of sex, gender, and marriage in iconic, stylized, and often idealized form. These were not limited to the Jewish reading public. Jeffrey Brooks has shown that the second half of the nineteenth century saw a marked increase in publication of Russian books directed to working-class, newly urban readers, "stories about banditry and crime, science and superstition, and romance," including "many tales about changing relations between the sexes," which were of particular interest "in a world in which the paternalistic values were contested."[95]

As Watt showed for England, Eastern European literary developments emerged from a close connection between new reading practices and sexual ideologies. Erotic experience is perhaps uniquely open to literary influence, given the resonances between the phantasms of imaginative literature and the idealizations of romantic love and their association with an internal and highly private sphere. The modern romance glorified love, embodied it in its distinctive reading practices, enchanted readers with the notion of enchantment, and trained them in the modes of aesthetic appreciation, courtship, and companionate marriage. As in other European settings, novel reading in Yiddish and non-Jewish European languages was associated in the Jewish world with a female readership. For Hebrew, however, this association was reversed, and it is a curious circumstance of Jewish literary history that the readership of such an exemplary romance as *The Love of Zion* was almost entirely male (although many women readers had access to the novel in its multiple Yiddish versions and other translations); that Lilienblum read, and perhaps translated, this novel to (rather than "with") "N" is no happenstance. This chapter began with a litany of examples of the effect Mapu's romance had on male readers—the one female memoirist who mentions the novel, Pauline Wengeroff, was an acquaintance of the author. But women also read novels in Yiddish and foreign languages. Iris

Parush's research presents documentation of the effects that reading these novels might have on young women:

> The influence on women was manifested in a wide set of changed behaviors that included girls refusing marriage to rabbinic scholars; secret alliances being forged with younger family members to promote enlightenment and secular education; traditional social arrangements being called into question; heretical tendencies; girls running away from home to seek an education; radical and "feminist" social perspectives being adopted; and, in extreme cases, girls joining revolutionary movements.[96]

Parush argues that the association between Jewish women and the reading of modern novels, mostly in Yiddish and European languages, can be attributed to, among other circumstances, "the benefits of marginality": the daily lives of girls were of such scant interest to the religious authorities that these girls were free to read much more widely than their brothers, for whom a traditional curriculum was dictated and policed; through this very marginality, women became "agents of secularization" in the larger Jewish world. Despite this freedom, the effects of reading on Jewish girls and women eventually became pronounced enough to draw rabbinic attention. Thus, Rabbi Gershon Henoch Leiner, the Radzyner Rebbe, excoriated secular literature in 1890 as "clownish degenerate tales and promiscuity and lewdness" and asked whether the effects of these promiscuous tales might be to devalue traditional marriage, since "is it possible that the maiden [who reads such books] will content herself afterward to marry a Torah scholar as is commanded by our rabbis of blessed memory for will she not scorn him in her heart?"[97] Parush is careful to avoid drawing a direct connection between reading novels and rejecting a traditional arranged marriage (although Katzenelson's description of how reading *The Love of Zion* rendered his prospective bride insufficiently beautiful to him makes precisely such a link), pointing to the condescension and stereotyping that often accompany reports of love-besotted female readers. Nevertheless, Parush acknowledges that "it is hard, for all that, to doubt that the heroines in these novels, the ones who run off with the handsome, prominent *maskil* and are rewarded by marriage to him, would have captured the imaginations of a great many women and would have come to be ideals for them."[98]

For all the overlaps between eighteenth-century England (in Watt's account) and mid-nineteenth-century Jewish Eastern Europe, the differences between these contexts should not be overlooked. As the nineteenth-century accounts of leaving home cited earlier have already signaled, the sexual modernization of Eastern European Jews was often an abrupt break rather than a gradual process, given the culture wars—attested in the autobiographies—between parents and children, particularly around traditional marital arrangements and their modern variations. However, Watt describes an English cultural setting that gave rise gradually and as if "organically" to new literary forms. Modern Jewish literature, moreover, drew more directly from French, German, and Russian literary models than from English literature, and the formal realism Watt describes as characterizing the English "novels of love" made only a belated appearance in Hebrew literature (the first Yiddish novel, Yisroel Aksenfeld's 1862 *The Headkerchief*, conforms much more closely than Mapu's works to the norms of literary realism).[99] The preferences for sentimental and melodramatic romances modeled on such popular French fiction as Alexander Dumas's novels and especially Eugène Sue's *Mystères de Paris* (read by thousands in Kalman Schulman's best-selling 1857 Hebrew adaptation) undoubtedly widened the gap so many writers perceived between Eastern European Jewish realities and the expression of romantic experience in Jewish literature. The distance between novelistic depictions of love and Jewish realities was a function of counterforces on both sides of the literature/life equation: writers were slow to adopt the conventions of literary realism, while social realities were slow to embrace erotic ideals.

Watt's genealogy of the modern novel suggests another important distinction. In Watt's view, the literary background of the eighteenth-century English novel is the courtly romance, which in turn secularizes Christian Mariolatry. As Lilienblum had pointed out nearly seventy years before the publication of Watt's study, the romantic worship of a woman (or women) had no Jewish prehistory on which to draw.[100] In commenting on the different marital customs and gender expectations of medieval Jews and Christians, Israel Abrahams similarly suggests that "the same events that gave chivalrous romance a commanding influence in the marriage customs of Christian Europe produced an exactly opposite effect in Jewish circles. There are two ends to a spear, and while the Christian knight handled the butt-end, the Jew was acquainted only with the point."[101] In other words, traditional (and perhaps also post-traditional) Jewish culture may be not only non-chivalric, but actively *anti*-chivalric, as Daniel Boyarin argues, constituting an alternative code of civility in which the ideal man is a gentle scholar rather than a "virile" knight. Reading Glikl of Hameln's loving descriptions of her husband as "devoted, reliable, gentle, and emotionally warm," Boyarin points out that "these were not the characteristics of a 'knight in shining armor.'" The ideal of a gentle scholarly man exists in Christianity, but only in the form of a monk; by contrast, Jewish culture views marital sexuality as perfectly compatible with male decency, spirituality, and gentleness. Boyarin writes, "The very qualifications that would render a young man fit to be a monk within European Christian culture—scholarliness, quietism, modesty, and a spiritual aptitude—are those that qualify him to be a husband in this Jewish culture."[102]

Boyarin's project is aimed at tracing the distinctiveness of Ashkenazic culture in its traditional forms, while viewing "modern Jewish culture, liberal and bourgeois in its aspirations and its preferred patterns of gendered life" as the result of Europe's "civilizing mission."[103] My own project is to complicate the view of modern Jewish culture that views this Jewish distinctiveness as largely ending with the adoption of European norms (except insofar as this adoption entailed distinctively Jewish ways of internalizing negative European attitudes toward Jews); modern Jewish culture is not simply the effect of a wholesale embrace and passive absorption of foreign models of gender and romance. While Stempenyu and his beloved meet on Monastery Road and Monish falls in love with a girl named Maria, they do so as outsiders to both the romantic values *and* the religious estimation of virginity implied in these names, even if their Jewishness has not entirely inoculated them against the charms of these streets and girls. Watt provides a suggestive model for understanding the co-emergence of new cultural models of sex and marriage and the eighteenth-century English novel, but the particular circumstances of the rise of the Jewish novel in mid-nineteenth-century Eastern Europe should warn us against assuming that this process worked similarly in the Jewish case. While chivalric romance might "organically" underpin modern (Christian) heterosexual courtship, the adoption of chivalric models in modern Jewish courtship necessarily involves the transgression of a highly charged religious-ethnic boundary. The lack of a long-established sacred ground as the basis for the secular modern "overestimation" of both celibacy and the (female) love object no doubt made it just a little harder for Jews to take either virginity or grand passion with the high seriousness required and lent Jewish literature a distinctive character. In establishing

Jewish variants of European romance, both Jewish sex-gender difference (the "married monk") and the long tradition of Jewish anti-chivalric critique inevitably played an important part.

Rather than reflect the congruence of religious background, social realities, and literary motifs that Watt shows for eighteenth-century England and Brooks for late nineteenth-century Russia, modern Jewish literature seems to arise from a series of mismatches, including the basic disjuncture between European literary models and Jewish attitudes toward women, literary traditions, and contemporary experience. To the tensions that necessarily arise from a gap between form and content, religious foundations and their secular translations, we might also add the distinctions between ideology and reality. Despite the ideological changes Freeze documents, many Jews—and perhaps most writers—were still ensconced in the marriages arranged in their youth or otherwise tied to a social order that was troubled but not fundamentally transformed by social liberalization or new cosmopolitan currents. Israel Bartal, in an essay analyzing the process of Jewish Europeanization, demonstrates that the ideal views of family, marriage, and masculinity that can be gleaned from the writings of nineteenth-century maskilim bore little relation to the lives these ideologues led: men of the Eastern European Jewish intelligentsia upheld theories of the proper male dominance in the family and its economy, but their memoirs amply reveal their real and perceived impotence in both sexual and economic spheres. The image of masculinity propagated in Haskalah writings, Bartal concludes, "was as far from the reality of family life in Eastern Europe as was Berlin from Shnipeshok [a suburb of Vilna] in Lithuania."[104] Speaking more specifically about the literature of the era, Alan Mintz points to "the radical tension between the new ideals of companionate marriage and the untransformed social institutions of courtship and marriage" that actually characterized mid-nineteenth-century Jewish life. Given the requirements of the genre,

> the relations between the sexes had to figure in the construction of the novel, if not as a central axis then at least as a crucial component. How seriously this requirement was taken—and how impossible its fulfillment—can be seen in the works of such Haskalah novelists as Mapu and Abramowitsch; "romance" is always present in the structure of the novel, yet it is a component which is most often comically detachable from the main thematic business of the novel, and bears no mimetic relationship to social reality.

> From the perspective of the [turn-of-the-twentieth-century] generation of Berdichevsky and Brenner, then, the allegiance to these generic conventions on the part of Haskalah literature perpetuated a lie. In the social and educational system of Eastern European Jewry, the romance of the novel hardly existed; indeed, it was a conspicuous absence.[105]

Mintz is undoubtedly correct in describing the gaps that separate nineteenth-century Jewish literature and social realities. Nevertheless, even if the generation of Berdichevsky and Brenner did not see it, the gaps that divided literature and life, Jewish modernization and the literature that emerged from it, were culturally generative, producing a literature that derived its energies from these very gaps.

Given the differences between nineteenth-century Jewish literature and the eighteenth-century English novel, Watt's project of bringing together a sociological reading of changing marital practices with a literary reading of the novel can provide only the broadest template for my own project. My immodest aim in this book is nevertheless to provide, in some sense, a Jewish counterpart to Watt's *Rise of the Novel*, reading the emergence of modern Jewish literature in the light of sexual modernization, Europeanization, and secularization. It is not only the different contexts that distinguish Watt's project from my own: Watt focused on three major eighteenth-century novelists—Defoe, Fielding, and Richardson—taking their contributions as the foundation for the English novel in its long history. I am interested in reading the first Hebrew and Yiddish novelists against the background of new marriage practices, but the argument I am making extends beyond the nineteenth to the twentieth century and beyond the novel to other related narrative genres (in particular, Hebrew autobiography and poetry and Yiddish closet drama for the nineteenth century, and theater, film, and the short story for the twentieth). To summarize my argument: Nineteenth-century Jewish literature, in a variety of secular genres, begins with the adoption of both European literary genres and conventions and European sexual conventions and ideals—to this extent, my argument resembles Watt's. But the Jewish adoption of European literary and sexual conventions was always partial and ambivalent, as I have begun to show. In the twentieth century, for reasons both literary and sociological, Jewish literature came to embrace what writers saw as traditional Jewish attitudes toward love and marriage, viewing tradition—or a modern imagining of "tradition"—as a source of erotic power. What began as a process of Jewish modernization and Europeanization was transformed into the literary discovery of "authentic" Jewish Eros. This literary discovery of "tradition," as it turned out, spoke for and to audiences beyond Jewish Eastern Europe and came to constitute a recognizable and distinctively Jewish voice within European and American literature. In the modern Jewish voices of Sigmund Freud, Bernard Malamud, Grace Paley, Lenny Bruce, Erica Jong, Philip Roth, and Tony Kushner, traditional Jewish attitudes and approaches to sex, marriage, and gender find surprising echoes. The persistence and redis-covery of traditional Jewish erotic attitudes in modernity contributed to the formation of a modern sexual counter-narrative to the Christian-chivalric models of love, most strikingly in psychoanalysis. With these developments, Jewish literature came full circle from its beginnings in Jewish Europeaniza-tion to its culmination, after Freud, in the "Judaization" of world literature. Traditional Jewish sexuality, reworked in its encounter with European forms that claim a very different genealogy, emerges, in the twentieth century, as a full-fledged Jewish counter-discourse that has moved into the center of the ways we understand sex.

CHAPTER TWO

Matchmaking and Modernity

> What has God been doing since the creation of the world? He sits
> and makes matches, assigning this man to that woman, and this
> woman to that man. . . . It is as difficult for the Holy One, Blessed be
> He, as the dividing of the Red Sea.
>
> —Bereshit Rabba 68:4

> The longing for destiny is nowhere stronger than in our romantic life.
>
> —Alain de Botton, *On Love*

Expelling the Marriage Broker

"For the maskilim," David Biale writes, "arranged marriage and the particular role of the *shadkhan* (marriage broker) constituted the most offensive
symbols of the mindless tyranny and seamy commercialism of traditional
Jewish society."[1] Such attitudes are on full display in the autobiographical
literature of the late eighteenth and nineteenth centuries, which details the
struggle of individuals against a mercenary and family-oriented marriage
system alongside the quest for education and Enlightenment. Salomon
Maimon's *Lebensgeschichte* (Autobiography), published in 1793–94 and read
widely in German as well as Jewish Enlightenment circles, provided a fierce
critique of early arranged marriage that got satirical mileage from both the
machinations of his parents' efforts to marry off their young prodigy (by
the time he turned eleven, his father had already sold him to the highest
bidder twice!) and the miseries of a marriage that included his move, as an
early adolescent, into a household dominated by a shrewish mother-in-law.
Maimon strikes the notes that would recur in Haskalah autobiography for

the next century: the commercial character of traditional marriage arrangements, sexual segregation as an obstacle to the development of normal relations between the sexes, the perils of early marriage and the premature sexuality dictated by this practice, the traditional wedding as a kind of tragicomedy, and even (in another maskilic theme) witchcraft as a cure for the sexual dysfunction that was a common if not inevitable by-product of these unions.[2]

Maimon's case accords with details of marriage arrangements we know from other sources: the gifted young scholar was a prize catch.[3] For a poor family such as Maimon's, the promise of settling their son's future early and the financial opportunities opened by their son's talents were tempting enough to encourage the kind of premature and enthusiastic overselling that lends Maimon's account its farcical character; and the young bride and groom were given no voice in the arrangements. The new couple's boarding for a period of some years with the bride's family, the source of much unhappiness for Maimon as for other young bridegrooms, was a necessary part of the marital arrangements, given the youth of the pair.[4] The very enticements of such a marriage, as Maimon suggests, were also cause for its ultimate failure: the young couple were suited to one another only by a set of external metrics, the union of so immature a boy and girl was a recipe for sexual and marital failure, and marriage in this system turned young boys not into little husbands but into manufactured orphans.

As is evident from the autobiographies, the practices described by Maimon persisted in nineteenth-century Eastern European Jewish society, particularly, as Immanuel Etkes has shown, among the scholarly elite, the circle of *Lomdim* from whom writers and intellectuals almost by definition emerged.[5] Mordecai Aaron Günzburg's *Aviezer* (begun in 1828 and published posthumously in 1864), which describes the marriage practices of an educated family, pivots around a boyhood interrupted by matchmaking: "I was eleven years old and the matchmakers that congregated in my father's courtyard to propose matches with rich men, honored men, reminded me that my childhood had come to an end."[6] The attempts of Günzburg's father to capitalize on his son's intellectual gifts and the family pedigree collapse when a relative converts to Islam (which Alan Mintz suggests is a euphemism for Christianity).[7] Given the decline in value occasioned by this "stain" on the family honor, the marriage brokers evaporate, and when they finally returned, "they brought ignorant families, and my father was ready to sell off his pedigree to a family with no name."[8] Like Maimon, Günzburg was initially unable to consummate his marriage; unlike Maimon, Günzburg makes his impotence a major focus of the autobiography, also describing, in graphic detail, the grotesque effects of the "cure" his mother-in-law concocted for his sexual troubles.[9]

The most novelistic of these autobiographies, Moshe Leib Lilienblum's *Sins of Youth*, also captures a comfortable childhood prematurely disrupted by the machinations of parents bent on marrying him off. On the day of his betrothal in 1857, at fourteen, Lilienblum writes,

> I woke up and was lounging in bed with the laziness of an only son when my father announced: "Arise, bridegroom! Why are you still asleep? Go to the synagogue, your mother-in-law is coming!" I couldn't make head or tails of what he was saying, and didn't try to, because I thought he was joking. . . . I prayed my prayers and with the group of boys my age climbed up to the roof of the synagogue, which I had never done before, to see whatever foolish things boys like to see. I climbed back down and went home, where my grandmother had a new story for me, the likes of which I had never dreamed. She told me that a rich lady had come from the city with her daughter, who was eleven, and she wanted to take me as a bridegroom for that daughter. . . . And then we went to the house of my mother-in-law's relatives, where the betrothal contract was to be written up. I sat on a bench in front of the assembled guests and from afar I could see a little girl, who looked to me not much older than three years old, and I understood that she was the bride.[10]

In setting these scenes on the vertically "split stage" of the synagogue roof and a series of domestic interior spaces, Lilienblum presents a marriage that commences through disconnection and incomprehension between parents and children and (more "horizontally") between prospective bride and groom; the curiosity that propels him up to the synagogue roof "to see whatever foolish things boys like to see" is not matched, for this particular adolescent, by sexual interests that might provide some motivation to wed. It is only on experiencing a nocturnal emission shortly after his betrothal that Lilienblum consents to be married, as a prophylactic against "Lilith and her demons." Describing the wedding that took place a year later and speaking to his younger self in the second person, Lilienblum makes bitterly clear that while his early marriage may have saved him from the torments of

Lilith, it was also the source of all his subsequent troubles and constituted the trauma that generated the autobiography:

> A great noise broke out: "Mazel tov! Mazel tov!"
> —Mazel tov to you, bridegroom of blood in the throes of trouble and horrific pain, Mazel tov to you for a life filled with despair and the reek of death, Mazel tov to you on your tragic biography, which is no more than the offspring of that very same "Mazel tov!"[11]

Lilienblum appropriates the mysterious and violent biblical story of "the bridegroom of blood" (Exodus 4:24–26) for the polemical purposes of condemning the barbarism of early arranged marriage, discovering in the story a means of viewing such a marriage as a bloody assault not on a virgin bride—as modern readers might expect—but on a premature bridegroom, who is subjected to something like the crude emergency circumcision performed (by a woman!) on Moses's son.[12] In linking his own "tragic biography" to this sexual trauma, Lilienblum suggests that this bloody union gave birth to texts as well as misspent lives.

It would not be difficult to make the case that the modern Hebrew and Yiddish novel was born from the same sociosexual trauma Lilienblum describes as the root of his biography, similarly participating in the painful *Kulturkampf* between the old way of organizing power in the Jewish family and the permanently traumatized if newly rebellious young victims of this system. Despite the struggle against arranged marriage shared by both autobiographical and fictional literature of the period, these genres took very different approaches to the issue. Tova Cohen, in her study of the image of women in Haskalah literature, stresses that this literature drew from both its sociological context and literary models: "On the one hand the image expresses a complex extra-literary reality . . . that includes social and ideological principles as well those connected with the personality of the writer himself. On the other hand this image is part of a network of literary conventions and functions and intra-literary traditions."[13] In distinguishing between extra-literary reality and intra-literary conventions, functions, and traditions, Cohen points out that while the bride in a nineteenth-century arranged marriage might well have been in early adolescence, the heroine of a nineteenth-century Hebrew romantic novel must be of age, since she functions by generic convention as both a victim—indeed, *the* victim—of the traditional system and an active erotic agent in her own right.[14]

While I have described as novelistic the striking scene of the young Lilienblum playing on the roof of the synagogue while his parents negotiate the terms of his betrothal to a little girl elsewhere in town, such a scene has no place in the novel as Mapu and his peers conceive it, which requires the courtship of attractive young adults at the first awakening of sexual desire. Nevertheless, the distance between the worlds described in this literature and those lived by its writers and readers should not rule out its real effects in transforming lives. As the testimony I traced in the first chapter abundantly attests, the novel both described the erotic lives of its characters and awakened erotic responses in its readers, creating libidinal energies that could be mobilized for social and cultural ends.

The generic conventions at play in the autobiography worked in rather different ways. Lilienblum's autobiography shares with the other autobiographies of the period the insistence that the protagonist in the marriage drama is completely sexually ignorant at the betrothal and thus an "innocent victim" of the arranged match; Lilienthal's first nocturnal emission thus comes *after* his betrothal. However, intra-literary motivations determine that the major events of *The Love of Zion* play themselves out between Tamar's seventeenth and eighteenth birthdays, the archetypal liminal period in a young girl's life when budding sexuality combines with innocence and virginity. This is roughly the age of other heroines, but by an equally strict set of conventions, the heroes must be a little older in the narratives of the period. While historians tell us that marital age was rising for all segments of the Jewish community during the nineteenth century for a host of sociological reasons, Jewish literature had already accomplished this revolution for internal literary reasons that may also have been bolstered by and certainly lent support to the delay of marriage among its readers.[15]

Other differences between the Hebrew autobiographies and the novels of the same period are equally instructive. The autobiographies (which like the novels, are nearly all authored by men) focus on the consequences of early arranged marriage on the development of young boys. Maimon set the pattern in this regard, too, casting his mother-in-law as the villain of the traditional marriage plot and taking the plum role of victim for himself—despite his later abandonment of his wife and children in search of enlightenment.[16] Lilienblum, who left his family for a time to pursue secular education (unlike Maimon, he suffered pangs of guilt for this abandonment), implicitly depicted his marriage as a near rape of the young groom by mobilizing a biblical intertext that could portray a quasi-sexual assault on an infant boy. Writing in 1910, Rabbi Yitzhak Nahum Twersky of Shpikov, the scion of the prestigious Chernobyl dynasty, described his impending marriage to the daughter of the Rabbi of Belz, which would entail his moving into the court in Belz, as being inducted into a harem. Twersky underlines the word "harem," as he says, to emphasize that "I am being married by coercion, against my will."[17] While traditional marriage is often viewed as an assault on the rights of women, these writers did not see it that way. Early arranged marriage, in this autobiographical literature, entraps talented young boys in a system that hampers their intellectual growth as well as sexual and emotional well-being; arranged marriage in this textual configuration is the enemy less of heterosexual courtship than of Enlightenment education and self-realization.

The Jewish novel juxtaposes arranged marriage not with the pursuit of education but with the ideology of romantic love: the marriage novel functions, as Watt explains, as the conveyor of the dogmas and rituals of this "religion," which places the highest existential value on romantic love rather than on (as in traditional ideologies) the construction of a family or (as in Haskalah ideology) the intellectual development of an individual. Despite the male authorship of nearly all Jewish literature of the period (and the largely male readership in Hebrew), the romance is oriented to female at least as much as male experience, associating love and sentiment—its primary concerns—with femininity in accordance with the bourgeois ideology of gender complementarity.[18]

This focus on female sentiment distinguishes it from the Hebrew lyric poetry of the day as well; as Lilienblum pointed out in an 1888 essay, that genre assumed or demanded a male authorial voice and recounted "*his* sighs for *her* blue eyes" rather than vice versa, in accordance with the exclusion of women both from Hebrew study and the European lyrical tradition, in which the poetic speaker was strongly associated with the (generally) male poet.[19] In the novel, however, the female rather than the male protagonists function as the particular victims of arranged marriage and the prime beneficiaries and even agents of the love match. Sitri's speech against arranged marriage in *The Love of Zion*, which serves as Mapu's maskilic manifesto against the practice, laments the young wife whose lack of marital affection leaves her withered "like a frost-bitten rose," reserving his sympathy exclusively for women rather than men caught in loveless marriages.[20] Thus, while such autobiographers as Maimon and Günzburg regularly describe the ill treatment they received at the hands of their mothers-in-law during the period of *kest*, those who wrote literature were much more likely to view arranged marriage as part of a system that combined parental control over adolescent children with the patriarchal control of men over women. Y. L. Gordon's maskilic citation and expansion of Genesis 3:16 in his 1875 epic poem, *The Tip of the Yud*, can stand in for broader trends in the literature of the day: "The hand of your father rules over you in your virginity / and upon departing his house— / your husband comes to dominate you."[21]

In a final distinction between the autobiographies and other literary works, the arc and pace of the autobiographies are shaped by their different generic affiliations. While the arrangements for marriage and the marriage ceremonies are described in detail in a number of Hebrew autobiographies, these descriptions are a prelude to the miserable consequences of arranged marriage, which unfold at far greater length, often without shying away from entering the unhappy marital bedroom. In nineteenth-century romantic narrative, it is the period before marriage that occupies center stage, with the arc of the plot ordinarily coming to rest at the end of the novel, under the wedding canopy, once the schemes of parents and villains have been thwarted and the happy union of the lovers can take place.[22]

In this basic comparison, the nineteenth-century Jewish novel has already begun to show its distinctive contours: While the nineteenth-century Jewish autobiography primarily (at least in its early chapters) emerges as a generational conflict, the prototypical Haskalah marriage plot takes shape along two perpendicular axes. The first of these, and the one that plays out in the foreground of the novel, is the "horizontal" field on which young people carry on a courtship and contend with the obstacles that painfully and deliciously delay their union; this axis is the one most closely modeled after European romantic patterns and the one that requires attractive protagonists who have reached their sexual prime. In this regard, the modern Jewish romance follows the teleological trajectory Peter Brooks describes as the engine of the novel, in which "plot [is] a form of desire that carries us forward, onward, through the text."[23] The second, "vertical" axis pits children against parents in an intergenerational ideological battle; this axis is more closely related to the struggles that shape nineteenth-century Jewish autobiographical literature. The Haskalah plot, borrowing from European and Jewish literary conventions, is an elegant and economic means of weaving together these two axes. Parents and other members of the older generation (among other villains, usurpers, and hypocrites) serve as the "blocking figures" that Brooks reminds us a romantic plot can hardly do without, while the younger generation serves as the ideological embodiment of a new social order, expressing the rightness of this order by virtue of youth, beauty, mutual love, and capacity to follow the European romantic script in the face of "Jewish" impediments—that is, Jewish parents. The romantic narrative thus combines the trajectory of romantic desire with the teleological "march of progress," achieving sexual fulfillment and Europeanized modernity under the very sign of Jewish tradition—the wedding canopy.[24]

While the conventions of the Hebrew autobiography allow the writer direct ideological excurses on the evils of the arranged marriage (alongside more neutral "ethnographic" descriptions of marital customs), Jewish narrative fiction typically mobilizes plot and character in the service of ideological argument. The romantic plot not only rewards the enlightened hero with a beautiful bride; it also stacks the deck against arranged marriage by having the matches proposed by parents involve eminently unsuitable couples or grotesquely unappealing prospective bridegrooms. That it is a prospective bridegroom who is regularly denigrated in these novels accords with the logic of the gender ideology that underwrites the romance, which insists particularly on both the beauty and the emotional delicacy of (all) brides and young women; the deformed or ugly bride (rather than groom) is a staple of matchmaking folklore and regularly appears in Haskalah autobiography as well. The first Yiddish novel, Yisroel Aksenfeld's *The Headkerchief* (composed in the 1840s, published in 1863) bridges the institutions of arranged marriage and the love match, but the beautiful bride is the constant in both scenarios. At the start of the novel the community, led by a corrupt Hasidic Rebbe, fines the protagonist, Mekhl, for a minor religious infraction and breaks off his impending arranged marriage to the beautiful Sheindel; Mekhl, after leaving the traditional world behind, forges the betrothal again on his own terms and manages to win back his bride from the eminently unsuitable second bridegroom to whom her parents have betrothed her.[25]

The same holds true for the Hebrew novels that followed: Mapu's *Love of Zion* rallies readers' objections to arranged marriage by having the beautiful Tamar affianced against her will to the morally repugnant and physically loathsome Azrikam. Sarah Feige Foner-Meinkin's 1881 novel, *The Love of the Righteous*, one of the few female-authored works of the period, is fueled by the protagonist's horror at seeing her friend Henrietta, a lovely and sophisticated Italian Jewish young woman, married off to a revolting Galician Hasid; Henrietta is so unhappy with her mate that she attempts suicide shortly after the wedding. In all these cases, the correctness of the love match is demonstrated by juxtaposing appropriate bridegrooms (handsome, kind, maskilic) with inappropriate ones (ugly, immoral, traditional), while a perfect (at least in the "bio-erotic" sense—her intellectual worth hardly matters) bride serves as both judge and prize in this contest between rival varieties of Jewish masculinity.[26]

But beautiful and articulate heroines could not alone carry the weight of reforming Jewish society. Because the nineteenth-century romantic narrative involved a national-cultural dimension, pitting European models of romance against those propagated by the traditional Jewish family, Haskalah writers often constructed older characters that could authorize "modern" ideas by lending them the patina of age; these figures generally represented the proper blend of tradition and modernity, as opposed to those characters in which tradition was a hypocritical mask for corruption (the maskilic "sage" also served a more European-literary function, as the "mentor" to the hero and/or heroine on his or her quest).[27] This mobilization of character was paralleled and reinforced on the linguistic and intertextual level in the search for distinctively Jewish (and thus "old" in another sense) sources for ostensibly foreign concepts. Establishing both the antiquity and Jewish character of the apparently modern concept of true love, *The Love of Zion* places its most direct critique of arranged marriage in the mouth of the wise Sitri, who contrasts the virtue and beauty of simple village life to the spoiled and artificial pleasures of the city. Describing "the son of Zion" (that is, the resident of Jerusalem) who "at noon is still asleep in his ivory bed," Sitri claims that

> even the pleasures of love, so sweet among village people, are corrupted for city dwellers, because pride and wealth are like an iron wall between them and their desires, alienating them from their own passions. I have seen those who love honor and wealth sell their tender, delicate daughters to some haughty noble who boasts of his ancestry and wealth. These poor girls . . . wither like frost-bitten roses when they fall prey to such heartless men, whom they loathe.[28]

In placing this encomium to the beauties of natural love in the mouth of an older man, Mapu militates against the ready notion that the pleasures of love are an invention of young people, thus productively complicating the Haskalah novel's larger tendency to map the battle between traditional marriage and modern romance onto a generational axis. And reversing the charge that the notion of marrying for love is a corrupt feature of urban modernity, Mapu also claims true and natural love for the simple villager. While city dwellers have lost the capacity to appreciate or enjoy love, their daughters, by virtue of their feminine "delicacy," retain this capacity and thus are the potential engines of the socio-erotic revolution Mapu implicitly recommends here.

Mapu's *Hypocrite* brings together the two functions of the determined heroine and the authoritative master of Jewish sources in one figure, Elisheva, who is that rarest of creatures, a female maskil (or maskilah). Like Sitri, Elisheva combats the system of matchmaking by framing it as a particularly debased form of urban commercialism, complaining to her grandfather about being treated "like a precious jewel that gets displayed on the street for all potential buyers, with a price put on it, and everyone who walks by turns it over to find its flaws."[29] Despite the contemporary setting of the novel, Elisheva manages to locate the features of the love marriage in the ancient past, demonstrating through textual acumen that the consent of the young couple, far from being a modern innovation, is a distinguished feature of biblical marriage practices. Elisheva discovers the authority for the right to choose her own mate in the Genesis story of Eliezer's journey to Padan-Aram to propose a match between his master's son Isaac and Rebecca. In response to Eliezer's proposal, Rebecca's mother and brother say, "Let us call the girl and ask for her reply. . . . 'Will you go with this man?'" (Genesis 24:57–58).[30] Elisheva may be evading her parents' wishes, but she does so by reaching past them, as it were, to an "enlightened" grandfather and to her biblical ancestors. She finds warrant for her position, remarkably, in the one passage of the Bible that most resembles a traditional Eastern European matchmaking scene: Eliezer serves as Abraham's agent in brokering a marriage for his son Isaac, in a scene in which the exchange of "costly gifts" plays as prominent (though only indirectly acknowledged) a role as it does in descriptions of Ashkenazic marriage arrangements. Moreover, while Rebecca's consent is solicited, she grants it before she lays eyes on her prospective bridegroom or even his father.

This same biblical proof text appears in Gordon's *Tip of the Yud*, where it is cited within a very different rhetorical performance. In a series of questions to the "Hebrew woman" to whom the poem is addressed, Gordon asks:

Why should you look at the one standing at your side,
To see if he is a hunchback or spindly, an old man or young?
It is all the same to you! You are not the one who chooses,
Your parents do the choosing, they rule over you,
Like an object sold from domain to domain do you pass.
Are they Arameans that they should ask the opinion of the young
    daughter?[31]

The cultural assumptions that underlie modern marriage—that marriage should be preceded by the meeting of a prospective bride and groom and built on mutual attraction and love—are invoked here only by indirection, with the narrator ironically taking on the voice of tradition in the form of citations from rabbinic texts, folkloric sources, and the spoken or unspoken attitudes that ground traditional practices. While Elisheva quotes Genesis 24:57–58 in support of consulting daughters in the matchmaking process, Gordon alludes to the passage in the voice of a traditionalist for whom this "liberal" practice should be dismissed by virtue of Rebecca's family's Aramean roots (or, we might say, European manners). The nineteenth-century struggle between Jewish and non-Jewish approaches to marriage, Gordon's traditionalist seems to argue, has precedents in the world of the Bible, and there as in nineteenth-century Eastern Europe, the notion of obtaining a daughter's consent in her marriage falls squarely into the alien camp.

In both its romantic and satirical modes, nineteenth-century Jewish romantic narrative was an active participant in the ideological struggle against arranged marriage, fighting this *Kulturkampf* using the weapons made available by the literary genres in which it participated. Taking full advantage of the cultural power of imaginative literature, writers attracted readers to the sex religion through the enticements of beautiful heroines, recruiting pleasure reading to the project of Jewish modernity. Borrowing heavily from European literary models, Haskalah literature also developed its own strategies for negotiating the national and religious tensions that characterized modernization and Europeanization within its Jewish framework. Mobilizing the authority of Jewish sources, writers of Jewish romantic literature used biblical citations (and older characters) to establish the Jewish provenance of the apparently foreign romantic conventions to which they were introducing their readers. It is in such ways that the nineteenth-century Jewish romance moved far beyond the question of whether young people should be allowed to choose their own mates, ultimately engaging the question of what might constitute the cultural character of Jewish modernity.

Reclaiming Arranged Marriage

Having argued that modern Jewish literature begins with and emerges from the rejection of arranged marriage, I propose now very nearly the converse: that it *also* begins with the (partial) recovery of the matchmaking system. *The Love of Zion* can serve to demonstrate both these points. Despite the status of Mapu's novel as an ideological manifesto for the importance of romantic love in contracting a marriage, the romantic plot that connects Amnon and Tamar relies to a remarkable extent on a marriage arrangement, one put in motion before their birth by the deep friendship between their fathers. When the young lovers meet, however, neither knows anything of this circumstance or of their family connections and compatible class status. It is not incidental to the romantic atmosphere of the novel that the initial encounter between Tamar and Amnon takes place far from the "hubbub of the city" in the pastoral "lap of nature"; Dan Miron suggests that this idyllic setting for the blossoming of young love has not only aesthetic significance but also "social associations, which derive from its distance from the socio-cultural centers of life and from its 'naturalness.'" The pastoral setting presents itself as outside the usual class structures of the city, a place where "the barriers between rich and poor fall, and the young lovers are equal before the laws of nature."[32] Families are conspicuously absent from this scene, though Tamar's maidservant serves as romantic accomplice and mentor (like the nurse in *Romeo and Juliet*) for Tamar, discreet chaperone for the young lovers, and even potential rival for Amnon's hand, as ostensibly his class equal; her role is thus split between enthusiastic champion of the ideology of romantic choice and tacit representative of the patriarchal class interests of her employers. Despite the apparent *mésalliance* from the social and class perspectives, the match between Amnon and Tamar is soon enough revealed—and from the start is known to the reader—to be an eminently suitable alliance, since not only is Amnon a son of the upper classes despite having been raised as a shepherd, but he and Tamar have also been promised to each other by their fathers, and the loathsome Azrikam is in fact a usurper of Amnon's role. This complex circumstance means that what looks from one perspective like Tamar's rebellion against her parents' wishes appears, once the facts come to light, as the truer fulfillment of her father's pledge, even if neither Tamar nor her parents realize this at first.

The ambiguous class status of Amnon as high-born shepherd has attracted some critical attention. In describing the ostensibly "egalitarian" setting for the initial encounter between Amnon and Tamar, Miron is quick to add that this freedom from social hierarchies should not be confused with "moral equality." Rather, in the pastoral setting

> there is a transformation of one class hierarchy (socio-economic) into another, which is in fact harsher and more arbitrary (the bio-erotic: nature favors only the beautiful, the attractive and the strong; the ugly and the weak are rendered more pathetic and miserable than they are in the midst of society). . . . In the long tradition of the romance . . . the encounter in the "pleasant place" is only very rarely infused with radical social content. On the contrary, in this literature it usually turns out that the apparent tension between these two hierarchies (the social and the natural) is an illusion. The full and successful love between an upper-class woman and a shepherd is unimaginable without the revelation, in the final analysis, of the hidden noble character of the beloved young man. The natural "nobility," it turns out, are also members (whether they know it or not) of the socio-economic élite, and their bio-erotic perfection combines in them with their social advantages into a single perfection, which is the rightful possession of all those who are "beautiful and good."[33]

Miron stresses that Amnon's ambiguous status in fact ends up reinforcing rather than undermining the novel's implicit class ideology. But it is also possible to argue that the belatedness of the revelation of the hero's hidden identity performs a number of important generic and ideological functions: On the level of plot, this belatedness delays the consummation of the love affair, serving as the obstacle that allows the author to spin out a book; ideologically, it also lends the relationship between Amnon and Tamar a veneer of naturalness flavored by the frisson of class transgression. That class mixing is entertained as an option before being ruled out complicates even while leaving intact the social conservatism of the novel. Finally, Amnon's hesitation at approaching a young woman who seems to be his social superior clears the field for Tamar to act as the initiator of their romance, in apparent defiance of the gendered rules of bourgeois courtship. Mapu's romantic plot, even if it ultimately naturalizes and polices both class hierarchies and the gendered choreography of bourgeois courtship, nevertheless opens the tantalizing possibility that sexual desire will overthrow both these regimes.

The notion that sexually transgressive as well as socially conservative impulses are at play in the Haskalah romance has recently been separately suggested by Olga Litvak and Yahil Zaban, who bring renewed attention to the intertextual role in *The Love of Zion* of the disturbing biblical story of Amnon's rape of his half sister Tamar in 2 Samuel 19. Far from "purifying" the biblical story of these horrific elements, as Joseph Klausner has it, Mapu's marriage plot draws from even as it reconciles and sublimates the violent sexual impulses of 2 Samuel: "Disarmed rather than suppressed," writes Litvak, "the power of sex must be disciplined in the name of 'love' and in the name of 'Zion.'"[34] While he also reads Mapu's novel as ultimately reconciling fantasies of incestuous violence with a religiously sanctioned and erotically "sublime" marriage drama, Zaban goes further in demonstrating that Mapu partially actualized such fantasies in *The Love of Zion*. The "information gap" opened by the proliferation of secret identities in the novel, a feature of its character as "a novel of intrigue," allows Mapu to stage the scene of incest through a "misunderstanding." In a central scene of the novel, Tamar and her twin brother, Teman, follow Amnon to a tent and witness through the fabric of the tent walls his apparently sexual revels with an older and younger woman whom they do not know are his mother and sister, Na'ama and Penina. The incest fantasy is fulfilled in the combination of two potential readings of this ambiguous scene: the first interpretation (available to the reader) understands the shadowy silhouettes to be a brother and his mother and sister expressing familial affection; the second interpretation (that of Tamar and Teman) reads the scene as Amnon's sexual betrayal of his bride with a pair of strange women. The incestuous reading combines these two (mis)interpretations, recognizing both the family connection between the figures *and* the sexual character of their interaction. Zaban shows that the fact that the two witnesses are *also* siblings in their sexual prime bolsters the power of this (ostensibly wrong) interpretation: "The scopophilia, the pleasure derived from watching a forbidden act, of Tamar and her brother Teman reveals the incestuous desire to the reader. Tamar and Teman are a brother and sister who witness a brother and sister kissing; Amnon and Penina reflect the hidden attraction between them."[35] These desires (as well as the homosexual attraction between the young men) are reflected and refracted, according to Zaban, in the emergence of two marriages from this constellation of attractive siblings: Amnon marries Tamar, who is Teman's twin, while Teman marries Penina, who is Amnon's sister.

The link between incestuous desire and fantasies of alternative parentage and kinship is spelled out in Freud's 1909 essay "Family Romances," which explicates the connection between romantic desire and children's fantasies about alternative parentage or kinship. "Once a child comes to know of the various kinds of sexual relations between fathers and mothers and realizes that *'pater semper incertus est'*" (or, we might say, "Mama's baby, Papa's maybe"), certain fantasies develop that combine sexual desire with fantasies about a different family; some of these fantasies closely resemble the rivalries over inheritance that drive *The Love of Zion*. Freud continues:

> An interesting variant of the family romance may then appear, in which the hero and author returns to legitimacy himself while his brothers and sisters are got out of the way by being bastardized. So too if there are any other particular interests at work they can direct the course to be taken by the family romance; for its many-sidedness and its great range of applicability enable it to meet every sort of requirement. In this way, for instance, the young fantasy-builder can get rid of his forbidden degree of kinship with one of his sisters if he finds himself sexually attracted to her.[36]

Marthe Robert has most brilliantly demonstrated the relevance of these psychoanalytic findings for the novel, which in Robert's view inherits and embodies the fantasies that make up the family romance; the novelist's subjection of "inventions to circumstance, utopia to temporality, and dream to experience, or, in Freudian terms . . . the 'pleasure principle' to the 'reality principle,'" represents "what the novel inherits long before it is transcribed." For writers and readers, according to this theory, the novel replays and fictionally fulfills the earliest fantasies of possessing solely what in fact must be shared (to read Oedipus a little more expansively than usual), thus, in Robert's words, combining "by magic the visible and invisible, dream and reality."[37] These psychosexual foundations are already apparent in the Bible (from which Mapu draws inspiration), for instance, in the suggestion that a bride might be a sister (as the Song of Songs names her), or an unwilling sister a compliant lover (as the biblical Amnon hopes). There may be a more particular Eastern European Jewish context at play in these fantasies as well. For a society in which parents were traditionally deeply involved with marriage and in which male writers were likely to know few women outside their family circles, the notion that a "family romance" underlies even apparently exogamous love relationships may be particularly illuminating.

Taken together, these analyses suggest that *The Love of Zion*, for all its orientation toward bourgeois marriage, achieved its cultural power because it also gave veiled expression to more complex anxieties and unruly sexual impulses, including those associated with the family romance. Both Litvak and Zaban view the reconciliation of transgressive and disciplined erotic impulses as ultimately serving national-historical aims. For Litvak, "the marriage of Amnon and Tamar represents the essential affinity— the marriage—of human will and historical reason."[38] Zaban, borrowing Claude Lévi-Strauss's insights on the construction of kinship systems on the basis of the prohibition of incest, views the exchange of women (especially sisters) as the initial act by which the tribe, the community, and the nation emerge from the "dark matter" of the primordial family.[39]

Litvak and Zaban, on the one hand, and Miron, on the other, offer two strikingly different insights into the persistence of the traditional family within the modern love plot. Miron insists that, despite subscribing to the ideology of free erotic choice, Mapu's novel demonstrates the continuing sway of certain conservative features of traditional marriage—those that maintain patriarchal hierarchies and class borders; Litvak and Zaban suggest that beneath the apparently conservative lineaments of Mapu's modern marriage plot lurks the most primal and forbidden sexual impulse of all. On the face of it, these seem like entirely incompatible arguments. Nevertheless, they serve as the double sides of a single dynamic, in which the modern love match is shaped by the traditional family in both its conservative-social and transgressive-libidinal dimensions. These interpretations of the novel, one exposing Mapu's social conservatism (shared by bourgeois modernity and the traditional marriage system) and the other laying bare the incestuous desires just below the surface of his marriage plot, together suggest that Mapu's championing of Jewish sexual modernity was complicated on both the ideological and psychosexual levels by impulses arising from a primordial social, sexual, and textual past. This aspect of *The Love of Zion* is signaled not only by Amnon's ambiguous class status, or by the veiled suggestions of incest among the (apparent) lovers, but also by the intense engagement of the novel—for all its affiliations with the rationalist ideology of the Haskalah—with the mystical nature and roots of erotic passion.

Unlike Amnon's true class status, the mystical character of his and Tamar's love is present from the initial encounter between the young people: Tamar is attracted to the singing shepherd because he resembles the man her grandfather dreamed she would marry, a dream described in a letter Hananel sends his son from captivity:

> I saw in my dreams a young boy with beautiful eyes, nobly dressed, a sword girded at his thigh, a helmet on his head, and raven locks curling on his brow, rosy cheeks, his forehead purer than snow, whiter than milk, and he rode up on a horse and stopped before me. . . . And when the youth heard me speak, he descended from his horse and took my right hand, saying in his gentle voice, "My soul that seeks out the soul of your daughter Tirzah's daughter Tamar, seeks you out in your captivity so I might redeem you and return with you to Zion to those you love, to live in the light of the Lord."[40]

Mapu mobilizes the resources of biblical Hebrew to produce an almost untranslatable parallel between Amnon's desire for Tamar (*nafshi tahshok benefesh Tamar*) and his desire to redeem Tamar's imprisoned grandfather Hananel (*tahshok nafsheha be'erets shvutha*)—a redemption that takes on both a political-national character and a bio-erotic one in continuing Hananel's line. Hananel's dream thus simultaneously establishes his own profound connection to the handsome youth who will rescue him and propels his granddaughter toward the young man who will redeem the paternal line. Tamar's love for Amnon in this sense *precedes* their encounter in the natural setting, beginning in the textual, cultural, and family sphere constituted by her reading of Hananel's letter. Their love, so apparently natural and unmediated, is produced, fueled, and refracted by the dream that is not only lineage but also (for her and for us) literature: "Hananel's letter was kept in Tirzah's chest, and Tamar read it as she grew up, and she would ponder Hananel's dream about her, and from thinking about it so often the vision began to grow within her, and she would see the image of the beautiful lad at night."[41] Given the priming of this pump, Tamar's initial encounter with Amnon thus comprises a unique and potent combination of "love at first sight" and déjà vu:

> "Leave me alone," Tamar replied [to her maidservant], "I'm rooted to this spot, because the pleasures of the visions I had in the night, those I saw in

my dreams, I now see in my waking life. Behold! I see the youth that my grandfather Hananel saw in his dream, in his form and description, nothing is missing. Set your eyes on the shepherd boy as he sings his song, see his raven-black curls, his white forehead; his red cheeks and gentle speech and charming lips. See how he is whiter than milk, purer than snow!"[42]

Tamar's attraction to Amnon has multiple causes: His beauty, reminiscent of the Grimms' Snow White, is sufficient of itself to spark her love (as it sparks the love of Tamar's maidservant). Beyond immediate perception, this beauty reaches her as recollected dream—a dream that is also a repetition of her grandfather's dream. Through the medium of the letter Tamar reads that is passed from grandfather to father to daughter, her encounter with Amnon produces the effect of literature come to life. Hananel's dream in turn derives from, keeps alive, and passes along to Tamar the vow of her father (and his son-in-law) to Amnon's father to marry their children to each other. Tamar's reading practices and her resulting erotic dreams pave the way for this love at first sight, alongside the desires, dreams, and commitments of her ancestors, which depend and imprint themselves on the apparently freely chosen attractions of their descendants, imbuing them with the character of preordained fate. Alongside the role played in Tamar and Amnon's love affair by the desires, hopes, and dreams of their elders, this love affair among descendants also reinfuses the love of their fathers and other intergenerational connections with the sexual energies of the young. Tamar's pastoral encounter with the shepherd "outside the social structures of the city" is thus fully interwoven with the desires and kinship commitments of her family and his, in ways both conscious and unconscious.

These features of Tamar's love for Amnon have the social function, as Miron asserts, of establishing Amnon's appropriately distinguished stock, but they also provide the mystical assurance that Tamar and Amnon are fulfilling a marriage vow and contribute to their encounter libidinal energies that derive from at least two prior generations of interconnected families. In this sense, Mapu indirectly reclaims a primary dimension of arranged marriage, the parental determination of the match, even while providing his readers with the requisite story of a modern and willful young girl determined to choose her own mate.[43] *The Love of Zion*, then, dramatizes the evils of arranged marriage while inventing uniquely literary modes of remembering, salvaging, and inventing its libidinal and social energies, thus marrying the theme of the mismatched or "star-crossed" lovers to the folkloric trope of a bride and groom who are destined for each other from birth.

The peculiar (some would say tortured) plot twists that enable the literary reappropriation of arranged marriage are shared in their main features with S. An-sky's *Between Two Worlds*, the play more commonly known as *The Dybbuk*, which similarly combines the betrothal vow of parents and the erotic rebellion of their children: *The Dybbuk* lays the by-then well-worn narrative structure of the struggle between arranged marriage and free choice over an antithetical and older Jewish tradition holding that love is fated (*bashert*) and marriages decreed in heaven. The young couple's love, like that of Tamar and Amnon, is an expression of the bonds of destiny and tradition—Leah and Khonen are meant to marry because their fathers had pledged them to each other before their birth, a pledge no less binding because one of the men has died and the other seems to have forgotten the entire episode. Ignoring the oath is no light matter; the children who have been pledged to one another do not marry, as Amnon and Tamar do at the end of *The Love of Zion*, but are more grotesquely united, first in Leah's spirit possession by Khonen and then, ultimately, in death. The term *bashert*, used in An-sky's play to describe this fated love, has a range of meanings, from "destined to be" (itself far from a transparent concept) to, more neutrally, "future spouse" and, more romantically, "beloved." For An-sky, the arranged character of the match is synonymous with mutual love—couples that are meant to be together because they have been promised to each other by their parents or God are soul mates or true lovers. But this association is not inevitable. In Gordon's *Tip of the Yud*, the notion that God is the universal matchmaker is coupled with the lovelessness of arranged marriage: What point is there to courtship or even the meeting between bride and groom if a woman's mate is chosen on her behalf even before she is born?

> Wretched thing, don't you know yet,
> That love in the heart of a Jewish girl there cannot be?
> Forty days before her mother gave birth to her,
> The Heavenly matchmaker found her a husband,
> So what good would it do her if she were to see him now?[44]

Puah Rakovsky seems to have similarly understood the notion of a fated marriage as the very opposite of romantic love, asking, "What Jewish girl would have dared consider a love match, when, ever since her childhood, she had been told that her match had been made in Heaven even before she was born?"[45]

Destined love, however, is understood entirely romantically in *The Dybbuk*. When the possessed bride, speaking in her dead lover's voice, shouts, "I have returned to my promised bride [*meyn basherter*] and will not leave her!,"[46] Khonen is expressing both the unbreakable character of his bond with Leah and his extravagant love for her. In *The Dybbuk*, An-sky thus takes the claims of sexuality and of tradition at their greatest distance and brings them together with maximum impact, combining a call for freedom from arranged marriage with an insistence on the real power of the ultimate arranged marriage. In doing so, An-sky suggests that the two derivations of the love between Leah and Khonen—one passionate, instinctual, and rebellious, and the other historical, traditional, and religious—are, in fact, one and the same.

As in Mapu's novel, the sexual attraction of the young couple is grounded in both mystical bonds that connect them before their birth and social and affective bonds that initially lead their fathers to forge a betrothal oath. Where incestuous impulses contribute to the desires that drive *The Love of Zion*, *The Dybbuk* is fascinated instead by the erotically charged homosocial connections that bind young men together in the yeshiva and the Hasidic court. David Biale reminds us that the opponents of Hasidism took aim at Hasidic men who left their wives and children for weeks on end to visit the Zaddik's court (An-sky, significantly, presents the oath of the young men as taking place at the Zaddik's court at the end of the High Holy Days, the occasion of a Hasid's longest absence from home); when a man affiliated himself with the Hasidic movement, the wife "bewailed the husband of her youth, who had left her like a widow, and her sons cried that they had been left as orphans." The *misnagdim* (opponents of Hasidism), Biale continues,

> did not believe that the abandonment of wife and children served any holy purpose; to the contrary, they believed that the extreme asceticism was a cover for erotic abandon, just as the mystical doctrine of intercourse with the Shekhina was a mask for licentious behavior in the court of the zaddik. The author of the anti-Hasidic *Shever Poshim* claims that when the Hasidim gather at Amdur on the fast of the ninth of Av, they would sleep together in the attic, use filthy language, and sing love songs all night. This homosexual innuendo was connected to the intense male fellowship of the Hasidic court.[47]

But these descriptions are found not only in anti-Hasidic invective. The Czech writer and friend of Kafka Jiří Langer, who lived intermittently from 1913 to 1919 among the Galician Hasidic community of Belz, records experiencing the Hasidic world as, in Shaun Jacob Halper's words, "an incubator of homosexual desire."[48] In his book on the eroticism of the Kabbalah (the fourth chapter of which is titled "Männerliebe"), Langer describes the atmosphere of the study hall thus:

> Here sit two young men, with beards just beginning to cover their chins, "learning" assiduously over thick Talmud-folios. The one holds the other by his beard, looks deep into his eyes, and in this manner explains a complicated Talmud passage. And there, two friends pace around the hall deep in conversation, while embracing one another [*sie halten einander umschlungen*]. The younger of the two rests his back against the wall, the elder has the entire front of his body literally pressed against him; they look lovingly in each other's eyes, but keep still. What could be playing out within their pure souls? They themselves don't even know.[49]

An-sky's description of Sender and Nissen's relationship draws from a similar understanding of the quality of profound attachment that could and perhaps regularly did connect young men in the study hall and Hasidic court. Although An-sky makes it clear that the love between the two men blossomed in their wives' absence, An-sky's play is far from "homosexual innuendo," since there is no trace of negative judgment in the play's presentation of this bond.[50] As opposed to both the *misnagdic* and Haskalah polemic that saw Hasidic male fellowship as a threat to the fabric of Jewish family life, and to Langer's emphasis on the profound (if inchoate) character of such attachment outside normative family systems, An-sky presents the love of Sender and Nissen as embedded in the traditional value system of Ashkenaz and even as reproductively fruitful. Just as he rescues the idea of arranged marriage from the very teeth of Haskalah critique, so too does he valorize its corollary—the "intense male fellowship" of the yeshiva and Hasidic court—as socially contributing to Jewish continuity rather than disrupting it. In the "trial" between the two friends that precedes the ritual exorcism of Khonen from Leah, Nissen's ghost, speaking through the rabbi, reminds his friend of their bond, a friendship that begins in the yeshiva and court and maintains its force and influence through their own near-simultaneous marriages (their wives are not mentioned in the phrase) and into the meeting, far in the future, of the two children resulting from these unions:

> Reb Shimshon: Sender ben Henya! The righteous deceased Nissen ben Rivke states in his claim in your youth you studied in the same yeshiva and that your souls were bound in loyal friendship. You both were married in the same week [*ir hot beyde in eyn vokh khasene gehat*]. Not long after, when you saw each other at the rebbe's during the High Holy Days, you pledged that if your wives became pregnant and one gave birth to a boy and the other to a girl, the two would marry when the time came.[51]

Golda Werman's translation of the last phrase, *vet ir zikh miskhatn zeyn*, smooths over some of the particularities of the Yiddish and of the kinship term it expresses. More literally, the phrase would be rendered as "you two [men] would be joined in marriage" or "you would become in-laws (through the marriage of your children)." The young men are described as study partners, friends, and spiritual companions, but this last phrase, and the proliferation of reflexive constructions, references to the life cycle, and the use of the physical term for an oath (*tkias kaf*, or handshake) all work to suggest that the bond between Nissen and Sender is also physically, sexually, biologically, and genealogically (re)productive. The concluding phrase, "to be joined in marriage," strengthens the already implicit suggestion that Nissen and Sender pledge their children to each other to forge the most intimate, quasi-marital connection available to two men in their society. And this connection, far from being sterile and deviant, is channeled through the sanctioned routes of Torah study, Hasidic life, Jewish marriage arrangements, and reproductive heteronormativity.

An-sky was able to celebrate the homoerotic currents that could contribute to rather than undermine traditional Jewish marriages by reconfiguring the Haskalah ideology that viewed arranged marriage as motivated by parents' concerns—mercenary at worst, practical at best—about class and prestige. These arranged marriages *are* in fact love matches, even if the love is between two fathers. *The Love of Zion* had already begun to discover and celebrate the potentially erotic role of family in the love match; marriages might be arranged through strong bonds between friends longing to become more than that. As in *The Love of Zion*, An-sky's play explores the ideology of romantic love alongside the persistent attractions of arranged marriage through a double emplotment: Sender's betrothal of Leah to a rich young man participates in the conventions that pit arranged marriage against romantic love; his prior betrothal of his still-unborn daughter to the still-unborn son of Nissen is a particularly dramatic form of arranged marriage. This betrothal, however, is also the polar opposite of arranged marriage in its more conventional depictions, describing the victory of young love (this time, between two young men) over practical considerations that include their actually having children! By setting the marriage arrangements among just-married young men and infusing the oath with mutual friendship as well as erotic attraction, An-sky recasts the generational opposition as a suppressed parallelism, in which fathers and their children are, quite literally, kindred spirits, expressing the same loving impulses in only apparently dissimilar ways.

Even Sender's opposition to Leah's match with the son of his dead friend is described as a resistance to his own attraction to the boy rather than a result of purely practical considerations. When Nissen asks, though the mouthpiece of Reb Shimshon who is conducting the "trial" between the two friends—one living and one dead—why Sender had never inquired who Khonen's father was and where he was from (normal behavior for a Jewish host, even one without a marriageable daughter), Sender answers:

> I don't know . . . I can't remember . . . but I swear that I was always drawn toward him as a son-in-law! This made me set such difficult terms whenever a match was proposed that the parents found it impossible to agree; three matches broke up this way. But the last time the family agreed to everything. (*Pause*)
> Reb Shimshon: Nissen ben Rivke says that deep in your heart you recognized his son and were therefore afraid to ask about his family. You wanted someone who could give your daughter a rich and comfortable life.[52]

Sender's halting response suggests that he drove a hard bargain for his daughter not because—or not only because—he wanted a son-in-law wealthier than Khonen but precisely because he was attempting to shield himself from his attraction to the boy. In this case, the stuttering attempts at finding a groom for his daughter are no more than a pathetic defense against the demands of memory and love—the love of his daughter for the poor yeshiva boy who eats at their table, Sender's love for the friend of his youth, and his attraction to the young man who is the son of his beloved Nissen. As I have argued elsewhere, if Sender sabotages his daughter's erotic desires, it is not because he doesn't understand or value them but because he cannot acknowledge that he once shared them.[53]

As in *The Love of Zion*, the romance in *The Dybbuk* takes shape within what Zaban calls "an information gap." But unlike Mapu's novel, this gap is the result of psychological complexities (Sender's "forgetting" of his friend) as well as external circumstances (Nissen's death) rather than solely attributable to the machinations of villains. In the court scene between Nissen's spirit and Sender that is the necessary prelude to the exorcism ritual, it is not the possessed woman who is on trial (she is not even present in this scene) but Sender, whose failure of memory is indicted, even as the content of this memory is brought back to consciousness; the past that is retrieved in the course of the trial is recognized as the cause for the corruptions and distortions that trouble the present. In An-sky's diagnosis, Leah's possession by the soul of Khonen is the result not so much of the erotic passion that unites the young couple as of her father's breaking of the pledge that he swore to Khonen's father. In displacing the love of the young from the center of the romantic drama, An-sky suggests that the search for true love must investigate the lives of parents as well as children, also laying bare the connections between parents and children that continue to haunt the erotic pathways of the young.

Despite the similarities between the approaches of An-sky and Mapu to the submerged connections between modern romance and traditional marriage, it is far more difficult in the case of An-sky to read this plot twist as a function of the writer's conservative stance. As is well known, *The Dybbuk* arises from an entirely different political-ideological and literary context from Mapu's Haskalah, that of An-sky's socialism and radical modernism. Nevertheless, the persistence of a kind of patriarchal conservatism within a more general political, literary, and sexual radicalism should not, of course, be ruled out: Gabriella Safran has intriguingly suggested that the nostalgia for arranged marriage implicit in *The Dybbuk* might have been occasioned by An-sky's longings for wealth and marital stability:

> The plot of the play turns on male upward mobility through marriage, which was once a common institution—at least anecdotally—among Eastern European Jews. Wealthy men would ask the head of the local yeshiva to choose his best student to marry their daughters, and in this way poor boys could become rich. . . . By the end of the nineteenth and beginning of the twentieth centuries, though, this custom was dying out, making Khonen's

frustration—he knows that he deserves Leah not only because they were promised to each other, but because he is the best student in town—realistic for the yeshiva students of An-sky's own time. An-sky himself, like Khonen, pursued women from wealthier families than his own, and was frustrated. As a radical, he could never admit to desiring a bride who would give him access to a comfortable life, but his play displays the tension between the radical's desire to gain credibility through asceticism and the human need for comfort and stability.[54]

As Safran conjectures, An-sky may have approved, for purely personal and "human" reasons, of at least one aspect of arranged marriage—the upward mobility at least anecdotally available to the most brilliant yeshiva students. Despite his abandonment of traditional observance, An-sky may have seen himself less as the beneficiary of the secularization of Jewish marriage than a victim of a process that worked to disadvantage him in the marriage game. This suggestion is both bolstered and complicated by Safran's reading of "the marriage politics" of the play in the light of contemporary Marxist discussions of marriage. An-sky's probable familiarity with the political analysis of Friedrich Engels and the anthropological research into the evolution of family structures of Lev Shternberg may have provided him with "the powerful vision of a society in which the claims of groups (or families) take precedence over the claims of individuals." *The Dybbuk*, Safran writes, is evidence that An-sky was "affected by [Shternberg's] search for living examples of the communalism of the past that could give a home for the revival of communalism in the future."[55] Safran proposes that alongside An-sky's personal stake in traditional marriage, he may have been inclined to judge it more positively in the light of the findings of his friend Shternberg that the Gilyak people of Sakhalin Island (where Shternberg was exiled for a time) practiced a form of

> cousin marriage, whereby children are assigned before birth (or at their birth, once it becomes clear whether they are girls or boys) to specific cross-cousins as spouses. This image represented the powerful vision of a society in which the claims of groups (or families) take precedence over the claims of individuals, and accumulated wealth has no effect on human fates.[56]

Arranged marriage as An-sky portrays it, then, might stand for a range of different psychological and political impulses, from the (presumably conservative) desire for a comfortable life and material reward for one's intellectual gifts to the (presumably radical) belief that traditional communal social arrangements could serve as egalitarian alternatives to bourgeois nuclear families. I would only add to Safran's argument that these alternatives have an erotic as well as economic character. For An-sky, Jewish arranged marriage—in its "purer" form, stripped of its modern capitalist orientation—revealed itself as a communitarian alternative to the alienations of modern marriage, both expanding bourgeois economic patterns to include other approaches to distributing goods and opening the bourgeois erotic range to homoerotic and heteronormative desires. Arranged marriage, understood correctly, represented not the retrograde impulses of a "cold" and mercenary patriarchal system but the simpler kinship system of a world still untouched by crass commercialism, the fetishistic attachment to individual autonomy, and the strict sex-gender rules of the "sex religion." The division An-sky presents *within* arranged marriage between a communitarian ideal (whether real or imagined, derived from within Jewish culture or borrowed from elsewhere) and the foreign capitalist practices that had corrupted it provides an opening for the reclamation of arranged marriage in the name not of conservative patriarchy but of radical sexual liberation and a future-oriented modern politics.

It is worth pointing out that the particular twist that characterizes Mapu's and An-sky's romances is not limited to these two works but instead draws from an ancient Jewish textual tradition about the force of betrothal vows that continues to make itself felt well into the modern era.[57] The motif of a marriage ordained by a vow begins with a rabbinic tale known as "The Weasel and the Pit" (sketched out in Babylonian Talmud Ta'anit 8a and more fully expounded in Rashi's commentary on the passage) and continues in a range of post-midrashic, medieval, Hasidic, and modern literary retellings.[58] The title of the tale type refers to the weasel and pit that are the only witnesses to a marriage vow contracted by a boy and the girl he saves from a pit; when the boy grows up, he breaks his vow and marries another woman. In the original version, the weasel and pit visit a series of punishments on the children that result from the "wrong match" until the vow is honored and the "correct match" is made. Ben-Ami Feingold traces the evolution of this tale in modern Hebrew literature, coining its distinctive twist the "double match":

> I use the term "double match" [*zivug kaful*] for a situation in which there is a match between a man and a woman that ends in a legitimate but failed

union, since it comes in place of and attempts to supplant, knowingly or unknowingly, a match that was preordained. I call the preordained match "the ideal match" and the match that supplants it a "real match." The intended match is not ideal in the ordinary meaning of the term, that is, that the couple is "suited" from a social or psychological perspective. On the contrary, the ideal match may be entirely absurd from this perspective, except that it has on its side from the outset a divine decree or the weight of fate, which human beings cannot control, as in "God sits and matches them to one another against their will."[59]

Naomi Zohar, who also analyzes the literary evolution of the tale, focuses on its appearance in the literature of the Haskalah, counting no fewer than fifteen German, Hebrew, and Yiddish Haskalah rewritings of the tale, of which the best known is Abraham Goldfaden's 1883 biblical drama *Shulamith*. Although Zohar does not consider Mapu's first novel among these rewritings, the question she puts to this literature is relevant as well to Mapu's less explicit use of the double match: "Why did the writers of the Haskalah," asks Zohar, "evince such great interest in the story of 'The Weasel and the Pit,' with its folkloristic character and interest in the workings of fate, talking weasels, demons and other destructive forces, as well as similar beliefs from which even the rabbis had already distanced themselves?"[60] Zohar begins to solve this conundrum by noting the distinctive transformations of the story in this period, in which the function of the weasel and pit (or the cat and well, in other variants) as guarantors of the betrothal vow is taken over by God himself, in a theological sublimation and "rationalization" of the magical dimensions of the folk tale. But at least as relevant to our study is her observation that the Haskalah writers who rework this story newly emphasize that the vow derives from and is an expression of romantic attraction: "The feeling of love is the necessary precondition for the entire relationship between the boy and girl. Only after the boy feasts his eyes on the girl's beauty does he fall in love with her, and only after that does he propose the vow as the condition for his rescuing her."[61]

In their citations and reworkings of the story, Haskalah writers thus reject the possibility of what Feingold sees as a distinct option for the tale in its longer history: an "absurd" match resulting from the betrothal vow. In this choice, these writers imply the unbreakable unity of romance and fate, the bio-erotic and divine dimensions of marriage. Relying on Miron's analysis of Mapu quoted earlier, Zohar suggests that the Haskalah version of the tale serves as a literary means of resolving romantic love not only with rational-ism and religious concerns but also with the social constraints embodied by family and nation. As in *The Love of Zion*, Zohar shows, the vow in the story of the weasel and the pit bridges the distance between the pleasant place where the young couple first meet and the social order within which they ul-timately marry, among the family that serves as "chief representative of class interests." In the Haskalah versions of the tale, the force of the vow takes on the additional social function of persuading the parents to accept the young couple's love. Zohar roots this harmony between the erotic and the social in the conservative ideology of bourgeois marriage of which Mapu is prime representative:

> The historical trajectory that concerned Mapu in all his writings also forms the precise concerns of the transformation of the story in all its [maskilic] versions. The problems of the appropriate relationship between sensual and erotic principles and the place of cultural and religious values in individual life, which concerns so many of Mapu's heroes, are also the problems of the heroes of the story of the weasel and the pit. Their personal decisions are always connected with historical and national considerations.[62]

While both Feingold and Zohar readily see in modern Hebrew and Yiddish literary versions of the double-match story the basic outlines of the Jew-ish adoption of bourgeois models of marriage, neither discusses the ways that Mapu and An-sky diverge from even as they adapt the story of the double match. *The Love of Zion* and *The Dybbuk* depend on a contrast between, in Feingold's terms, an ideal match and a real match, and both texts find ways to resolve tensions between Eros and the social-religious order and to "naturalize" the connections between the romantic, national, social, and religious dimensions of marriage. The major divergence from the folkloric tradition of the weasel and the pit lies in the fact that in Mapu and An-sky, the betrothal vow is contracted not by a young couple but by their fathers; it is this distinction that accounts for the longevity and power of these works when compared with other modern expressions of the double-match story. As in many variations of the folkloric story of the weasel and the pit, the vow in *The Love of Zion* and *The Dybbuk* is either villainously misdirected (in Mapu) or ambivalently forgotten (in An-sky). But the abrogation and forgetting of the vow, blamed in the weasel-and-pit tradition on the fickleness of young men, become an intergenerational dilemma for Mapu and An-sky—thus implicating tradition itself. For Mapu, the schemes of a villain and the exile of the family patriarch (who serves as repository of its cultural memory) are the root of the near failure of the match. For An-sky, however, not external forces but the ruptures, stutters, and amnesia that connect one generation to another are the root of the tragedy. It is this focus on psychological and cultural continuity and discontinuity that renders the play a major site for the rethinking of both tradition and modernity.

Placing the vow in the hands of the fathers has a number of other crucial ramifications: Because the older generation in *The Love of Zion* and *The Dybbuk* is the source of the ideal match while also blindly insisting on the real match, the love affair is presented as both conscious rebellion (against the real match) and unconscious submission (to the ideal match). Thus, while the modern literary permutations of the double-match plot illuminate a range of social and religious tensions around romantic love, the paradoxical and split plots developed by Mapu and An-sky bring the problem of arranged marriage into direct ideological play. A betrothal vow between fathers that is unknowingly played out by their children has the effect of simultaneously strengthening the repressive character of the vow (since it is contracted by parents rather than the young pair), the mystical power of the vow (since the children embody this power without ever having been conscious agents of the vow), and the erotic power of the connection (since it begins as a rebellion against social constraints).

In the case of Mapu, the generational split and resulting information gap, as Zaban suggests, allows for a staging of incestuous fantasies within a larger family drama; in the case of An-sky, the same circumstance allows for the staging of homoerotic currents in arranged marriage. The question Zohar poses to the Haskalah writers who retell this tale—why the attachment, by champions of Reason, to such irrational and supernatural beliefs?—is thus both sharper and more readily answered when it is directed to these writers. If a vow between two people has the irrational power to transcend the passing of time, a vow contracted by one person on behalf of another presents an even more irrational force in the courtship process. Yet, if the function of this tale is to provide social as well as divine warrant for the workings of romantic love—as Zohar asserts—placing the vow in the domain of parents more elegantly assures that the marriage will embody the social order even as it is energized by more primal and individual erotic impulses.

The motif in modern Jewish literature of the power of a betrothal arranged by parents might also be more broadly understood within the context of the representation and valuation of tradition in post-traditional culture. Vincent Pecora has shown that modern literature—particularly the novel—arises alongside the ideologies and processes of secularization while nevertheless playing a distinct and oppositional role within secularity. As Pecora writes, secular culture translated rather than negated "a religious worldview," just as it "struggled to resist the radical secularization that attended modernity." Citing Adorno on the "lost unity" of art and religion, Pecora insists that "every work of art still bears the imprint of its magical origin."[63] Given the persistence of religion, magic, and tradition within modern culture, secular culture acts as a brake on the Enlightenment "unfolding of reason." Pecora continues:

> Secularization might be best understood not merely as the implacable process through which (as in Hegel) reason unfolds, ruses and all, in its pursuit of universal comprehension. Rather, I want to approach secularization as something bound to take a more circuitous, partial, and uneven path, one filled with digressions that periodically call its basic (Weberian) premises into question, and that may provide, both for good and ill, a powerful resistance to any attempt to finish once and for all what Habermas has called the "project" of rationalized modernity. In particular, secularization can be considered simultaneously curative and distorting in the sense that its consequences can be understood to include both an enlightened liberation from dogma and an opening up of certain collective possibilities—redemptive revolution, nationalism, imperialism, racism—that could not have achieved their full and often destructive potential otherwise.[64]

Secularization should be understood, in Pecora's view, as involving an always ambivalent and incomplete process of rationalization; the unfinished and unrealizable character of this process is embodied in, among other effects, the "opening up of certain collective possibilities." Such an account powerfully illuminates not only Jewish modernity but, more particularly, the persistence of the "vow" tale in the literature of Jewish Enlightenment, in which a certain rationalization, Zohar demonstrates, is accompanied by religious (or even magical) and national impulses. In asserting the power of a forgotten vow and the persistence of the will of parents within the (also irrational) field of erotic choice, the domain of modern practice signals its openness to the "uneven" persistence and even reinvention of traditional and irrational possibilities, which cluster particularly thickly around both Eros and Jewish collectivity. As Pecora writes,

> The secularization through which magic or myth is eliminated by reason may never in fact be complete. This . . . is perhaps something to be acknowledged as the result of an irreducible set of needs in human and group psychology. One might then conclude that the society that produces Enlightenment never fully outgrows its desire for religious sources of coherence, solidarity, and historical purpose, and continually translates, or transposes, them into ever more refined and immanent, but also distorted and distorting, versions of its religious inheritance.[65]

In a philosophical-literary meditation on love, Alain de Botton suggests that notions of fate continue to shadow contemporary experiences of Eros as wishful correctives to the more evident operations of chance in the meeting of "true lovers."[66] Niklas Luhmann similarly observes that the metaphors implicit in terms like "falling in love" or "being made for each other" conceal a paradoxical tension between free choice and ineluctable fate.[67] Pecora might read such "superstitious" psychological inclinations on the part of lovers as evidence of the persistence of sacred conceptions of destiny within the disenchantments of secular modernity, an insight that acquires an additional national and religious dimension in modern Jewish literature. If the Haskalah novel took, in regard to the modernization of Jewish marriage, a rather "more circuitous, partial and uneven path" than is often acknowledged, modern Jewish literature emerges as the site not for the overthrow of a religious past and its oppressive systems but for their literary translation, cultural persistence, and ideological recovery. *The Love of Zion* properly situates erotic desire in the sphere of the autonomous individual who, on the brink of adulthood, determines his or her own erotic fate; nevertheless, the novel simultaneously displaces this desire "elsewhere," to the realm of visions, dreams, and signs. In asserting the continued force of parental desires, these dreams reaffirm for a new age both the "inchoate logic of collective life" and a longing for cosmic meaning. Such a view of the interconnectedness of individual and collective Eros does more than set limits to the program of sexual autonomy, as Miron proposes. It also redistributes erotic and cultural energies beyond the individual or couple to a range of intergenerational, collective, and mystical-religious sites.

The conservative character of the double match in *The Love of Zion* that both Miron and Zohar emphasize, which binds the erotic relation to the traditional family (and class), also—at least potentially—has the reverse effect, to infuse tradition, and the family, with the erotic energy generated by the love match. If this effect is submerged along with the incestuous fantasies of *The Love of Zion*, it rises to the surface in An-sky's radical modernism, which openly celebrates the eroticism of tradition, the passion that inhabits traditional forms precisely in their increasingly endangered "modes of transmission."[68] While Mapu's heroine, Elisheva, quotes strategically from the Bible to find Jewish grounds for her modernizing impulses, Leah is a more modernist modern in being passionately and aesthetically in love with what is old—Safran suggests that Leah is acting "as if she herself were a museum visitor" when she enters the synagogue and demands of the beadle, "Remember, you promised to show me the old embroidered curtains for the Ark."[69] Her aunt explains that Leah has promised to embroider a new curtain for the Ark for the anniversary of her mother's death, reviving what has apparently become a lost art: "She will use gold thread to work little lions and eagles onto the costliest velvet, just as they used to do in the old days." That this aesthetic-spiritual passion is also fiery and dangerous is made clear in the ensuing scene: After exchanging a word with Khonen, and taking up her aunt's invitation, Leah embraces the scroll and "kisses it with passion." Frade, taken aback, responds: "Enough, my child, enough! A brief kiss is all one may give the scroll. Torah scrolls are written with black fire on white fire!"[70]

Mapu dramatized the power of erotic desire through the fierce attack of a lion (and Amnon's equally fierce counter-attack in his defense of Tamar); Leah's lion appears as an embroidered figure on a threadbare velvet Torah covering, but it is equally dangerous. Rather than serve as religious and collective barriers against the anarchic perils of erotic freedom, the traditional past, the lost arts, and the Torah itself are themselves these erotic dangers, fully one with the passionate charge that connects young lovers. Against the suggestion that modern Jews must look outside their own traditions for erotic inspiration, Mapu dispatches a grandfather's letter in which Tamar finds the very image of her love. An-sky, a few generations later, sends a young girl a Torah scroll to passionately embrace in the presence of the boy she also desires. In both of these scenes, the textual and the sexual, the traditional and the modern, demonstrate that they are not so easily parted.

The Return of the Matchmaker to the Love Scene

If the modern reclamation of arranged marriage takes the form in *The Love of Zion* and *The Dybbuk* of a conflation of an arranged marriage and a love match, this recovery project does not embrace all aspects of arranged marriages. There is one clear loser: the matchmaker, whose services are apparently beyond reclamation, too damningly implicated in the commercial dimension of arranged marriage for modern (or modernist) rehabilitation. The destined union of Tamar and Amnon or Leah and Khonen is propelled not by the machinations of matchmakers but by true love and friendship between their fathers, who need no matchmakers to bring their children together or to guarantee that the match will be a passionate, blessed, and proper one.

It is striking, then, that matchmakers nevertheless continue to ply their trade and make their presence known in a variety of modern scenes, primary symptoms of Jewish modernity as an incomplete or ambivalent project. It is possible to argue not only that the matchmaker continues to play a role on the stage of the modern love match but even, more paradoxically, that the matchmaker is an *invention* of Jewish literary modernity. For modern Jewish literature—narrative, historiographical, or autobiographical—does not simply describe traditional practice *wie es eigentlich gewesen* (as it actually was). Talal Asad cautions that modernity, particularly in its literary projects, is not (only) what comes after tradition but (also) what invents, imagines, and re-enchants it. Secularization did not *break* with an "enchanted" world, the supernaturally infused world Max Weber and Peter Berger regard secularization as having "disenchanted"; rather, secular culture *produces* this enchanted world in retrospect, in the past that has been replaced and is incessantly remembered by an alienated (in its own view) and disenchanted modernity.[71] Asad, then, radicalizes Pecora's notion of secular culture as embodying the persistence and translation of religious forms and structures, insisting that secular literature entails the narrative invention of tradition. In this light, the modern Jewish novel can be understood as the site of the simultaneous abandonment and discovery of arranged marriage and the Jewish matchmaker, the place of both their passing and birth.

That this is so undoubtedly owes something to the nature of modern literature. Premodern documents record disputes and rulings on the practices and fees that surround the occupation, and the marriage broker lurks in the margins of folklore and rabbinic responsa, which—like the Hebrew autobiography—pay greater attention to the families and prospective mates at center stage. It is in modern literature that the marriage broker becomes a full-fledged character in his (and increasingly her) own right, even as other figures associated with traditional marriage, for instance, the *badkhn* (wedding jester), have retreated from cultural memory. Communal rules, responsa, and folklore abound with descriptions of unscrupulous match-making practice, but it is only with Shloyme Ettinger's closet drama *Serkele* that the marriage broker is granted a literary voice along with his fee. In Sholem Aleichem's epistolary novel *Menachem Mendl* (begun in 1899), the protagonist himself works for a time as a marriage broker, allowing the author to describe the occupation from the perspective of someone trying to make a living at it rather than from the point of view of romantic heroes for whom the matchmaker only gets in the way. Menachem Mendl, as a Jack-of-no-trades, is able to calibrate matchmaking with a long list of other pointless, "unproductive," and impossible Jewish professions: "As an occupation it may not be as respectable as writing, but it certainly looks better than trading," optimistically writes Menachem Mendl about the career on which he is embarking, reminding us of the commercial taint of the marriage "trade" while suggesting that the novelist and the matchmaker may be in roughly the same business, producing "happy endings" for a fee.[72]

That the ideology of modern love and the social institution of the matchmaker could and in fact did coexist in modernity might be demonstrated by the figure of the matchmaker Yona Toyber in S. Y. Agnon's *Simple Story*:

> Yona Toyber was a matchmaker. Though on the face of it he had never made a match in his life, no one in Szybusz had ever married anyone in Szybusz without his help. True, if someone mentioned that he had a marriageable son and was interested in so-and-so's daughter, Toyber would not even deign to reply, as if such things were beneath him. The next day, however, he would be sure to run into the young man in question, nor would the two of them have parted before there was such camaraderie between them that the young man's heart was putty in Yona's hands. Not that Yona ever laid down the law to anyone; it was enough simply to mumble a word or two and the rest simply happened by itself. No matter whom the youngster thought he loved, Yona could make him think otherwise, and whomever his parents thought he should love Yona could make him love, too, so that in the end, as it were, he fell in love with her all by himself and Yona simply gave his approval. There were some quite educated people in Szybusz who snorted at

the idea of arranged marriage without realizing that they themselves were a match made by Yona.[73]

In the figure of Yona Toyber (whose very name joins the Hebrew and Yiddish words for "dove" to create a pair of lovebirds), Agnon demonstrates the covert absorption of the institution of matchmaking into the very scene of modern love (and vice versa), with matchmakers now working in the shadows rather than out in the open. As Jacob Katz writes, the "virtually overnight" end to arranged marriages meant that "they were forced to adapt to the new social ideal. The marriage broker had to perform his duty discreetly."[74] That Toyber's successes are so easily assured despite the limits imposed on the open practice of his profession simultaneously suggests both the power and the fictionality of the love ideology. The youngsters, persuaded that love involves a free choice of romantic partner and the deepest expression of one's most primal being, are thus primed to misrecognize the influence of parents and the matchmaker-in-disguise they have recruited to shape this "choice."

The hybrid and liminal modern matchmaker, a feature of Jewish societies in transition, appears in numerous literary forms and contexts in the twentieth and even twenty-first centuries, becoming a figure of interest in his or her own right in the stage and film treatments of Sholem Aleichem's *Tevye the Dairyman*; Thornton Wilder's 1938 play, *The Merchant of Yonkers* (later revised as *The Matchmaker* and the basis of the 1969 film *Hello, Dolly!*); and such post-secular films as the 2007 *Arranged* and the 2012 *Fill the Void*, which portray matchmakers in the present-day Orthodox world. The differences between these literary matchmakers and those we know of from historical accounts, autobiography, or responsa are instructive: Hebrew autobiographies do not name the marriage brokers they mention and generally suggest that at least two brokers are required for a match, with each family represented by a different broker. Matchmakers swarm Günzburg's house when he turns eleven, he relates.[75] Avraham Ber Gottlober similarly writes that "in those days matchmakers would set their eyes on a boy who was learning Torah, and each of them would write his name in their notebook, with many girls surrounding him, some of them beautiful, some of them rich, some of them from famous families."[76]

However, the literary matchmaker Reb Yokhonon in *Serkele* is given the singular task of (retrospectively) approving a match on his own; increasingly, in the modern literary imaginary, it is one matchmaker, not many, who produces a match (the exception might prove this rule: it is only the presence of two matchmakers in *Menachem Mendl* that allows for the "absurd" results of their bungling efforts, which unite two perfectly suited young women). In the twentieth century, the role of the matchmaker harkens back to its rabbinic roots, becoming—as in God's matchmaking labors—a solitary, authorial occupation. This shift seems to reflect a fundamentally new conceptualization of the role: where the older model of multiple matchmakers represented marriage as a business proposition involving the calibration of two sets of external metrics, the single matchmaker embodies a view of marriage as involving internal and psychological factors, with a solitary figure who understands which individuals might forge a compatible partnership, embodying as well as producing a marital union.

The ideological shift from multiple matchmakers to one may find parallels as well in the transformation of the matchmaker from a male to a prototypically female figure. The matchmaking profession was for centuries a normatively masculine profession, with roots, according to Israel Abrahams, in the post-Crusade function of the head-of-yeshiva in reconstructing Jewish communities: "When Jewish society became scattered and disintegrated by the massacres and expulsions of the Crusading era, its scattered items could only be re-united by the agency of some peripatetic go-between" who was "almost invariably a male."[77] The twentieth-century literary matchmaker is increasingly gendered as feminine (and in the contemporary Orthodox world matchmaking has indeed become a largely female profession), reflecting the absorption of the "feminine arts" of relationship into the qualifications for the profession. Perhaps the most famous fictional matchmaker, Yenta in the stage and screen versions of *Fiddler on the Roof*, herself comically amplifies and transgenders the male character, Ephraim the Matchmaker, who plays a much more minor part in Sholem Aleichem's *Tevye the Dairyman*.

The proliferation of matchmakers in modern Jewish literature is not entirely explained by the partial absorption of the ideology of love into the matchmaking profession. Another reason the matchmaker may remain indispensable (narratively, if not sociologically) is that the matchmaker plays the important role of embodying the reality principle in relation to the fantasies of the love match. This role seems most clearly demonstrated not only by the matchmaker's attention to money, class, and other "practical" features of the match that the modern sex religion rules irrelevant;

the connection of the matchmaker with the occluded realities of modern love is also—paradoxically—signaled by the folklore that associates the matchmaker with untruth, with exaggeration and salesmanship. This aspect of matchmaking is abundantly attested in the Hebrew autobiography. As Avraham-Ber Gottlober described the occupation, the matchmaker "who was an expert in his work uttered many things, most of which were lies."[78] These exaggerations, by folkloric convention, serve as a transparent and pathetically thin cover for the unfortunate state of the marriage broker's "merchandise," thus allowing the "open secret" of the sex religion to (almost) speak.

Where the sex religion and marriage plot both assume and demand feminine beauty and perfection, relying where necessary on what Freud calls the "normal overestimation of the sexual object," jokes and stories that feature matchmakers reveal a horrified fascination with imperfect if not grotesquely deformed female bodies—the hump or clubfoot on the prospective bride is a veritable mainstay of this literature.[79] It is also Freud who shows us that these two attitudes are sides of the same sexual coin. If this is so, then the modern love match dialectically produces and psychologically calls for—can hardly do without—the matchmaker as its lying truth teller. That this is true in the sociological sense is the discovery of such historians as Marion Kaplan, who documents the submerged persistence of matchmaking within ostensibly modernizing German Jewish circles.[80] My own argument is that this holds true as well for Jewish literature. What is occluded in the ideology of romantic love—the inevitable imperfection of the "perfect match"—is broadcast (as it is concealed) in the more transparent exaggerations spun by the matchmaker. In the matchmaker, literature finds yet another arena in which the sex religion and arranged marriage, the beautiful fantasies and deflated realities of (Jewish) love, are permitted to speak their respective truths.

The most interesting matchmaker in modern Jewish literature may well be Pinye Salzman in Bernard Malamud's short story "The Magic Barrel," which appeared in the *Partisan Review* in 1954; in 1959, the collection of short stories with the same title won the National Book Award. As is the case for *The Love of Zion* and *The Dybbuk*, "The Magic Barrel" stands at the very heart of the Jewish literary canon. Malamud's work emerged as part of the renaissance of Jewish American fiction in the 1950s, which was at least partly stimulated by a new interest among Jewish writers in Yiddish literature, newly available in such canonical translation projects as Irving Howe's and Eliezer Greenberg's 1954 *Treasury of Yiddish Stories* (which included Saul Bellow's remarkable translation of Isaac Bashevis Singer's "Gimpel the Fool"). Julian Levinson describes this era:

> Yiddish literature gained a new lease among second- and third-generation American Jews for whom the language had suddenly become a poignant symbol for a distant but more "authentic" way of being Jewish. The American Jewish community, haunted by the Holocaust and dispossessed of the language of its forebears, was transforming into a self-conscious subculture defined through a connection to an "imagined" Jewish community— imagined both in Benedict Anderson's sense of a community defined more by the idea of commonality than by direct experience, and in the literary sense of a community whose self-understanding derives from the stories it tells about itself.[81]

"The Magic Barrel" was written in English, but it reads, in certain respects, as a translation from Yiddish, like Bellow's version of Singer's "Gimpel the Fool," which had appeared in the *Partisan Review* two years earlier. But while Singer's story was set in Eastern Europe, Malamud transported a Yiddish "type," the marriage broker, to New York of his own day. The story describes a young rabbinical student, Leo Finkle, who is approaching ordination. Finkle consults Salzman for the eminently practical reason that he "had been advised by an acquaintance that he might find it easier to win himself a congregation if he were married."[82] Finkle is embarrassed to take recourse to a matchmaker, who provides excruciatingly plain evidence that Finkle has failed to find and attract a woman on his own. Where Menachem Mendl updates the old occupation with an infusion of new urban capitalist practices (using a card system that resembles the paper chits of the period when he dabbled in the stock market), Pinye Salzman is even more clearly a "late" matchmaker, advertising in the Yiddish paper rather than contacting parents, dealing with young (or not so young) people rather than their families, and providing photos of his female "inventory" rather than documents of prestigious, which is to say, emblematically male, family trees. Nevertheless, Salzman also conforms to the stereotype, emblematized by Menachem Mendl, of the matchmaker as *luftmensch*, an impractical person with no actual occupation. Salzman's wife (as long suffering and sharp tongued as Menachem Mendl's Shaina Sheindel), when asked where her husband's office is, answers, "In the air." Leo persists: "You mean he has no office? "In his socks."[83] Yet when Finkle arrives back at his apartment, Salzman is there, appearing magically in Leo's home as if from the air.

The story follows a double trajectory that is cousin to the ambivalent embrace of arranged marriage in earlier Jewish literature—on the one hand, Leo Finkle is put off by recognizing, in Salzman, the activities of a "commercial cupid" with a barrel full of secondhand human goods, repeatedly wondering if "he did not, in essence, care for the matchmaking institution"; on the other hand, Finkle finds the woman of his passionate dreams through this matchmaker, even if Salzman ostensibly did not intend to include a photo of his "fallen" daughter Stella among the others he shows Finkle. Malamud—like Mapu, An-sky, Agnon, and a host of worried bourgeois Jewish parents—thus demonstrates that wild passion and matchmaking are not necessarily opposites but might work in secret consort. It is the matchmaker's barrel of photos, rather than the sexually free urban street or the landscape of untouched nature, that holds the image of Finkle's true love.

There are nevertheless significant differences between the world Malamud portrays and the ideological systems at play in these earlier texts. Nineteenth- and early twentieth-century Jewish literature had assumed that the major obstacles to the love match were parents and matchmakers; if only young people were left to their own devices, marriages would no doubt ensue. "The Magic Barrel" tells an entirely different story, that of a young man who, despite the opportunities represented by the modern city, has not discovered the means of finding a mate on his own. Rather than a matchmaker being imposed on him by his parents or society, Leo Finkle himself turns with ambivalence and evident shame to a marriage broker whose services he finds advertised in the newspaper. Finkle's circumstance is evidence not only of the unevenness of modernization, the persistence of traditional occupations within an urban landscape that would seem to preclude them (and indeed continues to marginalize them); it also points to the unfulfilled promise of the modern ideologies of love, which regularly produce aging bachelors and other romantic failures alongside more heralded successes. Malamud not only implicitly criticizes the romantic ideology on behalf of those it leaves behind; he also reverses a literary tradition that supplants matchmaking with a series of more romantic variations on how it might come about that boy meets girl.

In constructing a story that has Finkle discover passionate attraction in the figure of Salzman's daughter, Malamud draws the marriage broker into

the sphere of this passion, and not only because Salzman is "accidentally" instrumental in creating this bond. Finkle's attraction to Stella is signaled even
before he meets her, in his growing fascination with her father. And when the
rabbinical student sees her photo "among the discards in Salzman's barrel,"
Finkle "had a vivid impression that he had met her before." This feeling of
déjà vu, a regular feature of Jewish literary love at first sight beginning with
Mapu, emerges from both the overt physical resemblances and the inchoate emotional sympathies between father and daughter, which themselves
mirror and complement Finkle's relationship with his parents, who also met
through a matchmaker. Ideologically, Finkle's déjà vu suggests secret resonances between Salzman's occupation of marriage broker and his daughter's
less delineated role as rebellious daughter, sexual sinner, or even prostitute—
the evident generation gap between fathers and children cannot obscure
these connections. As belated expression of the intergenerational dreams and
magic that drive the erotic entanglements in *The Love of Zion* and *The Dybbuk*, "The Magic Barrel" represents the connection between fathers and their
apparently estranged children as a mystical engine of erotic love.

It is no surprise that the intergenerational workings of Jewish love are
matched by an intertextual web of Jewish literary allusion. Malamud acknowledged that the idea for his story came not from personal experience
but from his involvement with the "imagined community" of Yiddish literature: "The idea for the story itself, the donnée, came about through Irving
Howe's invitation to me to translate a story from the Yiddish for inclusion
in his and Eliezer Greenberg's anthology called *A Treasury of Yiddish Stories*."[84] Malamud declined, but the invitation reminded him of the Yiddish-
speaking home in which he was raised and stimulated his literary interest
in Yiddish culture. Lillian Kremer describes Malamud as participating in a
larger project of "transmogrifying" Yiddish literature into the American literary landscape: "Among the most successful of these contemporary transla-
tors is Bernard Malamud who has created a body of fiction incorporating
stock figures from Yiddish literature and folklore—recasting them, recloth-
ing them in modern dress, to explore themes of spiritual crisis."[85] Chief
among these stock figures is the marriage broker, of whom Kremer writes:

> Malamud draws this shadchan in broad comic strokes. A talkative humbug,
> with a genius for glossing over the physical and character defects of his cli-
> ents, Salzman is conceived in the traditional satiric mode, as lively, impu-

dent, given to exaggeration and banter. Yet, he is also touched with comic pathos, characteristic of the long-suffering Jews who populate Malamud's fictional world.[86]

In his notes on the development of "The Magic Barrel," Malamud makes clear, from the very first notation, that he intended to wed the familiar story of a courtship in which "the young man somehow gets the girl" with a rather different variety of narrative, one that involves both a miracle and a marriage broker (in Malamud's shorthand, M.B. or m.b.):

> The young man somehow gets the girl. Nor sure what the miracle is but he's got to do something that satisfies everyone but the M.B. He (the m.b.) has to be disappointed yet resigned. Once I work out the meaning of the piece I'll have the ending. Season with Chagall?[87]

The Chagallean seasoning is readily apparent in the story: In the ecstatic final scene, in which Leo Finkle finally meets Stella after persuading her father to arrange the encounter, the narrator relates that "violins and lit candles revolved in the sky. Leo rushed forward with flowers outthrust." If some of the images and atmosphere of the story are inspired by the folkloristic supernaturalism of Chagall, Malamud recounts that he learned about marriage brokers from a collection of Yiddish folklore by Immanuel Olsvanger that had appeared in 1947. As Malamud writes, "My reading in *Royte Pomerantsen* provided the six marriage anecdotes—two of which were very important."[88] Quoting from *Röyte Pomerantsen* (as Olsvanger transliterates the Yiddish), Malamud continues:

> From the first anecdote I got the basic idea for the story. From the second and one or two of the others, enough of the personality of the marriage broker to develop him with comparative ease. In other words, I recognized and understood him; I was able to recognize him in my past, though I had never met a marriage broker.[89]

Malamud's description of his "recognition" of the figure of the marriage broker replays the uncanny union of déjà vu and love at first sight at one remove, insisting that the marriage broker had survived his expulsion from Jewish modernity in a form available and attractive to modern literary appropriation in which matchmaking could be understood as miracle as well as commerce. Strikingly, it was folklore rather than fiction that made this appropriation possible. Olsvanger's collection of matchmaking humor (tales 12–17, as well as 22–23) revolves around the familiar stereotypes of the matchmaker's function as a "commercial cupid" who overpraises his clients' attractive qualities and minimizes their flaws; in this stereotype and in "The Magic Barrel," it is the prospective bride whose flaws (a hump, a limp, advanced age) are held up to scrutiny as they are concealed, the contrary of the romance's idealization of its heroine. Salzman indeed updates this folkloric trope in exaggerating one prospective bride's worldliness and sophistication while understating her age. But it is Malamud's genius to discover new ways that the matchmaker's stereotypical exaggeration might function as a tool for exposing social and psychological truths. Just as he recognizes that Lily has been misrepresented to him, Finkle, who is not given to self-scrutiny, also recognizes that he has been misrepresented to Lily—Salzman has given Lily the romantic impression that Finkle is a spiritual seeker rather than a dry scholar of Jewish law in pursuit of the professional advancement he is told will follow from marriage. This heightened portrait of himself leads to Finkle's crisis and subsequent transformation into the very being Salzman has painted and that a modern love story demands—a man capable of profound spiritual-erotic longing. Precisely the operations most criticized as venal matchmaking practices in folk literature thus work to erotically awaken a young man and render him ready for passionate love. Given that Salzman is to be credited, by dialectical logic, with awakening by inventing this passion, it makes sense that Finkle's passion will be directed toward Salzman's daughter, who bears some resemblance to her father even as she rebels against his sexual control.

In detailing the genesis of this story, Malamud cites in English translation the Olsvanger tale "Love Match" (called, in Olsvanger's transliterated Yiddish, "A Shidach fun Libe"), which recounts the efforts of a marriage broker to interest a young man in a "girl who's a regular doll. But really a pretty girl." When the young man declares himself uninterested, the marriage broker proposes other prospective brides, one in possession of a fortune, another with a distinguished pedigree of "twenty generations of rabbis," and so on. To each of these qualities the young man indicates his lack of interest, finally declaring, "Listen, mister, I don't want to hear anything more. I intend strictly a love match." The broker immediately responds: "Don't say another word. I can get you that kind too."[90] The straightforward opposition between an arranged marriage and a love match, for the matchmaker, is no opposition at all—even a love match can be arranged! In its humorous context, the story participates in the folkloric casting of marriage brokers as possessing seemingly unlimited rhetorical skills to turn obstacles to their own advantage; in this case, the matchmaker is able to treat the rejection of his services as a statement of what his customer requires and thus as a business opportunity. Malamud's reworking of the tale strikes a more delicate balance between arranged marriage and the love match: Malamud leaves open the question of whether Salzman only reluctantly agrees to Finkle's meeting his daughter or has engineered Finkle's infatuation with his errant daughter in order to "save" her by marriage to a rabbi, as Leo at one point suspects. As in Olsvanger's story and the "coincidences" arranged for their children by clever German Jewish parents in Marion Kaplan's research and in Yona Toyber's smooth manipulations, youthful passion may be just another tool in the skilled matchmaker's kit.

The critical interpretation of "The Magic Barrel" that views Salzman as a particularly devious marriage broker who manipulates Finkle into falling in love with Salzman's daughter derives some support from another of Olsvanger's marriage broker tales.[91] Tale 23 both conforms to and deviates from the familiar joke of the matchmaker desperate to marry off a deeply flawed prospective bride. While this flaw is by generic convention a deformity or disability, the matchmaker in tale 23 is hard at work passing off a promiscuous woman as a suitable bride. The tale, "No Persuasion Necessary" (Es Iz Nito Vos Ibertsureydn), describes the visit of a young man to the town of Kutne to do research on a prospective bride (a task traditionally left to the marriage broker or relatives rather than a prospective bridegroom). A few locals who know the young woman in question try to delicately warn him off: she's a girl, they let him know, who "with all the officers . . ." Another local tells him, "Stay away from her as from fire! With all the police officers!" And finally, an old man tells him, "with all the doctors . . ."[92] Returning to Vilna, the young man rebukes the marriage broker for proposing such a match. The broker replies: "Look here! All the officers, all the doctors in Kutne, you make it sound like Kutne is a city. But how big is the whole Kutne?" The marriage broker's minimizing of the defect in the bride by suggesting the demographic limits of her sexual escapades is a modern twist on the more common jokes about the matchmaker's ability to minimize a hump; the story intimates that such a woman, too, might be passed off or "saved" by a wily matchmaker. This story may have suggested to Malamud the figure of

Stella, Salzman's daughter, who is the very image of a streetwalker, standing "by the lamp post, smoking." Stella, we are told, "wore white with red shoes, which fitted [Leo's] expectations, although in a troubled moment he had imagined the dress red, and only the shoes white." Stella, like the prospect in tale 23, is both arranged bride (in white) and loose woman (in red); unlike Olsvanger's fallen bride, she is also the woman of Finkle's (troubled) dreams.

In its broadest outlines, "The Magic Barrel" recapitulates through Finkle the trajectory of modern Jewish literature from tradition to erotic awakening. Robert Alter reaches back further for a model of such conversion, writing that "the rabbinical student Finkle is led by the plot, according to sound Pauline principles, to turn away from the law, to which he has been devoted, for the sake of love."[93] But Finkle not only follows the move from arranged marriage to mad passion, from "the law" to love. He also brings along the traditional figure of the matchmaker, who represents, we might say, the (Jewish) "law" of the reality principle in its relation to the idealizations of (Christian) romantic love. Malamud's story places Salzman not outside the frame of the image of young love but just at its edge: As the famous last line of the story goes, "Around the corner, Salzman, leaning against a wall, chanted prayers for the dead."[94] The enticements of Malamud's story reside not only in the redemptive-erotic figure of Stella but also in that of her father, the owner of the "magic barrel" from which Stella's image materializes.

For Jewish American readers, distant from both the magical enchantments of Eastern European folk culture and the herring barrels of a previous immigrant generation, Malamud may have reminded them of a world they never experienced but that they nevertheless felt to be an uncanny part of who they were. Stella similarly appears to Leo as both a radical intrusion into the world he knows and "hauntingly familiar," and Malamud himself describes his encounter with Olsvanger's matchmaker in similarly paradoxical terms: "I recognized and understood him; I was able to recognize him in my past, though I had never met a marriage broker."[95] In these tales of (literary) desire, the trajectory from the old dispensation to the new, from the Law to the law of love, from the matchmaker to the modern love match, follows no straight path. From Mapu to Malamud it also seeks the powerful and impossible combination of tradition and love, the marriage broker and the young woman smoking under the lamppost who is his estranged and beloved daughter, his incarnation and overthrow.

The mysterious last sentence of the story, in which Salzman "chants prayers for the dead," has provoked a range of critical interpretations. Robert Solotaroff asks,

> Are the prayers for the dead that he chants in the last line of the story (as Leo rushes forward to meet Stella) for his own moral self? For Leo's future? Other readings offer themselves, but, within this line of reasoning, all lead to King Frederick William of Prussia's comment about the sympathy that Catherine II showed for Poland when the third partition erased that country from the map of Poland: "She wept but she took."[96]

Solotaroff's suggestion that Salzman is having it both ways—mourning a mismatch that he nevertheless ardently desires—emphasizes the figure of the matchmaker as a wily strategist who plays a double game (as of course all matchmakers do), making the best of a situation for which he feels moral despair. But Malamud also sees Salzman as an uncanny figure, magically taking up residence in postwar Jewish American literature, appearing in the ink of writers who had never met a matchmaker in the flesh. Olsvanger begins his introduction to *Röyte Pomerantsen* by suggesting that the book, for all its humor, stands as "a grim monument over the mass grave of a world that is no more."[97] Malamud, importing Olsvanger's marriage broker into the American postwar literary landscape, both gives the marriage broker new life and proclaims—indeed has the broker himself proclaim—his long-delayed, often-repeated, already-accomplished demise. If Jewish literature begins with the eviction of the matchmaker from the scene of the literary love match, Malamud's marriage broker—like Olsvanger's—manages to find a place for himself in the haunted shadows of the modern love scene, where he can keep an eye on what takes place under the streetlight.

The Dybbuk, like "The Magic Barrel," also ends with a ritual acknowledgment of death: *Barukh dayan ha'emet*—"blessed is the true judge," the pious formula recited on hearing of or witnessing (as is the case in the play) a death; this final line is appropriate for a play so steeped in death and in which a dead father and friend speaks from beyond the grave. Against the argument that each generation must be able to decide its own erotic fate, these narratives assert that the older generation continues to express its desires and exert its wishes on those who come after, arguing as well that the children and children's children hear—invent, imagine—the voices of their dead ancestors precisely in the wild idiom of erotic love. The matchmaker, exorcised at the outset of modern Jewish literature and repeatedly reborn in the generations that followed, reminds us that the erotic paths we follow and ties we forge are never entirely our own. Olsvanger's collection made the culture of matchmaking available to new audiences, who needed the marriage broker's services less for finding a mate than for finding a path to that erotic past. But it was Malamud who brought the matchmaker back into the Western literary tradition, even if his story ends with this matchmaker reciting Kaddish as if for his own death.

CHAPTER THREE

Pride and Pedigree

> Choosing ancestry is a serious business with major implications.
>
> —Robert Cover, *Nomos* and Narrative

Uprooting the Family Tree

Among the aspects of traditional arranged marriage most ridiculed by Haskalah modernizers was the importance accorded to *yihus* (also spelled *yikhus* or *yikhes*), generally defined as ancestry, lineage, or pedigree. In this regard, Jewish modernization was well in line with European norms; as Werner Sollors puts it, "By the yoking of love and marriage, betrothals were removed from the controls of descent (*déclaration de sa naissance*, definition of family by descent) and opened to the forces of consent (romantic love, serious intention to get married, founding of families through marriage)."[1] If, as maskilim believed, marriages were to be formed on the basis of consent, compatibility, and love, what conceivable relevance could there be in the pedigree of one or both members of a couple? In his 1863 autobiography, Mordecai Aaron Günzburg makes no bones about his disdain for the role played by *yihus* in the negotiations for his own marriage:

> If a matchmaker had a match to propose and came to my father, he would weigh the family ten generations back and if my father discovered that the

proposed match weighed a grain or two less than the honor of my father's household he would reject the match. And since my father was the one who owned the scales and the weights, he was the one who weighed and judged, and his self-love formed a weight of its own that could tip the scales in his direction; if the weight of the father of the proposed bride was heavier than he liked, he could lighten that of the proposed bride herself, who was presumably the primary object of investigation, though he asked almost no questions about her except whether she had healthy eyes and a straight nose—nothing more. This was the tribute he paid to the inanities of the land.[2]

Günzburg here excoriates not only "the inanities" of weighing a family "ten generations back" but also the inherent subjectivity and skewed calculus of such measurement. For all the rigorous neutrality implied by the elaborate metaphor of scales and weights, the owner of the scales could easily manipulate results in his own favor, whether he was assessing the pedigree of a prospective match or of his own family. In either case, pedigree was simply a wrongheaded and irrelevant measurement for the business of contracting a marriage: while family histories were carefully scrutinized, the qualities of the prospective bride or groom were almost entirely neglected, with no attention paid—as in the case of Günzburg's own match—to anything but the most superficial aspects of appearance or health.

Günzburg's metaphor of the scale draws attention as well to another contrast between modern marriage ideologies and traditional arranged marriage. While traditional arrangements and modern marriage could both be conceptualized as a kind of negotiated balance, this balance was viewed, in the love match, as a matter of complementary dispositions and harmonious mutual affection. The balancing act that resulted in an arranged marriage involved matching young people of similar status and negotiating such financial arrangements as *kest*; unlike the balanced mutuality of a love match (in its ideal form), the financial aspect of arranged marriage encouraged competitiveness from the outset, with each side attempting to gain an advantage through maneuvers that bore an unseemly resemblance to marketplace bargaining. Arranged marriage, in Alan Mintz's words, is "a set of transactions in which each family tries to maximize its three basic sources of 'capital': learning, ancestry, and money."[3] A more prestigious pedigree, then, could lead to an advantage in the financial negotiations. Such considerations maximized the temptation to exaggerate a pedigree; what raised the ire of Avraham-Ber Gottlober in his descriptions of traditional marriage arrangements was that they involved the competitive and narcissistic preening of two fathers rather than the mutual attraction of a young man and young woman: Gottlober writes: "The father on the bride's side does not fall short of the father of the groom in pride and haughtiness, marshalling proofs that the match is unworthy of his honor."[4] Such a competitive approach, however strategic it might seem, could be counterproductive, and indeed Günzburg tells us that "it was not easy to find a match that would suit my father, because he was extremely proud of his *yihus*, his wisdom and that of his son, who even—with all of his faults—was worth ten times the children of the rest of the householders, so that the matchmakers grew tired of finding a match he would like among the Jewish aristocracy."[5]

Given the incentives to inflate or even invent *yihus*, it is not surprising that family trees were flaunted by those who could claim descent from them and treated with skepticism by all others. In a characteristically ironic passage at the start of his autobiography, Moshe Leib Lilienblum repeats the family genealogy he learned from his grandparents only to deflate it:

> If my ancestors had recorded their lineages and kept these records, I could take pride before the distinguished reader who values high-born people with a long or short pedigree. My father's mother would always say that she was the great-granddaughter of two grand and wealthy rabbis (or even geniuses): R. Mordecai Tiktiner, who supported ten loafer-scholars (*lomdim-batlanim*) at his table so they could learn Torah, and R. Zvi Hirsch the Rabbi of Orla; when her paternal grandfather R. Shabtai, the son of the aforementioned Mordecai, married the daughter of the aforementioned R. Zvi, they measured out the gold coins by filling yarmulkes (a kind of cap worn under a larger hat); that branch of her family was among the most distinguished residents of the city of Brody, and she knew of one surviving member of the family by the name of R. Yosef Berakhiah. . . . My father's mother would tell this to me and the neighbor women each and every day, so it is possible that most of what she said is true. My mother's father was a priest of God, excelling in Torah and the fear of sin, who never uttered one lying word in his life, and he would say that my paternal grandfather had a family tree that went all the way back to Ezra the Scribe, but it was burned in the Great Fire (of when?) in Williampol (near Kovno).[6]

Lilienblum's autobiographical performance here is a complex one, recounting his own distinguished lineage, which combined wealth, learning, and antiquity in exemplary fashion while mocking the reliability of these ancestral reports and the pretensions of the reader who takes an interest in such lineage. In the assertion that "it is possible that most of what she said is true" in his grandmother's recitation of the family lineage, Lilienblum implies that such performances are suspect by their very nature. Even his maternal grandfather, who cannot be suspected of lying, proffers genealogical "truths" that are secondhand goods, with origins whose value increases but reliability decreases in proportion to their antiquity; moreover, evidence of this pedigree, which reaches back to Ezra (a scribe like his nineteenth-century "descendant"), has been lost in a fire whose very year has been forgotten. If his ancestors failed to keep or lost their ancestral records, Lilienblum compensates for this neglect in transcribing their words. Lilienblum thus lets his reader know that he is in possession of a distinguished pedigree even as he disowns it, projecting the estimation of ancestral status onto a preening grandmother and "the distinguished reader who values high-born people." Lilienblum's account is not only a quasi-traditional recitation of a distinguished family line: it is also autobiography, describing the remembered self from the perspective of the writing self, and auto-ethnography, recording both his lineage and the cultural value placed on lineage in his childhood environment. In this dense narrative performance, individual autobiography, family history, and collective ethnography can hardly be untangled from the unreliable narrators, mythical origins, and hazily remembered events they record and on which they depend.

The maskilic critique of the role of ancestry in marriage arrangements is abundantly attested in the Haskalah romance as well. In Mapu's *Love of Zion*, the wise Sitri excoriates the practice of those urban fathers who "sell their tender, delicate daughters to some haughty noble who boasts of his ancestry and wealth."[7] In one of his earliest exchanges with Tamar, Amnon laments the importance placed by his society on wealth and lineage, to the detriment of beauty and character:

> Amnon sighed and said, "Who is the man in this city that will consider my beauty as wealth, and the courage of my heart as family honor?"
> And Tamar said to him: "Who knows, perhaps a young woman might be found in this city that prefers your love to life, and cares nothing about your family tree?"[8]

This delicate exchange between the lovers acknowledges the realities of the marriage market while attempting to shift the principles that undergird it, recalibrating the relative value of (male) beauty and courage, wealth, and family honor. It does not occur to Amnon to hope for a prospective father-in-law who will discount status or money altogether; he yearns only for a man who is capable of converting Amnon's bio-erotic capital into the more traditional currency of wealth and family honor so that he can match Tamar's own considerable social and bio-erotic capital. Tamar opposes to this economy a simpler and more radical one in which a young woman rather than a "man in this city" serves as chief economist; her system has only two elements: (Amnon's) love and (Tamar's) life, with the first trumping the second in accordance with the extravagant romantic calculus set out by another young woman—The Song of Song's Shulamite, who declares that "love is stronger than death" (8:6). Tamar's calculus seems to be a feminine one, and it makes sense that women might have been less invested in a system so devoted to calculating male status. Indeed, it is echoed by her mother, Tirzah, who rejects her husband's "searching after Amnon's parentage," asking, "Why do you not search Tamar's heart, as my father did mine when he gave me to you? He asked me what I thought of you—I never thought of looking into your origin. I saw you, loved you, and decided to be yours; and only afterwards did I find out who you were."[9] Rather than choose a spouse after investigating his parentage, and only then falling in love, Tirzah makes it clear that the discovery of good parentage should or will follow (naturally?) upon the more immediate appearance of love (as it does with Amnon).

Yihus also makes an appearance in the Yiddish literature of the era, in which it takes on a characteristically sharper satirical edge. The major spokesperson for and representative of the *yihus* system in Shloyme Ettinger's 1861 closet drama *Serkele* is the title character, who as a callow nouveau riche has only recently escaped her status as a "miller woman"; Serkele inflates or invents a family background to suit her new circumstances. In one early scene, Serkele manages to inform the "modern" young man who is courting her daughter of the family's illustrious forebears, even as she acknowledges the irrelevance of such considerations:

> What? Family? What does she need to worry about family [*yihus*] for? Isn't my side of the family distinguished enough [*meyukheses*], after all? After all, the Rovshitzer Rabbi—heh? How about that?—a close relative, and the Preacher of Suaranyer, may he rest in peace, was related—a blood relation— to my uncle's mother-in-law, and the Chacham Zvi's mother-in-law's grand-

mother and her great-grandfather were on my mother's side . . . they were close relatives.[10]

Serkele's vague and stuttering recitation of this tangled chain of names and relations, which suggests that she is inventing distinguished connections on the fly, reflects her social climbing as it parodies the required recitation of family lineage in traditional marriage arrangements. It also expresses the confusingly transitional moment in which the play takes place: Serkele fully participates in her daughter's naïve embrace of modern ideologies of romantic courtship, even as she cannot entirely shake free of the sense that pedigree (her own if not the groom's) must still matter. Ettinger's play is commonly read as a satire of Jewish women's "false Enlightenment," ridiculing the pretentious attempts of Jewish women to imitate the rituals of European romance; but in this scene Serkele's pretensions are also native to the traditional world, and Ettinger's satire is directed at traditional estimations of *yihus*—as open to manipulation, associated with unearned status and false pride, market oriented in its view of marriage, and essentially irrelevant to the business of love.[11]

In his 1888 Yiddish novel *The Wishing Ring* [Dos vinshfingerl], S. Y. Abramovitsh similarly satirizes traditional society, describing the social aspirations of Leybtse the moneylender to gain the *yihus* he lacks by finding a budding young scholar with a pedigree to marry his young daughter:

> Leybtse wanted a son-in-law who had everything: A silken child from a prominent family, good and pious, with a head on his shoulders and steeped in aristocratic lineage (*eyngetunkn in yikhes*), so that God and man would envy Leybtse alike. . . . He looked and looked and finally uncovered his treasure; he found himself a Bentsye, a pale little boy with an emaciated face, just now bar mitzvah and already a candidate for hemorrhoids—in short, a jewel, the very thing he'd been hoping for.[12]

Abramovitsh achieves his satirical critique of arranged marriage by using Leybtse as a "focalizer" of the traditionalist view: Leybtse is gleeful at finding a "treasure" and "jewel." But the satirical portrait of a father falling in love with a prospective son-in-law is combined here with a different narratorial perspective, one that takes such attributes as physical appearance and health into account—"a pale little boy with an emaciated face . . . and already a candidate for hemorrhoids." Jacob Katz insists that "the outstanding characteristic of this society's approach to marriage was the extreme rationalism with which it calculated the chances of that 'proper match' to which each aspired in his own way. Such criteria as personal compatibility, not to speak of romantic attachments, were not considered at all."[13] Abramovitsh's complex irony helps us see, however, that arranged marriage also participates in the besotted idealism of love, even if it is a middle-aged man who rapturously describes finding the perfect mate for his daughter, and what counts as a treasure in this system is not a beauteous maiden or ravishing lad but an emaciated yeshiva student who spends far too many hours a day sitting.

As even this cursory survey of its various maskilic uses might indicate, the concept of *yihus* is far more ambiguous than its ready translation as pedigree or lineage implies. In their famous ethnography, *Life Is with People*, Mark Zborowski and Elizabeth Herzog propose that the usual translations fail to capture the multiple dimensions of the concept:

> [*Yihus*] relates to family background and position, but cannot be called pedigree, since it can be acquired currently as well as by inheritance, and does not necessarily require transmission "by blood." Essentially it is a product of learning plus wealth, of learning without wealth, or of wealth so used as to be translatable into the highest common denominator—the fulfillment of divine command.[14]

Zborowski and Herzog note that the term covers two distinct kinds of status. The first (*yihus avos*) is "inherited status," while the second (*yihus atsmo*) is the status attained by an individual who excels at scholarship, wealth, or philanthropy "through his own efforts." But even this taxonomy is deceptively simple, since "ancestor *yihus* cannot be retained merely by right of inheritance. If not constantly validated through activities of the individual himself, then his *yihus* dwindles." Among the ways that *yihus* may be acquired, Torah learning reigns supreme, as the gold standard that distinguishes those who are merely rich, powerful, and pedigreed from the true Jewish "aristocracy": "A wealthy and politically eminent family could really only attain *yihus* if one of its members was a scholar. Lacking such a scholar, a wealthy family could achieve that connection through a son-in-law. This phenomenon provided a pathway for social mobility, as a talented but poor student could marry into a rich family." If Torah scholarship is necessary for true *yihus*, then only marriage to a Torah scholar can secure this status for a family comprising daughters. For boys, to view the matter from the other perspective, Torah study accrues economic value as a pathway toward upward mobility. Zbrowoski and Herzog conclude: "However it may be defined, *yihus* is the badge and the measure of aristocracy. At the same time, to the extent that it is accessible to all and must be validated by the efforts of the individual, it bears witness to the principle that potentially all men are equal."[15]

In a recent and more subtle analysis of *yihus*, Glenn Dynner traces a series of historical shifts in the meaning of the term, with different groups holding disparate views of family distinction in accordance with their own class interests. Dynner notes that elite views of *yihus* as a "'sacred-biological' conception of nobility" long coexisted and competed with the conceptions of distinction as involving acquired Torah scholarship, a concept of *yihus* deriving from the medieval Tosafist school. Analyzing the operations of *yihus* within early Hasidism, Dynner suggests that while new Hasidic ideals of religious charisma initially displaced the traditional values of *yihus* as either inherited distinction or Torah scholarship, early leaders of the movement— who were themselves without family status—used the spiritual assets they had acquired on their own merits to bolster their family pedigrees through propitious marriages. Eventually, of course, Hasidic leadership produced its own *yihus*, in which inheritance rather than individual achievement played a substantial and at times even exclusive part. Given the shifting fortunes of the term, Dynner suggests that *yihus* came to encode, for traditional Eastern Europe, a "paradoxical conception of family status that might be inherited or acquired."[16]

Once one reads *yihus* as both a malleable and a contested term, it becomes clear that modern approaches to *yihus* might themselves be read genealogically, as continuing and recalibrating rather than overturning previous trends and currents. The Haskalah, Mordechai Zalkin has shown, produced both critiques of *yihus* as well as its own aristocracy, lineages, and prestigious family associations.[17] Nor is critique of *yihus* limited to Haskalah reformers. Nineteenth-century Hebrew autobiographies record traditionalist as well as maskilic critiques of *yihus*: Günzburg, for instance, adds to the description of his father's weighing of the family status of various prospective brides the rather surprising comment that his father did not particularly believe in the value of *yihus*, "since his discerning eye saw clearly enough that the pedigree and honor of the parents would render a match no more successful." Although he was ferocious in playing the pedigree game, Günzburg's father also tried to instill in his son the value of "self-pedigree, so that rather than being a moon who borrows its light from the sun around which it revolves, one should be a sun who bequeaths its own light unto others."[18] The ostensibly new Enlightenment estimation of individual achievement, then, might be discerned (if Günzburg's account is to be trusted), at least in this traditionalist father of a young maskil.

The class ideologies encoded in the *yihus* system have also been rethought since Zborowski and Herzog proposed that, by including Torah scholarship among the means of acquiring *yihus*, the system "bears witness to the principle that potentially all men are created equal." Shaul Stampfer subjects this widespread social myth to powerful deconstruction, arguing that the *heder* system in which all Eastern European Jewish boys were introduced to Torah study was essentially a conservative tool to maintain Jewish class stratification, "even though the popular image was that the educational system was open and every Jewish child could become a Talmudic scholar."[19] The *heder* instilled the *value* of Talmudic study and demonstrated to every Jewish child how difficult it was to achieve mastery, but Torah scholarship—by which was meant the ability to study the Talmud on one's own in a *bet midrash* after leaving the *heder*—was limited to those few who possessed the means to hire an *effective* teacher for their young sons. Stampfer summarizes:

> Jews in traditional Eastern European Jewish society saw the study of Talmud as a means of intellectual mobility, and not just that. They believed that a poor but brilliant Talmud student could become the son-in-law of a rich merchant, and thus rise instantly to the top of society. This meant that the religious élite could be regarded as a meritocracy in which membership is based on achievement and not family. . . . This was effective precisely because the reality was concealed.[20]

Demystifying the view of traditional Eastern European Jewish society as a (male) meritocracy, Stampfer understands the role of Torah study precisely as preserving class boundaries under the cover of Jewish meritocracy. Stampfer thus illuminates the structure of *yihus* as combining a spiritual ideology with a material base: Torah scholarship is the distinguishing mark of a member of the Jewish aristocracy, but a generally inadequate educational system ensures that wealth is required for students to study Torah. What distinguishes the traditional and modern marriage systems is thus not the presence or absence of an ideological superstructure obfuscating the operations of money and class in marriage but the content of this superstructure:

in traditional *yihus* it is Torah that serves this function, while in the modern romantic ideology it is love that exalts marriage over the material bases of economic life.

The role of women in the *yihus* system has not, to my knowledge, received the kind of attention that Stampfer pays to Torah study. It is apparent that *yihus*, in its reliance on women for its reproduction and as a system for arranging marriages in a patriarchal society, depends on what Claude Lévi-Strauss terms "the circulation of women" among men, and the absence of women's names in traditional genealogies is a symptom and by-product of their very importance; women function to forge connections between social groups and create an intergenerational line of fathers and sons. Lévi-Strauss writes: "Marriage alliances are not established between men and women, but between men *by means of women*, who are merely the occasion for this relationship."[21]

As Zborowski and Herzog describe it, since a woman "could not raise her social level" through the upward mobility ostensibly available to gifted yeshiva students, "her success in the 'matchmaking market' depended upon the *yihus* of her father and family, her economic attributes, and her physical beauty."[22] But the role of women as mere carriers of *yihus* understates their participation in or view of the process. It fails to account for Lilienblum's unnamed grandmother's role as the principal repository of the family names and its genealogical memory (real or invented), or of Serkele's recitation of her own, more clearly invented, family tree. These women (or female characters) might be seen as the "empty signifiers" that link wealthy fathers-in-law with brilliant sons-in-law, and fathers with sons, but in their genealogical performances (as narrated by male authors) these women wield the names of dead male ancestors to apparent social advantage, turning distinguished male names into the exchangeable and empty signifiers of *female* status.[23] Serkele is a female character imagined by a male author, and Lilienblum's unnamed paternal grandmother is an ancestor remembered (as she is effaced) by a male autobiographer; but they are also women who write their own family stories and invent their own ancestors. Both *Serkele* and Lilienblum's *Sins of Youth* remind us to remain alert to the ways that women author and produce *yihus*, even within their designated role of merely propagating, transferring, and reproducing it.

In the light of these complexities, it may be best to see *yihus* as a portmanteau term, covering different and opposing systems of values (inherited status versus individual achievement, wealth versus Torah), meaning different things in different periods and among different groups (priests and the families of rabbinic leaders, Tosafists and other elites, Hasidim and their opponents, men and women, fathers and sons, parents of prospective brides and parents of prospective grooms), and serving different functions (transferring status from one generation to the next, preserving family history, preventing incestuous unions). For all the differences among these functions and claims, *yihus* should also be seen as a relatively unified and coherent social structure and medium of exchange, functioning as a shared currency into which disparate values, classes, and family lines might be converted. This aspect is especially salient in marriage arrangements, in which it is precisely the flexibility of *yihus* that allows for the conversion of learning into wealth and wealth into learning, as well as the (paradoxical, retroactive) acquisition of ancestry in the formation of new family lines.

The flexibility and internal contradictions within the *yihus* system may also explain how and why it persists in modern marriage. As I have argued about other features of arranged marriage, the harsh critique of *yihus* in the literature and social arrangements of modernity should not obscure the ways that Jewish modernity continued to value, recover, and translate pedigree for its own purposes. The traditional world had already seen a variety of notions of what constituted family distinction, smoothing the way for the incorporation of newly emerging conceptions of the values *yihus* might express. Immanuel Etkes has shown that maskilim followed patterns set by traditional elites in forging social networks, family lines, and new varieties of inherited status.[24] Amnon's hope that his beauty and masculinity might be converted, by "a man in this city," into wealth and honor is also an accurate prediction of what came to pass once the values associated with the sex religion were integrated into the traditional marriage system.

As Freeze argues, the esteem for family lineage did not evaporate in modern marriage but was translated and modernized where it did not simply persist. Freeze suggests, however, that new possibilities of social mobility through secular education were crucially different from "the system of cultural prestige and male domination associated with Torah studies."[25] If a university degree could count as social capital, the traditional barrier that kept women from possessing *yihus* through their own intellectual merits was dealt a serious blow. Modernity thus both replicated the traditional system of social stratification and imbued it with new values, opening it up to (at least some) women and members of Jewish nonelites traditionally barred from participation. The social conservatism of the Haskalah may have been shaped not only by anxieties about what constituted its own Jewish status but also by the threat of encroachments by women and other nonelites. In this way, the ostensibly universal goals of the Jewish Enlightenment, which called for the transformation of society and individual self-betterment for all, stood in some tension with the desires of the new intellectual elite to guard its own hard-fought terrain.

It is against this set of competing cultural pressures that the maskilic representation of *yihus* should be understood. In their introductory essay on *Serkele*, Joel Berkowitz and Jeremy Dauber write that "there is no question that the appropriate groom is the enlightened figure, who once more [as in other maskilic dramas] is called Markus. And Markus, who aspires to adoption of Gentile culture as well as language, points the way away from current society, as symbolized by the arranged marriage system and the reliance on both *yikhes*—a word roughly akin to 'lineage'—and money."[26] Zehavit Stern has shown, however, that *Serkele* not only criticizes *yihus* but also subtly reinforces its value by having "the main villains of this play, Serkele and Gavriel Hendler, adopt a *yikhes* that is not their own." As Stern writes, "Indeed, *Serkele* does not do away with the notion of *yikhes* but endows it with a new meaning. At the opposite pole of Serkele, who flaunts her invented *yikhes*, is the impeccable Markus Redlekh, who keeps quiet about his noble lineage until the last part of the play, where we find out that his father was Zalmen (Solomon) Redlekh from Prague."[27]

Not pedigree itself but its flaunting or invention is to be denigrated. Just as Serkele suspects that her daughter's modern suitor might be interested in knowing about her distinguished ancestors, the author of *Serkele* seems to think that his readers would be relieved to learn that the poor tutor who is also the romantic hero comes from a line of decent, pious, learned, and *balebatish* (middle-class) Jews, if we are to condone and celebrate his marriage to the lovely Hinde. The poor and mistreated Hinde's own distinguished pedigree is similarly established before the marriage can take place: her learned and wealthy father makes a belated appearance at the end of the play, in time to prove that Hinde, too, comes from decent stock. But neither character may personally testify to this distinguished pedigree, which would be unseemly boasting and evidence of not understanding what truly counts in a marriage partner. It is thus left to a representative of the traditional world to supply this crucial information. Stern continues:

> Interestingly, it is the *shadkhn* [matchmaker], a much scorned figure in maskilic writing, who bears witness to Redlekh's lineage, and goes on to include the exquisite food in Zalmen Redlekh's house, the silver dishes, the Torah lecture and the pious wife. By serving as a source of information about the family and its *yikhes*, Yokhanan the *shadkhn* fulfills to a certain extent the traditional role of the matchmaker. His description of Markus' father suggests a new *yikhes* ideal, in which one is rich and dressed in a European manner and yet pious and a good scholar. This is parallel to and contrasted with Serkele's notion of *yikhes*, namely belonging to a lineage of Chasidic Rebbes. The ultimate maskil thus becomes the son of another maskil.[28]

How do we understand the curious persistence of elements of traditional marriage arrangements within the very literary works apparently designed to replace them? The social conservatism of the Haskalah is no doubt sufficient explanation, but Stern adds to this ready analysis a more interesting one. The ambivalent Haskalah attitude toward *yihus* reflects its own genealogical anxieties: "The new ideology endows the old term with a new content, but does not do away with it, as the need for proof of good origins is still (or even more) active. The young East-European Haskalah movement strives for a respectful lineage."[29]

In *A Traveler Disguised*, Dan Miron suggests that Sholem Aleichem supplied the patchy historical consciousness of Yiddish writers with a hoary past and chain of ancestors:

> The legend of Abramovitsh as the "grandfather" of Yiddish letters, which Sholem Aleichem launched when Abramovitsh was fifty-two years old (he himself was then twenty-nine years old) can be considered the basis of our conception of modern Yiddish literature as a literary institution. . . . People scarcely in their fifties he described as if they were tottering octogenarians. In this he camouflaged even from himself the shortness and scantiness of the tradition he was fabricating.[30]

The need to establish a distinguished past for secular Jewish literature was already an old problem by the 1880s, when Sholem Aleichem's genealogical mythmaking began. Indeed, the founding manifesto of the Eastern European Haskalah, Isaac Ber Lebensohn's 1828 *A Testimony in Israel* (Te'udah be-Yisra'el), can be understood as just such a *yihus brif*—a genealogical document demonstrating the aristocratic lineage and impeccable Jewish credentials of the ostensibly new program of Jewish modernization. As Immanuel Etkes points out in his introduction, Lebensohn devotes only a small part of the tract to laying out his main proposals to reform traditional Eastern European life through the study of Hebrew grammar and foreign languages and the "productivization" of the Jewish economy. The greatest part of the work focuses instead on "the justification of this program through the [rabbinic] tradition."[31] Etkes rejects the explanation that Lebensohn's disproportionate reliance on rabbinic and medieval sources is a stratagem for hiding a radically secularizing agenda from a traditional public; on the contrary, the rabbinic names cited in nearly every sentence of the manifesto satisfied "a weighty personal function in his spiritual world, saying: there is no contradiction between maskilic aims and the tradition!"[32] Lebensohn bolsters his ideological argument with a painstaking intellectual genealogy in order to demonstrate, to himself as to others, that Haskalah is not—God forbid!—a radical innovation but just the most recent iteration of a Jewish form of philosophical rationalism that could be traced from the biblical era until his own day. Etkes continues:

> A critical reading of this list [of rationalists] demonstrates that most of them were "recruited" through Lebensohn's anachronistic vision. However, the presence of medieval and Renaissance maskilim allowed Lebensohn to argue for, and as far as we can determine to believe in, a unified and continuous line of élite men who insisted on the pursuit of wisdom and science.[33]

Lebensohn's desire to establish an intellectual genealogy for Haskalah literature and ideas found multiple expressions in the movement that followed, in autobiography and literary history as well as other genres. The lineage of such literary characters as Markus, who is the representative of Haskalah ideas in *Serkele*, may have served to establish not only his own family line but also the proper ancestry of the movement more generally. The opening chapter of Mapu's *Love of Zion* also establishes the ancestry of Amnon (unknown to him or Tamar) as a descendant of Yoram, "a firm believer and devout worshipper of the one true God . . . and blessed with an abundance of earthly possessions."[34] Mapu here sets the template for beginning a Jewish novel by recourse to family history, in parallel with his recruitment of the status and antiquity of the Bible to ground its novelties in sanctified Jewish soil. *The Love of Zion* is thus both a rich expression of new romantic ideologies and a Jewish genealogy that traces romance back to the Bible. The impulse to record family trees, Glenn Dynner reminds us, often arises in the wake of historical catastrophes, serving as partial healing for ruptures of memory, transmission, and continuity. In the light of such analyses, we might recognize in the disparate genealogies of Lebensohn, Ettinger, Mapu, Lilienblum, and Sholem Aleichem primary evidence of and privileged response to family crisis and cultural disruption.[35] If, as Katz asserts, "sexual licentiousness [and] apostasy" were the exemplary "blemishes" on *yihus*, the Haskalah as a whole was challenged to establish its legitimacy against those who saw in it precisely these failings.[36] No wonder, then, that the literature of the Haskalah repeatedly takes the form of a *yihus brif*, demonstrating the "pure Jewish" roots and long line of distinguished ancestors of the movement and its champions, while attempting to eradicate the taint of illegitimacy, of trafficking in European ideas. That this pedigree, as Etkes notes, is imaginary and constructed should also not surprise us. In the discovery and invention of a distinguished lineage for their radical projects, Lebenson and Mapu are not so different from Serkele and Lilienblum's grandmother, who similarly plant proud family trees in the shifting sands of fallible memory and a rapidly changing world.

Literature and Lineage

There may be another, more literary reason for the persistence of *yihus* in modern Jewish literature, beyond its function of alleviating the genealogical anxieties of Jewish modernity and moderns: *Yihus* not only plays a role in Jewish literary texts; it also appears *as* modern Jewish literature. *Yihus*, that is, is *already* narrative in kernel form, providing traditional seeds for the blossoming of modern Jewish storytelling. If, as Yosef Yerushalmi famously put it, "history is the faith of fallen Jews," then the family history encoded in the *yikhes brif* became the faith that bridges the traditional past with those "fallen Jews" of modernity.[37] Alan Mintz suggests that nineteenth-century Hebrew autobiographers followed the model not only of those great individualists Rousseau and Maimon but also of premodern Jewish autobiographers "who attempted to confirm the worthiness and antiquity of their genealogies and to establish their own place within the cycle of family fortunes and misfortunes."[38] While geographic ties and traditional beliefs or practices might have been disrupted in the movement to modernity, family lines and genetic inheritance continued, providing an anchor in otherwise roiling historical currents. In a recent exploration of Jewish family, Jonathan Boyarin suggests that the notion (or joke) of Judaism as "ancestor worship" may "point to something that is characteristically Jewish, but by no means uniquely so: a sense of the continuing engagement of the dead (and especially our own ancestors) with the living that once was common in human culture, but that has generally been lost in the context of the 'privatized' culture of Western modernity."[39]

If indeed Jews maintain a particularly close connection with ancestors (or whether this apparent closeness is an effect of the Jewish grounding of this connection in a rich textual tradition), it should be no surprise that modern Jewish literature finds a privileged place for the family saga and incorporates family history into its many other genres. The connection between traditional genealogies and the family saga is sometimes particularly evident, as when novels append a family tree to the narrative (as in Thomas Mann's *Buddenbrooks*, John Galsworthy's *Forsyte Saga*, and Émile Zola's three family trees in the twenty-novel family saga *Les Rougon-Macquart*). What distinguishes the Jewish family saga from non-Jewish examples of the genre, according to Malka Magentsa-Shaked, is their sustained attention to "the enormous historical change which took place in the Jewish family and society as it moved into and through the twentieth century."[40] Such twentieth-century Hebrew and Yiddish family sagas as Israel Joshua Singer's *The Brothers Ashkenazi* and *The Family Carnovsky*, Der Nister's *The Family Mashber*, Isaac Bashevis Singer's *The Family Moskat*, A. A. Kaback's *The History of a Family*, and S. Y. Agnon's *History of Our Homes* express "the shock of history" through the story of what Thomas Mann terms, in the subtitle to *Buddenbrooks*, "the decline of a family." But in recording history through a family—even a family in decline—the family saga also suggests the continuity that is the guiding structure and hidden triumph of genealogical narrative in even its traumatized expression.

Writing at the very outset of the breakdown of the traditional Jewish family, Lilienblum apparently also felt the need to establish his genealogy, even as he deconstructed "the worthiness and antiquity" of this family line. Lilienblum begins by acknowledging that he did not inherit a written record of his ancestry and then proceeds to perform the exemplary "traditional" act of producing a *yikhes brif*. In this case, it is the modern autobiographer, as part of his efforts to assert an *individual* identity in rebellion against traditional expectations, who transmits in written form the oral memories of his grandparents. Interestingly, Lilienblum begins his work not with this ambiguous and ambivalent evocation of his pedigree, which is narrated in the second paragraph of his autobiography, but with the following opening passage:

> After my father divorced his first wife without paying her the sum specified in the marriage contract, since she had stayed overnight in the house of a Gentile without a chaperone, he married a second wife and after he had lived with her for five years they had their first and only son, the writer of this book, on a Monday morning, the 29th of Tishrei 5604 according to our calendar, or October 10 (or 22nd, according to the calendar used outside Russia), 1843.[41]

The autobiography begins, as is usual, with the autobiographer's birth, painstakingly recorded according to both Jewish and Russian calendar dates; but the double (or actually triple) birthday is preceded by a different doublet, that of his father's successive marriages. Lilienblum begins his autobiography not with the marriage of his parents but with his father's first marriage to another woman, which "the writer of this book" informs us was dissolved over an impropriety that, while not completely spelled out, has both a religious and sexual dimension—Katz, we may recall, considers apostasy and sexual transgression the primary "stains" on a family's *yihus*. I would suggest that the opening paragraphs of *Sins of Youth* present two different myths of origin, just as the creation of Eve (yet another sinning woman) is told through two accounts in Genesis (and mirrored by Lilith in rabbinic folklore) and just as every birth is the continuation of two different genetic lines (even if only one is recorded in patrilinear genealogies). Thus, along with the more conventional if unreliable pedigree provided in the second paragraph, Lilienblum also shows us another, similarly unreliable, prehistory for his own life story. His father's first wife is in no sense his mother, and her transgression is only sketchily recounted and, in any case, seems to have produced no direct offspring. But in beginning the autobiography with this story about his father's first wife, Lilienblum suggests that her story may be linked with his own through narrative logic rather than genetic kinship: her apparently sexual transgressions serve as a model for his own sins of youth, as in the autobiography's title. By bringing these twin genealogies together, Lilienblum suggests that both may play a part in the vagaries of his life, that he may be an imaginary bastard of this sinning woman as well as the legitimate offspring of his more pious parents.

The narration of lineage rather than its simple chronicling, I would suggest, is not a feature only of modernity, symptom of the spinning of straightforward genealogies into the more capacious shapes permitted by modern literature; it already resides in the tradition, in the interweaving of narrative and genealogical lists in Genesis, or in the rabbinic dictum that Jewish history forms a cyclical and repetitive pattern that expresses itself in descent, in which *ma'aseh avot siman la-banim* (the actions of the fathers are a sign for the children). While the genealogical list draws an apparently untroubled and neat chain of ancestors and descendants, the biblical narratives interwoven with these genealogies remind us that lineage can hardly progress without women, sex, and the complications these inevitably introduce into the reproduction of a male line. The patriline both depends on and conceals a sexual story, in which mystery necessarily prevails even without the hint of sexual transgression. The opening clause of Lilienblum's autobiography thus functions—just as the Bible often does—as pedigree and anti-pedigree, providing "neutral" information about the autobiographer's genetic line while demonstrating that genealogies can hardly be separated from the more obscure operations of human sexuality. Lilienblum's literary genealogy, like the book of Genesis, both presents his family history straightforwardly and multiplies the potential lines of ancestry and (dis)inheritance that surround and shadow it. Divorced and with her name expunged, Lilienblum's almost-mother nevertheless is given pride of place in the autobiography of the man who is a sinner like her, even if he also not quite her son.

Haskalah autobiography took an interest in *yihus* as part of its commitment not only to individual life stories but also to collective history and ethnography.[42] Among the more remarkable treatments of *yihus* in nineteenth-century Hebrew autobiography is Günzburg's historico-ethnographic narrative of the development of the *yihus* system, which is his lineage of lineage, genealogy of genealogy, produced as a lengthy digression from the story of his own marriage negotiations. This account is an early expression of the analysis of *yihus* undertaken by later historians of Jewish society and has much in common with them: a recognition of the class stratification encoded in the system, an analysis of the role of marriage in transmitting and "upgrading" status, and an attention to the ways that the policing of class boundaries is effaced in the system by what we would now call ideological superstructures. Günzburg's analysis nevertheless differs from those of later historians: He maps his reading of *yihus* onto the earliest biblical history rather than traces it to a later period in Jewish society, borrowing from this history an air of primordial legend and subjecting the Bible, conversely, to powerful secular critique. Rather than guarantee the special and deserved status of the Jews, the Bible—in Günzburg's deconstruction—is what Walter Benjamin would call a "document of barbarism,"[43] recording the triumphs of the powerful at the expense of the less powerful in and through an apparently neutral genealogical record.

Remarkably, while modern scholars typically distinguish Jewish conceptions of *yihus* from (Gentile) land-based inheritance systems by noting (among other distinctions) the important role Jewish communities accord to Torah study, Günzburg makes no mention of the Jewish valuation of scholarship, universalizing his analysis by grounding it entirely in economic conditions, beginning with the distinction between landowners and those who work the land:

> In the course of time, this difference [between landowners and peasants] became habituated, and rich people saw themselves as elevated and viewed the poor as lowly creatures who were born to work; the rich ate the best produce and lived in large dwellings and became soft and elegant and addicted to pleasure, while the poor worked as beasts of burden by day, were browned by the sun, unattractive and dark of spirit, eating the bread of affliction. The children that were born to these two classes of people inherited from the womb either a majestic and dominating spirit or lowliness and subjection— and these attributes became natural for them . . . so that the attributes that were originally accidental came to be considered an attribute separate from wealth and acquired through birth, under the new names of "the pedigreed" and "the ignorant masses" (*meyuhasim ve'amei ha'aretz*).[44]

Günzburg contends that purely contingent economic social differences became "naturalized" over the course of generations, so the different classes forgot the conditions of their own formation: children born to these two classes acquire different natures "from the womb," inheriting either a "majestic and dominating spirit" or "lowliness and subjection." Class character, then, is a product of historical circumstances that nevertheless imprints itself on and as human nature. This process is already well developed at the near beginning of recorded time:

> The pedigreed saw it as a detriment to their honor to marry with the ignorant masses, and took only women as pedigreed as themselves, but when they saw that the daughters of men were lovely, their desire came over them

and they decided, in twisted fashion, that these women were not good enough to be companions but were perfectly suited for lovemaking to satisfy their passions, and who would stop them from desecrating these women with their whoring? And they came to whore with them, and they gave birth to the Nephilim who were half-divine and half-human, elevated over their mothers because of their fathers' pedigrees but falling below (*noflim*) their fathers because of the lowly status of their mothers, and a new class of beings halfway between the pedigreed and the masses was born.[45]

Günzburg reads a further stratification of the *yihus* system beyond the simple binary of landowner/peasant in the mysterious episode in Genesis 6:1–4: "When men began to increase on earth, and daughters were born unto them, the divine beings [lit. "sons of Gods"] saw how beautiful the daughters of men were and took wives from among those that pleased them. . . . It was then, and later too, that the Nephilim appeared on earth—when the divine beings cohabited with the daughters of men, who bore them offspring. They were the heroes of old, the men of renown." By linking *yihus* with these human-divine sexual liaisons, Günzburg provides the lineage for a third, hybrid class and allows for a new pathway for reproduction, one occasioned not by the social desire to choose a partner from among one's class equals but by desire for women "not good enough to be companions but . . . perfectly suited for lovemaking" and who in their lowly status are apparently free for the taking.

Having begun by associating *yihus* quite straightforwardly with wealth, it remains for Günzburg to account for the presence of *yihus* without wealth and the underlying logic of marriages contracted between families with new wealth and those who possess only a distinguished pedigree. These very circumstances, we learn in an abrupt swerve from anthropology to personal history, stand behind Günzburg's own marriage:

> In this way did the root of pedigree begin to flourish from the root of wealth, and only after many generations was it distinguished from wealth, and in the course of time many wealthy people lost their wealth, and nothing was left but their pedigree, and the ignorant masses acquired wealth and they lacked nothing but pedigree, and so the structure changed and inherited status itself became a source of wealth, as poor pedigreed people sold their pedigrees for money to the greatest among the masses for gain. And I too, who had comparatively little in the way of pedigree, was sold to an ordinary man from a family of tailors who had amassed a little money, after which he showered me with gifts and offers of support at his table, but I found no

rest with him because my nature and that of the members of this family were entirely incompatible.[46]

Günzburg presents an odd and dense genealogy here, moving among a variety of positions as he traces a line from Genesis 6 to his own day: he begins with a quasi- or proto-Marxist anthropology that recognizes class and money as the material bases underlying the ostensibly natural distinctions in the characters of landowners and peasants; continues with a Lamarckian perspective on the possibility of inheriting such evidently social categories as class status; complicates this picture with a proto-Freudian view of male desire as split between women suitable for marriage (but perhaps less so as sex partners) and those desirable only as "whores" but not as wives; and suggests that the system is in flux, with distinguished pedigrees sometimes long surviving their original associations with family wealth. While Günzburg produces a potentially universal analysis by omitting mention of the role played by Torah scholarship in the Jewish *yihus* system, he nevertheless draws heavily from Jewish history by beginning with the primordial biblical genealogies of Genesis 6 and arriving, rather quickly, at the nineteenth-century Jewish marriage he was unfortunate enough to call his own. The genealogy of *yihus* he presents thus aims to explain one set of undeniably complex circumstances: the betrothal of a poor boy with some distinguished ancestry to a girl from a well-off but boorish family and—more painfully—the discomfort of the boy (the young Günzburg) with his uncultured in-laws, despite the apparent logic of the match.

The explanation for these circumstances exposes a system in decay, with pedigree no longer accompanying wealth but only the memory of wealth, and wealth wed not with cultivation but only with the desire to acquire such cultivation through marriage. In such a system, pedigree—even the "comparatively little" Günzburg possessed—could result in a tragic mismatch: while class differences could be the source of sexual allure, Günzburg's higher status unites him not with an alluring woman (his wife is unmentioned here) but with "an ordinary man from a family of tailors" whom Günzburg cannot abide "because my nature and that of the members of that family were entirely incompatible." While recognizing the artificiality of pedigree and the illusory quality of the superiority he acknowledges that he cannot help feeling, Günzburg demonstrates the very real anguish it has produced in his own case, in setting him off from his wife and her family by a fundamental difference in their very natures. The problem with Günzburg's marriage, then, is not that it fails to account for the compatibility of the couple in focusing on such "irrelevant" considerations as class. The problem lies at least in part in the fact that the system is no longer working as it should and once did, when it united members of equivalent class status and thus similar dispositions; instead, *yihus* operates to provide incentives for nonelite families who have acquired a little wealth to marry into the fallen aristocracy, despite the evident fact that such unions are mismatches precisely in the modern sense of uniting intellectually and emotionally incompatible partners (or families). *Yihus* itself is not the problem but its presently degraded state, in which culture, wealth, and lineage have ceased to be aligned and mutually indicative.

In Günzburg's remarkable account, narrative archeology serves to expose the history occluded in the *yihus* system, even as it provides a "talking cure" for his troubles by unraveling their causes (as indeed the doctor in the autobiography recommends that he do). *Yihus*, Günzburg suggests, is both false and true as a history of human development, indispensable and useless as a measure for contracting marriage, a record of continuities and disruptions, recollection and forgetting, that invites both reconstruction and deconstruction if we are to continue to make sense of who we are and how we came to find ourselves at the particular junctures we inhabit. The histories produced by those who have the status and disposition to explore the question of status and disposition will reflect the dialectic of truth and untruth that is lodged, by long convention, within the very genre of genealogy.

Jewish genealogical discourse, Günzburg attempts to show, intentionally obscures the role of class distinctions at its origins. But the role of women (and, more generally, reproduction) has been even more completely forgotten. This occlusion is perhaps the clearest sign that, as Donald Harman Akenson argues, "genealogical lineages and biological pedigrees can never be equated with each other."[47] Harman Akenson's analysis of the "plot" and grammar of lineage explores the codes that govern genealogy in different cultures, recognizing both the necessary presence of a "kernel narrative" ("a man and woman procreated and produced a child that survived") and the cultural factors that expand, rework, or obscure this kernel narrative; in Harman Akenson's view, patriarchal genealogies contain "an invisible nucleus—an Unnamed Woman—around whom that kernel revolves, no less real for being unseen."[48] This is not merely one missing figure. While ancestral lines branch out exponentially around both female and male ancestors, the individual lineage reproduced in patriarchal accounts privileges only half of all potential lineages, possibly missing others in its acknowledgment of only "legitimate" (or prestigious) ancestors in the myriad that might be counted. Among the functions of modern Jewish literature has been to expand and explore the telegraphic genealogies inherited from earlier generations and to expose what they conceal and ignore.

Serkele and *Sins of Youth* brought the voices of female literary characters into the more normatively male genre of Jewish genealogy, showing how these characters could produce male ancestors as well as reproduce male descendants. But it was not until the entry of women writers into the Jewish literary canon that the very notion of what constituted Jewish ancestry expanded to include foremothers as well as forefathers, giving fuller expression to the female experiences concealed in traditional male genealogies. These genealogies are necessarily literary as well as genetic, spiritual as well as biological, contending with the literary problem of finding poetic ancestors as well as the biographical problem of finding genetic lineages. In describing the literary dimension of the construction of pedigree, Ilana Pardes revises Harold Bloom's model of poetic influence, in which a "strong poet" must engage in an Oedipal struggle with a ghostly literary father, "a triumphant wrestling with the greatest of the dead,"[49] to account for the modern Jewish necessity of locating and celebrating rather than triumphing over precursors:

> In modern Hebrew literature in particular, due to the unusual circumstances of its emergence, the male poet surely has had to raise the dead. The difference has to do with the fact that for the modern Hebrew female poet, formulating tradition, or rather formulating a female literary past, is far more urgent and far more difficult: the dead haven't quite been born yet.[50]

Subjecting the pen name of the Hebrew poet Yocheved Bat-Miriam to a close reading, Pardes argues that the matronym "miraculously captures the very essence of this fluid literary mother-daughter relationship. If one bears in mind that Yocheved is the mother of Miriam in the Bible, then Yocheved Bat-Miriam is the mother who is the daughter of the daughter. Challenging the authoritarian structure of the patronym whose function is, as Freud and Lacan suggest, to prove and mark the father's paternity, the matronym floats between the mother and the daughter."[51]

While Pardes's analysis of Bat-Miriam's matronym suggests that discovered female "ancestors" could be the source of a new kind of poetic strength, it is clear from other works that female ancestry could also be seen as a burden and that literary modernity for women writers might require a wiping clean of the family slate rather than the persistence of ancestral memory. Among the most powerful and paradoxical poetic attempts to establish a female lineage even while breaking free of its constraints is the Yiddish poet Kadya Molodowsky's 1927 poem "Froyen lider" ("Women Songs"), which begins with an evocation of a line of female ancestors:

> The women of our family will come to me
> In dreams at night and say:
> Modestly we carried a pure blood across generations,
> Bringing it to you like a well-guarded wine
> From the kosher cellars of our hearts.[52]

Read in the context of Jewish genealogy and its modern literary offspring, Molodowsky's lineage emerges as a dreamed, matrilinear poetic account, linked not by a march of names but only by the blood that these nameless women carry to her "across generations." In this remarkable image, Molodowsky renders visible not only the genetic, biological, corporeal connection that binds one generation and the next but also the way that this blood is carried across through the piety and effort of Jewish menstrual law, in which women are both agents of Jewish continuity and objects of rabbinic control: the essential "passivity" of biological inheritance is thus translated, through the metaphor of Jewish blood as "well-guarded" kosher wine, into active cultural bequeathal. This bequeathal, moreover, is not through heterosexual intercourse, the usual means by which agency and reproduction are linked, but—in a reversal of the Bible's purely male genealogies— through female and matrilineal inheritance. Molodowsky's poem presents a variation on Jewish views of inheritance and more particularly of *yihus* as the transmission of both genetic material and religious status: the Torah study that more normatively transmits status between generations of Jewish men is here replaced by obedience to the sexual laws and food practices incumbent on Jewish women.

Despite these corporeal images, it is not only her biological ancestors who haunt the poetic speaker's dreams. While Harmon Akenson's kernel narrative of a genealogical plot dictates the minimum unit of such a narrative as a biological couple and their child, "Women Songs" finds poetic voice also for the woman who lacks both husband and (apparently) child:

> And one woman will say: I was an abandoned wife, left when my cheeks
> Were two ruddy apples still fixed on the tree,
> And I clenched my white teeth throughout lonely nights of waiting.[53]

While the other women speak through the blood they carry to their descendants, this woman is the only ancestor who is allowed direct speech; however, she, too, conveys the message that she has been obedient to the rules that govern her condition, even as she laments her unwilling sexual renunciation. While there is no evidence that this woman is part of the poetic speaker's direct ancestral chain, the poem continues by suggesting that she should also be considered a "grandmother":

> And I will go meet these grandmothers, saying:
> Like winds of the autumn, your lives'
> Withered melodies chase after me.
> And why should this blood without blemish
> Be my conscience, like a silken thread
> Bound on my brain,
> And my life a page plucked from a holy book,
> The first line torn?[54]

As Kathryn Hellerstein writes, "From the simile of women's pure blood as a binding thread (like the straps of the phylacteries, two small leather boxes containing prayers, worn by observant men during prayer), the speaker challenges with her metaphorical question at the end of the poem the way women's lives have been bound into the Book of the Law."[55] The poem, taken together, is a tour-de-force performance of shifting similes and metaphor, in which the tenor of one metaphor (kosher wine → blood) becomes the vehicle of the next (blood → phylacteries; phylacteries → conscience). In the question that propels the final lines, the inheritance that began as female and corporeal concludes with the archetypically masculine image of a holy book, *sefer*, to produce the final simile: (damaged) *sefer* → (disrupted) woman's life. This holy book is torn in the process of modernization and family estrangement, transgendered in its association with a woman writer, and partially recovered in the very act of constructing, and dreaming, a female poetic lineage. Zohar Weiman-Kelman argues that, while patriarchal history begins with the denial of the role of women in genealogical narrative, Molodowsky

> re-creates it at the same time that she attempts to reject it. Resist this bloodline though she might, the speaker/poet brings this line into being in her writing. As much as Molodowsky's modernist poetry, children's writing and Yiddish publishing projects separate her from the kosher lives of her foremothers, for today's reader these endeavors now serve as link, allowing us to connect both to Molodowsky and to her predecessors. For Molodowsky and the Jewish women of her time, becoming a woman writer meant breaking with tradition, but it is also what transmits to us the history of women, transforming the unwritten *farvelkte nigunim*, the "withered melodies of their lives," into poetry.[56]

Bat-Miriam and Molodowsky were not alone in constructing Jewish genealogies from a woman's perspective, exposing the fissures in the ostensibly smooth surface of Jewish patrilines as they recovered, resurrected, or invented missing female ancestors. Dvora Baron's 1935 short story "Family" (Mishpaha) is perhaps the most explicit and intricate literary meditation in modern Jewish narrative on the linked questions of lineage, family, and women's experience. The story is built around the charged question of what kind of story might be told of Jewish family that recognizes both the value of continuity and fecundity and the truth of women's experiences. By beginning with a moving and poetic translation of both biblical genealogy and traditional Ashkenazic patrilineage, and continuing with a focus on one woman within this larger scene, Baron rewrites the question of Jewish continuity as one of narrative coherence, searching for a pivot point and unifying motif between two interdependent yet apparently irreconcilable realms.

"Family" could be described as a short story with elements of an ethnographic case study; the case is of a Jewish woman who fails to conceive in the first ten years of marriage, a halakhic problem for which the rabbis normatively prescribe divorce. That we are meant to read this case within a context larger than Jewish law—that of universal genealogy and patriarchal culture—is evident from the first lines, which rewrite the primordial genealogies recorded in Genesis 4 and 5:

> Concerning the chain of generations, how it takes shape and grows, the Bible only tells us briefly that a certain man lived for so many years and he

begot a son, and then this son lived for so many years and he begot sons and daughters.

Link after link in a chain that never stops, for even if it breaks, it always renews itself. Such a genealogy looks something like this:

To Adam were born Cain and Abel and Seth; and Cain begot Enoch, the same Enoch in whose lifetime his father built a city. And Seth begot Enosh, and Enosh begot Kenan, and Kenan begot Mahalel begot Jared, and Jared lived 162 years and he begot—Enoch . . .

Another little Enoch, who probably ran about barefoot all day on the warm grass, and in the evening fell asleep on his loving mother's lap, just like that other Enoch, in whose lifetime the city was built.

In my shtetl, where people were named after their late forefathers, this pattern was even clearer.

There was the baker, for instance, from whom I bought my rye bread every day: he was known as Leyzer son of Chaim son of Meir.

Leyzer, who was sixty, only brought the water from the well for kneading the dough; it was his oldest son who baked and sold the bread, and he also had a young son who was still learning at the cheder—Chaim.

The family had been bakers for generations; the order of things only changed in that when one of the Meirs grew weak and full of years, he would go out to draw the water and his son, Chaim, would bake the bread, and when Chaim grew old, he would fetch the water, and his son, Leyzer, would bake the bread. . . . These were the generations of the family in the shtetl (*eleh toldot ha-mishpaha ba'ayara*).[57]

Baron begins by paraphrasing the genealogies in Genesis, taking particular note of the repetition of the name Enoch. That the Bible in its genealogical mode imagines male reproduction outside explicit participation by female partners and progenitors might already be gleaned from the repetition of the purely male divine-human "cloning" of Genesis 1:27 (in which God creates Adam "in the image of God") and Genesis 5:3: "When Adam had lived 130 years, he begot a son in his likeness after his image, and he named him Seth." What catches Baron's attention in the Genesis genealogies, however, is the repetition not of divine creation in human reproduction but of a name—a generational echo characteristic of Ashkenazic naming customs, but far rarer in biblical genealogies. The name Enoch appears first for Cain's son in 4:17 and then as Seth's descendent in 5:18. This repetition functions as a sign for what unites rather than distinguishes individuals and opens the door to Baron's own contribution to biblical history, in a scene that imagines one of these ancestors not in his prime or at the end of the (very) long life span Genesis permits these hoary figures before they are "gathered to [their] fathers" but as a small child, "asleep in his loving mother's lap." In this scene, the maternal caretaking that constitutes the hidden story of how any biblical character (or any person, for that matter) reaches adulthood is rendered visible as the universal background obscured in the individuality of a personal name.

The repetition of the biblical name Enoch also prompts Baron's reflection, in the next passage, on the recycling of names among shtetl families. Not only are names repeated in the same strict order, but each individual takes the role vacated by his father before moving on to the next life stage. The litany of names and occupations produces a distinctive form for a modern short story, in which the normative literary focus on individual characters, their unique predicaments, and their particular relationships gives way to something apparently premodern if not biblical, in which names signify not individual characters but larger social roles temporarily occupied by individuals whose individuality is thereby effaced or blurred. Narrative meaning, so linked in modernity with autonomy, choice, and conflict, and so associated (especially in the bildungsroman or *Erziehungsroman*) with a character's "vocation," gives way in this writing to a perspective that suspends as it hovers above the unique individual.

This structural or social perspective, which emerges from a focus on onomastic repetition, patrilines, and male occupations, is complicated in the rest of the story. The normative patriline, despite this powerful opening, rapidly becomes the backdrop for its primary concern: "Family" is devoted to the story of Dinah, an orphan girl whose genealogical past is not provided and whose reproductive role is put into doubt by her failure to conceive after she is married to Barukh. The neat symmetry and male cycle of the Meirs, Chaims, and Leyzers are retrospectively complicated by the story's continuation, which leads us to recognize that the perspective afforded by Jewish genealogy depends on even as it elides female experience. Baron's aim in the story, however, is not only to return female reproductive and genealogical experience to the scene of their expulsion but also to suggest alternatives to genealogy in constructing Jewish family and genealogies, alternatives that may be kinder to women and other outliers on the genealogical line.

Most of "Family" unfolds in the larger world of Dinah's extended kin, among girls and women whose relationships fall into no easily identifiable family patterns. Thus, when Barukh is gone from the house on business, Lieba, one of twin orphan girls being raised by a cousin, is brought in as

Dinah's companion, "and she would lean against Dinah gently, kiss the nape of her neck between her collar and kerchief, and call her 'Auntie' (*dodah*) even though she was only a distant relative."[58] The Bible mandates, in Levirate marriage, the "promotion" of uncles into fathers for the sake of perpetuating an endangered line; loose configurations of orphan girls, however, construct voluntary relationships not to perpetuate names they can never claim as their own but to form the affective, quasi-kinship bonds signaled by the term "Auntie." Later, Dinah plays with her sister-in-law's daughters, and

> the little girls, when they tired, dropped to the ground and leaned against her, their heads drooping in her lap like the sleepy vines curled around the stakes of the fence, and she—above the worry lines on her face her eyes misted over, and as she sat like that, restraining herself and yearning, it occurred to her that she could take one of these girls as her own. The kind Musha certainly wouldn't refuse to give her a child, and it was only right that she agree, for why should she have to bow her back under a precious burden that was too heavy for her to carry while the other woman walked around as if someone were scolding her, her idle, empty hands, as many people thought, making absolutely no contribution to the world.[59]

Hearing Dinah's stammering plea that she be allowed to raise one of these girls, "the big woman seemed to understand her and even shed a silent tear." In this and other scenes, the biological, legal, and genealogical connections between men and their sons give way to the more "fluid" relationships between women that Pardes argues is characteristic of the poetry and matronymic pen name of Yocheved Bat-Miriam (and of mothers and daughters more generally). It is consent rather than descent, proximity and familiarity rather than genetic (or botanic!) relatedness, that connects Dinah—the stake of a fence—with the "sleepy vines" that droop (like the biblical Enoch) in her lap.[60]

In narrating the network of relations that connect the women of the town, "Family" seems to deliberately resist presenting the type of family tree it so vividly provides for the generations of men counted at the beginning of the story. In contrast with the names and occupations that cycle through successive male generations, women of the same generation share both names and roles. There are, for instance, no fewer than three Liebas (the name means "love" in Yiddish) of roughly the same age in the town, "all the same height, with similar builds and features," and one of them, in a fateful scene at a family wedding, pulls Barukh away from Dinah and "drew him into the circle of dancing girls, Liebas and Mushas of her own age, who formed a chain, their arms linked, spinning and changing places in a dance that made the onlookers dizzy."[61] The circle of women reproduces on the "horizontal" or synchronic plane the more "vertical" or diachronic circle of Meirs, Chayims, and Leyzers, who take their turn filling a role in more orderly fashion.

This variety of family system holds both potential and dangers: while Dinah imagines that she might take the place of mother for one of her overburdened sister-in-law's young daughters, one of the Liebas correctly recognizes that the childless Dinah is also replaceable in her role as wife. The "circulation of women" in patriarchal societies described by Lévi-Strauss normatively values only the woman—in this sense an "empty" (if valuable) signifier—who can help two men establish kinship by reproducing a family line.[62] But from the perspective of these women, kinship takes a more flexible form, and their own roles as "exchangeable" partners may be expressed in the "adoption" of one mother's child by another, in the dizzying circles of a wedding dance that threatens to land one young woman in another's bed, or in the modernist prose of the writer who presses genealogical narrative into new and unexpected shapes. Read as modernist experiment, Baron's assignment of the name Lieba to multiple characters within a single story is a deliberate transgression of the convention whereby writers refrain from unnecessarily confusing readers. Confusion is in fact the targeted effect, the literary counterpart to the by turns hazardous and liberatory blurring of the imposed order of a patriline. Connected through uncertain, voluntary, shifting links with both dead ancestors and living kin (or replacements), the women of Baron's story open up the meaning of family beyond its normative patriarchal borders.

For all the promise of such flexible affiliations, the women in "Family" must eventually bow before the power of patriarchal Jewish law and the imperative of reproducing a male line. The failure of Dinah (and her husband, Barukh, although of course the assumption is that the failure is all hers) to conceive is the source of the tragedy of the story. This is not only private pain, the frustration of a woman's "natural" desire for children. In Baron's reading, failure to reproduce is also a threat to the social order and thus treated as transgression and rebellion even in as temperamentally mild and pious a woman as Dinah. That Barukh and Dinah love each other is irrelevant to their case, and propelled by the rectitude of "Wide Basya," the

female enforcer of the patriarchal order, a divorce is dictated on the grounds
of the evident unfruitfulness of this marriage. The ceremony plays out as
near comedy the tension between a divorce law that requires the consent
of the husband and the evident reality that the very notion of consent is an
illusion, in a field as hemmed in by social and halakhic pressures as this one:

> "You, Barukh, son of Avner," he was asked. "Are you giving this divorce of
> your own free will?"
>
> And then, for a moment, there was an anxious silence in the room. The
> woman, standing still, stretched one arm out in a groping gesture, like a
> blind man who senses an abyss nearby, and the old beadle came to the hus-
> band's aid.
>
> "Say 'yes,'" he instructed him.
>
> "Yes, yes," the man stammered in embarrassment.
>
> But the old man insisted:
>
> "Say 'yes' only once."
>
> And then he responded and said "yes"—only once.[63]

Only a scribal error in the divorce document saves the marriage, a kind of
positive mirror image of the mistake that more tragically renders invalid the
longed-for divorce document of Bat-Shua and Hillel in Y. L. Gordon's *The
Tip of the Yud*.[64] Like Molodowsky, Baron finds ways to translate the mute
biological role played by women in establishing Jewish family lines into the
textual realm: The rabbi "raised the parchment and before the awestruck eyes
of the people was revealed a letter, from which one end had been cut off, like
a limb amputated from a living creature, and it was bleeding ink and darken-
ing like a wound in the middle of the text."[65] Dinah, the "cut-off limb" of a
Jewish family tree, is saved only by a crack in patriarchal law. It is this crack
that allows the reunion of the loving, childless couple who are soon there-
after blessed with a male child (as is the case for those other "barren" women
so common in the Bible). The genealogical line continues, but the human
toll it has taken remains, retold by a woman writer who bears witness to both
the patriline and the feminine experience it depends on as it silences.

Dreaming of Ancestors

Sholem Aleichem's *Tevye the Dairyman* stories, which began to appear in
1904, have been taken as the archetypal depiction of the transition away
from arranged marriages to modern romantic unions. But the *Tevye* stories

are already a late expression of this transitional moment, when advocacy of romantic love could give way to assessments of a largely accomplished revolution. (It may be significant in this regard that, unlike Mapu, Lilienblum and other writers who suffered in arranged marriages, Sholem Aleichem succeeded in making a love match, eloping with Olga Loyeff, a young woman he met while working as her tutor.)[66] What sets the Tevye stories apart from the many earlier Jewish narratives of romantic love is not in fact the opposition between arranged marriages and free romantic choice—these are characteristic of dozens of earlier Hebrew and Yiddish literary works going back to the late eighteenth century. What distinguishes Sholem Aleichem's approach is that this story is told through Tevye's monologues, that is, from the point of view of a father rather than a son or daughter. This perspective differs both from the Haskalah novels that preceded his and from Sholem Aleichem's own earlier work, for instance, the 1888 *Stempenyu*, in which parents and parents-in-law play only the most minor and formulaic roles. Putting a father at center stage in the drama of young love radically defamiliarized what was, by 1904, already a familiar if not shopworn story.

The love between father and daughter at her prime moment of sexual awakening and erotic power expands the purview of modern ideologies of romance in complicated ways: it is heterosexually aligned but hedged by the incest taboo; moreover, the father's displacement by a younger man is foreordained by the conventions of the romantic plot and the dictates of both traditional practices and modern love ideologies. The necessary and inevitable displacement of father by suitor in a young woman's heart conditions the paternal role in the marriage plot: The relationship between headstrong young women and their fathers is typically recruited for the marriage plot primarily as an obstacle to the romantic attachment, which must remain the primary concern. Within this conventional romantic scenario, the love between fathers and daughters at this delicate moment is yet another that dare not speak its name. It is this love that, in the Tevye stories, is given full voice.

In his 1888 essay on "love poetry," Moshe Leib Lilienblum mocked the Hebrew writers of his day for focusing on romantic love to the exclusion of all other varieties, including the love felt by parents for their children. "Love is a natural human emotion," Lilienblum wrote, "and it expresses itself in many forms, the simplest and most common of which are the love between a man and a woman and the love of parents for children. . . . Nevertheless, it never occurs to our writers to write poetry about the love parents feel for their children."[67] It was Sholem Aleichem's particular genius to write not a poem but a series of short stories that staged *both* these "simple and common" forms of love—the romantic and the parental—at the moment of their greatest overlap and tension. In the process, he calibrated the price paid by parents for the conversion of young Jews to the religion of erotic love, thus mourning the victims as well as celebrating the victors of the romantic revolution.

It is not only parental love that has its say in the Tevye stories—more generally, the older generation and the ancestral line are also allowed to speak. The match between Tevye's oldest daughter, Tsaytl, and the tailor Motl Kamzoyl is stereotypically read as yet another account in the long victory of youth over their elders, romance over practicality, the sex religion over Jewish tradition. Tevye's invented dream, however, which turns the resistance of Tevye's wife, Golde, into an embrace of her daughter's choice, tells a rather more complicated story. As Shaul Stampfer has shown, many of the practices associated with traditional arranged marriage, including the use of a matchmaker and the "weighing" of *yihus*, were reserved for the scholarly and wealthy classes. Poor Eastern European Jews, who always constituted the great majority, did not participate in these practices, typically marrying later than the elites, among a local circle of connections and with no help from matchmakers; in small towns, the young bride and groom were likely to be acquaintances if not relatives. Tevye, it seems clear, has neither the pedigree nor the money to play the elite matchmaking game, and the match between Tsaytl and Motl perfectly fits the traditional lower-class model Stampfer describes. Indeed, despite his many daughters (I won't go into the vexed question of their precise number) Tevye has few dealings with a matchmaker until the end of the story cycle. Tevye's position outside the circle of élite matchmaking practices may be one reason that, when the rich Leyzer Wolf first approaches him, in the comic conversation in which they speak at cross purposes, he has no idea that it his daughter rather than his milk cow that the butcher is after.

The conversation is certainly meant as a wry commentary on the similarities between the marriage market in women and the meat market (an association that continues in contemporary dating rhetoric). But this association is not necessarily a critique of the commercial character of traditional marriage, as may at first seem. Tevye's problems wrapping his mind around this proposed match derive less from its character of uniting an old man—a butcher, no less—with a lovely young girl than because it hinges on the logic of uniting Leyzer Wolf's wealth with Tsaytl's youth and beauty. The logic of such a match is eminently familiar to modern adherents of the sex religion, even if it emerges from the suppressed commercial dimension of modern marriage rather than its overtly romantic ideology. Despite its mercenary character, it should not be confused with Jewish arranged marriages, in which the commercial transaction—in these cases quite explicit rather than concealed—takes a different form, prototypically uniting the wealth of a prospective bride's family with the status, pedigree, or learning of a young groom.

The exchange value of beauty—either male or female—is not entirely foreign to traditional Jewish matches, although according to Katz, good looks are a secondary consideration, once the more important considerations of class status and pedigree have been taken into account.[68] Thus, both traditional and modern marriage systems have their commercial dimensions, though what is bought in each case differs. In a traditional arrangement, a wealthy family with a marriageable daughter will be in search of a young man who can sit and learn in the local *besmedresh* as a living sign of the bride's family's wealth and religious commitments; in modern marriages, a wealthy older man will often seek a young woman who looks good on his arm, as a different form of conspicuous consumption. Both systems claim for themselves the virtue of social mobility, of allowing a talented but poor yeshiva student and a beautiful but poor daughter of a dairyman to rise in class through their distinctions (although, as Stampfer points out, in the case of traditional marriage this "rags-to-riches" tale was a social myth rather than real possibility).[69] The proposed trading of wealth for youth and beauty in the case of Tsaytl (and, later, Beilke), then, is a feature not of traditional marriage but of the modern sex religion, or perhaps more precisely of a mind-set in which the traditional marriage structure has been infected by the sex religion, that is, by the estimation (or overestimation) of physical beauty and sexual attractiveness in a woman over other, more "practical" considerations.

If Leyzer Wolf's proposed match with Tsaytl is evidence of a traditional marriage system in partial collapse, the romantic love Tsaytl shares with Motl, so thoroughly modern in appearance, still retains many features of the traditional match. When Tevye hears that the young couple is in love, he reconciles himself rather quickly to losing Leyzer Wolf's riches. As he asks Sholem Aleichem, "Who did I think I was, the great-grandson of Rabbi Tsatskeleh of Pripichek?"[70] (More literally, Tevye asks, did I have such a distinguished pedigree [*der groyser meyukhes vos ikh bin*]?) Without a pedigree, it is entirely appropriate and even traditional for his daughter to wed, as Stampfer would have predicted, a local boy within her own circles, with no wealth or property changing hands. Tevye, that is, is reconciled to his daughter's choice of a mate not despite its deviance from traditional models but precisely because it conforms to them perfectly.

While wealth and distinguished pedigree appropriately play no role in this match, family considerations are not completely irrelevant, as becomes evident from Tevye's invented dream: the dream serves the overt purpose of gaining Golde's approval for the match by scaring her with the threat of retribution against Tsaytl by Leyzer Wolf's vengeful (and dead) first wife. The dream manages to seal the deal not only by raising the specter of a first wife's jealous ire but also by uncovering a family connection between Motl and Tsaytl unmentioned up to this point. Golde's grandmother Tsaytl, brought back from the dead by Tevye for the occasion, congratulates Tevye on the match between her descendant and namesake, Tevye's oldest daughter, and Motl Kamzoyl, reminding Tevye—and through Tevye, Golde—that the young bridegroom is named after her uncle Mordechai. Grandmother Tsaytl does not spell out why Motl was so named, although the assumption in Ashkenaz is that such a name would be given after a deceased family member. While Grandmother Tsaytl does not specify exactly how the prospective bride and groom are related, she makes it clear that there is a long and meaningful family connection between bride and groom, hardly surprising for a local match far from any urban centers.

Golde's reaction to her husband's dream is similarly perfectly normative for a Jewish mother, giving thought, apparently for the first time, not only to Motl's pitiful lack of immediate material prospects but also to his family stock. Even though he's a tailor, Golde muses, "if he's named after my uncle Mordechai he doesn't have a tailor's soul."[71] Only this distinguished connection can account for her grandmother's "taking the trouble of coming all the way from the next world to wish us a mazel tov." Tevye's dream, then, supplies a distinguished forebear for a simple workman, as it provides a family genealogy—not Tevye's own but his wife's—for an ostensible love match. In bringing back the dead, Tevye undercuts at least one of the major tenets of the sex religion, which disdains the relevance of such ancestral recommendations in the choice of a mate.

It seems significant that Tevye's dream is the invention of a clever husband, and the writer who dreams him up, rather than an "authentic" communication from the past, even if the story leaves open the question of whether the genealogical narrative it transmits is *also* fictional. Tevye brings back the memory of an extended family network that includes his future son-in-law not in the context of the normal marriage negotiations in which they would certainly have been unearthed but only as a feature of the buried and forgotten past. In the dream, which is also a tale, a long-dead great-grandmother plays the role of family genealogist and even, in some sense, retroactive matchmaker. She gives her seal of approval to the match that unites her great-granddaughter with a member of their circle, an ordinary traditional attitude rendered remarkable only for having been unburied after being lost to memory. The narrated dream, told first to Golde and then to Sholem Aleichem, Tevye's conversation partner, thus serves both as the stratagem of a loving father to win over a reluctant mother and as an act of recuperative genealogy. As in *The Dybbuk*, the power of voices from the dead is mystical and erotic, revealing an ostensibly modern romance as the echo and fulfillment of insistent ancestral claims. But while Sender stands in the way of the young lovers, Tevye, even if he is barred from orchestrating the match, manages to reconcile the claims of generations past with the desires of those to come.

Tevye's dream, invented and staged for an audience of one, has reached many millions more in the stage and film versions of Sholem Aleichem's stories. Finding the lost connections between his daughter and her bridegroom, Tevye also unearths, invents, and imagines a much larger collective past at a time of crisis and rupture, forging the buried networks that turn strangers into cousins. In this sense, the 1963 Broadway production and 1971 film *Fiddler on the Roof* also serve as a Jewish family tree, repository of a dream that doubles as a genealogical narrative that can bridge the geographic and cultural ruptures of the twentieth century.

Fiddler on the Roof sheds light as well on the family resemblances between Jewish and other post-traditional cultures, far beyond the Pale of Settlement. Werner Sollors suggests that America is the land of romantic love by its very character and history: "American allegiance, the very concept of citizenship developed in the revolutionary period was—like love—based on consent, not descent, which further blended the rhetoric of America with the language of love and the concept of romantic love with American identity."[72] Indeed, Sholem Aleichem's daughters found enthusiastic devotees in America, where citizenship and love, romance and "consent" were closely aligned for Jews as for others. Nevertheless, *Fiddler*'s most extravagant and memorable theater may be not the weddings that emblematize this love but Tevye's genealogical dream, which lodges a story of descent rather than consent at the secret heart of its praise of romantic choice. As Yiddish folklore and Hebrew autobiographers know, narrated lineages are never to be trusted, and family genealogists are as likely as matchmakers to be exaggerators, performers, scam artists, and keepers of unreliable records. In their work, memory and fiction, dream and theater, commerce and love can never be strictly distinguished. But the record hardly matters. If history is a collective dream, then our shared fascination with this story of an invented and inventive ancestor may be enough to constitute us as kin even as it binds us as collective adherents to the modern religion of romantic love.

. . .

The sex religion in its European-bourgeois formations, as Ian Watt sees it, secularized and democratized a more elite and religiously infused Christian-chivalric romantic ideology. In the story Sollors tells of its American transplantation, romantic love worked to counter not only traditional forms of arranging marriages but also all arrangements that took into account descent, read in this context in the larger sense of ethnicity. It was in America that the ideology of romantic love, or marriage by consent, was nationalized, becoming an ideologically constitutive component of American identity. Even more dramatically, perhaps, this ideology was now reinfused with religious content and energies, so where the laws of descent had once been inviolable, now "consent is sacred and eternal." It follows, Sollors writes, that "citizenship by volitional allegiance was modeled upon the consent principle. Immigrants could thus be portrayed as cultural newlyweds, more enthusiastically and loyally in love with the country of their choice than citizens-by-descent.[73]

To the maskilic embrace of European models of literature and love we might add the enthusiasm Jewish immigrants felt for romantic love as the embodiment of the political-erotic freedoms of America. While Sollors dates the development of this story to the era of revolution, Jewish

American writers of later generations contributed to this ideology in significant ways. In the first decades of the twentieth century, debates on immigration and American citizenship were given shape by the enormously popular 1909 play by the Anglo-American playwright Israel Zangwill, *The Melting-Pot*, which helped popularize the term of the title and give it romantic form. The play describes the romance between the Russian Jewish David Quixano and the Russian Gentile Vera Revendal. Like Tsaytl and Motl, the pair are connected by old family ties; unlike Tevye's daughter and her fiancé, this "blood-connection" involves not kinship but violence: the pair are connected because, as it emerges, Vera's father was a participant in the very pogrom that killed David's mother and sister. As Sollors comments, Vera Revendal "is David's American melting-pot dream precisely because her father is David's old-world nightmare. . . . The Quixano-Revendal alliance is a union of opposites which redeems a specific family history, fuses the old ethnic antagonists 'Jew' and 'Gentile,' and bridges dichotomies of religion and class."[74] Within the sacred space of American consent, this pair becomes "a chosen couple."

The national-religious character of this "secular" romance rises to the surface in the epiphany described by David in the final scene, in which the reunited couple embrace on a rooftop against a glorious New York sunset:

> David: It is the fire of God round his Crucible. (*He drops her hand and points downward.*) There she lies, the great Melting-pot—listen! Can't you hear the roaring and the bubbling? There gapes her mouth (*He points east.*)—the harbor where a thousand mammoth feeders come from the ends of the world to pour in their human freight. Ah, what a stirring and a seething! Celt and Latin, Slav and Teutonic, Greek and Syrian—black and yellow—
> Vera: (*Softly, nestling to him*) Jew and Gentile—
> David: Yes, East and West, and North and South, the palm and the pine, the pole and the equator, the crescent and the cross—how the great Alchemist melts and fuses them with his purging flame! Here shall they all unite to build the Republic of Man and the Kingdom of God. Ah, Vera, what is the glory of Rome and Jerusalem where all nations and races come to worship and look back, compared with the glory of America, where all races and nations come to labour and look forward! (*He raises his hands in benediction over the shining city.*) Peace, peace to all unborn millions, fated to fill this giant continent—the God of our *children* give you peace.[75]

David's gestures point not only to the New York dusk or an American future but also to the American audience seated "below" the stage. The link between acculturation and performance, Americanization and the theater, is by now a familiar one, and it would not be difficult to make the case that Americanization was hastened and reinforced both by the overt message of *The Melting-Pot* and by the ways that theater itself—and not only the romances it staged—stood for the performative freedoms of romantic consent. Nevertheless, even as Zangwill's play brings two young lovers to a New York rooftop to signify a redeemed American future, it also presents the butchery of the Kishinev pogrom, if only as a memory of what has been left behind. In the decades that followed, it became increasingly clear that American theater was not quite ready to let sleeping (or murdered) ancestors lie, as evidenced by the reappearance of both shtetl Jews and their Cossack tormenters on the Broadway stage in *Fiddler on the Roof.*

Complicating Sollor's emphasis on America as the embodiment of romantic consent and exploring the attractions of theater for American Jews (as both participants and audiences), Andrea Most suggests that theater offered the "celebration of self-fashioning" and a range of other cultural practices and perspectives she calls "theatrical liberalism," which combines

> salient features of Protestantism, liberalism, Judaic rituals and attitudes, and the inherent theatricality of a nation in transformation. Characterized by a revolutionary embrace of theatricality as a viable social mode, the prioritizing of external action over internal intention, the celebration of self-fashioning as a uniquely American form of freedom, and the construction of a theatrical community based on obligation rather than rights, theatrical liberalism emerged as the hybrid liberal and Jewish worldview.[76]

Alongside the "freedom to shape the self" within the Americanization project that is such a salient feature of twentieth-century plays and films such as *The Jazz Singer*, Most notes the presence of "a set of obligations imposed by the covenant of The Theater, and shared by each member of a theatrical community."[77] American popular culture stages both communitarian obligation and individual rights, thus serving as an appropriate arena for the drama of Jewish Americanization, in which obligation and "external actions" continue to matter. It is within this American and Jewish American cultural history that Most reads Tony Kushner's *Angels in America* (the first part of which, *Millennium Approaches*, premiered in San Francisco in 1991, two years before the play was awarded a Pulitzer Prize). Kushner's play, in Most's view, serves as a commentary on the tension between obligations and rights, descent and consent, that haunts both Jewish Americanization and twentieth-century American theater, embodying "the late-twentieth-century ambivalence about the key principles and forms of theatrical liberalism."[78] Kushner does not eschew theatricality; rather, theatricality is emphasized, exposed, and celebrated (in a Brechtian stage direction, Kushner writes that "it's OK if the wires show, and maybe it's good that they do, but the magic should at the same time be amazing!").[79] What distinguishes *Angels in America* is that the self-fashioning of its characters is put on trial—literally, in the case of the particularly slippery character of Roy Cohn, who insists that he is "not a homosexual," given the clout he has in political circles. The theatrical cross-dressing and cross-casting should not blind us to the moral and even religious investments of the play, which revolves around the question of what we owe to our friends and lovers, what obligations accrue to a community built on sexual choice and voluntary affiliation.

It is in this context that Kushner's interest in genealogy and descent—precisely the dimensions normally marginal to the contingent assemblages of both theatrical and gay community—should be read. It might seem counterintuitive or presumptuous to read *Angels in America* as an example of the persistence of the genealogical impulse in modern Jewish literature—or to read the play as Jewish literature at all. Its major concern is not with heterosexual marriage or reproduction, the primary scenes for the recitation and unfolding of Jewish genealogy. Nor is it with the disruptions and catastrophes of Jewish modernity, except as part of a much broader social landscape. Like *The Melting-Pot*, *Angels in America* is interested in Jews only insofar as they are part of a multicultural America; the subtitle of *Angels in America*, *A Gay Fantasia on National Themes*, declares both its thematic interest in America and its "gay" stylistic affiliations. Kushner's more particular subject is the trauma of the AIDS epidemic in the harsh context of Reagan-era America, staged in a transparently theatrical, openly sexual, and stylistically "fabulous" production. The play's attention is trained less on traditional families than on the possibility of homoerotic friendships, sexual relationships, and ethical commitments in a community challenged by HIV infection, homophobia, and the indifference or hostility of the American political scene. Nevertheless, the scope of the play is not only synchronic and multicultural—staging the voices of ordinarily silenced or marginalized subcultures—but also historic and diachronic—laying bare the deep background of American religion and apocalypticism, recognizing past traumas behind present catastrophes, and finally, drawing strength from submerged precursors and dead ancestors. Stretching across the political spectrum and a fractious America, spanning earthly and supernal spheres, inviting dead ancestors and electrocuted victims onto the stage, *Angels in America* aims to tell a story about the AIDS epidemic that resists its relegation to the private experiences of unfortunate individuals or a marginalized minority.

Kushner's play ends with nearly as grand and religious a vision as Zangwill's and invokes many of the same themes. The final scene, set in Central Park in February 1990, brings together Prior, Louis (Prior's former lover, who abandoned him when Prior was diagnosed with HIV), Belize (described as "a former drag queen and former lover of Prior's; A registered nurse"), and Hannah (a Mormon mother visiting her gay son), in what Jonathan Friedman calls "the new extended family of the decade."[80] Prior speaks the final words of the play in his role of prophet for this new age, proclaiming,

> This disease will be the end of many of us, but not nearly all, and the dead will be commemorated and will struggle on with the living, and we are not going away. We won't die secret deaths anymore. The world only spins forward. We will be citizens. The time has come.
> Bye now.
> You are fabulous creatures, each and every one. And I bless you: More Life.
> The Great Work Begins.[81]

Despite the national-religious rhetoric (blessedly redeemed, in this case, by "camp") that he shares with Zangwill, Kushner envisions a very different American future in this scene. As opposed to the Rainbow Coalition David sees of "Celt and Latin, Slav and Teutonic, Greek and Syrian—black and yellow—," Prior's "fabulous creatures" are fabulous not because they happen to be a diverse group: an African American, a Jew, a Mormon, and a WASP. They are fabulous *also* because they have left these families and histories behind in a search for new configurations and communities, fabulous in their individuality and resistance. Nevertheless, this is *not* a story of the triumph of romance over historical prejudice, of consent over descent. Unlike David in the final scene of *The Melting-Pot*, who is with the woman "meant for him," Prior is not embracing his lover but praising and blessing a group that includes a straight new Mormon friend and two ex-lovers, who argue about Israel/Palestine in the moments before Prior's oracular pronouncement. The fractious connections among the group are not forged in the American "melting pot" (by then an entirely discredited notion) or at the first blush of young love. That love is behind them, and what heat there is, for Prior, is brought on by feverish nights alone with his disease. Unlike the love affair at the center of Larry Kramer's 1985 play *The Normal Heart*, in which political activism and caretaking are propelled by romantic attachment, Louis's breakup with Prior shatters the romantic contract that associates "to have and to hold" with "in sickness and in death." The questions of who will care for the sick, how scarce medications will be acquired, and how larger society will respond to the crisis of HIV are at the heart of the play, but these questions must be answered without recourse either to traditional families or to the romantic bonds of marriage or monogamy. The religion invoked in Prior's blessing is not David's "Peace, peace to all unborn millions, fated to fill this giant continent—the God of our *children* give you peace." Not children but friends, not God but a spinning world, and not fate but hard work is his message.

There is yet another difference between Prior's vision and David's. While the final scene of *The Melting-Pot* depends on leaving the past behind, it is part of the work Prior commands that "the dead will be commemorated and will struggle on with the living." Prior's primary reference here is to those who died prematurely of AIDS, whose memory must be carried on by those who survive even though "the world only spins forward." Kushner's play, as if in response to Prior's command, indeed recognizes the myriad ways that the dead "struggle on with the living." Like *The Dybbuk* (which Kushner restaged in 1997), *Angels in America* mobilizes the power of theater to enable encounters between the living and the dead; as does An-sky, Kushner recognizes that the stage might serve as a courtroom for victims denied a hearing in life. In *The Dybbuk*'s "courtroom," the dead Nissen lodges his complaint against the old friend who wronged him and his son; in *Angels in America*, Ethel Rosenberg pays a visit to the dying man who put her in the electric chair, allowing her to tell the story cut short by Roy Cohn to a new generation of American theatergoers. If Cohn is a prime representative of the self-fashioning American, Rosenberg's return

from the dead brings to light the communal consequences of such devotion to personal power.

It is not only theater that permits such attempts at rectifying injustice.
AIDS itself contributes to the construction of these stages and courtrooms.
Just as "spirit possession" is the only recourse of a silenced lover wishing to
plead his case and a young girl hoping to choose her own groom, the hal-
lucinatory fevers of HIV disease are the avenue for bringing back the ghost
of the woman Cohn robbed of voice and life. But it is the visitations of
Prior's ancestors, who appear to him in the throes of his fever, that provide
the AIDS epidemic with its deepest historical resonances. The two "prior
Priors," far from being shocked at their gay, diseased descendant, recognize in Prior the lineaments of earlier plagues: what this Prior calls AIDS,
they call "the pestilence," "the spotty monster," and "Black Jack." The shock
and horror that sometimes greeted the emergence of a gay rights movement
and rendered more difficult the response to the epidemic that followed is
countered, onstage and in the fevers of (invented) memory, by Kushner's
reminders of the (in this context, oddly comforting) truth that history, in its
repetitions, touches everywhere on the same human, mortal realities.

That memory and genealogy are woven into the fabric of *Angels in America* is evident from the opening scene: Kushner begins the play with a Jewish
genealogical recitation, participating in this way in the long Jewish tradition
(normally textual rather than theatrical) of starting an autobiographical work
by reciting a long line of ancestors, illustrious or otherwise. This genealogy is
set into another familiar trope, the Jewish auto-ethnography, which regularly
sets Jewish American family stories within the collective context of migration from Eastern Europe to the United States. The play opens with Rabbi
Isidor Chemelwitz eulogizing Sarah Ironson, the grandmother of Louis, the
play's main protagonist and apparent stand-in for Kushner. The rabbi refers
to the deceased by listing her descendants, present at the funeral ("beloved
grandmother of Max, Mark, Louis, Lisa, Maria . . . uh . . . Lesley, Angela,
Doris, Luke and Eric . . . Eric? This is a Jewish name?"). Louis, whom we
will soon get to know intimately, appears here in a long list of siblings and
cousins, the son of a (diachronic, Jewish) tribe rather than a proud (and self-
hating) member of "Queer Nation." The eulogy goes on to describe the history that Sarah and her descendants embody, a history, Chemelwitz insists,
that is both collective and cross-generational. It lives on in her children and
grandchildren and is no doubt well represented across the stage lights in

New York audiences. Sarah Ironson, whom the rabbi acknowledges he did not personally know, was

> not a person but a whole kind of person, the ones who crossed the ocean, who brought with us to America the villages of Russia and Lithuania—and how we struggled, and how we fought, for the family, for the Jewish home, so you would not grow up here, in this strange place, in the melting pot where nothing melted. Descendants of this immigrant woman, you do not grow up in America, you and your children and their children with their goyische names. You do not live in America. No such place exists. Your clay is the clay of some Litvak shtetl, your air the air of the steppes, because she carried the old world on her back, in a boat, and she put it down on Grand Concourse, and she worked that earth into your bones, and you pass it to your children, this ancient, ancient culture and home.[82]

With this speech, Kushner introduces the rhetoric of descent so central to ethnic discourse, placing Louis within this history in a way that negates his membership in any other; if we take the eulogy at face value, the very ambition of one of Sarah Ironson's grandsons to inhabit America (or of Kushner to write a play about it) is patently absurd.

At the very outset, *Angels in America* contrasts consent and descent, its broad American reach with "deep" Jewish genealogy and ethnography, making strong claims about the continuities that connect ancestor and descendant, separate them from their immediate national context, and potentially limit the self-fashioning freedom granted by the American romance, perhaps even in its homosexual variety. The scene in which Louis and Ethel Rosenberg say Kaddish in call-and-response fashion for Roy Cohn, at the prompting of Belize and punctuated by "You sonofabitch . . . You sonofabitch," perfectly calibrates the obligations and communal character of liturgy with the freedom of individual expression (and both are ethically meaningful).[83] But beyond the Kaddish and the printed script from which the rabbi reads, the play tells a different story, one of discontinuities rather than bred-in-the-bone inheritance, of Americanization rather than the persistence of Eastern European affiliations. For all the authority conveyed by the rabbi's Eastern European accent and by his full beard, Kushner undermines the potency of his narrative by various "stutters" in the performance. The rabbi acknowledges that he did not know the woman he is eulogizing; he reflects (in a metafictional moment) on her as a "type"; as if to challenge even the most determined theatergoer's suspension of disbelief, the stage directions instruct that this role, the very embodiment of Jewish tradition in its masculine form, be played by an actress (who also plays a Mormon); and in addressing a crowd that includes Louis with the description/injunction that they pass this descent "to your children," he makes it clear that he has no idea who or what Louis is, even as he claims to know his clay and bones. The tale Rabbi Chemelwitz spins, balanced between stereotype and idiosyncrasy, earnestness and parody, presents a genealogical argument for the persistence of Jewishness to a room full of not-so-Jewish descendants ("Eric? This is a Jewish name?"); among these, we learn in the next scene, is a closeted grandson who declares to his WASP boyfriend as soon as the funeral service is over that he knew his grandmother no better than the rabbi did. Louis may be part of this family, but the position he inhabits on the list of Sarah Ironson's descendants between Max and Mark, Lisa and Maria, obscures at least one essential truth of the man he is and the life he leads. Genealogy itself may be a form of theater, even when it claims to know deeper truths.

As if in parallel with this opening scene, *Angels in America* also stages another genealogical performance, this time not of a Jewish family line but that of Prior Walter, the WASP boyfriend Louis abandons soon after Prior tells him he is infected with HIV. Louis's ancestry is intoned by a eulogizing rabbi who is an outsider to the family, in the formal setting of a funeral. Prior's much more prestigious ancestry is narrated, at first mention, by Louis himself; in this sense, Louis's boast about his boyfriend's *yihus* is an evocation of the traditional use of lineage, in which status may be both inherited and acquired by marriage, as well as a decidedly posttraditional mobilization: Prior is a Gentile, and their relationship is far from a marriage, not only because same-sex marriage is decades in the future but also because Louis's loyalty will not long withstand the pressures of Prior's illness. We learn of Prior's lineage not at a funeral but in a hospital, where Louis (who shrugged off the rabbi's recitation of his own family line) proudly relates the Walter family history to the unimpressed nurse who is tending to his lover:

> Emily: Weird name. Prior Walter. Like, "the Walter before this one."
> Louis: Lots of Walters before this one. Prior is an old old family name in an old old family. The Walters go back to the Mayflower and beyond. Back to the Norman Conquest. He says there's a Prior Walter stitched into the Bayeux tapestry.

Emily: Is that impressive?
Louis: Well, it's old. Very old. Which in some circles equals impressive.
Emily: Not in my circle.[84]

Although it is Louis who plays the skeptic to the rabbi's attempt to trace Jewish history, it is Emily who expresses the archetypally American skepticism about the value of the old or of the past. The skepticism is pertinent in both cases: What connects the silent, dead Sarah Ironson with her verbose gay grandson? What remains of the Prior Walter woven into the Bayeux tapestry in his impoverished, abandoned, and ill descendant?

In contrast to these recitations of lineage by outsiders, Prior's ancestors also materialize in his bedroom during a lonely and feverish night, in which Prior is visited by the ghosts of two ancestors the script refers to as Prior 1 and Prior 2. The genealogical drama and comedy of the family line that begins with Sarah Ironson lie in the litany of increasingly Americanized names, in which names of dead ancestors have been ignored in favor of "Max, Mark, Louis, Lisa, Maria . . . uh . . . Lesley, Angela, Doris, Luke and Eric." Kushner cracks a different kind of joke with Prior Walter's lineage, a line of twenty-three Prior Walters. It is Prior's entirely male lineage that forms a closer (and more comic) analogue to biblical lineage than Louis's: this line of men even share the same name, as if they were carbon copies of one another (as Adam is of God, as Seth is of Adam) rather than having been born from mothers as well as fathers. Effacing the difference between father and son renders the erasure of women complete; but the very completeness of this erasure ends up backfiring, exposing it as a masculine fantasy of cloning-as-birth. What functions as an ideological erasure of women in the patriarchal imagination, taken to a campy extreme in the context of a gay "fantasia," is exposed as homosexual fantasy, the dream of a kinship line constructed exclusively of men. Nevertheless, in Prior's conversations with his ancestors, biological dimensions of descent rise to the ideological surface. That he is the end of the Walter line is evident: The prior Priors know that their descendant has no wife or children. But when they tell him he will "die alone," Prior answers, "I'm not alone."[85] To this rejoinder, the ancestors say, "We all die alone." At the heart of this exchange are both social and existential questions: In his premature death, and in his exclusion from, or refusal of, the reproductive imperative, Prior's death may bring a family line to a close. As Prior's answer implies, however, AIDS brought new forms of families, the voluntary affiliations and fractious alliances and one-night stands that shaped the social landscape of gay America in the 1980s and that come to his side even when he is abandoned by Louis.

The literature of the Haskalah began with the excoriation of lineage as a consideration in arranging marriage, suggesting a new era in which the individual and the couple would rightly forge bonds outside the interference of parents and without consideration of family background. But Jewish modernity provided reasons to rethink ancestral ties and construct arenas for the performance of new forms of family and community, of citizenship inclusive of "fabulous creatures, each and every one." Heterosexual romance was the privileged form of such "consent" for Zangwill, while Prior assembles in his loneliness and disease another kind of "voluntary family," with its youthful ardor already in the past, its components distinct rather than "melted," and no one category encompassing all of its members.

If Andrea Most is right that *Angels in America* embodies a certain American Jewish ambivalence about liberalism, this retreat from liberalism may also be a retreat from the ideology of consent, in which only those relationships built on love and choice ultimately count. In a crisis worsened by the alienations of modern life and the unsteady commitments that emerge from young passion, Prior is visited by his dead family, even if only in dream and vision. Loosed from its role in the arrangement of marriage, genealogy comes to signify a range of possibilities for configuring and giving meaning to the relationship between the present and the past, love and obligation, family and "family." In *Angels in America*, genealogy breaks free, once and for all, from its association with the imperative of heterosexual reproduction and Jewish continuity and from the illusion that we might establish our family lines with any certainty. Kushner's play is evidence that such a break with what genealogy once meant has not thereby rendered it expendable. On the contrary, it continues to speak and "struggle on with the living," across migrations, epidemics, and the evident fantasies of the stage, about the transformations that have rendered us unrecognizable to ourselves and made us virtual copies of those who came before.

CHAPTER FOUR

The Choreography of Courtship

> All the world's a stage,
> And all the men and women merely players;
> They have their exits and their entrances,
> And one man in his time plays many parts,
> His acts being seven ages. At first the infant,
> Mewling and puking in the nurse's arms.
> Then, the whining school-boy with his satchel
> And shining morning face, creeping like snail
> Unwillingly to school. And then the lover,
> Sighing like furnace, with a woeful ballad
> Made to his mistress' eyebrow.
>
> —William Shakespeare, *As You Like It*

> There seems to be no society in which members of the two sexes,
> however closely related, do not sustain some appearances before
> each other.
>
> —Erving Goffman, *The Presentation of Self in Everyday Life*

In the Time of Love

Writing to his fiancée Fromet Guggenheim in 1762, Moses Mendelssohn declared, "Your amorousness requires me in these letters to transcend all conventional ceremonies. For just as we needed no marriage brokers for our engagement, so we need no ceremonies for our correspondence."[1] In asserting his willingness to "transcend all conventional ceremonies," Mendelssohn announced his liberation from two rule-bound structures of his day: matchmaking and the correspondence between a betrothed pair. It was just this liberation from societal constraints on romance that was the hallmark of sexual modernity, and Mendelssohn, apparently prompted by Fromet's loving ardor, reveals himself here as elsewhere a Jewish cultural pioneer. David Biale understands Mendelssohn's remarks to signify more particularly that he was refraining from the "custom of writing formulaic letters based on literary models known as *egronim*" and comments that this freedom from formula would soon become a convention in its own right. "Paradoxically," Biale adds, "some of the maskilim were to compose their own letter formularies as ways of educating young Jews to greater romantic spontaneity."[2]

The paradox played out in Mendelssohn's conventional overthrow of convention speaks to a larger tension within the project of Jewish sexual modernization: even as modernizers rejected arranged marriage in favor of what they saw as the romantic "freedom" of young people to choose their own mates, the new era ushered in a set of rules for courtship and marriage that were at least as stylized as those they replaced.[3] These conventions—as Mendelssohn's linking of matchmaking and letter writing suggests—were both social and linguistic, which goes some way to explaining why the novel would become the primary channel for codifying and circulating the new patterns of romantic courtship that were supplanting traditional marriage, furnishing the sex religion with a written record of "its doctrine and its rituals."[4] As nineteenth-century autobiographies abundantly attest, the rapid social changes of the 1850s and 1860s brought new opportunities for young men and women to interact, interactions for which their traditional childhoods had ill prepared them. In this transitional period, the novel could expose the evils of traditional marriage, entice a traditional readership toward sexual modernity, ease the path from the negotiations of parents and matchmakers to the art of romantic conversation, lay bare the mysteries of what constituted the proper roles of young men and women in courtship, and chart the pace and stages of a modern romance.

Courtship indeed was the great innovation of the modern sex religion, manifesting itself not only as a set of social rituals but also as a new temporal phenomenon, a secular mode of differentiating modalities of time; both the rituals of courtship and the new temporalities it introduced were shaped by the conventions, plot, and even normative length of the novel. While in traditional marriages a bride and groom might first lay eyes on each other at their betrothal or even on the wedding day, courtship opened up an expanse of erotic experience between initial encounter and sexual consummation. In nineteenth-century arranged marriage, we learn from autobiographers, the time of betrothal could be sharply abbreviated, saturated with fear and dread, or ordinary in the sense that it involved no developing relationship between bride and groom. In the novel, courtship is a period of sharply heightened emotions that include delight as well as fear, eager anticipation as well as jealousy and longing, periods of prolonged waiting as well as intense moments of encounter; from the literary perspective, courtship (as Betty Friedan claimed was true of housework) expands to fill the space available. Courtship does more than add interest to a particular time in a young person's life; it also creates a life stage previously neglected or unknown among traditional Jews. The nineteenth-century Jewish novel paid homage to the period between sexual maturation and marriage, constructing a developmental stage in the lives of Jewish individuals that had often been prematurely foreclosed, drastically foreshortened, or stripped of charm and consequence.

The expanse of time that serves as the theater of romantic courtship is not entirely unknown in traditional arrangements: both arranged marriage and courtship concern themselves with sexual maturation, and both are driven by the same ultimate aim of contracting a marriage. These drives, though, are far from identical; it is generally the desires of the younger rather than the older generation that motivate the plot of the novel, while the desires behind traditional marriage arrangements—as Hebrew autobiographers repeatedly stress—are those of the older generation of parents and matchmakers, whether or not they also take the maturity and sexual interest of the young couple into consideration. Puah Rakovsky records that in 1878 or 1879, her parents began to seek a match for her:

> Along with my spiritual maturity, at the age of thirteen or fourteen, I was also physically well developed, and my parents started considering finding a match for me. Naturally they thought that a match was the only way to save me from my strong yearning to study and from my heretical thoughts. There was an even more potent factor: my child-love for my father's youngest brother.[5]

Despite her physical maturity, the match was made not because Rakovsky was interested in marrying (her ambition was to continue her studies) and not with the bridegroom she desired (the family agreed that Puah's uncle should wed her older cousin). It was precisely to forestall both these aims that her parents wanted to marry Puah off.

In contrast to the considerations of parents in traditional marriage, it is the desires of the young, according to Peter Brooks, that are the "machine" that normatively drives the plot of the novel, taking the double form of erotic attraction and (at least for young men) worldly ambition:

> Desire is always there at the start of a narrative, often in a state of initial arousal, often having reached a state of intensity such that movement must be created, action undertaken, change begun. . . . The ambitious heroes of the nineteenth-century novel—those of Balzac, for instance—may regularly be conceived as "desiring machines" whose presence in the text creates and sustains narrative movement through the forward march of desire, projecting the self onto the world through scenarios of desire imagined and then acted upon.[6]

In contrast to the desires of the young, which serve as primary material for the novel, Brooks views the desires of older people as performing a secondary function in the novel, to complicate rather than drive the plot: "the traditional comic structure—in theater and the novel—presents the resistance of an older generation of 'blocking figures' to the plotting of the younger generation seeking erotic union."[7] I would add to these fundamental insights that, despite the novel's "forward march of desire," erotic union cannot be the sole aim of either courtship or the courtship novel; nor should we underestimate the importance of the "secondary" function of complicating this consummation. The novel drives toward sexual fulfillment, but it generally thrives not only on sexual consummation but also on its *delay*, a delay that is supplied by the blocking figures requisite to a romantic novel and that it cannot do without. In staging courtship as a generational struggle, the Jewish novel recruits the opposition of parents in service of this delay, of literary "foreplay" as the intensification of erotic desire. In the slowed-down rituals of courtship and in the obstructions to courtship by internal or external forces, the romantic novel puts the brakes on the insistent trajectory that, in traditional elite circles, connected the onset of puberty with marriage. Stephen Kern in fact argues that "waiting" characterizes the predominant nineteenth-century erotic temporality, although "waiting for love to begin was particularly characteristic of women."[8] If the delay of marriage was a regular item on the maskilic agenda, the novel encouraged this delay not through ideological argument but through romantic plot. In the waiting from which love begins, in the stutters as in the propulsive drive of the erotic engine of courtship, the romantic novel intensifies desire (for the courting couple), spins out a story (for the reader), and implicitly makes the argument for the erotic payoff of a long courtship both in its complications and its ultimate success.

Walter Benjamin, in his critique of the notion of historical progress in *Theses on the Philosophy of History*, suggests that secularization vacated religious conceptions of sacred, cyclical, and messianic time, leaving only "homogenous, empty time" in their wake.[9] But if Watt is correct that modernity marshals religious impulses in its transfer of spiritual passions to the sex religion, then it is altogether appropriate to view this religion as having retained some sense of sacred temporality. It is romance that provides the strongest modern corollary to sacred time; in courtship, modernity opens the vistas of "romantic time," which far from being homogenous or empty, has a recognizable arc and is infused with charged experience (it also partakes of cyclicality, as the engine of reproductive desire). Like sacred time, the time of romance is ritualistic and rule bound. It shares with traditional marriage an anxiety about biological maturation, but even in its passive "waiting" mode it deftly turns this anxiety to spiritual and erotic purposes.

Traditional society—according to a ubiquitous Haskalah critique— forced young people into marriage at too early an age, leaving them no romantic time in which to develop. Shaul Stampfer has argued that the ubiquity of this charge in Haskalah discourse misrepresents Eastern European social realities, within which early marriage was limited to elite circles; moreover, far from being a long-established practice, early marriage was a fairly new style in the eighteenth and early nineteenth centuries even in these circles.[10] It is nevertheless true that the practice had a powerful effect on Haskalah literature and its most prominent writers. As Avraham-Ber Gottlober wrote in his memoirs, social pressures encouraged members of his circle to find mates for their sons even before they reached puberty: "Fathers would say: 'our son, may the Lord bless him, will soon be eleven years old and if we do not hurry to find him a good match, how will we be able to celebrate his wedding along with his bar mitzvah?"[11] Daughters were hardly exempt from such pressures: the Yiddish term *kale-moyd* (bride-virgin) for an unmarried pubescent girl captures the particular tensions of this stage, when marriage is already possible (*kale*) but not yet accomplished (*moyd*).

Roni Weinstein records similar anxieties for early modern Italian parents confronted by a daughter's sexual maturation:

> The new definition [in the early modern period] of the daughter as a girl whose "time had come," or as "fully grown," immediately created a need to proceed swiftly with the matchmaking process, hence the sense of a "pressing need." If a girl failed to find a mate in time, her value as a marriage candidate could go down, forcing her to marry someone beneath her or much older. A cruel hourglass was turned over from that moment on, measuring her family's success in finding her an appropriate partner.[12]

In contrast to the anxiety that greeted a young girl's sexual maturation, early modern Italian Jewish men married later and had more leeway in both the time of marriage and choice of mates. As Weinstein notes, "Whereas matchmaking marked the end of childhood for girls, implying their transition from their parents' tutelage to that of another guardian, men expected marriage to ensure them independence and recognition of their status as adults."[13]

For the traditional Jewish elite of nineteenth-century Eastern Europe, early marriage was the ideal for boys at least as much as for girls. It was this pressure to marry off sons before they could function in the adult world that the Haskalah targeted for critique: S. Y. Abramovitsh, in an 1878 essay, wrote that early marriage was the source of a host of economic ills, since young grooms "acquired" by a father-in-law spent their time in the study hall rather than learning a trade; at the end of their years of support, these husbands have "neither Torah nor the ways of the world [*derekh eretz*]" and are thus compelled to join the "legions of idlers, matchmakers, schoolteachers, and beggars who wander the streets asking for alms."[14] In including matchmakers in this list of pointless occupations, Abramovitsh exposes the vicious circle of unproductive masculine activity that is both the cause and result of early arranged marriage.

Among the critiques of early marriage are some that stress—generally from personal experience—the trauma of imposing premature sexual demands on young boys. Thus, Mordechai Aaron Günzburg laments his wedding at age fourteen:

> Adar 5 came. This was the end of my life! For my time was not the time of love [*ki iti lo et dodim*]. My work, alas, was the work of a man and my strength but the strength of a boy. Oh, fathers of my father! What were you

thinking when you sinned by placing the burden of a man on the shoulders of a boy! I was fourteen years old and never had been tempted to gaze at a maiden. I had no idea what happened when one added the feminine prefix "F-E" to the word "M-A-L-E" beyond what the Talmud had placed on my lips. My heart still lacked that desire nature puts in the hearts of men to uncover the secrets of the female sex, and I took no more pleasure in kissing a girl than I would have in kissing a beautiful boy. So why force nature to bloom before its time? It destroys a fruit to compel it to produce unripe seed, which fail to blossom and bear no fruit. Let nature take its course; do not awaken love before its time.[15]

Günzburg mobilizes here the biblical rhetoric of sexual maturity in Ezekiel 16:8, "your time for love [*et dodim*]," and the Song of Songs 8:4, "Do not wake or rouse love until it please!"; but while both these texts refer to young women, Günzburg directs his attention to male sexual development (indeed, both these passages have served as allegories of the relation between Israel as a male collective and God, and Ezekiel 16:6 is transgendered in its role in the Jewish liturgy of the circumcision ceremony: "By your blood live!"). To his warning against marrying off young boys, Günzburg also adds a caution against going to the opposite extreme, as he claims is done among "the Germans," who "do not marry until they are on the verge of old age—after wasting their youthful powers on whores and spending their strength on abomination." The result of late marriage, in Günzburg's allegoric language, is that "if he marshals to approach the fortress—that is, the charming lass—the king who cannot stand is with him. He prepares to build his father's house but his strength fails, he leans against his house but cannot rise." Having described these unpromising extremes, Günzburg concludes that the perfect age for marriage "for those innocents who have not yet eaten stolen bread" is twenty for a young man, when "nature has refined the ejaculations of semen into sparks of love," and fifteen for his bride. Despite Günzburg's careful calculus of what constitutes premature marriage and what overlong delay, the arbitrariness of the rules he draws from these findings is evident: by transgendering his biblical proof texts, Günzburg evades the biblical attention to female sexual maturity; this in turn allows him to rule that being married off at fourteen constitutes harmful abuse for a boy, while fifteen is the perfect age for girls to marry and ideally, the groom should be (precisely five years) older than his bride. For a writer clearly unsettled by the unpredictability of sexual desire and male sexual performance, the recourse to a strict time line for marriage may have provided assurance in the one quarter where it could be obtained.

The age of marriage, as Stampfer has shown, rose in the nineteenth century in both traditional and modernizing circles.[16] But if traditional systems placed pressures on parents to "settle their children's future" early, in Katz's terms, the advent of sexual modernization and the rise of marital age did not entirely alleviate these pressures, which now fell on parents and children alike.[17] Thus, while traditional and modernizing Jewish discourses differed on the question of the proper age for marriage, both assumed that there was such a proper age. If the presence of a marriage broker at the door could serve as signal that the matchmaking process should commence, what constituted such a signal outside the system of arranged marriage? How and when might a young man or woman's sexual interests begin to express themselves? And if early marriages were to be avoided, was it also the case, as Günzburg believed, that marriages could be contracted too late? What was the appropriate length of time for a romantic courtship? In addition to representing young Jews as what Brooks calls "desiring machines" that could set a plot in motion, the Haskalah novel gave voice to the post-traditional anxieties of a society in erotic transformation, suggesting time lines that might both intensify sexual desire and alleviate sexual anxieties. It also rendered youth newly valuable, a stage of life now signified by individualism and promise as well as instability and restlessness.[18]

In giving full expression to the temporal anxieties shared by traditional and modern marriage, the Haskalah novel might be contrasted with the late-antique Greek novel, which Mikhail Bakhtin views, in its focus on love and adventure, as blissfully oblivious to the march of "biological or maturational duration":

> At the [Greek] novel's outset the heroes meet each other at a marriageable age, and at the same marriageable age, they consummate their love at the novel's end. . . . When Voltaire, in his *Candide*, parodied the type of Greek adventure novel that was popular in the seventeenth and eighteenth centuries (the so-called "Baroque" novel), he took into account the real time that would have been required in such romances for the hero to experience the customary dose of adventures and "turns of fate." With all the obstacles overcome, his heroes (Candide and Cunégonde) consummate the obligatory happy marriage. But, alas, they have already grown old, and the wondrous Cunégonde resembles some hideous old witch.[19]

Unlike the Greek novel or its Baroque successors, the Haskalah novel circles insistently around issues of maturation and aging—particularly, as for
Bakhtin, of the female protagonist. Mapu's *Love of Zion* finds occasion to mention Tamar's age repeatedly and in a variety of contexts: Tamar enters the story
as a full-fledged character only when she turns sixteen, at which point we learn
that "Tamar was like a palm tree [called *tamar* in Hebrew] in her loveliness
and nobility, and when she was sixteen she was an altogether beautiful young
woman, and her face and walk and speech were pleasant and generous, and she
grew and blossomed in charm, and was a delight to her parents and beloved
to all who saw her."[20] Despite the narrator's presentation of Tamar as evidently
ripe for love (as indeed she shows herself to be in expressing her attraction to
Amnon in the following chapter), her mother sees her daughter somewhat differently. Trying to shield Tamar from her husband's attempts to compel her
to marry Azrikam, Tirzah stresses her immaturity and youth when she begs
her husband to "leave our daughter alone until she is eighteen or twenty."[21]
Yedidiah, angry at Tamar for spurning the man to whom he has betrothed
her and genuinely concerned about his daughter's marriage prospects (she has,
at this point, turned a little riper, at seventeen), sets a stricter clock running
when he exasperatedly warns his wife that they must do something about
their daughter, since "the time of love has come to Tamar [*et dodim hegiyah
le-tamar*]."[22] The phrase *et dodim* (the time of love) may transmit an undertone
of vulnerability and threat from its disturbing source in Ezekiel 16, where the
young woman ripe for love (an image of Israel in the desert) is also naked,
wallowing in her own blood and soon to become a "whore." On Yedidiah's
lips this phrase signifies not simply his daughter's readiness for sexual love but
also a system of values in which a curious, headstrong, and alluring daughter is
dangerous to herself, her parents, and the social order; marriage is intended not
so much to satisfy a daughter's erotic desires as to neutralize and obviate the
peril she poses to herself and others. Speaking to Tamar, Yedidiah thus treats
her approaching eighteenth birthday as a deadline (which is, for her, a death
sentence), after which she must part with her dangerous freedom: "Make
yourself ready for Azrikam your lover. In ten months you shall be eighteen,
and then you will be his, whether you want it or not."[23] In contrast to this
careful scrutiny of Tamar's age, the reader knows (roughly) Amnon's age only
by calculation. As in other novels, it is the heroine's age that attracts the most
persistent interest, comment, expectation, and anxiety, while the hero carries
the burden of age more lightly on his shoulders.[24]

Aside from the age of its romantic protagonists, the novel also takes careful measure of another sort of duration, that of the elapsed time between their meeting and the consummation of their love. If *The Love of Zion* can serve as template, the romantic time of the Haskalah novel can be calculated as spanning less than two years. This is the duration that separates the moment Tamar is introduced as a sixteen-year-old who, in her innocence, ripeness, and beauty, is an appropriate heroine for a romantic novel, from the wedding that takes place once she turns eighteen. This is also the period in which Tamar meets Amnon, falls in love, is (falsely) persuaded of his unfaithfulness, finally learns the truth of his loyalty, and is reconciled with him. During this time span, Tamar's thoughts are consumed with her love for Amnon, her pain at his "betrayal," and her fear that she will be wed against her will to Azrikam. These two years thus signify differently for parents and children: the "sociological" problems of the proper age of marriage or whether Tamar will find a mate are relegated to the realm of the parents, while she herself is concerned only with the vicissitudes of young love. While her parents' concerns about marrying her off have resonances with broader social debates about the proper age for marriage (Mapu seems to recommend that a girl marry within a few months of her eighteenth birthday), the milestones that present themselves to Tamar, the encounters, reversals, misunderstandings, intrigue, masquerades, and reunions, owe nothing to this sociological discussion and everything to the requirements of "true love," the intensification of sexual desire, and the exigencies of novelistic plot.

These (less than) two years—which pass so differently for parents and children—might also be contrasted with the larger cycle of events within which the courtship develops: the twenty-year exile of Amnon's father, Yoram, whose expulsion from Jerusalem sets in motion the loss of Amnon's rightful place among the nobility and as Tamar's true betrothed. Twenty years conventionally constitute the biological span of a generation, and indeed this is the time span that separates Amnon's conception and his arrival at the wedding canopy. This same period has a different significance for his father, who like Odysseus does not witness his son's coming of age: Yoram tells the son he fails to recognize that during his exile from Zion he has seen "nineteen years of evil, and I have grown old, faded, and bent in a foreign land."[25] When he is finally reunited with his wife, Na'amah, Yoram tells her, "For twenty years I longed for you, and all my sighs have now turned to eternal joy."[26] Na'amah is a secondary heroine—the most significant role permitted an older woman in a romance—and so, according to Tova Cohen, must retain her beauty even as her husband may be shown to have aged.[27] As in the Homeric epic (but not the Greek novel), Mapu registers the lapsed time of exile in the aging of a husband and the persistent love of a married couple, which adds poignancy to their long-delayed reunion. The passing of a generation, the pathetic aging of a man in exile from his country—these are both ruled out in the Greek novel and have no place in the romantic time that governs the relationship of the young couple: Amnon's exile and triumphant return, unlike Yoram's, last only for the months it will take to bring Tamar to her eighteenth birthday; that is, the return of the hero coincides with the peak of his military prowess and the bio-erotic perfection of bride and groom.

The two cycles, one of two years and the other of twenty, correspond to the double dimensions of Mapu's novel: the novel is a biblical-national epic, expressing the prototypically national themes of war, exile, and redemption and including such biblical characters as Isaiah and Sanherib. The romantic dimension of the plot borrows biblical names for characters who do not appear in the Bible. *The Love of Zion* allows Amnon to fulfill his worldly ambitions within the "masculine time" of war and heroic quest, but the novel is also, and primarily, a romance, occurring within the "feminine time" of sexual awakening and courtship and depicting the "private" realm of love and courtship. The romantic-individualist microcosm and national-epic macrocosm come together harmoniously at the end of the novel: Yoram's return from exile enables and coincides with the wedding of his son to the daughter of his dearest friend, Yedidiah.

National exile and return, and romantic encounter and marriage, are both well represented among the themes and genres of biblical narrative and are often twinned in the biblical imaginary; nevertheless, the Bible places greater stress on national history than on romantic time, generally weaving the erotic lives of individual characters into a larger national pattern. Mapu innovates by reversing these priorities, subordinating the "larger" epic to the "smaller" romance even as he resolves these two dimensions in one stroke: the last pages of the novel describe not only the return of exiles to Zion but also the reunion of the long-separated husband and wife, father and son, and two old friends, all of whom serve as celebrants of the marriage of Amnon and Tamar.[28] In foregrounding the trials of a loving couple over the tribulations of the nation, Mapu underscores the primary significance of "true love" as he recruits the most powerful elements of Jewish memory and history into its service.

The literature that followed Mapu's pioneering efforts deviated from his model in many respects, moving away from Mapu's stylized, archaizing, and idealized approach to romance and embracing sexual satire, psychological realism, and a range of other literary styles. In the decades that followed Mapu, the romantic-sentimental *embourgeoisement* in which he participated gave way to a series of more radical social and sexual revolutions. As in the European novel, more generally, the age of romantic protagonists was allowed to rise as their horizons correspondingly expanded. Nevertheless, in at least one respect the literature of romance, love, and sex has been remarkably consistent: literary interest has found itself repeatedly drawn to the sexual time that Mapu took as his primary focus, the period of months or years that separates our first glimpse of the literary protagonists from their passing into the far-less-interesting roles of full-grown married adults. This time period may be brief when measured against a life span, but modern literature regards it as a time of endless fascination.

Courtship and the Drama of Mutual Recognition

Within the vistas of romantic time, courtship—and the courtship novel—serves as a theater for staging not only a budding romance but also the gender roles of bourgeois marriage. The rituals and fantasies of courtship, ostensibly shielded from the harsher economic demands and realities of marriage itself, nevertheless are charged with establishing, choreographing, naturalizing, and investing with sexual energy the ideology that underlay the division and demarcation of the marital distribution of labor. It is among the pleasures and difficulties of modern courtship that it seeks to establish a union between a man and a woman, all the while insisting—in line with a major tenet of the sex religion—on the sharp and profound differences between the sexes. The "artificial distinctions" imposed on sex in eighteenth-century England, according to Watt, derived from new labor and market conditions, but they clothed these exigencies in a discourse that naturalized, interiorized, and sexualized gender roles.[29] As Watt argues, the ideology of gender complementarity also drew heavily on earlier Christian or chivalric cultural formations, although it was only with the rise of an eighteenth-century urban mercantile class that Christian or chivalric feminine ideals could be applied more widely and "democratically" to women as a group. Reflecting the bourgeois distribution of labor and infusing it with revived Christian-chivalric models, the novel casts men as "naturally" dominant in the economical and sexual spheres, while viewing women as inclined toward domesticity, modesty, and "delicacy":

> The [1740] appearance of [Samuel Richardson's] *Pamela* marks a very notable epiphany in the history of our culture: the emergence of a new, fully developed and immensely influential stereotype of the feminine role. . . . The model heroine must be very young, very inexperienced, and so delicate in physical and mental constitution that she faints at any sexual advance; essentially passive, she is devoid of any feelings towards her admirer until the marriage knot is tied.[30]

The delicacy of young women, in this view, is both "constitutional" and requires careful safeguarding. As Samuel Johnson declared, feminine delicacy "shou'd always be inviolably preserved, in eating, in exercise, in dress, in everything."[31] The emerging class structures that allowed for and determined these "natural" differences were submerged but, to Watt's discerning eye, remained never far from view. Thus,

> even Pamela's tendency to faint may be regarded as an expression of the changing economic basis of marriage: for since middle-class wives tended to be increasingly regarded as leisure exhibits engaging in no heavier economic tasks than the more delicate and supervisory operations of housewifery, a conspicuously weak constitution was both an assertion of a delicately nurtured past and a presumptive claim to a similar future. It is true that Pamela's humble birth hardly entitles her to this trait; but in fact her full possession of it only shows that her total being has been so deeply shaped by ideas above her station that even her body exhibits—to invoke the assistance of a neologism for which there is in any case a regrettable need—a not uncommon form of what can only be called sociosomatic snobbery.[32]

For all the differences in context, Eastern European Jewish society in the nineteenth century was undergoing a similarly rapid *embourgeoisement*—as "presumptive claim to a [bourgeois] future" if not as present economic or cultural reality. As did the conditions Watt describes for eighteenth-century England, new economic circumstances led to dramatic changes and even reversals in the gendered distribution of labor alongside new marriage practices; in the Jewish case, new cultural models appeared even in the deferral or absence of the economic or social preconditions for *embourgeoisement*. There is no need to rehearse here the substantial literature on the intersection between gender and Jewish acculturation.[33] It is by now abundantly clear that the Haskalah movement, while viewing itself as liberating Jews from traditional (and "unnatural") gender roles, advocated a conservative and bourgeois distribution of labor that relegated women to private domestic spaces and assigned them the role of "angel in the house" while insisting that men step up to the task of economic productivity and sexual dominance. Israel Bartal reminds us that these sociocultural ideals were aspirational rather than based on actual conditions.[34] But if reality was recalcitrant, a Haskalah novel encountered no obstacles to furnishing its male protagonists with productive occupations and heroic weaponry or its female protagonists with abundant household help and the leisure time needed for spiritual pursuits. As Tova Cohen writes, Haskalah writers used the novel to propagate bourgeois manners and an image of women as delicate and pure:

> Women, according to the understanding of this era, were distinct in their character and role from men; in her deepest essence she was closer to nature, to feeling, to family affection, and her place was in the home and within the framework of the family. . . . Since she was removed from the harsh working world, she was portrayed as more delicate and purer than the male. . . . Her weakness required that she be protected by a man, but in her emotional strength she was his conscience, and thus his guardian angel. The ideal woman in the literature of the period excelled in patience, delicacy, and modesty, and was the wellspring of love, warmth and solace for the man when he returned to the "shelter" of the home.[35]

Under the influence of this European model, the Haskalah also took aim at working women, reserving particular venom for the *eshet hayil* (woman of valor), who supported her unproductive husband while he learned Talmud unencumbered by occupational worries. Such financial arrangements, which serve as an only occasionally realized ideal for the traditional élite of the *Lomdim*, were the most glaring symptoms of the topsy-turvy distortion of proper gender roles in traditional society.[36] In an 1835 essay on Jewish education, Mordechai Aaron Günzburg praises Russian pedagogical methods over those of Jews, "which deviate from the natural custom." In Russian schools, "boys' energies are directed outward, while the girls use their energies in the home, so that 'the honor of the princess is within.'" However, "in our own territory the natural order is reversed and boys are hidden away in the schoolroom as in prison, while girls grow up within the world of commerce, and scorn the veil of shame that nature has drawn around them."[37] Leaning on the modern rhetoric that links the public sphere with men while assigning women to the private sphere, Günzburg suggests that Jews reverse this natural order by keeping boys imprisoned in yeshivas while encouraging girls to spend their time immodestly in the marketplace. Strikingly, Günzburg cites Psalms 45:14, "Kol kavuda bat melekh penimah" (The royal princess, her dress embroidered with golden mountings, is led inside to the king), a verse that is traditionally understood to signify and recommend the modesty of Jewish women, to praise the *Russian* approach of shielding girls and women from the public sphere. Here as elsewhere the Haskalah attempted to find support for their gender reforms by discovering canonical Jewish sources for ostensibly alien ideals. As novel as the protection of women from public life might seem in a culture that took working women for granted, by discovering biblical and traditional warrant for the notion of women's natural modesty, bourgeois innovations could be rooted in deep Jewish soil.

The distinctions between the bourgeois and traditional gender system are not exhausted, however, by the fact that they organize the family economy differently. More fundamental is the question of how these gender roles were understood: while traditional Ashkenaz idealized and esteemed female competence and male learning, bourgeois ideologies saw gender as natural and internal truths about individual sensibility. Moreover, bourgeois courtship establishes gender roles dialectically, through the encounter of two sexually differentiated individuals who are both categorically different and uniquely suited to each other. Courtship thus constructs gender through a drama of mutual recognition, in which the young woman witnesses and validates the masculinity of a potential groom, awakening this power through her beauty, just as the young man awakens her essential femininity. Traditional matchmaking also (and more openly) involves performance and evaluation (and thus invites exaggeration and masquerade), but the reception, interpretation, and evaluation of these performances are the tasks of parents and matchmakers rather than the young couple.

Thus, arranged marriage and courtship both interpellate subjects, but they do so differently.[38] It is the members of the older generation who collectively weigh family status, measure material assets, subject a young prodigy to an "oral exam," or frankly discuss the appearance of a young girl.[39] In the exam that precedes the betrothal of a young boy, the metrics used, normatively by a prospective father-in-law, are drawn entirely from the masculine realm—its educational values, cultural norms, and patriarchal ideals. In courtship, the gender performances as well as their reception are referred to the tastes of young men and women. Rokhele, in Sholem Aleichem's novella *Stempenyu*, reflects that her husband won the approval of the town schoolteacher and her own family but that she and her bridegroom had seen each other only once before their marriage, "and then only for maybe two hours, if that, and then only in the presence of a whole quorum of Jews, and even that was with the groom in one room and the bride in the other." As the narrator asks, "So who was he and who was she?"[40] It is precisely this mutual gaze, missing or marginalized in traditional arrangements, that in bourgeois courtship constructs masculine and feminine appeal most meaningfully across the gender line.

The distinction I am trying to draw here is a fine one, since it divides two varieties of heterosexuality. This effort has its precursors: In distinguishing the sexual structures of Ashkenazic culture from modern heterosexual ideologies, Daniel Boyarin refers to the traditional Jewish gender ideology as "heteronormativity," which in his usage signals the distinctive Ashkenazic combination of a universal imperative of heterosexual marriage that is nevertheless devoid of the homophobia and the "heroic," aggressive masculinity that generally accompany heteronormativity in most of its non-Jewish forms. Boyarin views the traditional Jewish gender order as an intentional deviation from Christian-European models of heterosexual masculinity, praising "gentle" Talmud scholars and their "powerful" breadwinning wives.[41] In a section titled "'Give Me a Bridegroom Slender and Pale': The 'Effeminate' Talmudist as Erotic Object for Women," Boyarin cites Yiddish folksongs in which young women describe their ideal mate as a "beautiful" and scholarly yeshiva boy, reading these songs as inversions of romantic assumptions that it is men who praise female beauty and that what constitutes attractiveness in a male is power rather than studiousness.[42] What remains intact in the evidence Boyarin marshals here is the cross-gender appreciation that is fundamental to modern courtship, the construction of gender (in whatever form) through what I am calling "the drama of mutual recognition." Without denying the existence and richness of a Yiddish folk tradition in which young women paint portraits of the men they hope to marry, I would suggest that the distinctive features of this folk tradition cannot be extended to the elite circles from which nineteenth-century Jewish writers emerged. Traditional heteronormativity among the learned elite joins young men and women in marriage not by reversing gender roles in the fashion of Yiddish folksongs but with no recourse at all to the desire of the young couple, to "sexual orientation," or to the mutual "cross-evaluation" of men and women. By foreclosing courtship and referring the evaluation of candidates for marriage to older adults, it also manages without interiorized or dialectically established models of masculinity and femininity.

In contrast to Boyarin's understanding of Ashkenazic heteronormativity, which views traditional and modern gender roles as inverse mirror images of each other, I understand Ashkenazic heteronormativity as simply lacking gender roles in the interiorized, dialectically related, and mutually constructed sense; this might be termed "heteronormativity degree zero," for its interest in uniting a boy and girl in marriage without taking into account their "complementarity" except in the biological and economic sense. The very notion of gender difference as interiorized sensibility (and not only the specific content of this sensibility) is part of bourgeois ideology; as Shmuel Feiner writes, while "maskilim recognized the value of women as human beings . . . the Haskalah in fact sharpened the distinction between the sexes."[43] Gordon is no reliable witness to traditional attitudes, but *The Tip of the Yud* may nevertheless capture something of the distinction between these two gender systems. The poem begins by describing the "Hebrew woman" as unknowable, her life unrelenting servitude: "You conceive, give birth, you nurse, you wean, / you bake and you cook and prematurely—you wither" (*Tahari, teldi, teniki, tigmoli*). The Jewish woman is presented as a series of successive actions or "performances" rather than a person in possession of feelings and experiences; the staccato rhythm of the Hebrew, in which each phrase is a single word and the tense hovers between the imperative and imperfect of continuing action, intensifies the impression of a human being as the sum of repetitive and successive actions imposed on her from outside. The next stanza reads:

And so what if you were graced with a feeling heart and beauty,
If the Lord gave you talent and intelligence!
For you, knowledge of Torah is a taint, beauty a detriment,

> For you, all talent is a deficiency, all knowledge a drawback,
> Your voice is indecency, your hair, a horror;
> And what are you in your entirety? A vessel of blood and excrement;
> Ever since Genesis, the snake's pollution rests inside you
> And like a menstruant woman, your people expel and banish you
> From the house of schooling, from the sanctuary of the Lord
> And from places of rejoicing—to express only lamentation.[44]

The distinction drawn here between the Hebrew woman who is a creature "graced with a feeling heart and beauty" and her image in the jaundiced eyes of rabbinic and post-rabbinic literature (from which Gordon of course culled the most damningly misogynistic material) is not only the difference between a positive and a negative image of a Jewish woman. The one drawn from the clichés of bourgeois romantic rhetoric claims to describe a woman's (metaphorical) "heart," while the latter is concerned primarily with the legislation—rather than description—of her body, voice, hair, and menstrual blood. Both aspects of the Jewish woman are filtered through a male perspective and heteronormative lenses, but the maskilic lens claims access to her interior being, while Jewish practice and law, which is not shy about legislating her activities from birth to death, nevertheless skirts the question of her essential nature.[45]

It is precisely traditional Jewish "heteronormativity degree zero" and *not* Jewish "queerness" that explains the recurring joke in Jewish folklore and literature: the matchmaker who proposes a match between two boys, or two girls. In *Aviezer*, Günzburg describes his father's scorn for the matchmaking practices of his day; so illogical and forced are these matches, Günzburg's father says, that "the only thing more crooked would be if they matched a male with a male."[46] These marriages are absurd (but not repulsive or condemned, and certainly not because they bring together two "effeminate" men) because the sex or even the character of the young couple is of (almost) no concern, of vanishingly small interest; there are no types involved, no sexual orientation, no effeminate men or masculine women—these two boys, or two girls (in other variations), are simply pawns to be moved across a marriage board by other people.

This joke found literary embodiment in at least two nineteenth-century narratives, S. Y. Abramovitsh's *Fishke the Lame* (1869) and Sholem Aleichem's *Menachem Mendl* (1896–1913). In *Fishke*, Abramovitsh lampoons traditional arranged marriage for its attention to characteristics other than the mutual compatibility of a bride and groom. When Alter goes into the matchmaking business, his focus on the fathers of the potential bride and groom—and more particularly on their wealth, the dowry, his fee—blinds him to the requirement that traditional Jewish marriage minimally unites a boy and a girl. Desperate to raise some cash for his own marriageable daughter, Alter clutches at the idea of becoming a matchmaker: "I had it! A nice piece of business—a match between two merchants, respectable men with stalls at the fair." With this plan in hand, Alter's way is clear:

> To make a long story short, I get going and things really start moving along. Quickly, the two fathers-in-law take a look at each other, one likes the other, they're getting excited, they want it badly. Nu, who could ask for anything better? The two of them panting, burning, really wanting it, they're ready! I'm just bursting with joy. I can already feel the fee in my pocket. . . . We're just about to break the pots for the betrothal when we remember the bride and groom, and what do you know? Believe me, it was a disaster. . . . Just listen to my misfortune, God really pulled a quick one on me this time: the two fathers-in-law each had—what do you think they had? They each had—a son![47]

Explaining the confusion that led to this oversight, and defending himself against the accusation that he has failed to understand the first (and nearly the last) rule of contracting a Jewish marriage, Alter continues, "Obviously, two boys don't take each other. A male and a female, that's the way it's done" (*a zokher mit a nekeyve vi der shtayger iz*).[48] The joke about contracting a marriage between two boys (or, in Sholem Aleichem's *Menachem Mendl*, two girls) has nothing to do with the masculinity of the potential grooms, whom we do not meet, or the queerness of traditional Jewish society. The joke is rather on the character of the heteronormativity that shapes traditional society, in which only the minimal factoid of biological sex plays a part and in which the qualifications of young people (particularly boys) are judged by two adult men who pant after a good match. In Claude Lévi-Strauss's terms, where marriages unite men in patriarchal society, with young women serving as objects of exchange, in Jewish society marriage unites families (and particularly compatible prospective fathers-in-law), with young people of either sex serving as "empty" objects of exchange.[49] If traditional heteronormativity regularly appears suspiciously queer to contemporary eyes, this effect is produced not by a *reversal* of proper sexual roles but (and more radically) by their neglect. Traditional Ashkenazic heteronormativity, in my reading, invests gender difference with so little individual, sexual, psychological, spiritual, dialectical, or romantic meaning that it comes close to treating all young candidates for marriage, of whatever sex (although not all families), as essentially interchangeable. It is this ideology that is most laughable—and heretical—from the point of view of modern adherents to the sex religion.

Perhaps by extension of this principle, traditional Jewish heteronormativity also reveals itself as curiously irresolute on the question of gender hierarchy. It is certainly true that traditional Jewish marriage is based on and ritually encodes patriarchy: a husband acquires a wife, hands her a marriage contract that only he signs (just as only he can end the marriage by handing his wife a divorce decree), and is circled by his bride under the canopy in an apparent performance of masculine centrality, if not dominance, in the marriage. But to these normative rituals, traditional Eastern European marriage added another, far less normative set. Salomon Maimon interrupts the description of his wedding ceremony with the following "digression":

> I had read in a Hebrew book of an approved plan by which one spouse might secure lordship over the other for life. One was to tread on the other's foot; and if both hit on the stratagem, the first to succeed would retain the upper hand. Accordingly, when my bride and I were placed side by side at the ceremony, this trick occurred to me, and I said to myself, "Now you must not let slip the opportunity of securing lordship over your wife for your whole lifetime." I was just about to tread on her foot, but a certain *je ne sais quoi*, whether fear, or shame, or love (*Furcht, Scham oder Liebe*), held me back. While I was in this irresolute state, I suddenly felt my wife's slipper on my foot with such force that I would almost have screamed aloud if shame had not restrained me. I took this as a bad omen, and said to myself, "Providence has destined you to be the slave of your wife; you must not try to slip out of her fetters." From my faint-heartedness and the heroic mettle of my wife the reader may easily conceive why this prophecy in fact came to pass.[50]

Although Maimon learned of this custom from a Hebrew book, his young bride also knew it and, moreover, had the advantage of not being too afraid, ashamed, or loving to go for it. Eschewing superstitious explanations for his wife's dominance in their married life, Maimon sees his own timidity as the first sign of a psychological inability to dominate his wife (although he managed to assert male privilege when he slipped "out of her fetters" and abandoned her); it is in this sense that the custom reveals its logic as marital diagnostic and self-fulfilling prophecy. Günzburg, writing decades after Maimon, describes a similar ritual:

> Among the warnings I was given, the first and foremost was to step on the bride's foot just as I was giving her the ring, which would assure my dominance over her all of our lives together . . . and this was an easy thing to comprehend, since reason and Torah dictate such dominance. But my shame spoke against daring to do such a brazen thing in public and show my desire to dominate the wife of my bosom, especially since I hoped to have a household like my father's, in which the reason of the father and the tastes of the mother harmoniously blended, solidly built on the foundation of mutual love without attempts at domination.[51]

Günzburg understood that he was supposed to step on his wife's foot at the moment he gave her the ring; in other words, along with the asymmetrical (and patriarchal) acts that normatively inaugurate the marriage, Jewish folklore offers a more brazen act that makes clear that dominance, not only partnership, is at stake. Unlike the rituals around the ring, however, this looser set of rituals may be performed by either the bride or the groom. Although the dominance of the husband, Günzburg believes, is warranted by "reason and Torah," and although he wishes for a marriage, like his parents', in which domination will play no role, he recognizes that neither masculine authority nor marital harmony is guaranteed.[52]

Pauline Wengeroff describes a similar custom in the context of her account of her sister's 1848 wedding, which took place when Pauline was fifteen. As she relates, the music stopped as the couple approached the doorstep, since

> it was time to see whether, and in part to make sure that, the bride stepped over the threshold first [*zu sehen und zum Teil zu bewirken, daß die Braut zuerst über die Schwelle trete*]. To wit: an old superstition held that whoever of the bridal pair first strides over the doorstep would have the upper hand throughout their married life. . . . Here, with us, this custom was discharged in cheerful good order, while among the simple people, this occasion very often became a hand-to-hand fray, in which the relatives of the bride tried to fight for the precedence of their protégée, while from their side, the relatives of the groom did the same.[53]

In Wengeroff's telling, this custom seems to be one that is (at least among more "cultured" people) not up for grabs but is designed to allow the bride to assert her dominance, at least in the home that the newlyweds are entering. That this is a custom designed for a bride rather than a groom may be suggested as well by Yehezkel Kotik's memoir; he seems not to have known of this custom at his own 1865 wedding, although the bride and her entire party are fully prepared for it:

> While we stood under the wedding canopy then, I felt my bride step on my foot. It never occurred to me that she had done it on purpose. Immediately after the ceremony, her relatives snatched her from my side and brought her to the house that she might be the first to set foot across the threshold. They considered it an efficacious means of ensuring that she would rule over me. Popular belief gave great credence to those sorts of things then. . . . At heart I laughed at the whole procedure, and deliberately let my bride step across the threshold before me. Why not? Let her enjoy herself![54]

The custom is curiously slippery: on the one hand, these memoirists suggest that either couple might win this game; on the other, all three male memoirists recall that their wives were the victors, and Wengeroff implies something similar. Why this was so, or so remembered, remains an open question: Maimon believed that something about his wife's *Heldenmut* (heroic mettle) stacked the deck against her fainthearted mate, and the three male memoirists suggest that they held back out of a certain chivalry—whether a native Jewish or rather a retrospectively imposed modern bourgeois variety. Wengeroff's account is clearest about the class dimension of how this game is played: with intense rivalry among "simple people" and with "good humor" among the elite, as Wengeroff's family certainly was; this good humor might explain why Wengeroff never tells us whether the bride succeeded in crossing the threshold first. Nevertheless, the suggestion in her account that all the guests at her sister's wedding were *invested* in seeing the bride "win" (even when they were related to the groom?) may help illuminate the ritual: The game only appears to be open in its outcome, and the victory of brides is in some sense preordained, perhaps as compensation for the patriarchal inflections of the more normative marriage rituals or as evidence that even in its traditional form, Ashkenazic culture recognized women as the more (physically or socially) powerful sex and unofficially embedded this recognition into its marriage ceremony. In either case, Ashkenazic marriage encoded two sets of rituals to be simultaneously performed, one normative and patriarchal, the other folkloric and either indeterminate in its outcome or secretly weighted toward wives, with the implicit and tacitly required cooperation of chivalric young husbands and bystanders alike.

The double marriage ritual, and the ensuing ritualized resistance to it, is not unique to Jewish culture. In *Anna Karenina*, Kitty and Levin similarly defy the recommendation of their friends that each of them race to step on the carpet in the church first, which will ensure the winner that he or she will dominate in marriage. In simultaneously refusing to play this game, Kitty and Levin imply that their marriage will be a modern one, built on a basis of harmony and complementarity rather than rivalry and domination, even if the urgings of their friends serve as evidence for the persistence of the traditional and folkloric within modern practices and ideologies.[55]

The foot-stepping custom constitutes a game that either partner may win, but the ritual misfire whereby the groom (regularly? by unstated convention or "open secret"?) fails to wholeheartedly play this game seems to also be part of the game, in both its traditional and modernizing forms. Along with the double character of the foot-stepping ritual, it also functions alongside and even simultaneously with other normative wedding rituals (the ring, and for Jewish weddings, the circling of the groom and the breaking of the glass) and literary tropes (Amnon's shooting of the lion, Tamar bestowing her ring on Amnon). In the absence of lions and other means available to novelists, the act of the bride or groom stepping on her or his partner's foot may be a public, and thus necessarily veiled, image of the private act of sexual intercourse. If so, it is an interesting one. Against the messages encoded in both normative marriage rituals and familiar literary tropes, this folklore suggests—it is the very point of the folklore to suggest—that asymmetrical sexual relationships are inevitable, but the question of which partner will dominate in the marital bedroom can be neither legislated nor predicted. Modern heterosexuality disdained this ritual (as perhaps Maimon, Günzburg, and Kotik, in their chivalry and "shame," were already beginning to do) on triple grounds: the first was that it encoded a bald rivalry that has no place within companionate romantic marriage; the second—more tacit—grounds was that it sinned against the modern ideology that the sexes are not interchangeable and thus potential rivals but are radically, harmoniously, and predictably different; and the third was that men were naturally dominant in marriage.

The distinction I have been drawing between traditional heteronormativity and modern heterosexuality is not, of course, absolute. The accounts of traditional marriage rituals I have cited are framed within the modernizing genre of the Haskalah autobiography; in this way, tradition is less what has been left behind in the modernization process than what modernity remembers and even invents as its own foil. If the modernization process, as Talal Asad has argued, is also the construction of a traditional past, then the past that is remembered—by literature, above all—is an inextricable part of modern culture.[56] The traditional formations of Jewish sex and marriage, whether invented or real, persist and are reinvented even as they recede, unsettling the ideologies of bourgeois modernity and putting the naturalness of its notions of gender identity into question. Nineteenth-century Jewish literature arose in a transitional moment in which competing notions of marriage and sexual difference coexisted, and which would claim the upper hand—or foot—could not always be predicted. It is this lingering traditional knowledge, that gender differences are not so easily established or harmonized, that may be detected just beneath the courtly surface of the modern Jewish novel.

Because the Haskalah novel tended to concern itself with romance more than married love, the question of the distribution of labor in marriage or educational institutions and occupational patterns was often secondary to the vicissitudes of courtship. But at least one major nineteenth-century Haskalah work deals very directly with the question of gender roles within marriage: Yehudah Leib Gordon's 1875 epic poem *The Tip of the Yud* records the courtship of Bat-Shua and Fabi, but, because Bat-Shua is already a working woman when they meet, it also discusses the economic arrangements the young couple anticipate after their marriage. Despite her depiction as a paragon of feminine beauty, modesty, and purity, Bat-Shua has been compelled by her husband's abandonment to support her family, an unfortunate condition that her budding relationship with Fabi, engineer for the new railroad that has come to town, promises to rectify. At the outset of their relationship, Bat-Shua occupies her small shop in Ayalon "like a soldier staunchly standing at her post / from early morning until after nightfall." While Bat-Shua is praised for caring for her children's needs in the absence of a male provider, the language that compares her role to that of a soldier (calling to mind the semantic connection between *eshet khayil* and *hayal*, the woman of valor and the soldier) conveys the unsuitability of this occupation for a lovely romantic heroine.[57] Unlike the traditional Talmud scholar (and the husband in Proverbs 31) who is happy to eat of the fruit of his wife's labor, Fabi encourages the woman he has chosen as his mate to abandon her post behind the counter of her shop; with marriage in sight, an image of their married life—painted by Fabi and gratefully accepted by Bat-Shua—begins to form:

> Fabi decided that after completing his assignment,
> He would begin to build railroads as an entrepreneur,
> Transfer his residence to the country's capital,
> And establish his home there in grand style.
> All this he confessed to her and did not keep it to himself.
> For her part, she was intending to abide by his wishes
> And place her children in the care of a trained governess
> And to prepare herself to become a homemaker at the appropriate time,
> But for now, to complement the deficits in her upbringing in her father's
>   house
> And to study music and writing, language arts and literature.[58]

Israel Bartal describes this anticipated marriage as uniting an "industrious and mobile economic entrepreneur, who builds the railroads that are part of Russia's transition to a capitalist economy," with "an educated house-wife, fluent in languages and able to play the piano."[59] Bartal stresses that Fabi's "rescue" of Bat-Shua should not be understood as an act of true liberation:

> Gordon observes Bat-Shua from the perspective of a man who has adopted the values of the European bourgeoisie. While the heroine of his poem is the victim of an oppressive social order that displays no interest in her inner world, her desires, her emotions, and her needs as-woman, her liberation from the bondage of traditional Jewish male society lies in her delivery from the hands of the "traditional" male to those of the "*maskil*" male. From one form of servitude, she is expected to pass to another—enslavement to the values of Central European bourgeois society—in which the male's domi-nation of her life is perhaps even greater than in the traditional Jewish so-ciety that the poet condemns. Such a woman merited the term *eshet hen* (a woman of grace), while her counterpart, who failed to meet the male demand to limit herself to the kitchen, the bourgeois salon and the marriage bed, was labeled a "domineering whore."[60]

In the social engineering implicit in such Haskalah visions as Gordon's, fan-tasies of class mobility and acceptance within the Gentile world are clothed in, channeled through, and combined with the naturalizing ideology of sex differences, with particular consequences for women. Even the poorest traditional Jewish woman, Gordon's poem seems to say, is potentially as lovely and delicate as those described in European literature, and once restored to her proper occupations—music and literature rather than buying and selling—will emerge as the truly feminine being God had always meant her to be. That this feminine nature is difficult to discern within Eastern European socioeconomic realities, and requires the retraining and restraint of Jewish women by modernizing men, begins to suggest the tensions that play themselves out in the genteel discourse of Jewish modernization.

Literature played multiple roles in the project of forging new models of Jewish womanhood, as it does in the "discovery" of Bat-Shua's feminine nature. First, it is a privileged domain for the exercise of feminine taste and the inculcation of the feminine "linguistic code" and thus among the chief occupations with which Bat-Shua will concern herself with after her marriage to Fabi. Literature also has the power to rectify the neglect and distortion of femininity in traditional society. Gordon's poem famously begins with the question "Hebrew woman, who knows your life?" (*isha ivriya, mi yeda hayayikh?*) and continues by praising these women for their feeling hearts and beauty while citing the rabbinic disdain for women:

> And so what if you were graced with a feeling heart and beauty,
> If the Lord gave you talent and intelligence!
> For you, knowledge of Torah is a taint, beauty a detriment.[61]

It is a blessing, the narrator wryly remarks, that Jewish women are kept ignorant of Hebrew and these offensive sources (although this poem is also in Hebrew); modern lives will free them from unattractive men and a masculine textual culture that devalues their gifts and introduce them to the belletristic literature that will serve as a truer mirror for their beauty and grace. In its praise for and attention to feminine beauty and delicacy and women's "feeling heart," Gordon's poem both establishes the gender code of modernity and performs the role of a romantic suitor, paying chivalrous attention to neglected traditional Jewish women as it narrates the story of the failed rescue of one of these women—who, in her beauty and in her victimization by a hapless husband, an unfeeling rabbi and a gynophobic textual tradition, can stand in for the condition of Jewish women more generally.

As chivalry always is, the poetic narrator's chivalry here is suspect, closely juxtaposed as it is with Gordon's marshaling of a torrent of rabbinic misogyny (of which I have reproduced only a taste). Gordon's praise for fine manners and feminine delicacy only draws into sharper relief the rage that drives his ferocious satire. Yahil Zaban has recently drawn attention to the distinctively maskilic tincture of high regard for "etiquette," "manners," and "delicacy" and an only half-submerged violence. Haskalah discourse was built, of course, on bourgeois class aspirations that were frustrated by a range of social, cultural, and political impediments and acted in consort with fierce ideological warfare and the competition for social power and authority against a series of opponents. The new norms and practices advocated by the Haskalah, in Zaban's view, competed for power in a complex social field and were themselves borrowed

> from the social stratum of power-holders in the European state: the local aristocracy, the urban bourgeoisie and the government officialdom. . . . The Haskalah offers new behavioral "currency," for instance, strolling in an ornamental garden or playing the harp, which have no value in traditional Jewish society. On the other hand, the Haskalah plays down the importance of manners based on traditional practices, such as religious scholarship and keeping mitzvoth, or creates the impression that Jewish social etiquette is fundamentally flawed.[62]

Literature played the role of teaching this etiquette (much of which was no doubt out of reach for most readers) while asserting its value within a Jewish cultural economy that had had no use for it. Thus, extraneous descriptions of settings that seem to be doing little to advance the plot of a novel may nevertheless be accomplishing the work, as their writers hoped, of advancing Jewish society. Describing such a scene in Gordon's 1868 novel *The End of Joy Is Sorrow*, Zaban argues that Gordon imposes a "regime of manners" in his novel to carve out a space for a modernizing elite:

> In the sitting room scene, refreshments are served by a Jewish servant with the ironic name Malkah ("Queen" in Hebrew). The very presence of the servant and the manner in which she silently performs her duties are also part of the class ritual conducted in the Maskilic household. The appearance of the servant emphasizes that the Maskilim are lords in their community, as they have people serving them. The fact that the servant is a woman, and that she is followed by Sarah, who calls the men's attention to the refreshments with the words *"Bi adoni,"* whose meaning, as aforesaid, is "please," but also "you are my lords," stresses how the regime of manners is meant to bridle and mold womanhood.[63]

In surveying this fictional Jewish society that understands the proper use of napkins and polite speech, Zaban argues that its regime of manners conceals as it "refines" the aggressions of the elite; the novel ends with a public lashing of miscreant Hasidim, an expression as well as a "correction" of the unruly sexual and social energies of a society in transition. The domestication of the "angel in the house," according to Zaban, similarly "reflects a masculine fear of an overflowing of the erotic and chaotic forces ostensibly embodied in the new womanhood." Manners thus encode violence as well as its restraint, antisocial impulses along with their civilized suppression.

These insights shed light as well on the role of courtship, and the courtship novel, in the acculturation project. The courtship scenes in Haskalah literature establish the gender differentiation on which bourgeois marriage rests not in nakedly economic terms but through refined notions of femininity; as Katz saw, in modern matches, money must be discussed only "behind closed doors" (and in a modern novel, only villains may be interested in money).[64] Gender complementarity must be signaled in sexual terms—but only indirectly, given the restrictions of "the female linguistic code" that governs the novel. As in the eighteenth-century English novel, the linguistic code in nineteenth-century Jewish literature forbids forthright discussion or depiction of sex, especially for women readers (thus preferring descriptions of faces over bodies). This bourgeois code was no doubt reinforced for Jewish writers by traditional codes of modesty in language and prohibitions against *nivul peh* (obscenity), which coexisted at least from the rabbinic period with more straightforward discussions of bodies and materiality. Thus, BT Shabbat records R. Hanan b. Rabbah's teaching: "All know for what purpose a bride enters the bridal canopy, yet whoever speaks obscenely [thereof], even if a sentence of seventy years' happiness had been sealed for him, it is reversed for evil"; and Maimonides warns that "we must not imitate the songs and tales of ignorant and lascivious people" and asserts that Hebrew is a holy language because it "has no special name for the organ of generation in females or in males, nor for the act of generation itself . . . and only describes them in figurative language and by way of hints, as if to indicate thereby that these things should not be mentioned."[65]

In traditional Ashkenaz, according to Stampfer, the avoidance of "public expressions of affection led to the creation of curious circumlocutions for the terms 'my husband' and 'my wife,' the most common being *mayner* and *mayne* ('mine,' masc. and fem.)."[66] To these taboos against direct sexual discourse might be added the solemnity and religious feeling with which marriage (and, implicitly, marital sex) was surrounded.[67] The Haskalah linguistic code was thus overdetermined by bourgeois and traditional attitudes and etiquettes and expressed itself as well in a sociosexual code that even as it allowed young men and women to meet without chaperones restricted premarital sexual activity to kisses and caresses. Of course, the refined and romantic code was an ideal rather than reality and functioned alongside other Jewish discursive patterns that addressed sexual matters more forthrightly. As occurred in the bourgeois etiquette Zaban studies, the discourse and practice of romantic courtship also concealed numerous less-than-civilized impulses directed toward both external (rivals, parents, traditionalists) and internal targets (the beloved woman).

The primal scene of modern Jewish courtship is undoubtedly the encounter between Amnon and Tamar in *The Love of Zion*. This scene could hardly be further removed from the material considerations of traditional matchmaking: It takes place outside Jerusalem and the scrutiny of parents; it is propelled by the young people's perception of each other's beauty—before they even know each other's names; it commences through the exchange of handmade garlands rather than through the weighing of assets and status; and it is accompanied by music and poetry rather than the coarse prose that governs traditional marriage negotiations. To drive home these differences, the song Amnon is singing that first attracts Tamar to him rings changes on the theme that the gifts of nature are free for the taking, available to rich and poor, peasant and prince alike: "To the poor man and prince does the sun its rays bring / together they take pleasure in the sweetness of spring."[68] By extension, the natural pleasures and sweetness of youth are also shared freely among all classes; the love between these attractive young people is thus rooted, from the start, in the "democratic" lavishness of nature rather than the stingy apportionment of society (although, as Dan Miron points out, nature in its bio-erotic mode imposes some equally harsh if not harsher laws).[69] Moreover, the pastoral setting works to naturalize the gender performances of the romantic protagonists. David Biale notes that the association of nature with modern romance found contemporary sociological as well as literary expression, with the modern era bringing new social practices that allowed young people to meet, not in the hills surrounding Bethlehem but in the woods surrounding the Jewish towns of Eastern Europe.[70] Such walks, prototypically held on Sabbath afternoons, not only shielded young people from the eyes of adults; they also encoded a host of significations about the erotic significance of bucolic settings, which challenged the social stratification of traditional matchmaking as they established the proper bio-erotic grounds for choosing a mate. As Wolfgang Iser suggests, they also embody existential options in presenting a "counterimage" to the more urban world suggestive of the "plasticity" of human consciousness, "a mirror to reflect the disfigurement caused by the incursion of the political world."[71]

Despite Mapu's mobilization of poetic rhetoric and pastoral setting in the encounter between Tamar and Amnon, it is not entirely true that this encounter is dictated solely by the mutual attraction of these young people or shaped only by their natural differences. Ma'acha, Tamar's servant, rebukes her young charge for speaking about love to a young shepherd, allowing us to see that rules are very much in play in this scene, both in the natural rule that insists that a young man must make the first approach to a young woman (since she herself has no base sexual desires but only, according to Watt, exhibits noblesse oblige in permitting her lover's importunities) and the more obviously social rule that holds that shepherds should refrain from making advances to high-born young women.[72] Even in "the lap of nature," class matters: Amnon rebukes his fellow shepherd for daring to gaze at a high-born woman, his friend in turn warns him against setting his romantic sights too high, and Ma'acha lets Tamar know that no mere shepherd could ever be worthy of her. The gender and class rules that accompany bourgeois courtship, as outlined by Watt and expressed in the novel by Ma'acha, Amnon, and Amnon's fellow shepherds, thus yield confusingly mixed messages in this circumstance, in which either class rules or gender norms must be overthrown for the love affair to commence; as it turns out, the overtly social class norms rather than the ostensibly natural (but of course also socially constructed) gender rules gain the upper hand at first, so Tamar reaches out to the young man who, as a shepherd (though not as a man), may not.

If Mapu insists that class can hardly be ignored, even outside the city and family, he suggests that other features of traditional marriage also continue to operate even in the most pastoral of settings. Mapu introduces into the romantic scene the disturbing possibility that young lovers are roughly interchangeable in a sexual relationship, the ideology that implicitly underwrites matchmaking in sharp contrast with the modern romantic notion of unique "soul mates." Amnon is just one among a band of shepherds who all notice Tamar's beauty, and Ma'acha is as taken with Amnon's beauty as Tamar is (and ostensibly it is Ma'acha who is the better match, as his class equal). Moreover, Amnon's song refers in the plural to maidens beloved by shepherds, and Tamar is eager to know whether this line is just a literary conceit or derives from Amnon's personal experience (although she is careful to disguise her anxiety about potential rivals as simple generosity, asking Amnon, "Tell me, please, who is your beloved? I wish to see her, so that I may repay her for the flowers I have deprived her of"). As his answer makes clear, Amnon is free from present or past romantic entanglements; in this, as in other respects, Amnon conforms to the ideology of perfect romance, which rules out as heresy the folk wisdom that "there are many fish in the sea." Nevertheless, the very need to establish that Amnon has never set eyes on another maiden he might consider as a spouse, despite singing of having seen "thousands of maidens," raises the specter of romantic alternatives even as it rules them out.

It is the appearance of a lion during the second encounter between Amnon and Tamar that establishes their relationship on the proper romantic footing, with Amnon's prowess with a bow and arrow allowing him to overcome his initially disadvantageous position. In this scene, sexual differences assert their primacy in romantic courtship, decisively trumping the class conditions that governed and constrained their first encounter:

Tamar raised her eyes and behold! A sudden fear and mortal terror, because from the bushes emerged a terrible lion. Terrifying was his appearance, his fur standing up on his shoulders like nails and his tail like a cedar, his eyes shooting fire, his jaws yawning like an open grave, his tongue red as fire, dry and bloodthirsty. The lion, creeping silently and directing his gaze toward the sheep on the other side of the stream, backed up and gathered his strength to make a running leap across the water. Quick as lightning Amnon aimed his bow at the beast, another moment and the lion let out an awful roar and then ceased, because Amnon's arrow had pierced his innards, and he fell dead no more than ten steps from where Tamar lay, faint with terror and shock. Amnon, who had gathered strength before the threat of the lion, now melted at the sight of the beautiful, fainting girl. He left his sheep and waded neck deep through the stream, standing still before her form. He called to her in a powerful voice, his tears dropping onto her cheeks, and he shook her until she awoke, and she opened her eyes and saw the corpse of the mighty lion, and heard the words of the young man saying, "Be calm, young noblewoman, do not fear. The danger has passed, for the Lord strengthened the arm of your servant and my arrow pierced the beast and he is dead; see, he lies in his blood before your eyes—look and be revived." . . . She took Amnon's right hand and said, "Your hand, dear boy, saved me from becoming a prey. Like a brother you were born to help me in distress, and like an angel you came to my rescue; your kindness is greater than I can meet, and beyond all thanks."[73]

The lion, as emblem of nature, brute force, and sex, short-circuits any reading of their compatibility that would subject it to social or economic consideration. Conquering the lion, Amnon demonstrates his own sexual prowess as the necessary prelude to his "melting" in the face of Tamar's power—her passivity and beauty as she lies in a faint. The scene, as many commentators have noticed, thus both anticipates Tamar and Amnon's sexual intercourse and conceals it through symbolism: the lion embodies and displaces first Amnon's sexual aggression and then, as prey, Tamar's sexualized vulnerability to Amnon's "arrows."[74] While Amnon and Tamar's bodies or genitals must not be mentioned—according to both Jewish and European linguistic codes—Amnon's arrows, the lion's red tongue, and pierced innards may describe them "in figurative language and by way of hints," to use Maimonides's terms.[75] Tamar's swoon confirms her "sociosomatic" propensity to succumb to a more powerful masculine force, correcting her initial portrayal as a sexually forward girl. In these and similar scenes, the novel establishes a code that can signify the bio-erotic dynamic that is the true driver of the romance of Tamar and Amnon, even as it displaces to nonhuman agents and modestly veils more open expression of these sexual energies.

Despite the bio-erotic character of the encounter between Tamar and Amnon, these initial scenes end not with an avowal of their mutual love but with Tamar's allusion to the awkward class imbalance between them. In insisting that thanks will not suffice in rewarding Amnon for saving her life, Tamar delicately reminds him of her father's riches, establishing a channel for money or other material goods to change hands and suggesting that Amnon's action might be mobilized (as indeed it soon is) to overcome not only a lion but also the disabilities of a social mismatch. That this reward, which remains unspecified, is guaranteed by Tamar's bestowal of her ring on the shepherd boy suggests that it may include sexual as well as monetary components (just as it continues to intrigue us with Tamar's regular refusal to play a strictly feminine role in bestowing rather than accepting a ring). Even while establishing the most primal of connections between the young people, Mapu (or Tamar) paves the way for a translation of this connection into economic terms, demonstrating that sexual attraction, if managed with appropriate circumspection, may enter smoothly into the economic gears of society, offering itself as a respectable part of the marital exchange system alongside money, honor, and family connections.

Gordon's poem might similarly serve to illustrate this function of courtship, as it did the ideal view of the marital distribution of labor. Alongside the bourgeois marital economy imagined by Fabi and Bat-Shua, *The Tip of the Yud* veils and anticipates their sexual lives: Bat-Shua is seduced by Fabi not by the attractiveness of his vision of her as bourgeois wife (though surely it would be nice for her to be able to rest her feet) but through the norms of erotic courtship, in which unseemly talk of money or work is replaced by military metaphor and veiled sexual images. Even as he "immodestly" opens the curtains on an intimate encounter between the two lovers, the narrator warns off those traditional readers who will misconstrue the "alien" language of romance:

> Begone, you women who spread malicious gossip . . .
> Incessant talkers and obsequious hypocrites.
> You do not know the language of the heart, the language of love,
> Lest you fill the streets of Ayalon with gossip and slander,
> In the event you might eavesdrop in back of closed doors
> And hear Bat-Shua answering Fabi lovingly:
> "Let the victor in battle carry away his captive—
> I am your maidservant, Fabi!"—as she kisses him.[76]

The words Bat-Shua whispers to Fabi, which Gordon characterizes as "the language of the heart, the language of love" that is so scandalously alien to traditional Jews, are also the language of battle (perhaps also alien to traditional Jews, either as practice or metaphor). In this (trite) metaphor, it is not the Jewish woman who (inappropriately) takes the position of soldier, as Bat-Shua does in her market stall, but—more properly—the man, whom she describes as having "conquered" her. While the narrator excoriates those gossips and "hypocrites" who would misconstrue the tenderness of such romantic discourse, the poem also clearly signals that such language is entirely foreign in its cultural context: What would a traditional Jew make of the idea that battle and courtship are related, not in the sense that either bride or groom may step on the other's foot but that a woman must be "captured" by a man? This allegorical scene, so distant as well from the calm domesticity of the marital scene Fabi paints, is nevertheless its necessary prelude: the relationship between harmonious marriage and the submerged romantic violence that precedes and undergirds it exposes erotic domination and economic hierarchy as the other side of companionate marriage. In the marital economy and on the sexual battlefield, husband and wife, men and women, play different and noninterchangeable roles, which courtship serves to encode and foreshadow.

In exploring the modern ideology of gender differentiation, Ian Watt reminds us that the ideology of natural male sexual and economic dominance and female sexual reluctance and economic domesticity conceals a more complicated interplay between sexual desire and economic interests, veiling—in particular—the economic dependence of bourgeois women on their husbands. Fabi's conquest of Bat-Shua functions as a poetic allusion to his sexual potency, but this rhetoric may also obscure the material conditions of this battlefield, in which it is certainly Bat-Shua who has the most to gain from their marriage (just as Tamar's beauty and propensity to faint in the face of lion attacks may conceal the truth that her family has some wealth and power that might ease Amnon's path in life). As Watt says was the case for eighteenth-century England, marriage was generally of far greater material importance for a young woman than a man; the fiction that men initially and more actively desire sex and so pursue marriage, while women must be "won over" before they "oblige" their lovers by marrying them, serves to conceal and compensate for this imbalance—as it flatters the female readership of the courtship novel.[77]

Werner Sollors shows how the very language of courtship conceals as it exposes the material bases for marriage: "Though the metaphors of 'courting' and changing one's 'state' allude to the dimension of property, the person who experiences romantic love in the courtship process does not care to be reminded of the mundane aspects of the choice of a spouse. Romantic lovers do not consciously want to think of 'property' when the 'pursuit of happiness' is at stake."[78] As in *Pamela*, the ordained passivity of Gordon's heroine, Fabi's "captive," masks any hint of her material interest in a marriage that would elevate an abandoned and impoverished woman (not to speak of her orphaned children) into a life of leisure. Courtship, which builds on and establishes sexual difference through a drama of mutual recognition, in this way also serves as an arena of choreographed misrecognition. Bringing the language of love to a field in which the language of parents and matchmakers had held sway, courtship both elevated the primacy of sexual attraction and allowed the language of love to cover a multitude of less romantic interests and realities.

Parodies of Courtship

Despite the sincerity and enthusiasm of its initial embrace of new romantic conventions, Jewish literature struck its greatest and most long-lasting successes not through the straightforward adoption of romantic ideologies but by means of their parodic displacement and heretical overthrow. In the very fervor of their acculturation, Haskalah writers also inevitably measured the distance between traditional Jewish culture and European ideals. Watt describes an English society that—however suddenly the new sex ideology took hold—quickly absorbed and naturalized new notions of gender and marriage; Samuel Richardson's Pamela is prone to faint at the appearance of male sexual desire, Watt writes, because she has thoroughly internalized the ideology of female delicacy.[79] That there was something risible about these romantic gestures was also apparent to English readers of the time, as evidenced by the 1741 appearance, a year after the publication of *Pamela*, of Fielding's parody *Shamela*. But if the moral hypocrisy and plot absurdities of *Pamela* were evident to English readers, bourgeois manners were not only absurd to Jewish readers; they were also transparently foreign—the term "German" (generally meaning German Jewish, or Berlin "modern") was immediately recognizable shorthand for certain kinds of bourgeois dress and behavior. Even as they presented themselves as expressions of an interiorized and natural gender subjectivity, the new rituals of courtship and their attendant gender norms were recognized by all as cultural imports.

It is precisely this effect, in which a required performance overtly reveals its origins in mimicry and thus is skeptically received as masquerade, that Homi Bhabha sees as characteristic of the colonial scene. In a scene that plays itself out everywhere colonial operations are in effect, colonizers first demand from the colonized that they imitate the "civilized" norms of the dominating culture and then suspect that the elicited performance is not homage but either deceit or mockery: "The menace of mimicry is its double vision which, in disclosing the ambivalence of colonial discourse, also disrupts its authority."[80] The required Jewish performance of European manners is inevitably shadowed by suspicion; the accoutrements of acculturation are not only borrowed (and thus "German") but also potentially meretricious or false (and thus "false Enlightenment").[81] By suggesting that (some) modernizing Jews were only pretending to absorb European values, the concept of "false Enlightenment" could draw attention to the ways that Europeanization was *inevitably* a matter of etiquette rather than ethics, manners rather than morals—even and perhaps especially when, as in its gender norms, it mobilized a universalizing and naturalizing rhetoric. The suspicion of false Enlightenment, ostensibly limited to a subgroup of shallow materialists, opportunists, and hypocrites, could spread to infect and denaturalize Enlightenment assumptions and performances more generally, casting them as symptoms of class striving rather than moral self-improvement; thus was Enlightenment modernization exposed, even and especially by its most fervent adherents, as a matter of shifting appearances and superficial borrowing rather than profound individual and collective self-transformation.

Suspicions about false Enlightenment circled with particular insistence, in Jewish Eastern Europe as elsewhere, around the modernization of women. Haskalah writers simultaneously propagated European ideologies about certain immutable truths about women's nature and signaled their acute awareness that this feminine nature could be borrowed, shed, and dissimulated. Shmuel Ettinger's closet drama *Serkele* presents a title character, who like Pamela, has risen into the bourgeoisie from the depths of the working class; like Pamela, Serkele is also prone to fainting. Unlike Pamela's, however, Serkele's fainting is transparently staged to achieve her own ends, central among which is Serkele's desire to appear as a delicate bourgeoise. Ettinger draws attention to the masquerade by interspersing one of Serkele's verbal tics, the phrase "Oy, I feel faint!" (*mayne koykhes*, literally, my powers), with her hearty curses, sexual voraciousness, and other "unfeminine" assertions of desire and power.[82] If Richardson seeks to demonstrate that Pamela is a fragile creature through and through, Ettinger uses Serkele's regular swooning to expose precisely the artificiality of her playing the delicate housewife as an example of the false Enlightenment of those Jewish women who adopt the outward manifestations of class status (by fainting at will) without possessing the inner characteristics that should occasion such performances (a delicate body or nature). To drive the point home, Serkele's affectations are juxtaposed with the real delicacy of Hinde, the niece Serkele has disinherited. Hinde is in love with Markus Redlekh, the young maskil

Serkele lusts after, and when Serkele interrupts a tender and spiritual love scene between the young couple, she shrieks at Hinde with unbecoming jealousy. Hinde responds not by cursing but by begging the maid to put her to bed: "I need to lie down, I'm completely overcome." To this evidence of another woman's delicacy, Serkele responds, "Just look at the way she pretends to be weak, the little bitch! Now she says she has no strength—just bring Redlekh back and she'll be strong enough. Oy, I feel faint!"[83]

In scenes such as these, Ettinger presents the modern gender roles that are so central to the Jewish project of *embourgeoisement* as transparently artificial performances; this hermeneutics of suspicion is internally reproduced within the play, since Serkele also (falsely) suspects Hinde of faking a delicate constitution. That is, Jewish *embourgeoisement*, dogged by the social phenomenon and literary excoriation of false Enlightenment, was from the first understood to be a form of cultural "drag," the adoption of a new garb rather than the embodiment of a truer way of being; given that this cultural drag so often involved the adoption of a new gender ideology, the cultural performance also manifested itself as drag in the more usual sense—as cross-dressing and playing against gender type.[84] Despite the widespread adoption of the bourgeois ideology of marital harmony, feminine passivity, and gender complementarity, in *Serkele* as in other Jewish cultural productions the traditional folkloric belief continued to assert itself that, with a small (mis)step under the wedding canopy, a bride as easily as a groom might permanently establish her dominance in the marriage.

Even *The Love of Zion*, in which the embrace of European models of courtship seems so seamless and sincere, presents a model of femininity that fits only awkwardly into the ideology of femininity as Watt and others trace it. Tova Cohen has noted that Tamar and Amnon both initially fail to play the gender roles prescribed by the European courtship novel, since it is Tamar who initially approaches Amnon, acknowledging in the first words she addresses to him that she finds him attractive and requesting a gift from his hand: "Pray give me the garland of roses in your hand, if your heart is as kind as your face is pleasant."

> Amnon's face turned pale when Tamar spoke to him and he said, "Certainly, my lady, if you will stoop to take it from the hand of your servant."
> And Tamar answered, "I heard the words you sang: 'Roses from the valley for the shepherd's crown, to place on the head of the maiden he chooses.'

Tell me, please, who is your beloved? I want to repay her for the flowers you made for her, which I have taken instead."

Amnon dropped his eyes to the ground and said, "By your life, my lady, I have not seen my beloved among the thousands of girls my eyes have seen until now."

Tamar replied, "Look, lovely boy! You will seek your beloved among ten-thousands and she will be more precious for that."

And Ma'acha her servant took Tamar's hand and said, "Stop, my lady! Let us go, for someone is coming and it would be shameful to be heard speaking so frivolously."[85]

It is Amnon who turns pale and drops his eyes shyly when his beauty is praised; European courtship especially prizes feminine beauty and grants young men the privilege of evaluating and appreciating it. Tamar's erotic initiative, in defiance of these norms, is partly explained and justified by her experience of Amnon's beauty as déjà vu: she recognizes in his face the boy described in a letter from her grandfather, recounting a dream in which just such a lad appears (the unlikelihood of such thirdhand recognition is among the elements of Mapu's plot that readers subjected to parody and derision). That is, female forwardness and the lineaments of traditional matchmaking (insofar as an older male chooses his daughter's—or grand-daughter's—mate) are united in this rejection of the norms of how courtship should proceed. Similarly, it is Tamar who rises early the next day and goes "into the fields"—a reference, perhaps, to the biblical Dinah's riskier forwardness—in the hope of seeing Amnon again. The young people's eyes meet in the reflection of the stream that separates them, but Tamar breaks their silent reverie by showing Amnon the garland she has woven for him, in yet another expression of female initiative. Amnon, perhaps reluctant to take a gift from her, objects that he cannot reach it:

"You see, my lady, the stream is running between us and I cannot reach the garland."

"If you cannot manage it, I have the strength," said Tamar [*im ketsara yadkha, lakhen yadi rav li*]. And she threw the wreath across the stream to where he stood.

"Beware, dear lady!" called Amnon, in a frightened voice.[86]

Until the appearance of the lion, it is Tamar who initiates every phase of their relationship, first requesting a present from Amnon and then bestowing one in return; reading Tamar's words to Amnon literally, his arm or hand (which is gendered feminine in Hebrew) comes up "short" while hers is "great" or "long." Cohen suggests that such deviations from the conventions of the ideal romantic heroine are ubiquitous in Mapu's work, "even to the point of these heroines taking the 'accepted' place of the man."[87] Thus, Tamar and Elisheva in *The Hypocrite* choose their own lovers and insist on their right to refuse to marry the men their parents choose for them. In describing her younger self, Elisheva says, "I was wild and gave my spirit free reign."[88] In contrast to these active heroines, we can point to Amnon's shyness and modesty, more typical characteristics of heroines than heroes and the foils that allow Tamar to play the active role. If Tamar and Elisheva may harken back to traditional models of female Jewish strength that maskilim were not quite prepared to abandon, Amnon's passivity accords with the traditional masculine ideal of the gentle and studious yeshiva boy, which he more fully enacts when he arrives in Jerusalem, where he is praised by Tamar's father for his quick wit: "Your tongue, Amnon, is like the rapid pen of a writer! May you continue to acquire wisdom."[89] These literary characters, then, may be transitional types, avatars not (or not only) of bourgeois modernity but of a society in flux. Evidence for the Haskalah as an arena for the negotiation of proper Jewish gender behavior and linguistic codes exists in a fascinating correspondence between the Hebrew writer Dvora Haefrati and Mapu, who asked that Haefrati read an early draft of the novel precisely to get the response of a woman reader; Haefrati's criticism was that "as a young woman I must remark on the matter of Tamar. [You wrote:] 'She threw a wreath of flowers to the bank of the second river.' [But] it's not the way of a modest young woman (*alma tsnua*) to throw such a distance."[90] It is not entirely clear whether she is objecting to the lack of realism of Mapu's portrayal—its distance from biblical, traditional, or bourgeois ideals or the realities of women's physical capacities—or to his praise of such a young woman as an ideal romantic heroine.

Mapu's ambiguous characterizations of his ideal heroine (and hero) may derive, then, from an ambivalent embrace of European models in the face of either their inadequacy to describe Jewish life or their lack of erotic appeal. It may be hasty, however, to presume that Tamar's resistance to playing the passive role in this courtship, as her servant counsels her, is an effect of the confrontation between Jewish and European gender norms. Rebellious heroines and passive heroes are not limited to Jewish literature, as the nineteenth-century readers of Shakespeare's plays in Hebrew translation certainly knew. Moreover, as Moses Mendelssohn's welcoming of Fromet

Guggenheim's "amorousness" might remind us, the ideology of modern romance embraces both strict gender roles and their (perhaps equally conventional) romantic overthrow. It was surely part of Tamar's charms for nineteenth-century as for twenty-first century readers that she is a rebel as well as an ideal heroine. *Embourgeoisement* may have been less schematic or complete than it is frequently portrayed.

. . .

The artificiality of the modern rituals of courtship, their borrowed quality and essentially literary nature, rises to the surface most fully in the transitional literature of the late Haskalah. On the face of it, Abramovitsh's 1878 Yiddish novella *The Travels of Benjamin the Third* serves ideological purposes similar to those of the Haskalah romance, though it negatively appeals for the adoption of modern romantic ideologies by satirizing traditional roles rather than presenting positive Jewish romantic role models.[91] *The Travels* recounts the adventures of two men, Benjamin and Senderl "di yidene" (Jewish woman, in a term often used to denigrate Jewish women's talkativeness and other stereotypical traits), who venture from their small town in the Pale of Settlement to search for the legendary and heroic Red Jews, using the often fantastic medieval literature of the "great Jewish explorers" as their eminently unreliable guide. The novella, which appeared in multiple Yiddish editions as well as in a Hebrew version in 1896, is a complex satire with multiple targets and has been read, for instance, as both a critique of Jewish political passivity and a deflation of proto-Zionist fantasies.[92] But it also functions as perhaps the most extended and complex treatment of the gap between two mutually contradictory gender ideologies within a society moving from the traditional to the European-bourgeois sex-gender system.

Benjamin and Senderl are depicted as inadequate, emasculated, or feminized Jewish men both in comparison with other men and in relation to their capable and strong wives. Senderl the Woman is also described as Benjamin's helpmeet and female counterpart, the practical partner to his dreamer *luftmensch*. Their farcical quasi-marriage, from one point of view, is an extension of the novel's extended parody of Cervantes's *Don Quixote*, itself a mock-heroic parody of the chivalric romance. Michael Gluzman writes of "a recognizable similarity in the narrative of the friendship between Benjamin and Senderl, who aspire to embark on a heroic quest, and the friendship between the Spanish 'knight' and his sidekick Sancho Panza, who leave on a heroic adventure in the chivalric style. . . . But what is represented by Cervantes as the flaw or madness of an individual is presented by Abramovitsh as a collective failure, given that Jewish society is represented as a forced consumer of fairy tales and legends."[93] In contrast with Quixote's emblematically European, heroically individualist pursuit of romance and adventure, Benjamin and Senderl are married men in flight from their wives; in this way, too, they are representative of the collective failures of their society. After all, which traditional Jewish man past adolescence could enjoy the luxury of a bachelorhood like Quixote's?[94] Their married state is no evidence of their success on the sexual field—they fear their virago wives and are intimidated by all women more generally. When Senderl appears disguised in women's clothing on the morning of their escape, Benjamin hides at the sight, only emerging from behind the windmill when he realizes that the terrifying woman is in fact his friend. Where Don Quixote turns simple peasant girls into noblewomen and paradigms of feminine perfection, Benjamin's sexual adventures include waking up in the embrace of a donkey and conducting a mock-sublime courtship—complete with references to the Song of Songs—with the cross-dressed Senderl. The erotic life of traditional Jewish men, in Abramovitsh's implicit diagnosis, is no more than a grotesque and degraded version of the valorized and sublime heterosexuality of both European literature and the Bible.

While suggesting that the literary conventions of romance and masculine dreams of adventure have no place in the traditional Jewish world, Abramovitsh nevertheless manages to introduce the rituals of courtship into his novella as part of its parodic repetition of European conventions and satirical reflections on the distance of shtetl Jews from these models. In Gluzman's sharp reading of the novella, *The Travels* is an expression of the position of Jews as Europe's internal colonized "other" and of the belated and imitative relation of Jewish literature to the European canon:

> Through this "colonial" narrative, Abramovitsh parodically comes to terms with the dominant literary models of European literature: with the chivalric romance, the typologies of which set the template in many respects for the relations between the sexes in European literature; with the traditional European novel and the love story at its center; and with the contemporary European novel, which repeatedly staged the encounter with "the other" in distant and exotic territories. This parodic "colonial" discourse allowed him

not only to come to terms with these literary traditions through distorted imitations, but also to present a new understanding of the Jew as colonial subaltern, inferior and strange within Europe.[95]

According to Gluzman, the scenes in which Benjamin persuades Senderl to leave his family and join him on his adventure should be read as parodies of European popular romances, particularly in their melodramatic and adulterous variations. Benjamin, we learn, "always felt kind of a little love for him" (*tomid gefilt tsu im epes a shtikl libshaft*),[96] and the scene in which he importunes Senderl to join him in his adventures is woven from a series of penny-dreadful clichés. Seeing Senderl sitting in the kitchen peeling potatoes, his face scratched and bruised from his wife's rough treatment, Benjamin begs:

> Stop peeling those potatoes, darling (*neshome mayne*), and come with me into the next room. Is no one there? I don't want any chaperone watching over us now—I want to bare my heart to you, I can't stand it anymore, my blood is boiling within me. Come, my heart, come quick, before she arrives and interrupts us before we're done.[97]

Abramovitsh's sexual innuendoes can hardly be missed here. And indeed, when Senderl's wife does interrupt them at an inopportune moment, she mocks them: "Just look at these two lovers, hugging and kissing while the goat is in the house eating the potatoes."[98] Relating this scene to the conventions of the European romance, Gluzman writes:

> In the chivalric romance the heroes, naturally a young man and young woman, have to escape from their families and contexts in order to realize their love. In the course of this journey, the romantic heroes experience exciting adventures. Since Abramovitsh's heroes are two men (even if one of them is called Senderl the Woman), the romantic plot cannot embody the heterosexual model of the European romance, and so the Jewish romance turns into a parodic mock-romance. The meaning of *The Travels of Benjamin the Third* is constructed, then, from an encounter and parodic dialogue of two intertextual models, one European and one intra-Jewish.[99]

Abramovitsh's satirical targets in *The Travels* are multiple: Abramovitsh excoriates a Jewish society in which arranged marriage produces heterosexual couples without the romantic connection and proper gender difference to underwrite these relationships; such partnerships produce marriages in which male dominance is not assured either by traditional Jewish patriarchy or by its European bourgeois counterpart; and in traditional Jewish society, which allows no room for romantic attachment between a young man and young woman, erotic connections may arise at least as easily between Jewish men as between marital partners. Abramovitsh thus takes the old Jewish joke that he introduced in *Fishke the Lame*, a marriage between two sons, to its absurd and hybrid conclusion, cross-breeding the clichés of the European romance with the homosocial worlds of Jewish men. Abramovitsh's critique is not exhausted by its attention to the flaws in the traditional Jewish approaches to marriage: When Senderl's wife excoriates her husband's romantic dalliance because it endangers not their marriage but their dinner, Abramovitsh also desublimates the romantic rhetoric that views love as the supreme of all concerns and thus adultery as a threat to marital harmony. In giving voice to the down-to-earth perspective of Senderl's wife, Abramovitsh also reverses the colonial gaze, putting the modern sex religion under critical Jewish scrutiny. In so doing, he ends up deflating the high rhetoric of bourgeois romantic ideology as well.

Although Benjamin and Senderl (and through them, traditional Jewish men as a group) are the primary and continual targets of Abramovitsh's satire, the army episode at the end of the novella also partially reverses the satirical charge. Benjamin and Senderl are predictably woeful at soldiering, but their very buffoonery exposes the ridiculousness of the soldiers they are trying to emulate; it is precisely this effect that Bhabha has in mind in describing the potentially subversive effects of even the most sincere attempts at colonial mimicry. In the final chapter, "No Longer a Bride, Once More a Maiden" (Oys a Kale, Vider a Moyd), the two men are kicked out of the army; in the narrator's words, "Looking at them, you'd think it was just a play, two Jews getting dressed up just to make fun of all the soldiers, making faces and showing how ridiculousness the whole this-and-that was."[100] In fact, Senderl and Benjamin do present an implicit challenge to the army, seeing army life not as the occasion for revealing their own masculine inadequacies but as the place in which men are stripped of such markers of proper masculinity as beards and side locks (and the narrator participates in this attitude in hardly bothering to name the pointless activities performed in the army, even if Yiddish terms could be found for them).

To drive this point home, Senderl, immediately before their abduction into the army, has a prophetic nightmare in which he is transformed into a woman, losing his beard, donning a housecoat, and pregnant with his first child; in fact, their uniforms hang on them "like women's housecoats," and when they wield their rifles, they look "like a male [a *mansbil*] messing around by the kitchen stove." After they try to escape and are captured, Senderl dreams in their jail cell that his grandfather had brought him a toy bow and arrow or a wooden sword, pinching his grandson's cheek and saying: "Toys! Go ahead, play! Go *bang, bang, bang*, little boy!"[101] The joke is partly on Benjamin and Senderl, but—unusually enough for a writer still ensconced within Haskalah circles—it lets us see that, from *their* perspective, it is the gender performances built into military service that are absurd, childish, and even effeminate. Jews enjoy weapons but see them—rightly, the novella implies—as childish pursuits to be put away once sober adulthood ensues. It may be significant that Senderl, the more "childlike" and "wifely" member of the duo, is less preposterous a soldier than Benjamin, who has a wily and spirited opposition to the absurdities of goose-stepping on command. Their discharge from the army is something of a qualified triumph—not at having achieved an ideal masculinity according to the Haskalah social model and narrative plot but at having recovered the dignity of the masculinity, degraded and laughable as it is, that was always theirs.

.   .   .

The parodic Jewish repetition of the discourse of European romantic courtship is a feature of both the Yiddish satire and the Hebrew realist novel. In Reuven Braudes's 1888 novel, *The Two Extremes*, which paints a broad portrait of the acculturating Jewish society of 1870s and 1880s Eastern Europe, Levi Suravin, a minor character nicknamed the "Englishman" for his cool demeanor, is described as approaching young women precisely through a calculated and distancing quotation of the now-established rhetoric of romantic courtship. As the narrator recounts,

> Once he met a young girl he liked, and he wanted to take her into his confidence and enjoy her company; a few days later he approached her and said:
> "My dear young lady! Imagine that I have already spoken fine words in your ear, already said something about the scattered sunbeams, about the lovely flowers and roses, the precious moon floating through the night and the twinkling stars, the verdant fields and birdsong, and already recited poetry about all these things—since all these things are just to get you to like me, I say: let's not bother with all that poesy—let the sun shine and the

flowers bloom, let the moon and stars light up the night and the birds sing in the sky—after all, that's what they were created for—and I'll tell you in simple human language that I like you and hope you like me, too, is there any chance of that?" . . .

The reader will clearly see that this woman, who was brought up on all the "fine manners" of the new generation, turned away from him scornfully, saying that he had dishonored and embarrassed her. . . . And Suravin also turned away from her, saying that she was foolish, and never spoke another word to her.[102]

Braudes rings changes here on the familiar trope of the falsely enlightened woman, who requires the "fine manners" of romantic convention rather than appreciates the "simple human language" of attraction. Here, as elsewhere, it is no surprise that it is the woman who demands this false language, given that this same romantic discourse also involves the idealization—or overestimation—of femininity as the primary site of beauty. It is in this way that sinning against the properly delicate and feminine linguistic romantic code or exposing its conventionality is so easily perceived as—or may actually be—an act of sexual aggression against women. That it may also be a distinctively Jewish form of sociosexual aggression, directed against the requirements of European romantic obfuscation as of European colonialism more generally, is suggested by the long history of Jewish skeptics who found romantic language so hard to swallow, from the narrator of *Monish* pretending to despair about the inability of Yiddish to capture the sublimity of romantic love, to Lilienblum, who had his doubts about what it was the Hebrew poets of his time actually adored.

These Jewish parodies and transgressions would soon themselves become as regular, expected, and conventional as the rituals and codes of romantic courtship. In a study of the stage and film career of Molly Picon, for example, Warren Hoffman argues that Jewish cultural proclivities for transgressing romantic codes explain why "Yiddish cross-dressing lasted longer than its English-speaking counterparts," reaching a pinnacle rather than declining in the 1920s and 1930s.[103] In the astonishing popularity of Picon, Yiddish audiences created a star who was celebrated for her refusal to play proper feminine roles rather than for her sublime feminine beauty—not only as a behind-the-scenes career strategy but often also as part of the plot. Even if Picon's characters are often returned to the norms of female dress and romantic love by the end of the last reel, films like the 1923 *East and West* and the 1936 *Yidl with His Fiddle* also gave audiences sufficient opportunity to enjoy the spectacle of cross-dressing: Yidl (or Itke) dresses as a boy in order to join a klezmer band and then proceeds to fall in love with a male band mate, which allows the film to play out the beginnings of their romantic attachment outside the codes of sexual difference. In this relationship, Jewish audiences delighted in a love affair between a young man and young woman freed from the trappings of femininity, romantic choreography, and (the masquerades of) sexual difference.

As Hoffman sees it, Picon's popularity derived from a new sense among American Jewish audiences of the price paid for *embourgeoisement*, particularly by newly domesticated Jewish women. Picon, in his reading, expressed a female longing to occupy male spaces and play male roles. But Picon's audience was not limited, of course, to women, and the rejection of the ideology of romantic courtship based on gender complementarity and gender differences may have appealed to Jewish men at least as much as to women—as Suvarin's disdain for the rhetoric of romance suggests. Indeed, Hoffman writes, Picon's work expresses both female longing to be a full participant in the larger male world and, in her antics and tomfoolery, a critique of these very same masculine roles as grandiose and empty. In these and other ways, Picon "implicitly demonstrates the ways in which Jewish male and female roles are theatrically constructed."[104]

Theater and film, with their emphasis on performance and visible exteriors, were a particularly rich medium for investigating acculturation and the exteriority and performative quality of gender roles and courtship (it's no accident that the boldest depiction of a woman's false Enlightenment appears in a nineteenth-century Yiddish play, just as the boldest and most positive depictions of a woman's transgression of bourgeois gender norms appears on the twentieth-century Yiddish screen). As Alisa Solomon writes, the process of acculturation entailed a capacity for mimicry and masquerade, so "the performance of the Jew on the stage of the modern West always plays on the tension between disappearance and difference."[105] For a society in which roles of all types were undergoing rapid and conflicted transformations, the lightness and transparency of Picon's gender performance may have been experienced as particularly liberating.

If the (apparent) love affair between two men in *Yidl with the Fiddle* is a twentieth-century cinematic offspring and positive reevaluation of the romance between Benjamin and Senderl, the traumatic sojourn of Benjamin and Senderl in the Czarist army has its own descendants. The 1878 *Travels of Benjamin the Third* finds surprisingly strong echoes in Woody Allen's 1976 film *Love and Death*, in which Allen plays a neurotic Russian intellectual, a failure at love, and reluctant (or cowardly) soldier in the Czarist army. The film more openly gestures to the nineteenth-century Russian novel than to Yiddish literature, and there is no reason to believe that Allen was aware of his Yiddish precursors. But no such intertextual borrowing need be demonstrated: The novella and the film that followed nearly a century later are related not through influence but through a kind of cultural isomorphy. Both are Jewish parodies of European literature, just as both are Jewish satires on non-Jewish (and more specifically, Russian) ideals of heroic, sexually masterful masculinity. While Benjamin and Senderl are Jewish men who, in being terrible soldiers, expose the irrationalities of military life and ideology, Allen sharpens the joke by presenting his protagonist as at least nominally a Russian man. That Boris immediately "reads" as "Jewish" is a tribute not only to Woody Allen's widely recognized persona but also to the fact that Abramovitsh's discovery of the comic power of cowardly Jewish men is an early expression of what would become a widely circulated, readily legible, Jewish cultural trope. The comedy of the film rests, as it does in the larger Jewish counter-discourse, on a kind of cultural combat between the logic of Boris's cowardice and the overblown masculine, militaristic, and patriotic sentiments of his friends and family. The Jewish/Russian (dis)connection is played in all directions, and some scenes are funny precisely because it is this patriotic discourse that is rendered in familiar Yiddish-Jewish intonations. Thus, Boris announces to his comrades: "Fellows, I'm a pacifist. I don't believe in war." "He doesn't believe in war," one "Russian" friend sarcastically echoes. "Napoleon, *he* believes in war."[106]

As in *The Travels of Benjamin*, the parody/satire also has multiple targets: The most immediate satirical target is the pathetic cowardice of the (Jewish or "Russian") man, but the logic of war also falls victim to Woody Allen's wit. Thus, Boris asks, "What good is war? We kill Frenchmen, they kill Russians, then it's Easter." The joke locates the back and forth of the Napoleonic war in the seasonal shift between winter and spring, so fateful on the Russian front. But it also mentions Easter, reminding us again that Boris is allegedly Russian Orthodox, however consistently viewers are tempted to view him as a Jewish man inexplicably born into a Russian family and caught up in the storms of Russian political history. Such double-talk and cognitive dissonance attend yet another exchange on the question of Boris's reluctance to serve. As his cousin pleads, "Boris, you're talking about Mother Russia," Boris responds, "She's not my mother. My mother wouldn't let her youngest get shrapnel in his gums." The stereotype of a Jewish mother, however, fails to apply. His mother, disgusted, pushes him away, calling him a coward: "He'll go and he'll fight. And I hope they put him in the front lines." Boris responds, "Thanks a lot, Mum." And turning to the audience (from whom he expects the sympathy and understanding lacking in his immediate environment), he adds, "My mother, folks." To his "manly" brother Ivan, who rhapsodizes over the medals he hopes to win, Boris responds, "Take it easy, Ivan. You've got to cut down on the raw meat." The long-operative cultural-ideological argument between the bellicose (or heroic) Gentile and passive (or gentle) Jew is transposed here to a fight between brothers.

Boris's "defective" masculinity also jeopardizes his romantic life, as the romantic ideology that associates militarism and sexual conquest would have predicted. Telling his lovely and unimpressed cousin Sonja that he's "not the army type," Boris adds, "I slept with the light on till I was thirty." His attempts at romantic speech—linked in the European imaginary as in the title of the film with notions of military valor—are similarly absurd: "And you, Sonja," Boris gushes, "you look more beautiful standing here than you do in person." Sonja also puts the lie to the conventions that dictate that the romantic heroine be modest as well as delicate and beautiful. When Sonja is propositioned by an army officer, the flirtation begins as required with her protestations of purity, but these fall apart with comic rapidity: "Come to my quarters tomorrow at three," orders the officer. "I can't." The officer begs: "Please!" Sonja replies, "It's immoral. What time?"[107]

Finally, the film deflates not only the rituals and values of army life but also the conventions of the military film. The absurdity of having Woody Allen play a Russian is matched by the transparent conventionality of having him meet, in the person of a bullying sergeant, the wildly anachronistic and entirely familiar African American figure, who fires commands and insults at the pathetic recruit.

> "You ignoramus!" barks the sergeant.
> "Ignoramus, sir," repeats Boris.
> "You want a dishonorable discharge?"
> "Yes, sir. Or a furlough."[108]

As in *The Travels*, the logic of war is rendered a Jewish farce, helped along by Woody Allen's performance of the role in the staccato rhythm of army speech and absurd exaggerations of stand-up comedy. Describing the impetus behind their fighting, the sergeant explains: "If we kill more Frenchmen, we win. If they kill more Russians, they win." Boris asks, "What do we win?" "What do we win, Private?" the sergeant erupts: "Imagine your loved ones conquered by Napoleon and forced to live under French rule. Do you want them to eat that rich food and those heavy sauces?"[109] What does it matter, to a Jew, which of these Gentile nations is in charge?

There is a fairly straight line, then, from Abramovitsh's satirical depiction of two Jewish heroes who are nevertheless execrable soldiers, thankful to be expelled from the army, to Woody Allen's depiction of the Russian Boris, who can't shoot straight and is quick to accept when threatened with a dishonorable discharge. The joke in both cases is partly on the failures of such men to perform romantically and militaristically. But this joke is a red herring (to invoke a ubiquitous culinary reference in *Love and Death*). The real joke is on the pointlessness, stupidity, and barbarity of Gentile romantic and military codes, separately and in their interconnection. A Jewish writer and a Jewish filmmaker, separated by a hundred years and many thousands of miles, thus stumbled on the same joke—one that would place Jewish soldiers in the Czarist army to fail on every level while succeeding on the only one that counts. In Vietnam- and feminist-era America, as in nineteenth-century Russia, it was Jewish men, precisely as pathetic lovers and lousy fighters, who could best make the case against the barbarities of modern civilization.

While *Love and Death* took war as its central ideological turf, Jewish writers also produced powerful deflations of romantic courtship. If Abraham Mapu had laid out the ideal arc that connected and separated the first meeting of young lovers and their sexual union, opening up an erotically charged space that the rituals of arranged marriage had entirely neglected, Erica Jong's 1973 *Fear of Flying*, with its famous—or infamous—fantasy of "the zipless fuck," reversed the long trajectory of Jewish literature-as-Europeanization by collapsing romantic time into the space of a few minutes and stripping it of its bourgeois falsities. As the protagonist of the novel, Isadora Wing, explains, the term refers to her fantasy of sex between partners who have just met, "zipless" because "when you came together zippers fell away like rose petals, underwear blew off in one breath like dandelion fluff. For the true ultimate zipless A-1 fuck, it was necessary that you never got to know the man very well."[110]

Jong's controversial novel is most often read within its more immediate context of the American second-wave feminism of the early 1970s.[111] Among the questions it raised when it exploded onto the scene was about the relationship between the "sexual revolution" of the late 1960s and the "feminist revolution" that shortly followed. As Alice Echols argues, women in the New Left felt both exploited and liberated by the "compulsory sexual ethic" within the movement; Ann Snitow, Christine Stansell, and Sharon Thompson summed up feminist critiques of the sexual mores of the 1960s: "The sexual revolution, radical women complained in retrospect, had been another male trick: the cool sex of the counterculture was a new version of men's old need to prove their property—now communal rather than private—in women."[112] In this charged atmosphere, whether books like Jong's were claiming for women the sexual rights and discursive freedom long reserved for men or were falling into sexual traps that kept them tied to men and male expectations remained an open question.

The Jewish dimension of this question is less often discussed. The New Left, the sexual revolution, and the feminist revolution that followed were not directed to Jewish concerns, and the overrepresentation of Jews among its participants was masked by the secular character of these movements (the "Jewish" religious revolutions sparked by these "American" revolutions are easier to see).[113] Nevertheless, an argument can be made that the visibility and enthusiastic participation of Jewish women—many of them second- or third-generation immigrants from Eastern Europe—in American second-wave feminism represent a late echo of the Jewish resistance to bourgeois gender norms I have been tracing here. That traditional gender norms persisted after secularization is the claim Paula Hyman makes to account for Jewish women's educational achievements in late nineteenth-century Russia: "Trained by the gender division of traditional Jewish society to take the initiative, at least economically; respected for their ability to manage; aware of the value attached to Jewish learning, from which they were largely excluded—Jewish girls often hungered for education and dedicated themselves to acquiring it."[114] If the legacy of these Jewish gender norms persisted for a generation or two beyond the point where Hyman discovers them, perhaps kept alive by American Jewish women's political and social activism, a Jewish sexual counter-discourse to the romantic sublime may

have also persisted despite and within Americanization and suburbaniza-
tion, breaking through in the sexual and feminist revolutions of the 1960s
and 1970s. Lisa Maria Hogeland reads Erica Jong as specifically combat-
ing women's "interpellation into romance," either by creating "alternatives
to the romance plots" or unmasking them as plots "in every sense of the
term."[115] But while Hogeland sees Jong as "interrogating" D. H. Lawrence
and Freud, David Biale aligns Jong with other Jewish cultural figures, male
and female, of her day, writing that "Jong's strategy is deliberately outrageous, a kind of female Lenny Bruce, in which the outrageousness is
specifically Jewish."[116] Jong's "specifically Jewish outrageousness" is outrageous, like Bruce's, in its function as Jewish challenge to the obfuscations
and euphemisms of the romantic sublime. But it is also outrageous (*more*
outrageous than Bruce) because Jong is a woman writer who defies the
feminine linguistic code, the stricter and longer-lasting form of this romantic discourse.

For all the simplicity of Jong's "zipless fuck," its heretical dimensions are
multiple: The erotic fantasy of Isabel Wing opposes and dramatically collapses the "romantic time" of bourgeois courtship; this fantasy rejects the
orchestration of gender roles that such courtship entails; and in its "indelicate language," it represents a sexual-discursive assault on bourgeois feminine ideals (as well as on Jewish discursive conventions), which could also
be interpreted as an ethnic assault on European-American-Gentile norms of
good breeding:

> The zipless fuck is absolutely pure. It is free of ulterior motives. There is no
> power game. The man is not "taking" and the woman is not "giving." No one
> is attempting to cuckold a husband or humiliate a wife. No one is trying to
> prove anything or get anything out of anyone. The zipless fuck is the purest
> thing there is. And it is rarer than the unicorn. And I have never had one.[117]

The absence Jong names of "ulterior motives" in the zipless fuck could
also be called social roles and gender norms. The sex between strangers
in this fantasy has nothing to do with marriage arrangements, occurring
outside the structure of both romance and adultery. It does not stand in
for other social relations, nor does it enter into their logic. Significantly, it
also has nothing to do with gender complementarity and difference—the
male and female partners do not take different roles or play out scenarios
of conquest and submission. In this fantasy, Jong imagines and longs for

sex stripped of all these elements and then acknowledges that such sexual minimalism is vanishingly rare.

From many perspectives, the ideologies underlying traditional marriage could hardly be different from those of Jong's sensational novel—not least the priority given in traditional Jewish society to modesty and the absolute avoidance of illicit sex.[118] Nor am I implying, as, for instance, John Murray Cuddihy does, that sexual foreplay is a feature of courtly or bourgeois romance rather than Jewish lovemaking: "Freud paid scant attention to sexual foreplay," Cuddihy writes. "To Freud's shtetl puritanism, fore-pleasure, like courtship, essentially, or courtesy—was a form of round-aboutness, of euphemism.[119] As Boyarin makes clear, traditional Jewish culture (which, in its sexual naturalism can hardly be called puritanism) encourages and celebrates marital foreplay. What it fails to appreciate is the combination, in romantic formations, of "merely spiritual loves between men and women" and the concealed violence of the chivalric views of women. As Boyarin writes, "Traditional Jewish culture may not have room for romance (and was cynical about it when encountered in either its medieval or modern forms), but it was not cynical about love between married couples."[120]

Boyarin's claims can help clarify how to read Jong's zipless fuck within the perspective of modern Jewish culture. Isabel Wing's fantasy is not a dismissal of *sexual* foreplay, contra Cuddihy's view of shtetl puritanism as allowing foreplay no part in Jewish approaches to marital sex. Jong seems to be dismissing the form of foreplay that takes place outside the bedroom in bourgeois courtship, postponing sex for the duration of the courtship, during which a veiled code for sexual intercourse is established that is infused with both ascetic (or spiritual) and aggressive impulses (although there is a *cultural* aggressiveness in both Jong's and Bruce's sexual forthrightness). It is this complicated foreplay that is foreign to Jewish sensibilities, not the forthright attention to the sexual satisfaction of the woman by the man that is legislated by Jewish law.[121] No direct line connects Jong's fictional fantasy with traditional Jewish approaches to sex: it is adulterous, immodest, and unconcerned with the establishment of a stable family or community. Nor is this fantasy recognizable as the product of the Jewish adoption of European sexual habits of mind. Traditional Jewish heteronormativity and Jong's wild and post-traditional heterosexuality both stand in sharp contrast to the modern bourgeois ideology of romantic love in many if not all of its features: feminine delicacy, the drama of mutual recognition, sex as the union of the active masculine and passive feminine principle, romantic love as the bonding of uniquely matched individuals, the necessity of veiling attraction and postponing fulfillment, and so on. In adopting the sex religion, Jewish modernizers may well have imagined that they were establishing what Watt describes as "the concept of courtship, marriage and the feminine role that has obtained most widely in the last two centuries."[122] Modern Jewish culture, at its beginnings and throughout, is evidence that something different, and rather more interesting, was happening.

Modern Jewish literature began with an embrace of the regime Watt describes but very quickly developed an ambivalent and critical version of its most prominent features. Indeed, by the end of the period I trace in this chapter, a recognizably Jewish counter-discourse had appeared, attained wide visibility, and was wielding enormous cultural power; this discourse was built on the critique of romantic courtship and of bourgeois ideals of femininity and masculinity. In its various manifestations, the Jewish romantic counter-discourse is heir to the nineteenth-century Jewish adoption of European models. Despite the enthusiasm of this cultural embrace, it gave way to ambivalence for a number of reasons: Adopting European manners quickly, promiscuously, belatedly, from literary as well as geographically disparate sources, rather than naturally and organically, undoubtedly rendered the artificiality of these manners more evident. As late participants in the production of European literature, Jews could also draw from different periods and genres of the novel. Their position in this literature as belated outsiders and as poor embodiments of its ideals may also have drawn them to both the internal criticism that already inhabited the novel from the very beginning and the countercurrents always present at the heart of bourgeois ideology. Critics such as David Patterson and Alan Mintz have suggested that the mimicry that often motivated Haskalah literature led to unrealistic pale copies of European originals.[123] That the act of copying could eventually result in explosive and colorful originality is the legacy we have inherited from Abramovitsh, Woody Allen, Erica Jong, and many others.

CHAPTER FIVE

In-Laws and Outlaws

> In American teaching marrying is just loving, but that is not enough
> for marrying. Loving is alright as a beginning but then there is
> marrying and that is very different. . . . Sometimes it needs a sister of
> the man to make his marrying and sometimes the mother of the girl
> who is to be married to him.
>
> —Gertrude Stein, *The Making of Americans*

> Forget the Name of the Father! Think about your uncles and your
> aunts.
>
> —Eve Kosofsky Sedgwick, *Tendencies*

Nuking the Jewish Family

Discussing the connection between narrative style and constellation of
characters in Saul Bellow's work, Robert Alter writes that "from the early
fifties onward his novels and stories encompass not isolated individuals and
overmastering parents but a welter of disparate squabbling, ambivalently
loving siblings, uncles and aunts, cousins near and distant. This attraction
to familial sprawl is inseparable from the zest, the panoramic sweep, and
the element of formal looseness in Bellow's fiction."[1] Bellow's thickly populated fiction, teeming with characters, ideas, and talk, is both stylistically
and demographically expansive, matching a maximalist style with a density
of human networks. Bellow occasionally comments directly on these networks, for instance, in a 1984 story called "Cousins," in which the complexity and "stickiness" of an extended Jewish family is both theme and setting.
The protagonist, Ijah Brodsky, reflects on the role played in his life by "Jewish consanguinity—a special phenomenon, an archaism of which the Jews,
until the present century stopped them, were in the course of divesting

themselves."[2] In Brodsky's view, his continued connection with a large, quarrelsome, and demanding network of cousins begs explanation, given the trend in modernity that social historians call "nuclearization," in which complex family networks are reduced, under the pressures of urbanization, migration, and *embourgeoisement*, to much smaller forms.[3] The shedding of cousins and other distant relations, so visible throughout the modernizing world, was at least partially halted in the Jewish case, according to Brodsky: "The world as it was dissolving apparently collapsed on top of them, and the divestiture could not continue."[4] If it is true that the eighteenth-century English novel, describing the construction of the nuclear family around the kernel of a romantic pair, provided ideological support for nuclearization at its outset, then Jewish American narrative at the end of the twentieth century may bear witness to the incompleteness and partial reversal of this project. In Brodsky, a character whose primary literary role is cousin rather than lover, husband, son, or father, we may discover a guide to the concerns of this chapter, which follows the divestiture of extended family in the literature of Jewish modernity and records its perhaps surprising persistence and return.

The narrowing of extended family is not of course unique to Jewish modernity. Modernization took similar routes in a variety of contexts, with new labor conditions, increasing urbanization and industrialization, and the concomitant rise of romantic ideologies; all of these conditions contributed to the narrowing of the family circle in a variety of national and colonial contexts. Ian Watt claims the reduction of the family structure as an integral part of the new bourgeois marriage: "on marriage the couple immediately sets up as a new family, wholly separate from their own parents and often far away from them; extended kinship ties lose their significance, and the conjugal family typically becomes an autonomous unit."[5] Historians have demonstrated that the transformations Watt sees in eighteenth-century England reverberated through Eastern European family life a century later, in Jewish as in non-Jewish circles.[6]

The abandonment of the extended family in favor of the nuclear model, while not the most visible feature of romantic modernization, may nevertheless be its most crucial one. In traditional marriage, the most significant kinship effect of a match, according to Stephanie Coontz, was the cementing of a relationship between in-laws. The connection between the parents of the bride and groom, who both contract and are then linked by traditional marriage, may in fact be its aim and raison d'être. As Coontz argues, "Since the dawn of civilization, getting in-laws has been one of marriage's most important functions. . . . It converted strangers into relatives and extended cooperative relations beyond the immediate family or small band by creating networks of in-laws."[7] I would point out that Coontz uses the term "in-laws" in a larger sense than usually intended in standard English usage, which typically limits the term to the "diagonal" relationship of a husband or wife and the parents of the spouse. In Coontz's usage "in-laws" refer to the "horizontal" relationships that connect the two sets of parents and their families beyond. Such extended networks, in Coontz's view, are particularly important for nomadic and transnational societies, where they function to provide family connections, economic partners, and safety zones in times of need:

> Marriage was certainly an early and vitally important human invention. One of its crucial functions in the Paleolithic era was its ability to forge networks of cooperation beyond the immediate family group or local band. Bands needed to establish friendly relations with others so they could travel more freely and safely in pursuit of game, fish, plants, and water holes or move as the seasons changed.[8]

Marriage produced the extended family networks that, in Coontz's summary, nomadic societies needed for survival; it is no coincidence, then, that societies that depended on such extended networks exerted particular control in the contraction of marriages:

> Among the aborigines of Australia, marriages were traditionally arranged when girls were still in their childhood and were strictly controlled by elders. Because of the scarcity of food and water in that harsh environment and the need to travel over long distances to ensure survival, Aboriginal elders had to ensure that their community's children were distributed in ways that gave the community family connections to the land and resources wherever they traveled.[9]

While Coontz's analysis focuses on the prehistoric and aboriginal functions of marriage, her analysis may apply to Jewish family formation as well. Beatrice Weinreich's study of Yiddish kinship terms makes a similar case for the relative importance of in-law relationships in Eastern European Jewish society, as compared to those relationships in the populations among whom Jews lived. While Jews shared a host of kinship terms with Germans and

Slavs, they also developed a set of Hebrew-derived terms that distinguished Jewish arrangements from those of the communities among which they lived; Weinreich argues that it is precisely this Hebraic element in Yiddish kinship terminology that "lends itself to sociological interpretation." The importance of extended family in traditional Jewish society, according to Weinreich, is reflected in Hebrew-derived terms to signal degrees of cousin-hood (for instance, while the term for second cousin, *glid[ge]shvesterkind*, is shared with German, the term for a second cousin once removed is derived from Hebrew *sheyni-beshlishi*, literally, second with third). While terms for son-in-law, mother-in-law, and so on are similar to those in German, Wein-reich draws attention to the presence in Yiddish and absence or rarity in German or Slavic languages of terms that designate more-distant kin and in-laws at greater remove, such as those that pertain to "the ego's children's in-laws," which is to say, the relationship between individuals whose chil-dren are married to each other, who are known in (Hebrew-derived) Yid-dish as *mekhutanim* or *makhatonim*.[10]

Quoting Zborowski and Herzog's ethnographic account of Jewish family life, Weinreich claims that it is a distinguishing feature of traditional Jew-ish society that *mekhutanim* "claim and render the obligations of kinship" while serving as sources of family status accrued through marriage rather than strictly by descent.[11] The "thickness" of such kinship ties, Weinreich continues, is no doubt reinforced and justified by the institution of *kest*, the terms of which are arrived at by the negotiation between both sets of parents and which literally embeds the young couple within the home of one set of parents for an agreed-upon period of maintenance. The term *mekhutanim* describes a structural rather than affective relationship, signaling that fam-ilies connected through the marriage of their children take part in a set of conventions, obligations, and transfer of status that constitutes a third space, a degree or type of connection beyond or between biological descent, sexual partnership, and friendship. Marriage creates family both backward (to a previous generation) as well as forward (to grandchildren) and thus radiates "outward," as well.

Coontz's argument for the particular utility of in-laws for nomadic popu-lations may also apply to Jewish societies. The family networks achieved through marriage, along with those constituted by cousins, may have been particularly important to Jews, given their economic and geographic mo-bility and the displacements of the medieval and early modern period in which traditional Ashkenazic culture took shape.[12] Jacob Katz suggests that extended family connections were indeed a distinctive feature of traditional culture, in some sense taking the place of "property of permanent value—such as real estate," which was generally absent from Jewish family holdings:

> As we have seen, Jewish society profited economically from its unity despite geographic dispersion—in other words, from the fact that Jews could use their shared language and culture to maintain contacts with other Jews living in distant lands. Kinship ties among even distantly related individuals provided further such advantages . . . in many circumstances. The Talmud student traveling from center to center in pursuit of his studies, the rabbi who accepted an appointment in a new kehilla, and even someone seeking a match in a distant city all required local support, if only to provide them with information and the like.[13]

Despite the evident usefulness of extended family for a mobile society, and perhaps especially for a young couple taking their first steps in adult life, such family structures were reduced not as an unintentional side effect of modernization and the adoption of the sex religion, as might be supposed, but through deliberate rejection on both ideological and personal-psychological grounds. Among the particular targets of autobiographical excoriation and ideological critique was the practice of *kest*; the experiences reflected in these texts are most often of a young groom compelled to live for a period of time with the parents of his young bride. The practice of the young groom moving into the bride's home is not universal—Pauline Wengeroff describes living with her new husband's family for the first four years of their marriage.[14] (Patrilocal marriage, unusual among traditional Eastern European Jews, is by far the more common arrangement in other traditional societies.) Immanuel Etkes explains the prevalence of Jewish matrilocality by pointing to the underlying logic of *kest*, in which the bride's father could convert material wealth into spiritual assets through the acquisition of a son-in-law who could "sit and learn" after the wedding:

> Given the young age of marriages and because the newly married couple had no independent means of support, it was common for them to spend the first years of their married life in the bride's parents' home. . . . Because the talents and achievements of the groom were accorded great value in the marriage market, it was common for an affluent father who yearned for a scholarly son-in-law to undertake to support the groom's studies.[15]

The problem with such arrangements, for modernizers, was not only their conspicuously economic character (even if clothed in love for Torah) and the disdain they showed for the new romantic ideals. More damaging, for those autobiographers who spoke from personal experience, was that they ripped a boy away from his immediate family and required him to lodge with a family of strangers. As Etkes writes, "The groom was a boy of thirteen to fifteen who was forced to leave his parents' home after his marriage. In many cases that separation was a cause of suffering and pain."[16] The autobiographies regularly describe the resulting ill will that arose between the young groom and his mother-in-law in particular. Salomon Maimon speaks of repeatedly coming to blows as a young bridegroom with his wife's mother.[17] Mordechai Aaron Günzburg reports being poisoned by his mother-in-law in the course of her attempt to "cure" his impotence. In describing the tensions that often arose in these "combined" families, David Biale speaks of the psychological "splitting" evident in the autobiographies between an unfailingly loving family of birth and the "bad" family into which a young groom was thrust.[18]

While hostility between young grooms and their mothers-in-law is widely attested, young grooms and their fathers-in-law seem often to have enjoyed warmer relations. Günzburg, who suffered bitterly at the hands of his mother-in-law, says that, in the first weeks after the marriage, "my father-in-law's love was the whole of my desire."[19] Y. L. Peretz's first marriage—which was arranged—failed, but before it did, he forged a poetic collaboration with his father-in-law that resulted in a coauthored Hebrew book that was Peretz's first publication. Premodern Jewish literature is also filled with descriptions of such relationships, characterized by intellectual connections that begin with the older man's attraction to a smart young man and culminate in mutual adoration. The description of the marriage of the Besht (Rabbi Israel Baal Shem Tov) in the early nineteenth-century collection of legends about the founder of Hasidism, *In Praise of the Baal Shem Tov*, describes his future father-in-law's amazement at the Besht's subtle explication of a difficult passage in Maimonides. Listening to the younger man, "Abraham's soul became attracted to the Besht's soul and their souls were in accord." The deal was sealed after the Besht renders a just decision in a dispute: "Rabbi Abraham was in awe of the Besht and loved him very much." Discovering he was "in need of a wife," Rabbi Abraham offered him the hand of his daughter, despite the Besht's lack of distinguished lineage.[20] The role played in romantic literature by the initial rapturous encounter between a young man and young woman is here assigned rather to two men of different generations who similarly fall in love as prelude to forging a marital bond.

The connections between young men and their (prospective) fathers-in-law were inevitably also the subject of literary scrutiny and satire, even if writers more typically focused, following generic convention, on the relationship between a young man and woman. To the other excoriations of arranged marriage in *The Tip of the Yud*, the poet Yehudah Leib Gordon adds a subtle dig at the importance of the impression the young groom made on his prospective father-in-law rather than on his young bride: When Bat-Shua is fifteen, her father seeks a groom after *his own* heart (*hatan ki-levavo*) rather than hers.[21] The point is satirically and linguistically reinforced in the description of how the father-in-law "falls in love" with the young Hillel. After Hillel gives a brilliant sermon on a Talmudic passage that discusses "the cleaving of two uteruses" (*hidbik shney rehamim*), Bat-Shua's father, Hefer, "hears and, enamored, his heart cleaved to the deliverer of the sermon (*vatidbak nafsho ba-doresh*), saying 'Indeed he alone is the bridegroom for my only daughter / He alone will say *kaddish* after me, he is to be my son and heir.'"[22] Gordon uses the root *d.b.k.* (to cleave, a root-word with a range of erotic and theological significances) twice in stanzas 21 and 22 of the poem: the first usage describes the anatomical anomaly or malformation of a "double uterus," in which the fallopian tubes join incompletely or not at all; the second describes the phenomenon of a middle-aged man falling in love with a young boy as prelude to acquiring him as a son-in-law who is also quickly promoted to son and heir. In bringing these two passages together, Gordon suggests that the practice of having a father-in-law choose his daughter's mate is as grotesque and unnatural as a double uterus, a union not of gender complements but of two identically sexed organs or individuals.

The most direct literary critique of *kest* and in-law relations may be Sholem Aleichem's 1888 *Stempenyu*, in which he sets out to describe a Jewish marriage under the threat of an adulterous affair, recounting the travails of a newly married young woman living with her husband's family who is tempted by the erotic attention of a wandering klezmer musician named Stempenyu. The novel suggests that she has been left open to this temptation by the unnaturalness of her living situation; in this regard, *Stempenyu* conforms with the Haskalah tradition of novelistic critique of traditional

marriage practices, although it is rare in directing this critique to the practice of *kest*. For reasons that are no doubt obvious, the practice of *kest* is
represented in great detail in Haskalah autobiographies from Maimon on,
but it makes only rare appearances in the modern novel, which much prefers to view the young couple as an independent unit in which parents are
cast in the role of romantic obstacle rather than postmarital bursar or cook.
More unusual still is Sholem Aleichem's focus on what *kest* looks like when
it is the young bride who moves into her husband's childhood home. The
Hebrew autobiography of the nineteenth century focuses obsessively on the
trauma of such an uprooted young groom and seems to have spared not a
thought on its effects on the young bride, whether similarly uprooted or
merely compelled to share her parents and bed with a newly acquired, eminently immature "brother" in the form of a husband. (Pauline Wengeroff's
memoirs are an exception in this regard as in so many others.) Why would
Sholem Aleichem choose to explore the ill effects of *kest* through its workings on a bride? This deviation, I would suggest, is an effect of the influence
of the genre, which invites attention to a young bride's predicament and
views the threat and allure of adultery as particularly interesting when it is a
beautiful young woman's virtue that is tested.

Kest plays a surprisingly pivotal role in *Stempenyu*, given that its major
focus is not on Rokhele's home life but on what transpires outside the home
between the young wife and the wandering musician of the title. Rokhele
ultimately resists Stempenyu's charms and saves her marriage, a feat accomplished only because she also decides to persuade her husband to move out
of his parents' house. In the chapter titled "Rokhele Returns to the Correct
Path," the couple is finally reconciled after Rokhele falls ill, horrified by
how close she had come to consummating her passion for Stempenyu. As
her husband and his mother hover over her in distress, Rokhele entreats her
husband to ask his mother to allow them some time alone.

> "Mother, excuse me, but would you be so kind as to leave us to ourselves?"
> asked Moshe-Mendl. He went to the door with his mother, and then re-
> turned to Rokhele's bedside.
> "Tell me, what ails you, my soul?" asked he, in a voice that was full of real
> concern and tenderness, for the very first time.[23]

After Rokhele's feverish near confession, the two open their hearts to one
another for the first time, the narrator pointedly tells us, since they were

married. This heart-to-heart ends with Rokhele turning to her husband with one request:

> "Enough of this *kest* already, Moshe-Mendl; you're no sitter in the study-hall, we have some money, thank God; let's move to the city, to Chmelnitz, there with my friends, my family, with you—things will be good; we'll be alone together. I've had enough of eating *kest*, it makes me sick, it's not ko-sher, I can't take it. We're here with your people but total strangers to each other. . . ."
>
> Moshe-Mendl sat and listened in wonder. Then he swayed a bit again and continued to sing "Elijah the Prophet." "Okay, why not? Elijah the Prophet, let it be this week!"[24]

And sure enough, we learn in the next chapter, the young couple set up their own household "alone together" and the husband tries his hand in business with the help of his wife (though he assures his parents that she remains at home when he travels to fairs). Moshe-Mendl's loving parents, left behind, mourn the abrupt end of their arrangement, with Dvoshe-Malke asking her husband, "Who ever heard of such a thing, no more than one year of *kest*?"[25] Nevertheless, the reader is assured of the success of this new modern phase of what began as a traditional arranged marriage by the birth of a young son, a year after the couple strike out on their own. We learn of the birth from a letter written by the proud new parents to the grandparents, who remain, even at this crucial juncture, safely ensconced back in their own shtetl with no visit invited or planned. Moshe-Mendl's letter ends with warm regards for his uncle, aunt, and various other family connections, and Rokhele adds to these her own loving wishes. She breaks off her writing, however, when she hears the newborn awake from a nap, turning away from this constellation of relatives toward the smaller family that she has made her own.

Stempenyu captures a transitional moment in the history of the Jewish family, one that has otherwise evaded attention. Literature more generally did the work of "reducing" the extended family through focus rather than plot or argument: the very attention to the young couple does the work of arguing that it this relationship, this variety of love, that is the most interesting, significant, and worthy of notice, as opposed to, for instance, the varieties that connect parents-in-law with the new couple, grandparents and their newborn grandchildren, or—in Bellow's story—a network of cousins. Nevertheless, in the generations that followed, parents and in-laws and aunts and cousins occasionally swam back into focus, not only on the periphery of the nuclear family but sometimes even at its center. It was in these literary works, in which the pull of romantic love vied with the claims of family and the demands of tradition, that modern Jewish culture acquired some of its most distinctive shapes.

.   .   .

In 1904, sixteen years after the publication of *Stempenyu*, Sholem Aleichem began to publish the *Tevye the Dairyman* stories, which constitute a radical departure from the earlier work precisely in their ideology of family. Where *Stempenyu* advocates for the nuclear family as the unit best designed to ensure the love, stability, and reproductive fruitfulness of a young couple, the *Tevye* stories record the price paid for the nuclearization of the Jewish family by those excluded in the new arrangement. *Stempenyu* recommends modern marriage not only for the sake of love and companionship but also as a way to guard against sexual temptation, which it sees as an indirect effect of the lack of privacy for the young couple in traditional arrangements that hamper the development of intimacy between them. The *Tevye* stories take nearly the opposite position by viewing these arrangements from the perspective of those displaced in the triumph of the nuclear family. The Tevye stories have often been read as depicting at least two parallel or overlapping sets of concerns. The first of these is the marriage of Tevye's daughters, while the second is the growing threat of anti-Semitic violence, culminating in the expulsion from Anatevka of Tevye and his immediate family.

Reading these two trajectories in the context of nuclearization, it becomes clear that Tevye's apparently personal troubles with his daughters and the larger political issue of the rise of anti-Semitism in late Imperial Russia are linked both through Pertchik's radicalism or Chava's intermarriage and the post-traditional marriages of each of his daughters. Traditional marriage may well have been an adaptive mechanism for dispersed Jews: Israel Abrahams suggests that the institution of the matchmaker arose in the wake of the Crusades as a response to both geographic dispersions and the disruptions of the genealogical narratives; matchmakers served, among other functions, as the genealogical memories and repositories of a community in crisis. As Abrahams writes, "When Jewish society became disintegrated by the massacres and expulsions of the Crusading era, its scattered items could only be re-united by the agency of some peripatetic go-between. There was nothing essentially unromantic about the method, for the *shadchan* was often a genuine enthusiast for marriage."[26] The modern Jewish marriage plot thus differs from both Watt's description of English marriages and the patterns of post-Crusades Ashkenaz: It arises with an urbanizing and secularizing commercial class, as the English novel does. But it expresses as well the Jewish traumas for which traditional marriage practices might have served as corrective.

It may be a function of the fact that Tevye already operates in a post-traditional society that even the marriages he would like to contract lack the larger in-law relations that are, according to Coontz, the primary mode and ultimate reason for arranging marriage. The parents and especially fathers of these young men, Tevye's counterparts and prospective *makhatonim*, are missing because the young man has been orphaned, as seems to be the case for Motl and Pertchik (although Tevye mentions that he knew Pertchik's father, who was a cigarette maker); or because the suitor is already an adult male, and an independent economic unit, as is the case for Leyzer Wolf and Podhotzur; or because the father-in-law (the term hardly applies) is a Cossack. When Hodl and Pertchik announce to Tevye that they have cho-sen to marry, Tevye responds, "Excuse me, but when was the engagement party? It's rather odd that you forgot to invite me to it, because if she'll be your wife, I just might be your father-in-law (or, in the Yiddish, *a shtikl mekhuten*)."[27] Into his daughter and Pertchik's announcement, Tevye inserts precisely the kinship term that their embrace of modern engagement prac-tices rule out.

Despite the lack of *makhatonim* with whom Tevye might forge relation-ships, the stories conceal, in distorted form, many of the practices of tradi-tional marriage. On the face of it, Tevye does not get to choose the young men his daughters will marry—the whole point of the stories, it would seem, is that his opinions on the matter are entirely irrelevant, as the sex religion holds. But this appearance is deceptive. For all the modernity of his daughters' romances, it is Tevye as often as not that introduces the young man into his household of beautiful young girls. In the case of Hodl's en-gagement to Pertchik, it is Tevye who meets Pertchik first, growing fond of him in the venerable fashion of prospective fathers-in-law with smart young men: "We talked on and on," Tevye relates about their conversa-tion after Pertchik comes to house for dinner, "because something about the little fellow appealed to me. I'm damned if I know what it was, but it did. You see, I've always liked a man (*ikh hob lib a mentshn*) I can have a Jewish word with; here a verse from the Bible, there a line from the Talmud, even a bit of philosophy or what-have-you."[28] So too was ignited the love between the Besht and his father-in-law, over the Besht's explication of Maimonides and acumen in settling a dispute. Although his maneuvers are more veiled than Rabbi Abraham's, Tevye's appreciation for Pertchik is surely what induces him to introduce the admirable young man into his house full of marriageable daughters. It is precisely this kind of parental orchestration that Marion Kaplan calls "the fine art of coincidence," by which German Jewish nineteenth-century families camouflaged their matchmaking maneuvers: "Conscious of the growing contradictions between social ideology and social reality, some [Jewish] parents 'covered up' traditional, arranged marriages. Others arranged circumstances where certain young people could meet each other." When an engagement resulted from these efforts, it was declared a "real love match."[29]

It is part of Sholem Aleichem's genius to present the Eastern European Jewish world-in-transition through just such a drama of overlapping and conflicting social codes. Tevye's conversation with Pertchik is both a replay of the Talmudic "tests" that promising sons-in-law were put through by older men and a radical rewrite of such rabbinic displays of brilliance. Although Tevye, as always, liberally sprinkles his side of the conversation with Jewish quotes, Pertchik displays his own wit by undercutting all of Tevye's assumptions, both magnifying and evading the older man's interest in him (the Besht, we might recall, similarly "plays hard to get," although this game is justified by the narrator's explanation that he had not yet "revealed himself" when he meets Rabbi Abraham). Hitching a ride on Tevye's cart and letting it slip (intentionally perhaps) that he knows who Tevye is, Pertchik is nevertheless unwilling to satisfy Tevye's curiosity about him. Tevye relates the frustrating conversation that ensues:

> "Tell me," I say, "since you seem to be a personal acquaintance of mine, just who exactly are you?"
> "Who am I?" he says. "A human being."
> "I already guessed as much," I said, "because you didn't look like a horse to me. What I meant was, whose child are you?"
> "Whose child?" he says. "I'm a child of God's."
> "I knew that, too," I say. "After all, it's written *vaya'as eloyhim*—and God

made every creeping thing. I mean, who's your family. Are you from here-abouts or from elsewhere?"

"My family," he says, "is the human race. But I was born and raised around here. You even know me."

"Then out with it!" I say. "Who is your father?"

"My father," he says, "was named Pertchik."

"The devil take you!" I say. "Did you have to take all day to tell me that? Are you Pertchik the cigarette maker's boy, then?"

"Yes," he says. "I'm Pertchik the cigarette maker's son."[30]

Sholem Aleichem presents a conversation here in which the two partici-pants (as so often in his work) are speaking at cross-purposes: one of the participants is playing "Jewish geography," while the other pretends not to understand the rules of this game as a form of principled protest against it. From his perspective, Tevye takes a natural interest in his young pas-senger, not only as a father of marriageable daughters but also as an inhab-itant of a social universe in which family connections provide a shortcut to crucial information and mutual aid. For Pertchik, Tevye's attempts to locate him in a knowable Jewish universe rubs against both his individual-ism and universalism—his modern inclination to see himself as "his own man" and his instinct to resist Tevye's Jewish urge to classify or claim him. When it nevertheless becomes clear that Tevye knew Pertchik's father, this relationship opens up new avenues for intellectual connection in shared class experiences. As does the dream that establishes that the tailor Motl can claim an old family connection with the girl he loves, Tevye's acquaintance with Pertchik's father might also smooth the romantic path for Pertchik and Hodl, however persuaded the young couple are that their love is entirely of their own making. Tevye is a master of this game; he is no fool, although his apparent blindness to the ways of modernity forms a useful mask behind which his own taste in young men (which is not so distant from his daugh-ters') might continue to function.

I do not mean to sentimentalize the extended family or arranged mar-riage, as Tevye and, more to the point, Sholem Aleichem do not. As folk wisdom knows, in-laws are no picnic. Perhaps it is relevant here that al-though Sholem Aleichem's own marriage began as rebellion against parental interference, he was compelled by his disastrous failure to establish him-self as what Watt would call "an independent economic unit" to accept his mother-in-law's financial help and then her presence in his house; she was willing to fork over the money to save him from creditors but, after she moved into his house, refused to exchange another word with him. Tevye's relationship with the one son-in-law he acquires with the help of a matchmaker, Beilke's Podhotzur, is even more unpleasant: When Tevye goes to visit his daughter, the doorman refuses to let him in. On the verge of leaving, he catches the eye of a maid:

> Well, she noticed me, opened the door a crack, and asked me in Yiddish, "Who are you looking for?"
> "Is this the Podhotzur place?" I said.
> "Who are you looking for?" she asked again, raising her voice.
> "When you're asked a question," I said, raising my voice louder than hers, "it's considered polite to answer before asking one of your own. Is this the Podhotzur place?"
> "That it is," she says.
> "In that case," I say, "you and I are practically related. Please be so kind to tell Madame Podhotzur that she has a guest; her father Tevye has arrived and has been standing outside like a beggar for quite some time, because he failed to pass muster with that silver-buttoned sheygetz of yours, who isn't worth the nail on your little finger."[31]

Beilke has risen in the world, but Tevye may not follow. While her rich husband is perfectly happy to wed a poor young beauty, his willingness does not extend to her unpresentable father, whom he pays off to leave town. Tevye's sense that Beilke's maid is nearly kin derives not only from her connection with his daughter but also from a shared Jewish and class connection; and indeed their shared language does get him in his daughter's front door. But he can go no further, since the rules of Tevye's universe do not apply to the Podhoretz marriage. Tevye's ability to forge an in-law relationship even with a young communist devoid of the slightest interest in such traditional arrangements fails to work in the case of this capitalist son-in-law. Katz points out that the relationship among in-laws ideally acts as a set of structural obligations in a Jewish economic universe that includes richer and poorer members of an extended family; these obligations continue to operate whether or not they are also built on affective connections.[32] Although Beilke marries Podhotzur precisely in the hope of lifting her father out of poverty, for this modern marriage the presence of a beggarly father-in-law is a bridge too far. The price Tevye pays for acceding to the choices of his daughters—and really, what choice does he have?—is not primarily of his patriarchal authority, as the Haskalah writers had described the intergenerational battle. The price he pays is this: When Tevye is expelled from his home, he has nowhere to go, no *makhotonim* to turn to. That we have no English term by which to translate this term, or even register its absence, means that even this absence has fallen prey to cultural amnesia. Thus, Tevye's loss is also, and perhaps even more profoundly, our own.

The Return of the Family to the Scene of Its Expulsion

The 1959 publication of *The Little Disturbances of Man*, and in particular, "Goodbye and Good Luck," the first story in Grace Paley's inaugural collection (and the first she published), brought a strikingly innovative stylistic idiom into American fiction.[33] Paley's authorial voice, as distinctive and unique as it was, was also recognizably part of a larger shift in American letters. As Julian Levinson describes the "Jewish American Renaissance" of postwar America,

> This was a period that witnessed the rise of a new generation of Jewish writers, critics and scholars to national prominence, among them Delmore Schwartz, Saul Bellow, Harold Rosenberg, Leslie Fiedler, Isaac Rosenfeld, Paul Goodman, Bernard Malamud, Grace Paley, Allen Ginsberg, Philip Roth, and Norman Mailer. All were noisily interceding in a literary climate presided over by T. S. Eliot's icy persona, in which John Cheever's terse *New Yorker* style had seemed the only imaginable way to write fiction.[34]

Levinson's description of the cultural shift in American letters makes it clear that what changed with the entry of Jewish writers into the American literary arena was a matter of style in multiple senses: Jewish writing exploded Cheever's "terse *New Yorker* style," as Jewish writers "noisily" interceded in an atmosphere dominated by "T. S. Eliot's icy persona." Along with Bellow and the other writers Levinson lists, Paley's forging of an idiosyncratic, brash, and noisy English literary idiom was at least partially indebted to and inflected by the Yiddish of the earlier immigrant generation. In describing her move from poetry to the short-story form, Paley spoke of having found another "ear," that of the Eastern European Jewish immigrant milieu in which she was raised:

> I understood I'd found my other ear. Writing the stories had allowed it—suddenly—to do its job, to remember the street language and the home lan-

guage with its Russian and Yiddish accents, a language my early characters knew well, the only language I spoke. Two ears, one for literature, one for home, are useful for writers.[35]

While Paley talks here about the language of her childhood milieu, she also records Bellow's role in expanding the literary options available to a writer starting out when she did: Bellow "freed the Jewish voice in some ways that I didn't even recognize, but his was all about men. Still, for Jews who are crazy about the English language, he was the one."[36] Reviewers also took note of the similarities between Paley's work and Philip Roth's, whose first story collection, *Goodbye, Columbus*, appeared in the same *annus mirabilis* of 1959; according to a reviewer of both publications, Paley's work "stems from the same soil as Mr. Roth's."[37] Like Roth, Paley was not only testing the prevailing norms of English literary style; she was also challenging accepted images of what it meant to be a writer and what constituted the proper material for literary prose, in the openness and earthiness with which she narrated sexual experience and the life of the body. In Paley, even more than Roth, these transgressions—of American sexual convention and of conventional English style—went hand in hand.

Levinson's canon of participants in the Jewish American Renaissance lists both men and women as representatives of a zeitgeist and a common rooting in second-generation immigrant culture. Nevertheless, the openness about sex that was one of the shared characteristics of this generation of Jewish American writers also opened sharp fault lines between its male and female members, reflecting larger tensions in Jewish American, and American, culture.[38] Paley traces one of these fault lines, in implying that Bellow's usefulness as a liberating model for her own Jewish voice was limited by his exclusive attention to male experience. Her own literary experimentation included more radical explorations of the possibilities of Jewish prose style and a pioneering attention to the ordinary experiences of working-class women; this focus has secured Paley's role as a founding figure of second-wave American Jewish feminism and her place in the canons of American Jewish and feminist fiction.[39] Paley's innovative literary style and her attention to the voices of women on the social margins are in fact intricately related. Paley's first short story, "Goodbye and Good Luck," provides an important tool for the critical analysis of her distinctive voice by locating its idiom within a particular cultural history and within a particular set of family relations—that which connects a childless aunt with her niece. As in Bellow's work, a maximalist English style was wedded to a willingness to include a more extended family of characters than literary decorum usually dictated. Family relations are also an important semantic resource for conceptualizing the dynamics of literary transmission, inheritance, and influence; the description in "Goodbye and Good Luck" of a diagonal connection between aunt and niece provides us with the tools to trace the inherited, transfigured, and invented Jewish kinship and cultural legacies that energize and distinguish Paley's work.

Paley's inaugural story is not only stylistically distinctive—even within a generation famed for its noisiness, verbosity, and maximalism; it also is unusual in what might be termed Paley's "generational stance," in presenting this new voice as the expression of a middle-aged aunt, representative of a generation whose time, in many ways, seems to have passed. "Goodbye, Columbus," the first and title story of Philip Roth's 1959 collection, features a more familiar narrator and protagonist in Neil Klugman, an educated and ambitious young man, whose conflicted sexuality and class strivings converge in his attraction to the wealthier Brenda Patimkin and from whose perspective the story is told. Rather than take the young writer's traditional prerogative and present a critique of the moral failings of society from the perspective of a young protagonist who functions, in this sense, as representative of the writer and the writer's generation, like Sholem Aleichem in the Tevye stories Paley allows an aging generation to have its say, placing a younger character in the position of receiver and listener. Paley steps onto the literary stage with a story that focuses not on the alienation of the young (or not *only* the alienation of the young) but on the sexual rebellion of an earlier time, as remembered by Lillie's aunt Rose. Paley's idiom is more experimental than Roth's, but it constructs its idiosyncratic style by reaching back to an earlier generation of Yiddish-inflected English speech. It is perhaps fitting that, in "Goodbye and Good Luck," the most evident stand-in for Grace Paley, who spoke of finding her literary voice precisely by discovering that she had two *ears*, is Lillie, who (unlike such famously voluble Jewish narrators as Roth's Portnoy) never utters a single word.

"Goodbye and Good Luck" takes the form of a nearly uninterrupted dramatic monologue, with Rose Lieber (in Yiddish, this last name might be rendered as "lover" or "dear") relating her life story, and present good fortune, to her niece. The story begins with an assertion that Paley claimed, in an interview, to have once heard from her real-life aunt: "I was popular in certain circles, said my aunt Rose."[40] The last four words of this sentence, the only words in the story that are *not* Rose's direct speech, are presumably Lillie's, who is thus both the audience for and implied narrator of Rose's narrative. Rose's opening remark is directed to a niece she hopes will be able to see beyond the image of an apparently lonely, single, childless, middle-aged, and overweight woman, an image of Rose forged in Lillie's more conventional immediate family; Rose speaks in order to present Lillie with a different image of her aunt from an alternative and more generous perspective. Rose's popularity "in certain circles" was achieved precisely by refusing to follow the rules of the culture in which she was raised and by which she is still judged, and her conversation with Lillie is an opportunity to set the record straight about how she got to the place she is now. Thus, Rose relates her first experience in the work world, at a factory: "A long time ago I said to the forelady, 'Missus, if I can't sit by the window, I can't sit.' 'If you can't sit, girlie,' she says politely, 'go stand on the street corner.' And that's how I got unemployed in novelty wear."[41] Aunt Rose's next attempt to find work lands her a job selling tickets for shows at "the Russian Art Theater," in fact, a Yiddish theater. There, she meets an established actor, Volodya Vlashkin, whose attentions she at first bashfully permits and then warmly welcomes, as she becomes persuaded of his genius and talent. Rose recounts to Lillie his invitation: "And you, Miss Lieber, please, I suggest Feinberg's for a glass of tea. The rehearsals are long. I enjoy a quiet interlude with a friendly person." Vlashkin is treated like royalty at Feinberg's and served on a tablecloth embroidered "Here Vlashkin Eats." With "the Valentino of Second Avenue" in pursuit, Rose becomes Vlashkin's mistress and moves out of her mother's home:

> The sad day came, I kissed my mama goodbye. Vlashkin helped me to get a reasonable room near the theater to be more free. Also my outstanding friend would have a place to recline away from the noise of the dressing rooms. She cried and she cried. "This is a different way of living, Mama," I said. "Besides, I am driven by love."
>
> "You! You, a nothing, a rotten hole in a piece of cheese, are you telling me what is life?" she screamed.[42]

After recounting this exchange with her mother, Rose goes on to admit that her mother did know something about life, given her ugly marriage to an

ugly man. It was just that unhappy circumstance that motivated Rose to decide "to live for love." Describing her father, Rose says, "He never washed. He
had an unhappy smell. His teeth fell out, his hair disappeared, he got smaller,
shriveled up little by little, till goodbye and good luck he was gone and only
came to Mama's mind when she went to the mailbox to get the electric bill."[43]

When Rose crosses paths with Vlashkin's wife for the first time, she feels
pity and guilt. "Poor woman, she did not know I was on the same stage
with her. The poison I was to her role, she did not know." Rose leaves Vlashkin that night, saying, "I am no home breaker."[44] Later, Rose tells Lillie, an
actress from the theater company publishes a tell-all autobiography

> in which she says certain things regarding Vlashkin. Such as, he was her
> lover for eleven years, she's not ashamed to write this down. Without respect
> for him, his wife and children, or even others who also may have feelings in
> the matter.[45]

While Rose disapproves of the actress's lack of discretion and is hurt to
hear that she was not Vlaskhin's only dalliance, she has no harsh words for
Vlashkin himself: "Now, Lillie, don't be surprised," Rose continues. "A great
artist like Volodya Vlashkin . . . in order to make a job on the stage, he's got
to practice. I understand it now, to him life is like a rehearsal." She goes on
to remember how it felt to see him onstage, in a play in which his character,
an older man, was in love with a much younger woman:

> What he said to this girl, how he whispered such sweetness, how all his hot
> feelings were on his face . . . Lillie, all this experience he had with me. The
> very words were the same. You can imagine how proud I was.[46]

Eventually, Rose explains, the theater fell apart, and the actors found
other work or went on to English-speaking roles in film or on Broadway.
But "Vlashkin himself, no place to go, retired." And then, Rose, "fat and
fifty," receives a phone call from her long-lost lover, letting her know that
his wife is divorcing him and asking Rose to dinner. After a renewed, late-
life rekindling of their old romance, and at Rose's insistence, Vlashkin proposes. Rose asks her niece to

> tell this story to your mama from your young mouth. She don't listen to a
> word from me. She only screams "I'll faint. I'll faint." Tell her after all I'll

have a husband, which, as everybody knows, a woman should have at least one before the end of the story.[47]

While the story revolves almost entirely around Rose, it also indirectly presents her niece Lillie, whose reactions to what she is hearing can be gleaned at moments in Rose's monologue. Rose, having grandly described her decision to break with her mother and live for love, interrupts her story to say, "Don't laugh, you ignorant girl." Describing the heroic efforts of a suitor, in the days when "young girls wore undergarments like Battle Creek, Michigan," Rose invites Lillie to compare Rose's to her own experience with men, in an age of more accessible underwear: "Nowadays I suppose it is easier, Lillie? My goodness, I ain't asking you nothing—touchy, touchy."[48] Aunt Rose is also keenly aware that Lillie's mother has no conception of the rewards or pleasures of the path Rose has taken, feeling nothing but pity and contempt for her: "Poor Rosie!" (these are, not coincidentally, a mirror of Rose's feelings for Vlashkin's wife).

With deft economy, then, Rose's dramatic monologue, so richly expressive of her own experience, is prismatically shot through not only with the words and attitudes of those whose path Rosie crosses—the forelady, her mother, her boss, Vlashkin, and through Vlashkin, Yiddish melodrama—but also with the attitudes of the people to whom the monologue is directed: first of all Lillie, to whom Rose is speaking; but also Rose's sister (and Lillie's mother), whose own life has taken a more conventional route and to whom Rose wants Lillie to direct the happy news of her imminent marriage; and finally the readers, whose responses may have been foreshadowed or forestalled by the range of reactions to Rose already embedded within the story.[49] Thus, although "Goodbye and Good Luck" is most directly about Rose and the vicissitudes of her on-again, off-again relationship with Vlashkin, this story is refracted through the relationship Rose has with the various women in her life: her mother, sister, and niece. It is Lillie who has pride of place within these potential respondents to Rose's story: Lillie not only hears Rose out but also—despite the evident mixed feelings with which she listens to Rose's tale, and in contrast with Rose, who resists publicizing her story beyond the family—writes it down.

The conception of literary transmission as structured along the lines of an aunt-niece relationship is a notion borrowed and transgendered from the writings of the Russian Formalist Viktor Shklovskii. Revising an earlier model of literary dynamics that connected literary generations through patterns of filial mimicry or rebellion, Shklovskii posits that "the legacy that is passed on from one literary generation to the next moves not from father to son but from uncle to nephew."[50] That is, authors acquire literary techniques not (or not only) from their literary "fathers," or canonized precursors, but also from their literary "uncles," writers marginal to the literary mainstream in their own time and who had no immediate descendants but who nevertheless belatedly supply new options for younger writers in search of alternatives to the dominant techniques inherited from a previous generation. By such intergenerational recovery, literary techniques may shift from the margins to the center of a literary system, even encouraging reassessments of literary history. In Shklovskii's model (also called "the knight's move," for its oblique lines), writers are not limited to being feeble epigones or strong rebels; they may also be enterprising nephews who seek to expand their literary inheritance beyond the father-son binary, discovering forgotten uncles at the far end of the family table who had no immediate heirs and actively forging rather than merely passively inheriting family relations in adopting these older writers as precursors.

The notion against which Shklovskii was arguing, that literary transmission is a kind of patriarchal family struggle in which the battles take place within the nuclear family, is most closely associated, on the American scene, with Harold Bloom, who mobilizes Nietzsche and Freud to construct a model whereby young poets, laboring under "the anxiety of influence," overthrow the strong poets of previous generations—generally through a creative misreading of their work—in a necessary Oedipal assertion of their own strength.[51] Feminist critiques and revisions of both Formalist and Bloomian models of literary transmission have pointed out that both models exclude women from the one arena in which even patriarchal culture has normally allowed them a place—the family. Feminist recognition of the role of gender in the literary family dynamics has had dramatic effects on how literary inheritance, transmission, and canonization are conceived. While young male poets, as Bloom assumes, may indeed feel the crushing weight of strong precursors, women writers contend with a nearly opposite set of conflicts. As Sandra Gilbert and Susan Gubar argue, women writers struggle less with the power of strong fathers than with the absence of strong mothers, that is, with the lack of female precursors or cultural warrant for female authorship.[52] Against Bloom's anxiety of influence, Gilbert and Gubar posit an "anxiety of authorship," with nearly opposite results: where male writers need to cut their precursors to size, women writers need first of all to find these precursors, recovering, appropriating, constructing, or inventing a literary matrilineage rather than either adopting or overthrowing a paternal inheritance.

Gilbert and Gubar's revisions of traditional theories of literary transmission are addressed most directly to Bloom; but their insights about the necessity for women writers of constructing a matrilineage rather than contending with the paternal line has some interesting overlaps with Shklovskii's uncle-nephew model: both theories suggest that precursors may be discovered rather than merely inherited, and Gilbert and Gubar's argument that less powerful women writers are resurrected by women writers in search of precursors can easily be reformulated as precisely the shift from the margins to the center of a literary system that Shklovskii considers so fruitful a process for literary development. While Bloom's model relies on the notion of powerful precursors, and thus lends itself to mapping onto patriarchal cultural systems, Shklovskii's uncle-nephew model embraces the generative value of marginal, underrated, and neglected precursors and thus is more easily transgendered to account for aunts and nieces as well as uncles and nephews, as Chana Kronfeld has advocated.[53] As a theoretical tool that extends the bourgeois boundaries of nuclear family, the uncle-nephew/aunt-niece model allows for a more culturally specific and historically contextualized analysis of the metaphorical (but not only metaphorical) family models that underlie theories of literary transmission. That is, the uncle-nephew model expands the notion of what might constitute literary family and inheritance by recognizing the existence and productivity of other kinship models beyond the (historically contingent) nuclear one. Finally, the uncle-nephew/aunt-niece model has the benefit of providing a more precise and flexible notion of what constitutes literary influence, a point that Michael Baxandall has made in relation to his own field of art criticism:

> "Influence" is a curse of art criticism because of its wrong-headed grammatical prejudice about who is the agent and who the patient: it seems to reverse the active/passive relation. . . . If one says that X influences Y it does seem that one is saying that X did something to Y rather than that Y did something to X. . . . If we think of Y rather than X as the agent, the vocabulary is much richer and more attractively diversified: draw on, resort to, avail oneself of, appropriate from, have recourse to, adapt, misunderstand, refer to, pick up, take on, engage with, react to, quote, differentiate oneself

from, assimilate oneself to, assimilate, align oneself with, copy, address, paraphrase, absorb, make a variation on, revive, continue, remodel, ape, emulate, travesty, parody, absorb, extract from, distort, attend to, resist, simplify, reconstitute, elaborate on, develop, face up to, master, subvert, perpetuate, reduce, promote, respond to, transform, tackle . . . —everyone will be able to think of others.[54]

To translate Baxandall's insight about influence into the metaphor of literary transmission as family inheritance, the aunt-niece model more clearly allows us to see the literary family as a construction, adoption, appropriation, transmutation, and so on, not simply something a writer is born into and has no choice but to accept or reject. Queer theorists have argued for just such an understanding of the family as a social construction, a contingent and conventional invention even in its most "natural" heteronormative configurations; we are just beginning to feel the reverberations of this shift in fields that build entire conceptual frameworks on such family metaphors as origin ("the Founding Fathers"), kinship (Judaism and Christianity as "sister religions"), and inheritance ("the legacy of the Enlightenment"). Within this changing landscape, cousins and in-laws, childless aunts and bachelor uncles, might be particularly "good to think with," denaturalizing the family "from within" in reconfiguring lineage as consent rather than descent. As Eve Kosofsky Sedgwick writes,

> Because aunts and uncles (in either narrow or extended meanings) are adults whose intimate access to children needn't depend on their own pairing or procreation, it's very common, of course, for some of them to have the office of representing nonconforming or nonreproductive sexualities to children. . . . It might therefore follow that a family system understood to include an avuncular function might also have a less hypostatized view of what and therefore how a child can desire.[55]

For Kadya Molodowsky in *Women Songs*, it is a childless agunah in the poetic speaker's family—who may well be an aunt—who "has the office" of bitterly complaining against women's treatment by patriarchal law and representing an imagined community of ancestors beyond the strict patriline.[56] The aunt-niece relation functions as a middle position in these literary and critical discourses, splitting the difference between biological and marital or constructed dimensions of family and thus providing a constructed or even queer kinship line within the natural family. The avuncular line, as neither entirely inside nor outside the psychological positions and legal rules governing parent-child relations, opens possibilities for how we might imagine the movement from one generation to the next—or from the present generation to the past it remembers, adopts, and invents.

Such an aunt-niece relation may stand, in fact, at the (constructed) origin of Jewish women's literary history, if we consider the memoir of Glikl of Hameln (1646–1724), the first autobiographical text we possess that was authored by a Jewish woman, to represent such an origin. (This origin is constructed not least because Glikl mentions another such autobiography, one that has been lost to history.) The memoir found its initial audience in German translation, after circulating among Glikl's direct descendants for about two centuries, through the agency of the Jewish feminist activist and translator Bertha Pappenheim, who, as a descendant of Glikl's sister, was thus a niece at some remove.[57] In this case the aunt-niece relationship describes not only the family relationship between the memoirist and her translator but also the "swerve" that connects the private circulation of what Glikl intended as a kind of family history and ethical will and the publication and reception of this document as a major resource for early modern Jewish and women's history. The "knight's move" might also describe Pappenheim's own translational shift between Yiddish, or Judeo-German, and modern German, a shift echoed as well in the indirect connection between the pious instruction that constitutes an ethical will and the document of female empowerment that Glikl's memoir becomes in the feminist appropriation and recovery for which Pappenheim provided the initial impetus. To rephrase this relation with Baxandall's tools, Pappenheim not only promotes and copies Glikl's work; she also adopts and transforms it, establishing the legacy that she "inherits."

"Goodbye and Good Luck," as a story told by an aunt to a niece and a story told by a niece about an aunt, also involves a diagonal kinship between speaker and listener that functions as the channel through which Rose's narrative legacy is transmitted. Paley's unique literary idiom might be described as similarly diagonal, representing a creative swerve between Yiddish and English, the linguistic interference of Rose's native Yiddish in her English conversational style, and in the innovative English prose idiom that is the hallmark—beyond "Goodbye and Good Luck"—of Paley's oeuvre. Another indirect line connects Rose's sexual experiences, on the margins of conventional, petit-bourgeois Jewish immigrant culture, with those of her niece, as a member of a younger generation of Jewish Americans who, in rebelling against the constraints inherited more directly from their parents, created a new set of sexual norms within American culture writ large. It is Paley's insight that what appeared to cultural observers as a radically new form of sexual expression might have indirect roots—whether remembered or imagined—at the margins of their parents' Jewish cultural context. As a young writer, Paley discovers, mobilizes, re-creates, and celebrates the marginalized experience and distinctive idiom of a childless Jewish aunt, finding within this experience and voice an alternative not only to the speech patterns of a more acculturated generation of American Jews but also to the cultural legacy of nuclear family and bourgeois marriage offered by Lily's mother and grandmother.

If the aunt-niece model allows us to read the interplay between innovation and inheritance in Paley's fiction, "Goodbye and Good Luck" also functions as a potential intervention in the theoretical understanding of the aunt-niece model. With Rose and Lillie at hand, we might also ask what an aunt-niece relationship looks like in the flesh, as it were, rather than view the aunt and niece as purely structural kinship terms, ready to be filled by any marginalized precursor and the literary descendant who remembers her. The relationship between aunts and nieces, for all this specificity—and Rose is nothing if not specific—also takes shape within a history of the family, subject to shifting cultural modes and norms and in dialectical tension with those norms that shape the more widely acknowledged, valued, and studied relations between parents and children. The psychoanalytic focus on the apparently universal dynamics of the family has tended to obscure its intricate connection to such processes as nuclearization, *embourgeoisement*, urbanization (or suburbanization), and, for Jews, Europeanization, integration, and Americanization. Freud's focus on the charged triangle of the mother, father, and child, so instrumental in naturalizing the construction of the modern family, was thus also a *product* of the formative processes that produced the Central European Jewish family. It is telling, for instance, that by the nineteenth century, the biblical commandment of Levirate marriage, in which the brother of a childless man is required to marry his widow if he dies, to "redeem his name," was made legally akin to incest in places like Germany and Austria.[58]

The immigrant and post-immigrant experience that was the context for the emergence of the Jewish American Renaissance was, like Freud's Vienna, a site for the ideological constitution of the Jewish family *as an ideal* along middle-class nuclear family lines, as well as for a sustained critique of the attendant conventions and oppressions of this configuration. Nevertheless, Freud's own family situation belied the neat structure of the nuclear family, which perhaps never entirely matched the cultural realities of family life, for Jews or for anyone: the family in which Freud was raised included half siblings from his father's earlier marriage, governesses who may sometimes have been more than that, and an uncle who exerted considerable and lasting influence for both good and ill.[59] Nor were such complications excluded in the family Freud built with Martha: the Freud household also included Martha's never-married, childless sister, Minna Bernays, who has long been rumored to have shared Freud's bed as well as his house and who often looked after the children in their mother's absence. The diagonal option Minna presented to Freud's children was not only the refusal of the marital and reproductive imperatives (an option taken up by Anna Freud, who was in so many other ways her father's daughter) but also the maintenance of Jewish practice in an otherwise adamantly secular environment—Minna was the only one in the family who refused to be cremated.[60]

The remarkable configuration of the Freud family, in which aunts as well as parents represent cultural options to the children they jointly raise, and where traditional practices are maintained in concealed form alongside more secular ideologies, may stand in for the larger structure of Jewish modernity. Jewish modernization and *embourgeoisement*, so closely tied to the rationalization and "normalization" of the Jewish family, are enlarged, haunted, and challenged by a variety of "supplements." Religion itself might be understood as just such a supplement, persisting even as it is pushed to the corners of modern Jewish life. God, even in traditional Jewish cultural formations, might indeed be more like a bachelor uncle than the father to whom he is more frequently likened. Kadya Molodovsky (sometimes spelled Molodowsky), in a 1940 poem recounting the place of religion in her family life, describes the God of her childhood as just such a great uncle: "My God, like a beloved great-uncle / you lived in every corner of our house."[61] The image of God as a great-uncle mobilizes a range of religious and family associations: God is everywhere in the traditional Eastern European Jewish home, but his power and presence are avuncular rather than paternal or patriarchal. He resides in the corners, taken for granted, domesticated, humble, and perhaps increasingly unwelcome as the Jewish family is reduced, nuclearized, and modernized.

Where psychoanalysis has often been silent on the nature of relations beyond the parent-child connection, literature and folklore have persisted in
recognizing the power of these family ties, praising God as a beloved great-
uncle, detecting danger in the presence of Gertrude's brother-in-law or Sigmund's sister-in-law, imagining a queer "ancestor" in an old-maid aunt or a
chain of "prior" Prior Walters, or bringing back long-dead great-grandparents
to affirm the legitimacy of a young person's romantic choice. The Bible already knows this game, tucking one sister rather than the other into Jacob's
bed and discovering, in the geometry of Levirate marriage, a way to salvage an
endangered paternal line by the strategic substitution of a compliant uncle for
the not-quite-father. Deuteronomy 25:5–6 proclaims that when a man dies
childless, his brother must marry the widow, with their firstborn son taking
his deceased uncle's name so as not to "blot out his name from Israel." The
slippery terminology involved in describing this arrangement—who is the
uncle, and who the father?—might enlarge our understanding of Shklovskii:
Even in the rigid confines of biblical law, the role of uncle and father may be
interchangeable, shifting according to the deployment of different fictions.
The nephew may be a biological son, while the uncle may be, from one perspective, the father, while the father is actually an uncle. If not genetics but
the impulse to refrain from blotting out a father's name determines biblical
lineage at crucial moments, the line between biological ancestry and legal fiction is not so distinct. With kinship and fictionality so closely connected, it is
no surprise that literature may function as a writ of legal adoption. From this
perspective, "Goodbye and Good Luck" is the felicitous female expression
of an ancient impulse, keeping a family name alive with the help of blood-
lines and the freedom of the imagination: "Goodbye and Good Luck" fulfills
Paley's/Lillie's biblical obligation not to blot out the name of her childless
aunt. Rose's concluding refrain to Lillie, "tell this story to your mama . . . tell
her . . . tell her from Aunt Rose," echoes the biblical compulsion of transmitting the Jewish story from "generation to generation"; here, though, the command to tell it to your children is turned on its head: Lillie is enjoined to tell
Rose's story to her sister, Lillie's mother, even as the story moves outward to
larger circles of readers—relatives, descendants, or otherwise.

As Baxandall reminds us, to speak of the influence of an earlier rather
than a later artist is to get this relationship backward, failing to see the
agency of the ostensibly influenced artist in choosing, shaping, and otherwise engaging with the work of the precursor. This insight should warn us

against the temptation to read in Rose's speech patterns, and in Lillie's or Paley's, "transcription" of them, the deforming effects of Russian and Yiddish on proper English. The unconventional idiom of "Goodbye and Good Luck" should rather be read as a stylized mobilization, by a literary niece with her own literary agenda, of the less deliberately unconventional idiom of an earlier generation. Paley's style certainly registers as inflected by Yiddish (and perhaps also Russian), a reading invited by evidence that Rose is a native Yiddish speaker. Rose makes English grammatical mistakes presumably typical of her generation of immigrants, saying, of her earlier years, that "I wasn't no thinner then, only more stationary in the flesh" and speaking of her "independence"—by which Rose means the paper flowers by which she makes a living—as "blooming, but it didn't have no roots."[62] In "recording" such immigrant speech, Paley is practicing a form of dialect writing, a literary practice with deep roots in American letters, which found many practitioners among Jewish writers who were immigrants or children of immigrants. As Hana Wirth-Nesher writes, "In works by authors such as Abraham Cahan, Mary Antin, Anzia Yezierska, and Henry Roth, the writer would often weave Yiddish or Hebrew words into the novel accompanied by a variety of strategies for translating the phrases into English for American readers."[63] Writers of the immigrant generation faced the difficulty of rendering in English different varieties of speech—Yiddish, Russian or other foreign languages, and Yiddish-inflected English; the strategies by which this speech was rendered into English ranged from Rosten's low-register comic "Yinglish" to Henry Roth's significantly more artful use of broad dialect writing for the street English of immigrant children and a lyrical and high register to "translate" the Yiddish of David's mother.[64]

Paley, writing a generation later, was less compelled to forge an English literary style from immigrant English; in this sense, her entry into the American literary arena with a voice that signaled an already fading cultural idiom was a choice, the conscious adoption of an older style for new purposes. Indeed, Rose's Russian or Yiddish-inflected idiom registers not as a retrograde, "ethnic," and obsolete deformation of English but as an energizing of English, with turns of phrase that strike the reader less as a greenhorn's mistakes or as Russian or Yiddish calques than as provocative, novel, and fresh turns of the English language.

That linguistic and cultural codes, literary and sexual convention, grammar and gender are intricately connected is the general insight about language and culture I have been exploring in this book; in "Goodbye and Good Luck," these spheres are brought into particularly intricate conversation. The speech strata represented in Rose's monologue—the curses her mother hurls at her as she leaves, the romantic clichés of the popular Yiddish stage, the sexual "girl talk" Rose tries to share with Lillie, the fusty euphemisms with which she describes her erotic longings—are hardly separable from the sexual mores they express, reflect, and embody; the formal circumlocutions by which Rose describes her relationship with Vlashkin (her "outstanding friend") bear a family resemblance to the bulwarks of ladies' undergarments of the period—preventing easy access to naked flesh and bare reality. Rose, navigating among the sexual and discursive possibilities of home life, the work world, and the Yiddish theater, undergoes a kind of transformation that is both literary and sexual: When Rose explains why she is leaving her family, she combines a straightforward explanation with a romantic cliché: "'This is a different way of living, Mama,' I said. 'Besides, I am driven by love.'" Preceding the grand statement of love with the casual "besides" has the effect of rendering Rose's words as a visible quotation. Literature, and perhaps the performing arts above all, served the acculturating Jewish masses as a sentimental education, providing models of romantic love and bourgeois gender roles. That these stand in potential conflict with more indigenous attitudes toward sexuality is evident from Rose's mother's angry response, with its drastic drop in register: "You! You, a nothing, a rotten hole in a piece of cheese, are you telling me what is life?" In this drop, Paley's story echoes Peretz's "Monish," which similarly shifts in register from "my love, my life," to such foodstuffs as licorice pretzels and goose schmaltz.

That what is at stake in these romantic choices involves both sex and literature is made explicit throughout the story, in Rose's curious and illuminating tendency to read and recount her life through the lens of theater, and vice versa. Thus, Rose describes Vlashkin's marriage as a play, in which the wife has a leading role: "Poor woman, she did not know I was on the same stage with her. The poison I was to her role, she did not know." And in describing her imminent marriage, Rose says, "I'll have a husband, which, as everybody knows, a woman should have at least one before the end of the story."[65] While Rose chooses what might appear as an unconventional life, she makes it clear that this choice is of a different set of conventions, those of high romance against the more pragmatic realism that imbues domestic life. Rose's resistance to a scheme that would privilege life over art, her juxtaposition of the conventions that govern the culture in which she was raised and those of the one to which she aspires, have an ironic, self-deflationary effect. To hope for at least one husband before the end of the story is both to submit to cultural convention and to denaturalize it by recognizing its conventionality. The message of this short story, that resisting traditional role models may yield conventional connubial happiness, veers from both traditional and antitraditional models of sexual morality, since Rose, a home wrecker, nonetheless desires and finally achieves the usual prize of a husband and home. Rather than champion Rose's rebellion, or watch her pay the usual price for popularity "in certain circles," "Goodbye and Good Luck" has the most traditional of happy endings, with Rose achieving—in a final twist—the perfect bourgeois dream.

"Goodbye and Good Luck" thus presents a range of sexual (as well as literary) models available for appropriation by a younger generation, beyond the obedience and rebellion explored in other Jewish works from the nineteenth century onward. The older members of the cast of characters that populates the story include not only conformist parents, insistent on seeing their children shepherded to the marriage they both champion and disparage, but also the aunt who has taken a different path, by which she redeems and disowns the sad marriages of her mother and sister. Rose suggests that Lillie, like her aunt, has had some sexual experience ("Nowadays, Lillie, I suppose it is easier," she says to her niece), but she also assumes that Lillie will follow in her mother's footsteps ("honey, you will no doubt love and marry one man and have a couple kids and be happy forever till you die tired"), and the implication is that she hopes to show Lillie that other choices are there for the taking.[66] Nevertheless, Rose's rebellion is of an earlier time, shrouded in euphemism, dated sentiment, and the bohemian gestures of the Yiddish stage. For the younger generation, sexuality—like the new styles of underwear—is more accessible, less stylized, freer of grand sentiment; we can recognize this world in Lillie's reaction to Rose's story and in the larger atmosphere in which Paley found her literary voice. But Rose's world is not simply a period piece: her story, in presenting both the Yiddish theater and bourgeois marriage as varieties of performance, and in its embrace of both romantic rebellion and the happy ending of marriage, serves to call into question the assumptions of the sexual revolution on the horizon, which sometimes failed to see the ways that rebellion could slide into conformity and sentimentality and that sentiment and conformity could nevertheless provide comfort and victory. If conformity and rebellion are the two options for a son or daughter, Rose provides a third option for her niece and Paley's readers, one that cheerfully draws from both.

While "Goodbye and Good Luck" is her fullest expression of the powerful potential of the aunt-niece dynamic, Paley wrote and spoke about this form of family and literary kinship in a number of other stories, essays, and interviews. The title of the story "In This Country, but in Another Language, My Aunt Refuses to Marry the Men Everyone Wants Her To," published in 1985, remembers both a marginalized figure of the previous generation and a now-forgotten vernacular, bringing them into English and into a new generation for whom such female empowerment has become a central rallying point. In interviews, Paley has suggested that the stories she heard from her aunts, above all others, taught her to be "a story hearer," the necessary prelude to becoming a storyteller: "My father talked an awful lot, when he had time, and my aunts told stories. Mostly people, as they get older, begin to defend their lives in some way. They say, I did this and this and this and why I did it. My aunt especially lived in constant defense of her life."[67] Why Paley's aunt might have felt she needed to defend herself is made clearer in a later interview: "it seemed that my aunt was very much hurt by coming to this country." Paley continues:

> She was hurt in the sense that although we did live in an extended family that was not really considered good once you came to the United States. You are supposed to just be a mommy and daddy. I don't think she thought of it that way. But that idea, which was socially there, made her feel a little bit as though she didn't belong here or there. . . . She never married and that also was considered pretty bad and also somehow her fault. Well it was her fault, she didn't like anyone. She just liked my father. And so the idea that she should really be somewhere else made her very angry. . . . I think one of the first stories I wrote was "Goodbye and Good Luck." It's not about her, it's really not. But it's about her. It's about me thinking about her, a little bit about her stubbornness and so forth.[68]

"Other Mothers," which appeared in a special issue on motherhood in *Feminist Studies* in 1978, presents the aunt not, as in "Goodbye and Good Luck," as a foil for the mother but as part of a constellation of mothers, described in kaleidoscopic, impressionistic fashion: an American-born, a Russian-born, and a Polish-born mother, "granddaughter of a fair-haired hooligan"; a "first mother" and "second mother," who discuss the effectiveness for "family planning" of pajamas versus nightgowns; a grandmother who "speaks not a word of English"; and a trio of "sister-aunts." The world of Paley's story, of a 1950s Bronx childhood, is indeed populated almost entirely by mothers: "The men are inside. The men are sleeping, are talking shop. They have gone to see if Trotsky is still sitting on a bench in Crotona Park. The street is full of mothers." Among these "mothers" is an aunt, "the one who was mocked for not having married, whose beauty, as far as the family was concerned, was useless, because no husband ever used it."[69] This aunt, whom her niece, the first-person narrator, calls "the sister-mother," gives her niece a piece of advice in the longest conversation addressed to a child in the story:

> Darling, she said, I know you want to go to the May Day parade with your friends, but you know what? Don't carry the flag. I want you to go. I didn't say don't go. But don't carry the flag. The one who carries the flag is sometimes killed. The police go crazy when they see that flag.
> I *had* dreamed of going forth with a flag, the American flag on July 4, the red flag of the workers on May Day. How did the aunt know this? Because I know you inside out, she said, since you were born. Aren't you *my* child, too?[70]

The mother's sister is thus a kind of partner in parenting, but a particularly fluid and flexible one: the aunt is "on the worried mother's side," identifying with her sister in her concern for the child they share; but her identification is also with her niece, knowing without being told that she wants to carry the flag (any flag!), and wanting her niece to go to the parade—as if in her place—even as she worries for her safety.

Paley's literary blurring of the ostensibly clear boundaries between mothers and all others is a paean to the pleasures of group parenting, a recognition of other configurations than the Oedipal triangle. But her description of this motherhood beyond the nuclear family also functions as a protest against a male-dominated literary canon, where the singled-out mother is routinely mocked by "her son the novelist": "What use was my accumulating affection" for these mothers, the narrator laments, "when the brains of the opposition included her son the doctor and her son the novelist?"[71] In this sense, Paley's celebration of mothers, her defense of (Jewish?) mothers against the denigrations of novelist and doctor sons, and her recognition of a variety of modes of motherhood beyond the biological uncover new axes for what Gilbert and Gubar call the "secret sisterhood" of women writers, who ease the woman writer's isolation and provide support for her enterprise.[72] The sister-mother, or mother-aunt, is just such a "secret sister," equally committed to the daughter-niece's survival and to her rebellion— even if she prefers that the dangerous job of carrying the flag is delegated elsewhere. Describing her participation in the budding feminist movement, Paley writes:

> I had been reading the current fiction, fifties fiction, a masculine fiction. . . . As a grown-up woman, I had no choice. Everyday life, kitchen life, children life had been handed to me, my portion. . . . Every woman writing in these years has had to swim in that feminist wave. No matter what she thinks of it, even if she swims against it, she has been supported by it—the buoyancy, the noise, the saltiness.[73]

That Paley was part of a revolution seems impossible to deny, even if—as she writes—she was hardly aware that it was happening. Nevertheless, this revolution was, from the very outset, already declaring itself as something different from the Oedipal struggles outlined by Freud and Bloom. As the narrator of "Other Mothers" learns, she is not the first in her family to want to carry the flag in the May Day parade or, as Lillie comes to see, who is "driven by love." Nor does the story of Paley's legacy, of the flag she carried in American letters, end with her own work. Aside from her readily visible role as a strong precursor for a generation of women writers, we might also add the more diagonal inheritance Paley bequeathed as an experimenter with English style. This inheritance is perhaps most apparent in such Jewish American master stylists as Jonathan Safran Foer and Gary Shteyngart, but it may be heard as well beyond the circle of Jewish American writers. The act of writing, for Paley as for these other writers, begins not with the overthrow of the dictatorial father but with an act of creative discovery and literary adoption, letting the mother-aunts and secret sisters tell their stories through hers and letting them find, in the niece's words, their most powerful echo.

Freud, of course, was interested in group as well as individual psychology, and ancient Israelites if not modern Jews were a privileged collective subject of psychoanalytic inquiry; nevertheless, the particular configurations of Jewish extended family have generally remained unexamined either in psychoanalysis or queer studies.[74] Freud's analysis of the relations between son-in-law and mother-in-law in *Totem and Taboo* is psychosexual rather than structural, weaving the dynamics of in-law relationships back into the nuclear family rather than allowing his focus to expand beyond the reduced family.[75] The focus on the psychosexual individual, sexual couple, and nuclear family in both psychoanalysis and queer studies has left the analysis of broader and more complex Jewish kinship structures and social configurations to playwrights and short-story writers. It is An-sky, who "analyzes" a spirit possession by unearthing the relationship between the father of the possessed girl and the father of the boy who is possessing her, who might count as the theorist of Jewish family systems, just as it is Grace Paley and Saul Bellow who expand the possibilities of inheritance and maturation to include the influence of aunts as well as mothers and fathers, cousins as well as lovers and friends. Modern Jewish narrative, so dedicated at its outset to expelling the intrusive families that stood in the way of modern romance, finally became a stage on which these cousins and aunts could crowd and on which their voices could resound.

CHAPTER SIX

Sex and Segregation

> The characters in my novels are my unrealized possibilities. That is
> why I am equally fond of them all and equally horrified by them.
> Each of them has crossed a border that I myself have circumvented.
> It is that crossed border (the border beyond which my own "I" ends)
> which attracts me most. For beyond that border begins the secret the
> novel asks about. The novel is not the author's confession; it is an in-
> vestigation of human life in the trap the world has become.
>
> —Milan Kundera, *The Unbearable Lightness of Being*
>
> Women are requested to walk on the opposite sidewalk.
>
> —"Modesty" sign in Beit Shemesh, Jerusalem (2011)

Tearing Down the Wall

In explaining in his autobiography why his firstborn child was born three
years after the wedding, Salomon Maimon delicately acknowledges that his
marriage long remained unconsummated. This circumstance, however private and individual it might seem, owed everything, in Maimon's estimation, to the social conditions in which he was raised:

> In my fourteenth year my eldest son, David, was born to me. At my mar-
> riage I was only eleven years old, and owing to the retired life common
> among people of our nation in those regions, as well as the lack of social
> contact between the sexes, I had no idea of the essential duties of marriage,
> but looked on a pretty girl as on any other work of nature or art. It was
> therefore natural that for a considerable time after marriage I would have
> no thought about its consummation. I used to approach my wife with trem-
> bling as an object of mystery.[1]

Among the reasons for his sexual ignorance at marriage, according to
Maimon, were the striking fact of his youth (which one might have pre-

sumed sufficient in itself as explanation), "the retired life common among people of our nation in those regions," and "the lack of social contact between the sexes." Indeed, the strict separation of boys and girls and the lack of opportunities for social mingling were visible and distinguishing features of traditional society, especially in the learned circles from which Jewish writers tended to emerge. Sexual segregation was not merely a by-product of the commitment to Torah study for Jewish men and the exclusion of women from such practices; rather, sexual segregation is intrinsic to the ideology and social organization of the traditional Jewish elite. Tova Cohen describes the primary rationale for the ramified set of strictures that constitute sexual segregation as the need to guard against (male) sexual thoughts:

> The root of the extreme sexual segregation that characterized traditional Jewish society was the halakhic concept of "modesty," and its aim was to provide a fence around any situation that could lead a man to have sexual thoughts about a woman. This conception found its expression in such legal rulings as "a man must never do anything that will lead him to thoughts about women" (*Sefer ha-hinukh*, commandment 168), or "A man must distance himself greatly from women" (*Arba turim*, Even ha-ezer 21). In order to create this distance from women Jewish law fixed methods of separation between men and women in all gathering places: at prayer, at celebrations, and in education. The principles of sexual segregation were adhered to in different measures at different times, but were certainly characteristic of the circles of *lomdim* in the nineteenth century. In general, traditional life in the small towns of East Europe dictated almost entirely separate lifestyles for boys and girls, from early childhood, and defined separate realms for the two sexes.[2]

As Maimon's diagnosis of his marital impotence makes clear, there was a price to be paid for such extreme segregation: separating boys and girls left no room for the acquaintance that might lead to mutual understanding and normal sexual relationships; a strictly sexually segregated society produced marriages between strangers, not only in the sense that each spouse was an unknown quantity to the other but also in that his or her entire sex and the facts about sex, more generally, were shrouded in mystery. As Shaul Stampfer writes, until the shift to modernity

> men and women occupied adjacent but different cultural worlds in eastern Europe. In the early nineteenth century, for example, there were no opportunities in eastern Europe for mixed social activities involving married

men and women. There were no evenings of dancing or eating in restaurants which, in some societies, enable men and women to be together casually. Jews ran taverns but did not frequent them. Enjoying food and drink was permissible, of course, but within a meal in honour of a holiday, or at a religious event such as a wedding or circumcision. At these events there was a great deal of social supervision.[3]

Sexual segregation organized traditional Jewish life for young people from elite circles before marriage, but even engagement did not much change matters. In writing about his wedding in 1865, at the relatively mature age of eighteen, Yehezkel Kotik describes his keen desire to see and speak with his bride-to-be but relates that his father, a strict Hasid, allowed the betrothed couple no opportunity to meet. While others (including other men) were permitted a glimpse of the bride, such attempts were specifically ruled out for him:

> Upon her arrival in the town, the entire family, young and old, rushed to see her, with the exception of myself. In fact, everyone, the whole town, young and old, rushed to see the bride, and they all happily told me what a beauty she was . . . ; not a pockmark was visible on her face . . . but I, on the other hand, was full of anger at not being allowed to get so much as a glimpse of her. . . . Early the next morning, before the women gathered there, I managed to see her. She was, indeed, beautiful. Although I felt embarrassed, I nevertheless plucked up enough courage to wish her mazel tov and ask her how she was feeling. I wanted to sit down and keep looking at her beautiful face but [my friend] Aryeh-Leyb pulled me away by the hand, saying "Come, it is forbidden to visit with the bride now."[4]

Marriage itself did not spell an end to the traditional rules that forbade mingling between men and women, and even—in public spaces—between a husband and wife. Pauline Wengeroff, who pays close attention in her memoir to the initial cracks in the walls that separated women and men, relates that among the first signs of modernity in her life was the choice made by her sister Eva (the same one who had been the last to be engaged in the old fashion) and brother-in-law sometime in 1848 or 1849 to walk through town together on a Sabbath afternoon, when, traditionally, "the men, of course, were completely separated from the women. As the Bible says, 'if you go right, I go left.' God knows how many centuries this custom had held among the Jews!" Her father, seeing the "scandalous, revolutionary deed" of the two "sinners" on the street outside his house, rapped on the window and called to Pauline's sister: "You return at once! Your husband can go by himself! For Jewish women, and certainly for my daughter, it is unseemly to walk next to one another, and in broad daylight, yet!"[5]

The maskilic critique of sexual segregation went far beyond Maimon's description of its deleterious effects on marital sex. In a remarkable reversal of the traditional assumption that the intermingling of the sexes leads to forbidden sexual thoughts if not actions, maskilim argued that it was precisely the separation of men and women that encourages sexual immorality; traditional society, in their view, was not guarding against sexual transgression but promoting it in its zeal to separate men and women. Drawing on new bourgeois notions of masculine and feminine nature, maskilim argued that a segregated society corrupted men by keeping them away from the "civilizing influence" of women and impeded the development of women's natural modesty when it stopped them from socializing with men. Commenting approvingly on the new salon society emerging in late eighteenth-century Berlin, Isaac Euchel noted that "precisely the crossing of traditional sexual boundaries" was the best means of educating both young men and women in morals and proper behavior: "Whenever one treats a woman with respect the roots of modesty in her heart are raised and she will be very afraid of lowering herself by listening to coarse talk and desire. And so it is good for a man to spend time in his youth in the company of such modest women as these, who become a powerful fortress for his tongue and lips against speaking coarse words."[6] The norms of salon society, along with the edifying company of members of the opposite sex, produced both courteous men and modest women.

The role women play in reinforcing the rules of polite speech among men came up again in an epistolary exchange between Moshe Leib Lilienblum and Miriam Markel-Mozessohn, who accused Lilienblum of speaking too coarsely in his autobiographical writing; Lilienblum took recourse in the fact that he wrote in Hebrew, defending himself by reminding her that she was the only woman who could read such books, so there was no need for him to "to watch my speech and my writing in the holy tongue (which is not foreign to such expressions, in the spirit of antiquity)."[7] Genteel mixed company was the necessary condition for the new bourgeois norms of social and discursive modesty, and in the absence of female readers, Lilienblum considered himself free to speak with the sexual frankness he considered (contra Maimonides) native to classical Hebrew sources.

The traditional segregation of men and women, in its sexual dimension, was not directed equally at men and women, since it was clearly designed to control male sexual thoughts; the fact that traditional synagogue architecture shields women from the male gaze, while keeping men in full view of women, is sufficient testimony to this asymmetry. Modernizers also tended to focus on the effects of sexual segregation on men, even when they understood these differently than traditionalists: Maimon and Euchel directed their attention largely to the price paid by men kept from social interactions with girls and women, slighting these effects on women.

But the barriers separating men and women had other functions beyond the sexual, and many of these had far greater ramifications for Jewish women's lives. Sexual segregation worked not only negatively, to stop sexual mixing, but also "constructively" and differentially to distinguish masculine and feminine spheres, investing masculine ones with special value while relegating feminine activities to the margins; sexual segregation was a system that worked to grant intellectual and religious status to men by keeping women from participating in valued activities. In this sense, women suffered, and men benefited, from segregating the sexes. Discussing the role that educational segregation played in constructing this gender hierarchy, Iris Parush writes that traditional education "took upon itself the task of upholding the patriarchal gender hierarchy." While in the world of practical affairs, women worked in such public spaces as the shop and marketplace,

> the educational system re-established the uncontested superiority of the men by shifting the gender axis of public and private from matters of economy and income to the realms that were, by its lights, truly important: Torah study and the spiritual life. In these realms, traditional Jewish society kept women confined to the private sphere of their homes or to the margins of the synagogue's public space—to the women's section, namely to the *Ezrat Nashim*. Men, by contrast, were positioned in the public sphere—in the *heder*, at the yeshiva, in the study rooms and the main halls of the synagogue.[8]

Sexual segregation thus had linguistic and epistemological as well as sexual ramifications, barring women from accruing cultural capital, limiting their access to the most esteemed Jewish sources, and redistributing sociocultural value from the economic to the intellectual spheres. In Haskalah writing, it was Yehudah Leib Gordon, in *The Tip of the Yud*, who concerned himself most directly with the exclusion of women from the world of Hebrew and Jewish learning, taking full measure of sexual segregation as it shaped female rather than male lives. In a bitter twist, Gordon writes that the exclusion of women from Torah study might actually work in their favor, not because women are left free to read secular literature (in Parush's sense of "the benefits of marginality) but because women who cannot read rabbinic texts are thereby shielded from rabbinic misogyny.[9] Quoting and exaggerating the venom of these passages, Gordon writes:

> It is a good thing you do not know your fathers' language,
> That the house of your God is locked in your face,
> For now you cannot hear the blessing of those who scorn you,
> Blessing the One "Who did not make them a woman" every day.[10]

The exclusion of women from "the house of [their] God" is a mercy, in Gordon's view, since what transpires in this house is scorn and mockery against women. That men should speak so coarsely of women in their absence is perhaps predictable, given the maskilic understanding of the role played by the mingling of the sexes in guarding against indelicate speech. Indeed, the sections of the poem that pile the rabbinic quote upon quote still shock with their crudity: Hillel, Bat-Shua's callow and preening future bridegroom, gives a bar mitzvah sermon on the topic of "the cleaving of two uteruses" and demonstrates that he knows that "a woman is acquired in three ways"; his attitude toward the actual woman in his life is evident from his abandonment of Bat-Shua and their children. In contrast to these public discussions of obscure gynecological conditions and to the halakhic means of "acquiring" a woman (through money, a wedding contract, and intercourse) in discourses *about* women spoken only among men, the words that arise behind closed doors between Fabi and Bat-Shua are the "refined," exalted, and mutual "language of the heart, the language of love" (even if they also express, in barely veiled fashion, the language of sexual aggression and war).[11]

For all its focus on the price paid by women for traditional sexual segregation, Gordon's poem also sheds light on the epistemological ramifications of sexual segregation for male writers, who are barred by the walls erected between men and women from ever truly understanding women's experience. In this sense, sexual segregation is not only a social problem (especially for women) but also a literary problem (especially for men): *The Tip of the*

Yud begins with the question of the possibility, for the implied male writer, of gaining entry into the perspectives of Jewish women:

> Hebrew woman, who shall know your life?
> You came in darkness and in darkness you go.
> Your sorrows and joys, your hopes and desires,
> Are born within you, and inside of you they end.
> The earth and its fullness, all good things and pleasures,
> Are reserved for the daughters of other nations,
> But the Hebrew women's life is eternal slavery,
> Never leaving her store to go here or there;
> You will conceive, give birth, nurse, wean,
> Bake and cook and before your time, wither.[12]

Gordon does not hesitate to describe Jewish women's experience as harsh and devoid of pleasure, but this description is necessarily qualified by the speaker's concession that he has no direct access to the internal experiences of the women whose lives he claims to describe. The darkness of Jewish women's lives thus has two irreconcilable meanings: they are dark in the sense of being joyless (although Gordon also writes that the Hebrew woman experiences joy as well as suffering, even if this experience dies within her) and dark in the sense of being unknown, at least to the male writer. That Gordon also apostrophizes the "Hebrew woman," ostensibly speaking directly to her, while writing in a language Jewish women are generally barred from understanding, constitutes this poem as a self-negating performance, a cultural project doomed from the start. The social structures and epistemological effects of sexual segregation pose a challenge to the writing of modern literature, which after all demands the portrayal of full life worlds inhabited by women as well as men and which is exemplified by a discourse that connects men and women. Sexual segregation also in itself evades description, since a single participant in the system will by design be privy to its character in only one of the two distinct realms it creates.

Sexual segregation was particularly challenging for the romantic novelist, who was required to describe both male and female characters and, more particularly, a young female protagonist who meets an unattached young man. Given the structures of the traditional society in which most Haskalah writers were raised, a Jewish writer was likely to really know only a handful of women: his mother, his wife, his mother-in-law, and a sister or two. As Cohen writes, a prospective writer "had very little opportunity to meet unmarried women, the prime subject of literary characterization."[13] S. Y. Abramovitsh laments this very circumstance when he writes that "we never made love to charming young women . . . and never learned how to waltz with young maidens at balls." The handicap posed for Abramovitsh by this absence of romantic opportunity is less personal than literary, since the lack of these experiences made it hard for him to imagine writing a novel: "In short, all the material that could entice a reader—is lacking among us."[14] This may be at least one of the reasons for the long delay of this literature—noticed by Alan Mintz among other literary scholars—to produce realistic representations of Jewish life.[15] The memoirs Parush has collected of nineteenth-century Jewish reading practices demonstrate the distance between the social realities of readers, male and female, and the literature they devoured, openly or in secret. Y. Y. Trunk recalls such a sexually segregated scene in his memoir of growing up in a Hasidic setting:

> The daughters of the Kallischer Rebbetzin . . . were favored with an aristocratic education. Both knew Polish and German, read the works of Schiller and were versed in the great novels. In the home of Rabbi Yehoshuele Kutner—a place where the smell of books broke forth from the dusty cabinets into all the surrounding rooms and merged with the smell of groats that grandmother Priva prepared for meals—the aristocratic daughters would sometimes sit by the windows and read thick Polish and German novels, their eyes streaming tears, sighing at the passionate loves depicted in them. Rising from the courtyard below was the sound of the Talmud in sing-song from the beit midrash students, merging with the joyful clamor of the children of the poor at the municipal "Talmud Torah" school.[16]

This rich and novelistic description (as if the novel were exercising a contagious effect) draws on the image repertoire of fairy tales and, more specifically, images of princesses locked in towers, awaiting rescue by their lovers. But this scene diverges from the genre in describing the more general and collective architecture of sexual segregation, in which young women are separated from their male counterparts, spiritually as well as physically, since their minds are occupied with an entirely different world of images and characters (that Trunk himself was engaging in prodigious efforts of imaginative projection, in this scene as in others, is no doubt also evident). The Talmudic singsong and clamor of the children penetrate the soundscape of these daughters, but their quieter sighs and tears will not be heard below.

What distinguishes the female reading world is romance, which depends on the interaction between women and men—exactly what this physical architecture is designed to preclude.

If Haskalah writers saw sexual segregation as an attempt by traditional forces to suppress the development of healthy relations between men and women, they nevertheless maintained, in altered form, many of the strictures and structures of sexual segregation, especially those that excluded women from "male" texts and intellectual pursuits. This exclusion, as Shmuel Feiner writes, inhered in the ideology of the movement:

> From its inception until almost its final years, the Haskalah was virtually an exclusively male movement. Those who launched the Enlightenment revolution of the eighteenth century were young men in their twenties and thirties who never imagined the possibility of women being in their ranks. . . . The stereotypical character of women as driven by emotion and desire, as opposed to the man who was guided by reason, did not allow him to see her as a candidate for joining the "covenant of the enlightened ones."[17]

The persistent power of cultural and intellectual sexual segregation to invest male spheres with status survived the Haskalah and continued to shape the reception of women writers in later generations of Jewish literature. Perhaps it is not surprising that Dvora Baron, the foremost Hebrew woman writer of the modernist period (she was a Yiddish writer as well), set a number of her short stories within the sexually charged architecture of the synagogue/study hall. Baron acquired the linguistic tools to become a Hebrew writer by participating as a young girl in the classes that her rabbi-father taught the boys of the town as she sat enclosed in the women's section. Baron never directly describes these exclusions and transgressions in her fiction, but she nonetheless often revisited the segregated spaces of traditional Jewish life, and their continuing reverberations are everywhere apparent in her work.[18] In a 1908 story, "Genizah," Baron describes the ritualized burial of damaged Torah scroll from the perspective of both physical and textual-intellectual segregation: thus, the procession to the cemetery begins with the beadle's shout, "Women to the side," while the respect and care with which the Torah and other canonical "male" texts are treated is juxtaposed to the disrespect toward the Yiddish women's *tkhines*, the personal prayers written for and sometimes by women, which the narrator's older brother deems unworthy of ritual burial, flinging a copy of their mother's tkhine collection to one corner as a "filthy rag!"[19] Sexual segregation is exposed in this story as a mechanism not for separating men and women and "guarding" against (male) sexual thoughts but for marginalizing and devaluing women and their books. More recently, the Israeli writer Amalia Kahana-Carmon argued that contemporary Hebrew literature was similarly structured as a traditional synagogue, in which the supplications of the individual are pre-ordained as trivial or inferior when compared to the central act of collective prayer. Since Hebrew literature must speak for and of the collective, it is men whose voices are central to the literary arena, while women's speech is deemed peripheral:

> Being a woman, her one place in this arena is in the *ezrat hanashim* (the women's gallery). As a passive observer, she does not contribute anything. Someone else, acting in the name of all Israel, speaks also on her behalf. And so, anything that is likely to happen to the woman seated in the women's gallery will be defined ahead of time as peripheral, a hindrance, and a deviant incident.[20]

Kahana-Carmon's outrage may be generated not only by the marginalization of women in the "synagogue" of Hebrew literature but also by the very persistence of a religious structure in the ostensibly secular and progressive environment of Hebrew letters (the persistent tensions between Orthodox and secular Israelis no doubt exacerbates this critique). Her diagnosis of the sexual politics of Hebrew literature and its reception suggests that sexual segregation is a physical and spatial feature of traditional life as well as a cultural condition that shapes Jewish culture in its modern and traditional forms. This condition can be shown in the collective realm, governing how collectivity and community are understood. But it also inevitably shapes the individual—writer or reader, man or woman—who occupies and is oc-cupied by this collective space. Kahana-Carmon, writing in 1989, speaks of the ghostly persistence of sexual segregation in the collective, secular Israeli sphere. The push to sexually segregate and remove women's voices and bod-ies from public spaces in Israel—buses, community events, the radio—has only grown fiercer in the decades since.[21] Sexual segregation, overturned as part of Jewish modernization, Europeanization, and secularization, persists not only invisibly and psychosexually but also more aggressively and physi-cally, long after the maskilim first tore down the partitions between men and women and refurbished the women's gallery for other cultural uses.

The Erotics of Sexual Segregation

The role of sexual segregation in maintaining the status of textual traditions, religious spaces, and ritual performances traditionally associated with men may be sufficient explanation for the persistence of segregation in open or disguised form in secular and post-traditional Jewish culture. But sexual segregation persisted and was reimagined for other reasons as well. Precisely in an era that finally saw widespread sexual desegregation in both the social and the intellectual spheres, twentieth-century writers began to mine traditional practices for their literary potential, recognizing a host of erotic possibilities even in the most sexually segregated space of all—the synagogue, which was ostensibly designed to keep sexuality from intruding on sacred male activities. Thus, while the daughters of the Kallischer Rebbetzin spent their days in a sexually segregated world devouring romances about heterosexual encounters, their daughters, granddaughters, and great-granddaughters might well have sat in sexually desegregated theater and film audiences, watching with equal passion scenes set in the purely male worlds of a Hasidic court, a yeshiva, or the main section of a synagogue. Beginning with Abraham Goldfaden's early cabaret skits featuring singing and dancing Hasidim and continuing with such enormously popular plays and films as *The Dybbuk* and *Yidl with the Fiddle*, men and women flocked to the "secular synagogue" of the theater to watch scenes set in the segregated architecture of the traditional synagogue or in the entirely male spaces of the Hasidic court, the yeshiva, or the traditional klezmer band.[22] These cultural phenomena form a chiastic image: In one, the "aristocratic daughters" of the Kallischer Rebbetzin sat in separate women's quarters, sobbing over Polish or German novels and dreaming of love. Decades later, in the theaters of Warsaw and New York's Second Avenue, modern mixed-sex audiences fell into collective erotic dreams set in these now-abandoned homosocial spaces. What had seemed utterly devoid of appeal to nineteenth-century writers seeking juicy romantic plots reemerged now infused with nostalgic eroticism. Literature, in both cases, reflected not immediate social realities but their lacunae, the "counter-image" of urban modernity that only literature could provide.[23]

Nostalgia for traditional social structures was not, of course, an exclusively Jewish phenomenon: Hebrew and Yiddish modernisms shared with their international counterparts an attraction to eroticism and archaism in their overlap. Among the most distinctively Jewish expressions of this more general interest is the fascination with the eroticized space of the synagogue. The synagogue is a particularly charged site for such literary depictions: the Torah scroll is materialized and eroticized in synagogue ritual—the man who recites the blessing over the Torah reading is called the *hatan torah*, or bridegroom of the Torah; the Torah is tenderly cloaked, processed, kissed, and danced with; and the scroll is inscribed on parchment, that is, on animal skin. Moreover, like the relationship between God and Israel (or Jerusalem), the relationship between Israel and the Torah has often been figured through heterosexual metaphors that could be revivified by modernist writers. For all the erotic potential of Jewish ritual, such efforts to reinfuse tradition, the synagogue, and the Torah with their lost erotic currents were also a potentially explosive intervention in an architecture that ostensibly also continued to encode and enforce sexual segregation, exclusively male religious leadership, and, more or less explicitly, the separation of sexual and religious activity.[24]

That despite its segregationist architecture the synagogue could function as a site for romantic encounter is evident, for instance, in An-sky's 1919 *The Dybbuk*, which locates at least one meeting between Chonon and Leah at the most sacred site of all, the Holy Ark. It is no coincidence that this scene begins with Chonon singing the Song of Songs—a text central to the modernist recovery of the erotic signification of biblical texts obscured by layers of rabbinic interpretation (and one that Ilana Pardes argues continues to shape Zionist, and world, culture).[25] Leah and her aunt enter the synagogue where Chonon is studying and singing not to pray, which would be an open transgression of traditional norms. They come, outside the time of official prayers, to admire the velvet covering of the Torah scrolls rather than investigate what is written within them; the women thus participate in the (modernist) appreciation of aesthetic elements of sacred space lost in the rabbinic focus on liturgy, ritual, and text, acting, as Gabriella Safran writes, as museumgoers rather than worshippers.[26] The recognition of the erotic, literary, and aesthetic power of biblical texts, traditional practices, and religious spaces opens new channels for female and male appreciation for and participation in synagogue life: Freide warns Leah not to touch the Torah not because women are "impure" or "unclean" (as some medieval prohibitions against women touching a Torah imply) but because the Torah is an object of danger and power.[27] An-sky's aim in this scene is to reinfuse tradition with erotic energies; the meeting of Chonon and Leah within this sacred space completes a circle that encompasses both religious practice and romantic love, simultaneously demonstrating the mystical and religious powers of Jewish Eros and showing the erotic attractions of Jewish religious practices. In *The Dybbuk*, the dangers and appeal of Eros and Torah, sexuality and tradition, do not stand at opposite poles of Jewish life but as its intertwined and potent center.

In mining the sexually segregated structures of traditional Ashkenazic life for their literary-erotic potential, An-sky was implicitly recognizing that the separation of men and women, boys and girls, ostensibly a means of sexual control, could also function as an engine of sexual excitation. The interrelationship between sexual control and excitation, and the notion that "repression" may generate as well as subdue sexual energies, is by now a familiar one. In volume 1 of *History of Sexuality* (1976), Michel Foucault argues for just such a revision of the broadly accepted cultural narrative that views modernity as having liberated society from Victorian restraints on sexuality. In Foucault's analysis, the modern period (including the Victorian era) was part of a longer historical process that amplified as it scrutinized sexuality, with new sexual discourses arising alongside ramified mechanisms for subjecting the sexuality of children and deviants to policing and examination. These changes, far from "suppressing" sexuality, created sexually charged connections among individuals linked in multiple networks of power/knowledge, cultural expectations for people to view themselves as sexual beings, the imperative to speak "the truth" about their sexual desires, and an invitation to view such (compulsory) speech as a daring form of "sexual liberation." As Foucault puts it, "Western man has been drawn for three centuries to the task of telling everything concerning his sex," and this imperative to sexually confess, which prides itself as a break with taboos, is in fact a submission to cultural requirements. Foucault continues: "This carefully analytic discourse [on sex] was meant to yield multiple effects of displacement, intensification, reorientation, and modification of desire itself."[28] Sexual confession, in other words, *generates* rather than suppresses or controls desire; it is itself sexual, multiplying and intensifying the variety and character of sexually charged human connections and lending erotic excitation to a range of asymmetrical pedagogical, medical, and family relations.

Foucault's challenge to the assumptions that modernity brought a new era of sexual liberation has some bearing on the study of Jewish sexual modernization, which has for a decade or two explored the related question of whether sexual secularization liberated traditional Jews who had been kept from the free exercise of romantic choice or instead subjected economically active Jewish women to bourgeois domestic constraints while robbing Jewish men of their religiously ordained status and "feminizing" them in relation to European counterparts.[29] Foucault's work has specific ramifications for the study of sexual segregation: That sexual segregation may be construed as a tool for energizing as well as controlling social relationships is perhaps evident from the fact that the nineteenth century saw the rise of both secularization and particularly ramified forms of sexual segregation in the Hasidic court and the yeshiva movement; these homosocial spaces, bulwarks against the sexual attractions of modernity, did so by providing their own sexual attractions. Rather than view Jewish modernity as the overthrow of sexually repressive regimes by more "liberated" ones, it could be argued that modernity brought multiple and simultaneous attempts to sexually re-energize Jewish society, in Hasidism, in the new bourgeoisie, in the yeshivas that grew and flourished in the nineteenth century, and in the "voluntary segregation" of the secular youth movements that arose at the turn of the twentieth.[30] In all of these, what appears from one perspective as sexual control appears from another as the "intensification, reorientation, and modification of desire itself."[31]

The persistence of sexual segregation in modern Jewish movements and the return to the traditional architecture of sexual segregation in modern Jewish narrative seem to be evidence of a widespread recognition of the erotic potential of these structures. Among the most interesting literary explorations of sexual segregation is "The Animal in the Synagogue," Franz Kafka's only story (probably written in 1923) that takes place in a recognizably Jewish world. "The Animal in the Synagogue" is an unfinished story, a parable without a moral, about a pale blue-green marten that inhabits a small, dying synagogue and has done so for as long as anyone can remember. As I have discussed elsewhere, the animal in Kafka's synagogue is a stubbornly opaque figure, resisting all interpretation by the congregants who mull over its origin, motives, appearance, and proclivities and by the reader, who searches in vain for what this animal, as a literary figure, might symbolize or mean.[32] Yet precisely because it resists meaning, the animal is an engine that generates narrative, speculation, dogma, law, and eventually ritual—tradition, in other words, in what Walter Benjamin calls its "transmissibility" rather than truth.[33] "The Animal in the Synagogue" reflects Jewish tradition making not only in its diachronic aspect, in the movement from one generation to another, but also in its synchronic aspect, in the mechanisms of social differentiation by which a tradition is constructed at a given moment in time. The interpretations that arise around the animal, in the absence of other informational contexts, are shaped by the particularities of the architecture within which the marten moves. In speaking of the animal, the congregants simultaneously trace the contours of their social world:

> The animal does not dare to go down below where the men are, and it has never yet been seen on the main floor that holds the Torah Ark, the pulpit and other central features of the religious rituals that are the ostensible focus and purpose of the synagogue. If it is stopped from getting on the lattice of the women's compartment [*das Gitter der Frauenabteilung*], then at least it wants to be at the same height on the opposite wall.[34]

In Kafka's narrative, what the animal means is less important than how it means: it acquires significance within and through the structures it disturbs. Thus, the men debate the halakhic ramifications of its presence in a synagogue, speculate on its origins, and plot its removal; the women watch it and feign fear to disguise their erotic fascination with the creature, which in turn prefers to spend time on the same level that is designated for them. In traversing and violating the boundaries between the sexes, the animal presents a different series of distractions, dilemmas, and diversions for the women and for the men:

> To be sure, it is only the women who are afraid of the animal, the men have long ceased to bother about it, one generation has pointed it out to the next, it has been seen over and over again, and by this time nobody any longer wastes a glance on it, until now even the children, seeing it for the first time, do not show any amazement. It has become that animal that belongs to the synagogue—why should not the synagogue have a special domestic animal [*Haustier*] not found anywhere else? If it were not for the women, one would hardly be aware of the animal's existence any more now at all.[35]

The animal not only calls our attention to the architecture of the synagogue; it also symbolically reorganizes it, displacing the traditional male center as the legislated focus of attention and reconfiguring the concentric, closely guarded circles of the Holy Ark, Jewish men, and, at the periphery, Jewish women. The normative, sacral content of religion, a community of men praying to their God with women as spectator-participants, is disrupted by and subsumed to the sexual drama of men watching women ogling a strange beast. It is impossible to resolve the question of the symbolic relation of the animal to God, to the Torah, to men, to women (polar opposites? secret doubles?); Kafka maps these relations only in spatial terms. Nor does Kafka invite us to read "animality" or "carnality," in its romantic or sexual essence, in this particular blue-green creature, whose very color seems to signify exotic difference from the natural features of the animal world. For all the uniqueness of this story and Kafka's style, the constellation of concerns in this story is not unfamiliar. "The Animal in the Synagogue" shares with a wide range of Jewish modernist works (including others in Kafka's oeuvre) a fascination with the processes of tradition and its breakdown, with the tensions between the temple and the leopards that break in, the carnal and spiritual, men and women, and normativity and transgression. More particularly, the story can be read as an ambivalent symptom of the long death of tradition and, more particularly, of traditional sexual segregation, which produced new literary life even as it repeatedly ended. In this regard, the animal in Kafka's synagogue can be said to inhabit the Jewish modernist project in its wider expression.

S. Y. Agnon's 1919 "The Tale of the Scribe" (Agadat ha-sofer) represents the Hebrew writer's most direct exploration of the question of the relationship between religion and sexuality, the animal and the synagogue. The protagonist, Raphael the scribe, views his work as a rigorous ascetic practice, with little of the sensual joy in the craftsmanship it entails, in contrast with another of Agnon's signature characters, the craftsman Ben-Uri in "Agunot," who neglects his wife while reveling in the pleasure of carving a synagogue ark to hold the Torah. Neither man finds a happy balance between his religious calling and his marital duties or desires; for Ben-Uri, the focus on his craft trumps his interest in women, while for Raphael, God himself seems to come between his wife and him. Miriam returns home from the ritual bath that normatively serves as a prelude to marital intercourse,

> and when Raphael returns home after the prayers and sees his wife in her true beauty reflected in the mirror he is immediately attracted to her. He goes toward her to make some pleasing remark. But when he is near her, His Name, may He be blessed, flashes before him out of the mirror. Immediately he stops and recites devoutly and in holiness, "I have set the Lord always before me," and shuts his eyes before the glory and awe of the Name. Both turn away silently. He sits in one corner and studies the *Book of Splendor*

and she sits in another corner reading the women's prayerbook, until sleep invades their eyes.[36]

There may be a deliberate irony in Raphael's reading the Zohar, a text that imagines cosmic unity through the figure of marital intercourse, rather than actually approaching his wife. While either one of the textual traditions they are immersed in might lead them to holy sex (a topic available not only in the Zohar but also in the Yiddish prayers women addressed to the matriarchs—who also had husband troubles), this segregated textual world functions as a set of parallel tracks that never meet. To deepen the irony, the name of God Raphael catches sight of in the mirror hangs beside a fertility amulet written for Miriam's mother by a Rabbi Simon interweaving the name of God with a "Gentile" proverb: "When the cow is young and healthy why should she not give birth to a calf?"[37] For Miriam as for Rabbi Simon, God is entirely embedded in the natural order of the universe; but Raphael sees neither the young cow nor his pious wife, reading God's divine power as a warning against sex rather than its enabler or equivalent. Although the story makes clear that his approach to sexuality is far from normative from a Jewish perspective, Agnon leaves open the more psychological question of whether Raphael's asceticism should be read as extreme piety or as a cover for sexual ambivalence or even perversion. The sensuality of traditional Judaism that Raphael labors to keep at bay is evident everywhere, but he either misinterprets or fails to notice it, even in his wife, Miriam, with her longing to embrace a child and her connection to religion through its physical touchstones—embroidered proverbs, folk rituals, talismans, the daily work of sustaining her pious husband.

Their different approaches to religion, as ascetic or sensual practice, are emblematized in the scene in which Raphael recalls, after his wife's death, the circumstances of their meeting and betrothal. The encounter takes place, significantly enough, in the synagogue on Simhat Torah, the holiday in which the Torah as material object is most lavishly on display, loving partner to communal rituals of ecstatic embrace. The sexually segregated synagogue on this night, as frame for the embodied and eroticized Torah, becomes an arena of spiritually transfigured passion in which young girls and boys "hold the scroll, caressing and embracing and kissing it with their kosher lips that have not tasted sin."[38] Even the grown women, whose segregation is designed to ensure the separation of religious practice and sexual desire (and whose intellectual alienation from the holiday prayer service is guaranteed by their ignorance of Hebrew), are drawn into the Simhat Torah procession by the broad sensuality of its symbolic gestures, leaning "from the windows of the women's gallery into the study hall and their heads were perched like a flock of doves on the ledge of the wall."[39] The imagery of the Song of Songs infuses this scene, suggesting that the architecture of sexual separation is also a mechanism for erotic attraction and display—the latticework does not hide the women from the male gaze, as its ostensible function dictates, but provides their faces with an ornamental architectural as well as erotic-textual frame.[40]

This episode precisely calibrates Raphael's brand of ascetic piety against the more typical religiosity of his community and future wife. Something about his posture as he holds the Torah has a chilling effect on the ecstatic dance of the old Hasidim, who cease their dancing "although their hearts were consumed with fire."[41] Miriam's response to the vision of Raphael in the scene in which they first meet is diametrically opposed to that of the Hasidim, arousing not a frozen awe but a literally fiery passion:

> And Raphael held the scroll in his arm, walking in the lead with all the other youths following him around the pulpit. At that moment a young girl (tinoket ahat) pushed her way through the legs of the dancers, leaped toward Raphael, sank her red lips into the white mantle of the Torah scroll in Raphael's arm, and kept on kissing the scroll (ve-nishka et ha-sefer meneshikot piha) and caressing it with her hands. Just then the flag fell out of her hand and the burning candle dropped on Raphael's clothing.[42]

The Torah, in this scene, is implicitly conflated with the young man holding it as a single embodied object of Miriam's fervent devotion, an identification reinforced by the use of the same Hebrew word (me'il) for the Torah mantle and Raphael's caftan. (Later in the story, Raphael similarly conflates the Torah and his wife when he literally converts her wedding dress into a parokhet, the curtain that hangs before the Ark.) Miriam's kiss is rendered in the language of the Song of Songs 1:2 ("Oh, give me of the kisses of your mouth"), the text at the epicenter of the protracted collision, and collusion, of the sensual and the religious in Jewish tradition.[43] As if to make the point that the easy coexistence of sex and religion is native to this traditional scene, the rabbi jokes that the damage Miriam has inflicted on Raphael's caftan can be made good by betrothing them. Agnon revises here the maskilic excoriation of early arranged marriage, suggesting the eroticism of a marriage that emerges from the wild desires of a little girl and a sympathetic and worldly rabbi (Agnon does not explicitly tell us their ages, but while Raphael seems to be at least an adolescent, Miriam is described as being young enough to not be confined to the women's section; she is thus certainly prepubescent, and perhaps considerably younger). Where the writers of the Haskalah had bitterly criticized early marriage, Agnon suggests that the betrothal of Raphael and Miriam arises from the rabbi's recognition of the claims of sexuality, even in the very young. Passion and piety, for Miriam and the rabbi (though not for Raphael, the object of Miriam's pious passion), might as readily feed as negate each other.

Raphael imposes his asceticism on Miriam and their marriage, but the story suggests, in the final surreal and fantastic scene, that Miriam's spirit and the power of sexuality must ultimately triumph. While Miriam initiated the fateful embrace that began their marriage, the dying Raphael finally shows his hand and belatedly welcomes this embrace, hallucinating a scene in which "the young girls come down from the women's gallery to the House of Study hall to watch the youths dance. The youths continue to circle the pulpit and the girls reach out with the tips of their fingers toward the Torah scrolls in the hands of the youths."[44] As Raphael's reverie continues, the Torah scrolls themselves begin to dance around his vision of Miriam. The story ends with these lines: "Suddenly a tongue of flame leaped up and illumined the room. Its light framed the face of Raphael the scribe who sank down with his scroll. His wife's wedding dress was spread out over him and his scroll."[45]

In this last passage, the identifications that have propelled the story come full circle, from Miriam's conflation of Raphael with the Torah scroll he is holding, to Raphael's clothing the Torah in Miriam's bridal dress, and, finally, Raphael's transvestite transformation into Miriam. The Torah, as flexible medium for these transformations, ultimately becomes the channel not for sexual union but for a more solipsistic merging, in a scene that renders mourning as either melancholic absorption of the dead or masturbation. The problem of Raphael's asceticism remains unresolved: Is it a religious stance, a misunderstanding of a religion that insists on the acceptance of sexuality, or a "modern" sexual problem, deriving from Raphael's psychosexual vacillation between his desire to have and his desire to be his wife (or her child)? One larger question Agnon raises in this story, however, is directed to the nature of traditional sexual segregation, the theater for both Raphael's asceticism and his wife's frustrated sensuality. How much is traditional Jewish sexual segregation to blame for what separates this particular man and woman?

For modernizers like Maimon and Günzburg, the answer is simple: a society that first separates young boys and girls and then brings them together with the expectation that they will get right down to (reproductive) business does irreparable harm to a marriage and to the individuals within it. Agnon suggests that sexual segregation is a different structure than may at first appear, connecting men and women even as it ostensibly separates them through the very religious rituals around which the entire community, male and female, circles. Agnon dramatizes the question of the nature of sexual segregation by assigning different perspectives on the relationship between God and Eros to husband and wife; for Raphael, God functions as an ascetic principle, while for Miriam, God and Eros are one and the same. Agnon tips his hand in the ending, which exposes Raphael's religious "sublimation" as an illusion, a chimerical and inhuman struggle against the inescapable force of erotic desire. Miriam wins, but too late to do her any good. This view, psychoanalytic and traditionalist-Jewish in its skepticism about asceticist hopes, also encapsulates Agnon's sexual modernism more broadly.

The traditional gendered architecture of Ashkenazic life had divided men and women into two worlds so separate that no one participant could claim to know the culture as a whole. But what separated moderns from what they had left behind created another, perhaps equally unbridgeable gap. Like the barrier in the synagogue, the screen that veiled the traditional past from modern eyes did not preclude its infusion with fantasy and desire, producing enchanted images in which the unseen exerted as much fascination as what was exposed when the barriers fell.

Queer Architectures

The modernist literature I am surveying discovered the means to stage heterosexual passions within traditional structures. But segregation, read through Foucault (and not only Foucault), amplifies *both* heterosexual and homosocial eroticism. The circulation of sexual energy through traditional structures and practices ensures a bisexual distribution of sexual energy, in which marriages might (and did) as easily commence by Rabbi Abraham's falling in love with the Besht as by Tamar's falling in love with Amnon. Both homosocial spaces and heterosexual transgression could thus yield erotic connections and fortify community. The reduced family and companionate marriage of bourgeois modernity put all of its erotic eggs into one romantic basket, privileging the heterosexual couple over all other forms of connection. However, the traditional Jewish sexual system links a partially de-eroticized heteronormative sphere (insofar as marriages are arranged) with a partially eroticized homosocial sphere (insofar as same-sex relationships are energized by a range of erotic connections). Despite and through the mechanisms of sexual segregation, these spheres are both distinct and connected in multiple ways—marriages unite a man and a woman, but they are often forged in homosocial spaces and serve to bolster homosocial connections by promoting the links between men into kinship ties. The ties I am describing link individuals in potentially far wider networks than bourgeois marriage, connecting individuals not only horizontally, as in a marriage that joins two men (Nissen and Sender, for instance, in An-sky's *Dybbuk*) when their son and daughter marry; but also diagonally, through the relationships between fathers-in-law and sons-in-law (Tevye and Pertchik, for instance); and vertically, in the bonds forged by a couple that produces links that are expressed and embodied in future generations as well as retroactively, in their parents and families. On the broadest level, the bisexual distribution of energy in a sexually segregated society contributes to the construction of a community; the nuclear family championed by nineteenth-century modernizers and that continues as a model today (even in many LGBTQ circles) creates the strongest bonds between a couple and their children, at the expense of all others.[46]

The sociological and literary return to traditional practices and structures, including sexual segregation, was at least partially motivated by an implicit recognition of the price paid for modern marriage. If this price has not registered more directly, that may be because twentieth-century perspectives on gender and sexuality focus attention on the gender identities and psychosexuality of individuals and couples, leaving larger systems of sexual organization unexplored. Thus, the cross-dressed female characters in Yiddish film who transgress the boundaries of male homosocial spaces are regularly (mis)read as evidence of the perceived effeminacy of Jewish men or of the homosexuality of these characters. But homosocial desire is not limited to "homosexuals" and is not universally characterized by a *reversal* of normative sex-gender roles. For post-traditional Jews expressing cultural alongside psychosexual desires, homosociality is at least as powerful a draw, as is the desire to shed gender roles altogether. The attractions of homosocial spaces for literary characters, and the attractions of a sexually segregated world for its readers and viewers, are simply incoherent or invisible in worldviews dominated by bourgeois ideologies or their queer responses, even as these spaces continue to exert a powerful literary and even sociological pull.

The homoeroticism of sexual segregation was not the discovery of such modernist writers as An-sky, Agnon, and Asch but was part of the literary critique of traditional life from the very outset of the Haskalah project, beginning with Joseph Perl's 1819 Hebrew satire, *Revealer of Secrets*. Perl's work is both a satire on Hasidic life and a parody of Hasidic literature, replete with rabbinic approbations and "learned" footnotes to the most popular Hasidic works of the day. Along with the venalities and corruption of Hasidic leaders and the superstitions and naïveté of their followers, the novel aims to expose the sexual irregularities of the movement. The novel is told in the form of letters between Hasidim trying to recover an anti-Hasidic German book that threatens to damage their reputation (Perl himself had authored just such a tract a few years earlier, but it had been suppressed by the censors). *Revealer of Secrets* includes some pivotal female characters, and the recovery of the anti-Hasidic book depends in part on the relationship between a Jewish woman who belongs to the Hasidic sect and a Polish nobleman who possesses a copy. But the novel derives much of its comic energy not from this (it turns out, innocent) relationship but from an acute recognition of the distinctive erotic character of the Hasidic movement. Perl's regular comic strategy is to expose the "abnormal" erotic world of Hasidism and to literalize the spiritual love the Hasidim feel for their eminently unworthy leader. The first letter begins with a paean to the Holy Rebbe, "Lamp of our Generation," and with a fulsome description of the rapture of the writer, Reb Zelig Letitchiver, in hearing the rebbe pray. "I could go for days without eating and drinking," writes Reb Zelig, "to hear his holy speech." But this pleasure is not only spiritual. Reb Zelig continues:

> But our holy *rebe* wanted to smoke his pipe and go to the outhouse. I gave him the pipe but I wasn't privileged to light it for him because while I was giving our *rebe* the pipe, another of our Faithful scrambled to light it. When

I saw that it wasn't our *rebe*'s wish to be accompanied to the outhouse, I went home overjoyed that I am worthy to be among our *rebe*'s people and that G-d gave me the privilege of hearing great things from our rebe that day.[47]

Although Zelig's exalted love for his rebbe leads to his transcending his own desire to eat or drink, he fully accepts the carnal appetites of the rebbe, longing to light his pipe and accompany him to the outhouse—a kind of outrageous reductio ad absurdum of the Hasidic principles of *avodah she-ba-gashmiut* (worshipping God on the material plane) and of the imperative to emulate and learn from the leader in all his actions, including the most mundane. Letter 4 makes it clear that the odd combination of spirituality, carnality, and devotion that characterizes the relationship between a Hasid and his rebbe extends even to the sexual domain. Trying to quell Reb Zelig's melancholy by suggesting that it has roots deeper than his anxiety about the anti-Hasidic book they are seeking, Reb Zanvel (whose "corrupt" and Yiddishized Hebrew Dov Taylor's translation aims to capture) diagnoses his condition as "lovesickness":

> In your letter I seen you're very melancholy—it should never be worse!— about the *bukh*. I'm surprised on you! I'm the one who don't got the good fortune to be by our holy *rebe* every day, to see him and his face, shining like a mirror (*aspaklaria*). . . . But you see him and you hear when he sings and still you become melancholy sometimes, G-d save us! This must be 'cause you're lovesick for our rebe more then for women, and you're concerned he shouldn't have aggravation, G-d forbid! over the *bukh*.[48]

Perl's footnote to this passage does not cite either Song of Songs 5:8 ("For I am faint with love" [*holat ahava ani*]) or David's famous threnody for Jonathan in 2 Samuel 1:18–27 ("Your love was wonderful was your love to me, more than the love of women"), although both texts are in the immediate background of this letter. Instead, Perl cites a collection of teachings by Rabbi Nachman of Bratslav, which clarifies that "the essence of attachment is love—that [the Hasid] loves the *tsadek* with perfect love so that his soul is bound up with the other's, to the point that through his love of the *tsadek*, his love of women is abolished."[49] Perl's intent is clear—while the passage from Samuel might have lent biblical warrant to the passionate devotion one man might feel for another, the Hasidic text suggests that the love Zelig feels for his rebbe is prescribed "cultic" practice rather than an emotional choice, and moreover an extreme and unnatural form of abolishing the "natural" love men should feel for women. In this novel as in other anti-Hasidic discourses, Hasidism emerges as a fanatical zeal that supplants normal attachments, perhaps even manifesting itself in actual "perverted" behavior.[50] Perl's intentions in this critique of Hasidism are to invalidate the movement, and his readings of Hasidic texts deliberately ignore their translation of sexual concepts into spiritual, mystical, and religious realms, a translation that has a history much longer than Hasidism itself. It is nevertheless the case that Perl may *also* be an astute reader of Hasidism in its erotic structures, and writers in generations that returned to Hasidism as a resource for modern Jewish literature and experience did not so much invalidate his insights as transvalue them, celebrating the pleasures available in sexually segregated structures rather than decrying them as perversions. Jiří Langer took this interest in the homoerotics of Hasidism further than most, distinguishing it sharply from the heteronormativity in which it is usually embedded; this interest, as extreme as it appeared to his assimilated Prague family, was entirely within the mainstream of Jewish modernism in its attraction to the archaic and traditional precisely for their erotic power.

If Perl and the authors of anti-Hasidic tracts revile Hasidic sexual arrangements for supplanting family connections, An-sky's *The Dybbuk* explores the multiple overlaps between Hasidic homoeroticism and passionate heterosexual love. As Sholem Asch showed in his 1907 play *God of Vengeance*, the traditional sex-gender system that connects same-sex and heterosexual spheres could also shape Jewish culture in its modernizing moments.[51] Asch's play takes place not in a Hasidic court but in a Jewish brothel and juxtaposes bourgeois heterosexuality and lesbian romance rather than Hasidic homosociality and heteronormativity. Like *The Dybbuk*, it also prominently features a Torah scroll, but rather than serve as an emblem of religious-erotic-aesthetic fascination, this Torah scroll has been commissioned by the brothel owner in an effort to present a respectable public face and win his "pure" daughter a rabbinic bridegroom. In the 1923 obscenity trial against the English-language Broadway production of the play, Rudolph Schildkraut, who both directed and played Yankl, defended the play against charges of immorality by pointing to Yankl's yearning "for something higher and more beautiful," as evidenced by his desire to bring a Torah scroll and pious son-in-law into his home and thus "arise from his fallen state."[52] Implicit in Schildkraut's defense of the play as aspiring to traditional piety and bourgeois respectability is the assumption that the lesbian scenes that transpire in the basement brothel represent all that is "fallen" in the play, while Yankl's bourgeois/religious aspirations represent the play's moral core.

What Schildkraut does not acknowledge, however, is that the play has no sympathy for the class aspirations masked by his spiritual hopes. The characters repeatedly expose the awkwardness and falsity of Yankl's attempts to stage-manage his reputation by acquiring a learned son-in-law for his daughter. In Yankl's hands, the Torah is a clumsy and hollow trophy; the scribe and matchmaker he hires strain to understand what their rich bene-factor is trying to do with the scroll: "You mean," asks Elye, the match-maker, "that when you marry the girl off you'll give her the Torah scroll for a dowry, right?"[53] With such transparently manipulative attempts to simu-late a traditional Jewish life, and such blatant ritual-social misfires (Torahs are communal rather than private property and have no place in a bedroom or a dowry), Yankl cannot entice the proper crowd to gather at his home for a celebration of his Torah scroll, to serve in his private play as both audience and extras. The prospective groom, for whom this elaborate production is orchestrated, never comes close to materializing.

What is at stake in the charges of dramatic inauthenticity, on the part of both Asch and Yankl, cannot be confined to the strictly theatrical. Because the authentic performance of Jewish religious traditions is at issue here, im-plausibility is inextricable from impiety, tawdriness from blasphemy, falsity from religious and ethical betrayal. Remarks made by the presiding judge at the 1923 trial confirm the suspicion that many Jews besides Peretz were shocked less by the prostitution or lesbianism than by the odd and cava-lier treatment of a Torah scroll, which Yankl pushes into the hands of the matchmaker in the final act when it becomes clear that he has no further need for it.[54]

But Yankl's transparently staged performance of (apparently half-forgotten) religious customs is not the only performance of Jewish "folkways" in the play. Alongside Yankl's awkward and artificial attempt to signal and guarantee the chastity of his daughter, Asch presents another, more natural conflation of Jewish tradition and Jewish sexuality in a scene that transpires in the brothel downstairs. The erotic contact between Rivkele and Manke in the second act is enacted as what would be called, in modern sexual par-lance, a "scene"—a transparently staged, extended sexual fantasy. As in the sham piety that Yankl is frantically trying to stage upstairs, Asch presents us with theater within theater and, more specifically, with a theatrical staging of tradition within a corrupted modern space. The two girls play out their scene in a brothel, which might be considered an appropriate setting for such sexual scenes; they are not customer and client, however, but close girlfriends (or performing the roles of close girlfriends) whose intimate female companionship gradually shifts toward a reenactment of the shy embrace of a bride and groom behind the backs of the bride's respectable parents, a passion that is both transgressive and half-legitimated by their status as betrothed couple.[55] This performance, it should be noted, is not entirely removed from the bourgeois fantasies of Rivkele's parents upstairs, who also dream of a distinguished and pious groom for their lovely daughter:

> Manke: Let me comb your hair like a bride, hair parted in the middle with two long braids. (*Combs her hair.*) Would you like me to, Rivkele? Would you?
> Rivkele (*nodding*): Yes, I would.
> Manke: You will be the bride, a lovely bride. It's Friday night. You're sitting at the Sabbath table with your father and your mother. I'm the bridegroom, your bridegroom come to visit you. . . . Would you like that, Rivkele? Would you?
> Rivkele (*nods*): Yes, I would.
> Manke: Wait, wait. Your father and mother have gone to bed. . . . Bride and groom have met at the table, we're embarrassed. Right?
> Rivkele (*nodding her head*): Yes, Manke.
> Manke: Then we draw close to each other: You're my bride and I'm your bridegroom. We embrace. (*She puts her arms around her.*) We're pressed together, and we kiss very quietly, like this. (*They kiss.*) We blush, we're so embarrassed. . . . It's good, isn't it, Rivkele?
> Rivkele: Yes, Manke, it is.
> Manke (*lowers her face, whispering into Rivke's ear*): And then we go to sleep in the same bed. No one sees; no one knows; just the two of us, like this. (*She presses Rivkele to her.*) Would you like to sleep the whole night through with me, Rivkele, in the same bed?[56]

This love scene between Manke and Rivkele is, by the standards of its day, a daring and explicit evocation of lesbianism, transgressive of New York state obscenity law and perhaps also of the norms of Jewish cultural modesty. But the scene between Manke and Rivkele is not an extreme version of the commercialized sex that is the normal order of business at the brothel— as linked criticisms of the play's depictions of prostitution and lesbianism imply—but its reverse. While Yankl is shamming a traditional Jewish life upstairs by attempting to buy himself respectability and thus a pious son-in-law, his daughter and his most alluring prostitute are imagining themselves into such a life, not for profit or social respectability but purely for its erotic pleasures. The scene the two young women enact is a persuasive and loving performance of Jewish tradition and folk practice, the primary site of traditional reference in a play that otherwise reduces Jewish marriage, Jewish piety, and a Torah scroll to a series of stage props. Yankl's attempts at providing Rivke with a bridegroom are performed by the appropriate person—the bride's father—but through corrupt or inappropriate means: crass commercialism, the construction of a social facade, the reduction of a Torah scroll to an empty fetish. Manke may be the wrong person—or the wrong sex—to stage-manage Rivke's introduction to (quasi) marital eroticism, but the cultural materials she draws from are taken from a traditional repertoire: the charged atmosphere of Friday night, with its potent mix of the spiritual and sexual. Moreover, while Manke "directs" the love scene with as much persistence and attention as Yankl invests in finding Rivkele a groom, she makes sure to seek Rivke's consent at every stage of the scene, taking this consent as erotic fuel.

Act two of Asch's theater within a brothel within a theater is his most profound tribute not only to Jewish tradition but also to the enterprise of its (modern) staging and performance. The performance of tradition by actors whose roles can never be seen as natural or authentic and whose gender bars them from the more sanctioned arenas of Jewish ritual performance, but whose erotic investment in the roles they don is beyond question, opens tradition itself to new performative possibilities. Asch's play thus resists the privileging of tradition over its theatrical reenactments, by implication deconstructing the opposition between theater and tradition altogether. By having tradition so transparently—so outrageously—staged, *God of Vengeance* paradoxically transforms the secular theater into a legitimate and "authentic" site of Jewish performance, we might almost say, of Jewish observance.

That Yiddish theater serves, in some sense, as a site of ritual performance, a "secular (desegregated) synagogue," has been noted before.[57] With the geographic displacements and social disruptions of modernity, theater and film perform important roles analogous to and sometimes substituting for religious observance. Ideally, they keep alive not only the "correct" performances of religious customs (otherwise Peretz would not have been so outraged by Asch's "sins" on this score) but also the very structures of traditional life, including those that organize sex and gender. Plays like *The Dybbuk* thus provided images for modern desegregated audiences of such segregated spaces as the synagogue and the Hasidic court, channeling the pleasures native to such spaces for theatergoers who regarded them as lost. *God of Vengeance* stages both the lost eroticism of a tradition that was fading and the nostalgia for this lost eroticism and the attempt to revive it in the most degraded urban space imaginable—a brothel. It does so by re-creating two lost spaces: that of the heterosexual attraction between a young bride and groom (transposed to a lesbian scene); and that of the erotic atmosphere that could infuse traditional homosocial spaces (re-created in a brothel temporarily empty of men). Moreover, while most Jewish modernists focused on the homosocial eroticism of sanctioned male spaces, Asch discovers an erotically and religiously vibrant female world within the most nakedly corrupt heterosexual spaces imaginable—a brothel. The love between Manke and Rivkele that arises even in this fallen world draws from twin dimensions of traditional Jewish eroticism—the shyness of traditional brides and grooms and the erotic fantasies that develop among young girls imagining what lies before them. In aligning ethnography, ritual, and tradition with theater and sexual fantasy, Asch announces the (homo)erotic powers of both tradition and its modern reenactments.

The erotic possibilities of sexual segregation were also visible to Dvora Baron, despite her more frequent focus on women's exclusion from Jewish textual and ritual spaces. Such marginalization was in intent and general effect both painful and unjust, as Baron persisted in showing; nevertheless, sexual segregation could also work positively, to construct regions of pleasure and social connection. "Fedka," published in Hebrew and Yiddish in 1909, describes a town in which all the adult Jewish males have left to seek their fortune "abroad," in the New World. The town is not entirely devoid of men, only of husbands: the title character is the saintly, gentle (and Gentile) postman, who brings the townswomen news from their husbands overseas. The notion of a shtetl abandoned by its entire male population is obviously fantastic, but it is not entirely without historical or sociological grounding. Such processes as urbanization, proletarianization, and mass migration (the historical phenomenon in the immediate background of Baron's story) shook the traditional Jewish family to its core.[58]

Bluma Goldstein has written about male adventurism and wife abandonment in Jewish literary and historical modernity,[59] and the writers discussed here include an inordinate number of such adventurers: Salomon Maimon abandoned his wife and family in search of Enlightenment and education, as did (less permanently) Moshe Leib Lilienblum. In early twentieth-century New York, the *Forward* featured a "Gallery of Disappeared Men" that included the pleas of children and wives to their missing men. Jewish literature of the era reflects these realities (or aspirations): Benjamin and Senderl leave their wives behind in search of the Red Jews in Abramovitsh's *Travels of Benjamin the Third*; the plot of Y. L. Gordon's epic poem *The Tip of the Yud* hinges on another such abandonment; and Sholem Aleichem's *Menachem Mendl* consists entirely of letters exchanged by a wife and her husband, who is traveling the Jewish world in search of a living. Dan Miron argues that the *agunah* appears regularly in shtetl fiction as more than a reflection of social realities; she also signals the affinity between these tales and the metaphysical narrative of the people of Israel in exile, emblematized by the figure of the widow or abandoned woman in biblical and midrashic literature. The shtetl, Miron suggests, "was Jerusalem in her fallen state, and yet it was still Jerusalem—the Jewish polity par excellence."[60] The abandoned woman is not only collateral damage in the movements of modernity and the most visible victim of halakhic patriarchy; she is also the most potent symbol for the national catastrophe of exile in its much longer reach.

Baron's shtetl tale is faithful to the language and many of the details of the midrash in Lamentations Rabba 3:21, which describes Israel as God's wife, abandoned after her husband "journeyed abroad." The abandoned woman is mocked by her neighbors, who say, "Go! Marry another man!," but she remains faithful to her husband, reading and rereading her marriage settlement—the Torah—in the absence of the man who bestowed it upon her. When her husband finally returns and praises his wife's faithfulness, she replies: "My master, O King! If not for the large wedding-settlement you wrote me, my neighbors long ago would have led me astray."[61] While Baron seems to be referring to this story, she rejects both its tragic tone and pious conclusion. Nor, like other works of shtetl literature, does she take the desertion scene as occasion for reflecting on Jewish marital dysfunction, showing us neither weeping women nor viragoes (like Benjamin and Senderl's wives or Menachem Mendl's Sheina Sheindl) pursuing their browbeaten husbands. Instead, she imagines a female

population that wears its abandonment lightly, helped by the pleasant circumstance of being collectively in love with the postman, who fully returns
their affection and ardor. Fedka of course has the important function of
bringing the mail, and like the abandoned woman in Lamentations Rabba,
these women too are ardent readers of their husbands' words. But far from
Fedka being merely the vehicle for the more evidently important relationship that connects the wives with their husbands in America, his postal
deliveries become the occasion for an ongoing flirtation with the women
who depend on him for a range of masculine and Gentile services: not only
opening letters that arrive on the Sabbath but also unscrewing recalcitrant
bottles and, as the story hints, providing sexual comfort and diversion. On
the Sabbath, Fedka postpones his delivery until the afternoon, strategically timing it to coincide with the languor of the post-chulent nap: "The
shutters are closed, the house is stifling and dark. Women and girls dressed
in nightgowns and slips try to scurry away, but Fedka hushes them, wav-
ing his arms. 'Sh . . .' As if absentmindedly his hand grazes a soft heaving
breast; on his face he suddenly feels a panting breath that makes his blood
sizzle: 'Fedka-a-a . . .'"[62]

In "Fedka," Baron reverses the nearly universal perspective that privileges
the masculine journey over the experiences of the women left behind, uncovering a store of hidden compensations in a shtetl emptied of Jewish men.
"Fedka" both mobilizes and undoes the metaphorical structure that in the
classical shtetl literature views the shtetl as a fallen Jerusalem. By describing
the mutual attraction between a non-Jew and the women left by their Jewish husbands, Baron in effect gives new voice to the "neighbor women" of
Lamentations Rabba who urge the deserted women to take their husband's
absence as license to find another man. As David Stern points out, the suggestion of the neighbors (Gentiles?) may not be a taunt but "a perfectly
accurate view of the state of the marriage" and "a perfectly neighborly ges-
ture"; it is Stern's reading of the parable as critique of the divine "husband"
(rather than praise for the faithful wife) that finds expression in Baron's
rewriting of the narrative.[63] Lamentations Rabba ultimately prescribes the
text—both marriage contract and Torah—as a substitute for husbandly affections; Baron, however, suggests that the postman may serve as erotic
substitute for the texts he delivers. Baron, then, takes up the recommendation offered by the neighbors, and through these neighbors by the rabbis,
that an abandoned woman should find her comfort where she can.

Baron's radical rereading of Lamentations Rabba is also a rereading of traditional sexual segregation. Modernist writers like Agnon explore the eroticism of traditional Jewish life by staging erotic encounters in the synagogue and imagining how the partitions between Jewish men and women could energize rather than quell sexual desire. Baron depicts the enticements of a Jewish women's space unseen by men—in effect, an entirely female shtetl. This shtetl, which is in structural accordance with the notion of a feminized collective abandoned by its (divine) husband, deviates from the tragic, redemptive, national model by rereading abandonment as freedom, separation from men as liberation from patriarchal constraint, the women's section as the center rather than the margins of the world. Reading God's "wife" more literally to denote a *female* Jewish collective, Baron stages an erotic scenario that dissolves both ethnic borders and the ineluctable narrative of religious teleology. In this scene, the homosocial and the heteroerotic work together to produce these pleasures. Privileging the present (man) over the absent (men), the visible over the textual, immediate pleasure over future redemption, Baron also invites us to recognize the grand religious narrative of Jewish exile as having prematurely foreclosed the pleasures of Diaspora and the company of Gentiles. And she does so precisely by producing a modern midrash, grounding her declaration of freedom from the sacred text in the unexplored potential of sacred texts, in the lines attributed to "others" within rabbinic scenarios. In focusing on the recommendations of the neighbor women rather than strictures of the marriage contract, and on the women left behind rather than the men who travel on, Baron invites us to read both modernity and the Jewish national epic entirely differently.

. . .

The discovery of the erotic potential of sexually segregated spaces was not solely a feature of high modernism. The twentieth century saw two enormously popular films that appealed to audiences at least partly by showcasing homosocial worlds—the 1936 Yiddish musical comedy (directed by Joseph Green) *Yidl with His Fiddle* and Barbra Streisand's 1983 musical drama *Yentl*, which was based on Isaac Bashevis Singer's 1962 short story "Yentl the Yeshiva Boy." *Yidl with the Fiddle* features the Yiddish star of the stage and screen Molly Picon as a young woman who disguises herself in male garb to play in a klezmer band. Picon's role here harkens back to the female transvestism of such earlier stars of the Yiddish stage as Pepi Littman and to other plays and films in her own wildly successful career.[64] As occurred in other plays and films in which Picon starred, the popularity of the film derived from the delight audiences took in watching the boyish Picon's antics. The film opens by introducing us to the fiddle-playing, motherless Itke, a girl who cross-dresses and takes the name Yidl in order to travel more freely and safely after she and her father have been evicted from their home. The pair are soon joined by two other musicians, and together the four make up a traveling klezmer band.

Yidl's strategic cross-dressing should be understood through the recognizable figure and subgenre of the "temporary transvestite," the conventions of which are summarized by Chris Straayer as "simultaneous believability of this disguise to the film's characters and its unbelievability to the film's audience . . . a progression toward slapstick comedy and increased physicality; heterosexual desire thwarted by the character's disguise; accusations of homosexuality regarding the disguised character; romantic encounters that are mistakenly interpreted as homosexual or heterosexual; an 'unmasking' of the transvestite; and finally, heterosexual coupling."[65] *Yidl with His Fiddle* conforms to each of these conventions: Itke/Yidl is clearly a girl in the viewers' eyes but unrecognized as such by her fellow musicians; Froim's disgust at her mooning adoration of him might qualify as a veiled "accusation of homosexuality"; the film revels in the physical comedy of Yidl's drunkenness in her attempts at matching her bandmates drink for drink; she is publicly "unmasked" in a pivotal scene; and the film ends with the young man and woman—now "properly" attired—united as a bourgeois heterosexual couple on their way to America. Such a progression permits the audience to enjoy the apparently homosexual love scenes between the cross-dressed Yidl and her beloved Froim, all the while knowing what Froim does not, that the figure swooning in his arms is a woman and not the irritatingly effeminate but still adorable young boy that Froim thinks Yidl is, and that the pair will soon enough be united according to appropriate gender and sexual models. *Yidl with His Fiddle* thus gives the audience the frisson of watching an apparently homosexual romance develop while remaining secure in the foreknowledge of a properly heterosexual happy ending: marriage, musical celebrity, and a first-class voyage to the *goldene medine*—America, the golden land. In this as in other films, the queerness of traditional Jewish gender is allowed its moment before it is ultimately overcome.

If the transvestite career of Molly Picon and, more particularly, *Yidl with His Fiddle*, matches a widespread and readily recognizable model of how ostensibly bourgeois audiences nevertheless regularly enjoy a kind of flirtation with homosexual transgression, this queer flirtation takes on particular significance in the Jewish case. Yidl speaks directly to Jewish modernization as the transformation of traditional Ashkenazic gender roles, sexual practices, and marital structures, traversing in a single (comic and "deviant") story the much larger meta-narrative of modernization as sexual transformation. Warren Hoffman writes that "Picon's work speaks to the numerous changes in race, gender, and sexuality that the Jewish community at large was experiencing. The success of cross-dressing becomes a metaphor for the passing and cross-dressing behavior that Picon's assimilating behavior was arguably going through as well."[66] The agility of Picon's movement from role to role and the cinematic framing of these movements within a romantic comedy that ends well (with a successful romantic pairing and a ticket to middle-class society) was a way of mirroring, encapsulating, and comically easing the difficult traversals that had brought the viewing audience to where they were.

The film might illuminate both the social and geographic displacements that characterize the culture it addresses and from which it emerges and some of the literary history I have been tracing here. The backstory of *Yidl with the Fiddle*, as retold in Picon's autobiography, records a tension between the director's original ideas for the film and its eventual shape: The story as first conceived featured a bride in an arranged match who runs away from her wedding to be with her lover with the help of the bohemian musicians hired to play her wedding. When it became clear that Picon was both unsuited for and uninterested in playing such a conventionally attractive (that is, feminine) young woman, the plot was revised to relegate the escaped bride to a brief subplot of the main story, which now more prominently featured the klezmer band in which a cross-dressed Picon played the fiddle.[67] With this story at front and center, Picon had the opportunity to parade her bag of gender tricks, charming the audience not in the exalted role of bride but as a young woman freed from an onerous husband and the choreographed courtship, the staged and complementary gender roles that are the prelude to modern marriage and the staple of modern literature. In the negotiations between a rather conventional director and his less conventional star, the play recapitulates some of the history I have been tracing in this book: At first, the only possible romantic story involved that staple of Haskalah narrative, the tension between arranged marriage and true romantic love. But what interested Picon in this configuration was neither the wedding nor the scene of romantic bliss. Where Picon wanted to be, and where audiences wanted to see her, was in a klezmer band, a "third space" whose erotic potential remained unimagined in the Haskalah plot, the European romance it borrowed for Jewish purposes, and the many epigonic echoes of this marriage plot.

Picon's cross-dressing, read so regularly either as queer gender performance or (homo)sexual play, is thus also the traversal of different *social* structures. The one that wins out sees her hand in hand with Froim, alone with him and gazing lovingly into his eyes as they sail off to America. But this happy ending lasts hardly a minute before the credits roll. The real treat of the film, for the moviegoer as for Picon and Yidl, is the time Yidl and Froim spend together not as a couple but as part of a larger traveling band of musicians, sharing a barn, playing drinking games and singing bawdy songs, stealing food from the kitchen at the wedding they have been hired to play—activities that stand at the furthest remove from the choreographed courtship, gender complementarity, and the drama of mutual recognition that characterize bourgeois romance. The love affair between Froim and Yidl has the power it does because it partakes of the directness, physicality, and earthiness that is by convention permitted among men and ruled out by the linguistic codes and gender ideologies that shape bourgeois heterosocial discourse.

This affair also fails to conform, until the "happy ending," to the binarism of the (complementary) couple—the band travels as a foursome, with the multiple requirements of musical harmony dictating their interactions rather than the binarisms of gender. Yidl is able to know Froim far better than the runaway bride with whom Froim has an entirely conventional romantic flirtation: while the "heterosexual" pair progress in intimacy in carefully calibrated moves, Froim and Yidl sleep side-by-side in a barn the very first night of their acquaintance, with Froim's leg flung casually over Yidl's excited and terrified body; they make music, drink in taverns, and curse at each other in ways ruled out between proper men and women. The freedom from sexual harassment that Yidl's male garb allows thus also grants her entry into the easy physical companionship that develops among an all-male traveling band. In this space, Yidl is at once performing as a boy and liberated from the apparently more onerous codes that govern, for a young girl, what Erving Goffman calls "the presentation of self in everyday life."[68]

The difference between the relationship the cross-dressed Yidl has with Froim and the proper bourgeois couple they become is not (or not only) the distinction between an apparently homosexual flirtation and a clearly heterosexual romance but between a relationship that finds its pleasures beyond the couple and outside the ideology of gender complementarity and one that rests entirely on those foundations. The attractions of such homosocial spaces as the film lovingly stages have been misread, it seems to me, by an automatic recourse to the language of sexual orientation. The popularity of the film testifies to the fact that in post-traditional societies, homosocial desire has a far broader range of significations than a discourse grounded in minoritarian sexual orientation can begin to recognize. What *Yidl with His Fiddle* stages is the nostalgia for the spaces and social relations made available by traditional sexual segregation and vacated in bourgeois romance (and, in some ways, also forgotten in its queer overthrow).

A half century later, Streisand's film *Yentl* (1983) achieved equal popularity by replaying the same "temporary transvestite" plot. After the death of her father, Yentl cashes in her inheritance, brushes off the attention of neighbors and matchmakers, clothes herself in her father's garb, and sets off to fulfill her desire to study in a yeshiva. Dressed as a boy, she succeeds in her plan, although—as with Yidl—romantic complications ensue. The story on which the film is based, however, does not entirely conform to the "temporary transvestite" plot. While Yentl reveals her female body to her study partner and friend Avigdor, she has no desire to revert to dressing like a woman in order to become his wife, and this undressing is no prelude to a heteronormative happy ending. The criticisms of the film were largely directed at Streisand's resistance to such irresolution: Singer ends his story on a tragic note, with Yentl leaving town for an unknown destination, leaving behind his friend Avigdor and former wife Hadas joined in a mournful marriage, in which they name their firstborn Anshel after their disappeared friend. The film version of *Yentl* ends with a scene that echoes the final shot of *Yidl with His Fiddle*, although Yentl (presumably as befits a modern woman) is alone on board a ship to America. In Streisand's revision of Singer's plot, she is now dressed as a woman; the implication is that in the freedoms of the New World, she no longer has to cross-dress, as was necessary for her to participate in the masculine activities of the tradition she is leaving behind.

Streisand's ending bolsters some of the interpretations of Singer's story that view it as directed against traditional society. David Biale, for instance, reads Singer's story as a critique of the suppression of both female intellectual aspirations and romantic love in modern society: "the traditional Jewish world, Singer intimates, could not accommodate either the liberation of women or modern romantic love without tragic consequences."[69] Nancy Berkowitz Bate similarly judges that "according to the narrow sex role definitions of her era, Yentl can live neither as a man nor woman, homosexual nor heterosexual."[70] In these readings, Singer (or Singer and Streisand) is a belated critic of Jewish tradition, championing its rebels as he excoriates its gender roles and oppressive structures. These interpretations stand in some tension with others that mine the film and story for their "queer" content and view Jewish tradition as queer rather than patriarchal and homophobic. For Marjorie Garber, Yentl's cross-dressing embodies the movement of modern Jews between lands, cultures, and gender systems:

> The transvestite is a sign of the category crisis of the immigrant, between nations, forced out of one role that no longer fits (here, on the surface, because a woman can't be a scholar; but not very far beneath the surface, because of poverty, anti-Semitism, and pogrom, Jewish as well as female) and into another role, that of a stranger in a strange land.[71]

These category crises are sexual as well as geographic and historical, reflecting the gender trouble visited on traditional Jewish masculinity in its confrontation with modern bourgeois masculine ideals (although of course Yentl is a female character). In Garber's summary of this difference, "one mode of Jewish 'manliness' mandated a life of study; another accepted a definition of 'manhood' based upon martial values and physical perfectionism." As elsewhere in the queer studies literature, Garber's analysis rests on notions that modern Jewish anxieties about defective masculinity are closely linked with circumcision. Drawing attention to the fact that when Yentl/Anshel orders a suit, the tailors who take his/her measure are *Schneiders*, cutters ("a word that Freud points out is related to the verb *beschneiden*, 'to circumcise'"), Garber continues: "Are Orthodox Jewish men, ritually circumcised, really any different from women? the film seems, teasingly, to ask."[72] Although Singer relates Yentl's cross-dressing to the fact that she was "unlike any of the girls in Yanev—tall, thin, bony, with small breasts and narrow hips," this transvestism is linked less to the "manliness" of this female character than to the "femininity" of the Jewish man she is so easily taken for:

> The secret—open to the audience and the reader—of "Anshel's" gender tells a double-edged story about the "manliness" of Torah study and scholarship. In Jewish tradition there is no higher calling for a man. . . . In the case of Yentl, is the "real" story one of a woman who needs to "become a man" in order to study Torah—or the story of a Torah scholar who is "revealed" to be a woman?[73]

Echoing and explicating Garber, Daniel Boyarin writes:

> On one hand, it is clear that the one who is cross-dressed is the girl, Yentl, who dresses as a boy in order to study in the Yeshiva; her very study is cross-dressing as well. On the other hand, the fact that she is indistinguishable as a girl dressed as a boy owes something to the effeminate or cross-dressed nature of the boys vis-à-vis European norms of manliness in the Yeshiva as well.[74]

This interpretation focuses primarily on the traditional gender roles that "improperly" link ideal masculinity with scholarship rather than physical prowess. Within one widespread understanding of the relationships between gender roles and sexual orientation, a "wrong" gender performance correlates with "deviant" sexual inclinations; it is no surprise, then, that, as Garber writes, the scene in *Yentl* between Streisand and Amy Irving "smolders with repressed sexuality,"[75] a homoerotic subtext that for Garber also correlates with the position of Jews as the Asiatic others of the Central European imaginary.

However well this analysis correlates with contemporary understandings of the relationship between gender performance and sexual orientation, or with the queer studies analyses of Jewish male effeminacy, the notion that Yentl escapes detection because Torah scholars are themselves already effeminate has no basis in Singer's story, which instead notes the pleasure Yentl takes in her inaugural excursion, as Anshel, into a world of young Jewish men:

> It was the first time that Yentl had ever found herself alone in the company of young men. How different their talk was from the jabbering of women, she thought but she was too shy to join in. One young man discussed a prospective match and the size of the dowry, while another, parodying the

manner of a Purim rabbi, declaimed a passage from the Torah, adding all sorts of lewd interpretations. After a while the company proceeded to tests of strength (*oyspruvn di koykhes*). One pried open another's fist; a second tried to bend a companion's arm. One student, dining on bread and tea, had no spoon and stirred his cup with his penknife.[76]

These young men are not the delicate Torah scholars Garber and Boyarin describe. They talk about Torah among other subjects, but they do so with no delicacy at all. Yentl is fascinated with their company, gratified to be admitted into their circle, and identifies with their conversational interests over those of "her own sex"; it turns out, though, that she is attracted to the smartest and kindest of the group, Avigdor, who becomes her friend and protector. What constitutes the "gender performance" of any of these men? And where in the story or in its narration is the sexual stigmatization Garber sees as so critical and painful a feature of modern Jewish masculinity?

The approach to "Yentl the Yeshiva Boy" laid out in Garber and elsewhere leans heavily on the discourse about homosexuality that associates it with cross-dressing and other deviant sexual performances, but there are other sexological approaches that might illuminate the story before us. Eve Kosofsky Sedgwick describes a "contradiction between seeing same-sex object choice on the one hand as a matter of liminality or transitivity between genders, and seeing it on the other hand as reflecting an impulse of separatism . . . within each gender."[77] In the "third-sex" model (associated with Magnus Hirschfeld and his Wissenschaftlich-humanitäres Komitee, Scientific-Humanitarian Committee), behaviors that fall in the "middle" of the gender spectrum correlate with homosexual desire, while in the "separatist" model (associated with the also-Jewish Benedict Friedländer and his Gemeinschaft der Eigenen, Community of the Special or Fellowship of Individuals), the converse is true, and (male) homosexuality is the expression of the highest degree of masculinity. The homosexual in this view "was seen as the founder of patriarchal society and ranked above the heterosexual in terms of his capacity for leadership and heroism."[78] These differences were not merely theoretical: Hirschfeld's Komitee included men and women, but Friedländer's Gemeinschaft was exclusively male. As Sedgwick adds, the logic of such separatism is clear: "Far from its being of the essence of desire to cross boundaries of gender, it is instead the most natural thing in the world that people of the same gender, people grouped together under the single most determinative diacritical mark of social organization, people whose economic, institutional, emotional, physical needs and knowledges may have so much in common, should bond together also on the axis of sexual desire."[79] In this view, homosexuality entailed no necessary stigmatization and might manifest itself as a noble, pure, and exalted calling.

Sedgwick's interest is in recognizing the "intractable, highly structured discursive incoherence" at the heart of the "most generative and most murderous plots of our culture," the discourses linking gender and sexuality.[80] Without claiming a greater coherence or more benign effects for Ashkenazic culture, it is worth pointing out that Ashkenazic culture might also represent a third way within both the homosexual-heterosexual binary and the "transitivity"/"separatist" models of homosexuality. The yeshiva world Singer is describing falls somewhere between the separatist and third-sex models: Yentl is described as "transitive" in her physical resemblance to a man and spiritual aspirations to be (like) one, and at least her relationship with Hadas could be characterized as a lesbian marriage. Nevertheless, Yentl's most passionate attachment is to Avigdor, (clothing aside) an apparently heterosexual attachment. But it is the arena in which these relationships play themselves out that seems most distinctive, and least acknowledged. Yentl, Hadas, and Avigdor all live within a separatist world, and one in which separatism, far from bearing sexual stigma, carries with it the valuation of masculine speech and activities that Yentl shares with the young men whose company she keeps. Yentl's "social" desires to live among men and study Talmud governs *both* of her (bi)sexual "romantic" investments; her attraction to Avigdor can hardly be separated from her longing to study Talmud with him. In "Yentl the Yeshiva Boy," after Anshel has confessed to Avigdor that she is actually Yentl, a woman in male dress, their friendship and mutual love rapidly become awkward: "their intimate talk, their confidences, had been turned into a sham and delusion," Avigdor feels. But soon enough the friends and study partners enjoy renewed intimacy, debating the halakhic ramifications of the problem of "Avigdor spending another moment alone with Yentl." As romantic opportunity, the problem of Yentl's being a woman produces nothing but discomfort. But as halakhic argument (precisely the field that would appear to foreclose such mixing of the sexes), it leads them back to the friendship they knew as study partners:

> Gradually the two went back to their Talmudic conversation (*beyde khaverim hobn genumen shmuesn un lernen*). It seemed strange at first to Avigdor to be

disputing holy writ with a woman, yet before long the Torah reunited them. Though their bodies were different, their souls were of one kind. Anshel spoke in a singsong, gesticulated with her thumb, clutched her sidelocks, plucked at her beardless chin, made all the customary gestures of a yeshiva student. In the heat of argument she even seized Avigdor by the lapel and called him stupid. A great love for Anshel took hold of Avigdor, mixed with shame, remorse, anxiety. . . . For the first time he saw clearly that this was what he had always wanted: a wife whose mind was not taken up with material things.[81]

Avigdor's stereotypical denigration of women as materialistic, one impetus for his great love of Anshel, exposes a contradiction internal to Western heterosexual ideals. As Stephanie Coontz writes, the doctrine of sexual difference arose in association and tension with the sentimental discourse of companionate marriage among the nineteenth-century European bourgeoisie. "The conviction that men and women had inherently different natures remained an impediment to romantic love and intimacy, making men and women both complementary figures and driving a wedge between them."[82] But this same obstacle is no obstacle at all over the pages of a Talmud; Jiří Langer's description of the Hasidic study hall of early twentieth-century Galicia (discussed in Chapter 2) suggests that the "customary gestures of a yeshiva student" allowed for physical intimacies of the most passionate sort. Anshel's cross-dressing should be read neither as a symptom of his (or her) homosexual orientation nor as evidence of the "effeminacy" of Jewish men. Anshel's cross-dressing is a strategy for evading the choreography of bourgeois gender relations; such cross-dressing allows (indeed, is the only structure that allows) a young man and woman to encounter each other within the "democratic," aggressive intimacy native to Talmudic argument, and foreign to the "civilized" choreography of bourgeois gender performance. Modernity is thus no solution to the dilemma posed by Yentl's impossible, multiple, transgressive, traditional desires. Anshel's drag swings both ways, sexually and culturally, and should be read more "bisexually," as the impossible combination of modern and traditional social spaces and the erotic pleasures each of them holds. Singer's story and Streisand's film did not find their success they because they criticized traditional social structures that kept women from participating in valued male activities but because they imagined ways for their stars and audiences to participate in pleasures unavailable elsewhere in modern life. Reading from East to West, Yiddish drag emerges not as a move toward modern freedoms but as a strategy for finding the way back to the structures abandoned in the secularizing drive. In drag, the disparate sexual cultures of traditional Ashkenaz and its modern successors could argue their respective positions as ferociously and passionately as only Talmud study could allow.

Afterword

After Marriage

> I still want your body,
> That body young and true,
> They can bury your soul, love,
> I've soul enough for two.
>
> —Heinrich Heine, Lyric Intermezzo: "I cannot forget it"

In 1888, S. Y. Abramovitsh declared to Sholem Aleichem that Jews had a distinct sexual culture, that "the circumstances in which a Jew can love are entirely different from those of other people. The Jewish people today have their own character, their own Jewish spirit with its distinctive customs and habits, different from other peoples'."[1] What was this difference? And if Abramovitsh was correct in diagnosing Jews as sexually different, even after secularization and the abandonment of halakhic practice, has this difference persisted?

Persisted where and in whom? More than just the ordinary passage of time separates the traditional and post-traditional Ashkenazic Jews of the nineteenth century from their dispersed descendants; any cultural after-effects of their secularization are similarly fractured, prismatically separating into different components or turning back to "recover" elements of the Eastern European past apparently jettisoned and forgotten. The very notion of describing "Jewish culture" is rightly viewed with skepticism in contemporary academic discourse as retrograde, nostalgic, "essentializing," liable to fall into the "booster-bigot trap." David Hollinger, who identifies this trap, insists on recognizing "the internal diversity of ethnoracial groups and the contingent, historically specific character of the culture these communities present to the larger society at any given moment."[2] Evidence that I risked such pitfalls is the entirety of this book; my main defense is that I stand in a line of diagnosticians of Jewish sexual culture, and in presenting their notions along with mine, I hope to relativize my own (explicit and implicit) theories along with theirs. This is a book about Jewish discourses around sex and marriage rather than about Jewish sex itself. Nevertheless, the very structure of my book, in which each chapter concludes with a section that describes the recovery of a traditional sexual practice ostensibly overthrown in the Haskalah (arranged marriage, pedigree, the extended family, sexual segregation), suggests that the distinctive sexual character of Ashkenazic culture (whatever that might be) either "persists" in diasporic expression or "returns" through conscious reclamation and memory construction.

Although this book begins with a sociological-literary analysis of modernization as *embourgeoisement*, most of the examples for the recovery of traditional Jewish practices and customs are literary. There is some logic to this. This recovery was often literary, and just as in the Haskalah, literature did not reflect realities but served "compensatory" functions; for example, Bernard Malamud depicted a marriage broker in "The Magic Barrel" without ever having met one in the flesh.[3] This view of tradition as filtered through absence, loss, and nostalgia represents secularization as the uncontested norm, failing to recognize that traditional Jewish practices also simply "continued" (although not "unbroken"). With these warnings in full view, I nevertheless cautiously address the question in this afterword: What persists of the traditional Ashkenazic sex-gender system in the post-Ashkenazic cultures of our own time?

In the previous chapter, I argued that traditional sexual segregation, initially understood primarily as a form of sexual control, came to be seen as holding erotic attractions for both literature and life. Sexual segregation, which the nineteenth-century modernizers believed they had laid to rest in the name of a desegregated bourgeois society, indeed persisted in such "modern" phenomena as Jewish youth movements and has even increased in contemporary life, less as a literary trope than as a dramatic form of social engineering. Witness, for instance, recent attempts by *haredi* communities in Israel to impose segregation far more widely and publicly than was ever accomplished in even the strictest Eastern European Jewish circles. The violence that greets women who transgress the rules of segregation in buses and public spaces, and the move to erase images of women from public advertisements and women's voices from the airwaves and public meetings, testifies to the sexual aggression and misogyny that underlie at least some of these segregationist impulses (that segregationist efforts function as political assertion by a growing demographic on various public stages is also undoubtedly true).[4] But sexual segregation is not only about sexual control and the exclusion of women from high-status masculine activities; it is also the mechanism for the production of (eroticized) homosocial spaces. No doubt the attraction of these spaces is among the reasons for their expansion and persistence, as primary characteristics and social sites of our post-secular age.

The erotics of sexual segregation, which undoubtedly functions differently in different contexts, may help explain one particular conundrum Debra Kaufman describes: the return of significant numbers of secular, liberal, and feminist women to religious practice. Writing of feminists who join Hasidic groups, Kaufman asks, "What maintains these women's commitments to a past not of their own making and to a patriarchal present? How can one conclude that these women's lives are anything but oppressive and 'alienated'?"[5] Acknowledging that these newly Hasidic women represent themselves as the guardians of a tradition from which they descend (if not individually, then as a collective) against a materialistic, individualistic, and self-indulgent dominant culture, Kaufman also concludes that the social practices of Orthodox Judaism, along with those of "evangelical theology and institutions, may be flexible resources for renegotiating gender and family relationships."[6]

Among these flexible resources might be counted the power of homosocial organization for women (and men) of a variety of sexual, political, and cultural orientations and histories. Feminism, from one point of view, is the ideological challenge to the strict gender hierarchies and masculinist exclusions of Orthodox life, which leads to the very question Kaufman raises: How can avowed feminists willingly join a society so committed to patriarchal practices? But from the perspective mobilized in this book, feminism presents itself as ideological cousin to homosocial desire and thus allied to (many) traditional social structures rather than in necessary opposition to them. It is at least possible, then, that conservative Orthodox communities, with their genius for same-sex rituals and practices, satisfy one particular aspect of feminist desire—what was referred to, in a now-bygone time, as "sisterhood." I would caution against the assumption that homosocial desire is a cover for the psychologically "deeper" dimension of sexual orientation (and against the secularist bias that slights the power of "purely" religious impulses). Our social desires may be as profound as our sexual impulses or political stances; they are certainly productive of political and religious affiliation and also may be productive of sexual orientation.[7]

The paradox sociologists confront in the phenomenon of the turn to conservative religious communities is no paradox at all. It may be patriarchal social formations, segregating the sexes ostensibly in the name of sexual control, that nevertheless are most effective at producing and sheltering homosocial communities and thus satisfying the homosocial desires that more secular, liberal, and modern formations leave unfulfilled because unacknowledged. Through a range of religious and cultural practices, these homosocial communities sexualize human connections both across gender boundaries and within homosocial spaces. My attention to the homosocial dimension of the traditional Jewish sex-gender system is not intended to slight homosexual desires. Jiří Langer's embrace of Hasidism as, in Shaun Halper's words, "an incubator of homosexual desire" stands as evidence that, despite the halakhic prohibition against sex between men (and perhaps also women), a society that distributes social and sexual energy "bisexually" may in some regards be more hospitable to gay men and lesbians, precisely because the concept of sexual orientation plays no part in this system.[8] Of course, I do not mean to slight the real discrimination and pain that queer individuals and communities have experienced and continue to experience in Jewish and other settings, as part of traditional halakhic constraints or secular liberal homophobic environments.

The weight of my argument in this book is not, however, on the persistence of traditional Ashkenazic culture in contemporary religious Jewish communities. What I have repeatedly drawn attention to is the more surprising evidence of the persistence of at least some features of this society among post-traditional and secular Jews. The emergence in the past few decades of "Queer Yiddishkeit," a mystifying phenomenon to some unsympathetic observers, raises particularly acute questions about the relationship between the sexual character of traditional or secular Yiddish culture and this contemporary phenomenon.[9] That early twentieth-century Yiddish circles included open homosexuals and even what Jeffrey Shandler calls "homophilic" subcultures is by now well established. Nevertheless, there are other ways beyond direct lineage to draw connections between the artists, writers, and activists who identify with Queer Yiddishkeit and these earlier Yiddish-speaking cultures. Speaking of "parallel systems of alterity," Alisa Solomon names some correspondences: "diasporism; rootless cosmopolitanism; a penchant for transgression, border-crossing, and being proudly, defiantly different; standing as a challenge to broader societies' sense of 'certitude and power.'"[10]

But of course no direct lineage need be established. Queer perspectives have allowed us to see with ever greater clarity that kinship is necessarily an "invention," and any defense of the "pedigree" of Queer Yiddishkeit is surely unnecessary. Against the fetishization of Yiddish cultural "continuity," Shandler argues for the value of "the contributions made by other forms of social contact [than those forged in the family] to cultural, and therefore linguistic vitality—including the vitality generated by 'scrambling' in response to discontinuity."[11] He also reminds us that "although Yiddish culture is often vaunted as a 'golden chain' forged by an unbroken succession of biological generations, it might be better understood in the modern era as proceeding through cohort generations, manifest in youth organizations, religious movements, political parties, trade unions, literary circles, educational institutions, various immigrant, refugee, and survivor associations, and so on."[12] The questionable legitimacy of Queer Yiddishkeit as an offspring of traditional Ashkenaz is thus answered by new understandings that render the constructedness of all genealogies more visible.

I would just make one intervention to this understanding of what might be considered the persistence of Yiddish culture in contemporary Jewish life. The persistence or reclamation of traditional Jewish culture in contemporary queer formations often privileges both categories in their "minoritarian" status, to use Eve Kosofsky Sedgwick's distinction.[13] The minoritarian stance characterizes the wave of publications that emerged from the extraordinarily dense intersection connecting queer studies, postcolonial theory, and Jewish studies: In these writings, the "parallel lines" of Jewish and queer identities meet at the stigmatized Jewish male who is both feminized and viewed as homosexual within the European societies he faces and wishes to enter. The argument I make in this book, in contrast to minoritarian approaches, might be termed "majoritarian" in at least three senses:[14] My reading of the queerness of traditional Ashkenaz (and its secular diasporas) is majoritarian in taking a wide view of what constitutes its sexual difference, encompassing not only improper Jewish gender performances and inappropriate attachments between men or women but also Jewish heteronormativity and traditional Ashkenazic marriage and kinship patterns. These patterns are also queer, if by queer we mean the specificity, contingency, distinction, unnaturalness, and even oddity of all sex-gender systems, including heteronormative ones; of course, they are also queer in relation to other European models. But while the minoritarian view tends to privilege the transgressive or subversive aspects of culture-as-subculture, the majoritarian view allows us to take full measure of the conservative, patriarchal, and normative dimensions of traditional and post-traditional Ashkenazic culture, recognizing the ways in which elites within this culture wield power in relation to other classes and groups within Ashkenaz (even if these elites also suffer stigma in a larger European context). One part of the claim I am making is that modern Jewish sexuality—as experience and discourse—has been culturally powerful, not only marginal, and sometimes culturally powerful in its very marginality and queerness.

My approach is majoritarian in yet another sense: Gershon David Hundert argues that, for Jews in Poland-Lithuania in the eighteenth century, the term "minority" hardly applies, since "most Jews lived in communities that were quite large enough to support the living of the dailiness of life in a Jewish universe."[15] This life in a Jewish universe persisted through the dramatic processes of modernization and Europeanization and was even enriched in what Benjamin Harshav calls the "polysystem" of secular Jewish Eastern European culture.[16] Taking the measure of Eastern European Jewry by how it was viewed by the Central European "colonialist gaze" (whether or not transvalued by queer pride) slights the self-confidence of even modernizing Jews, who are perfectly capable of aspiring to be more European while deftly "reversing the colonialist gaze." As Haskalah literature teaches us, Europeanization often proceeded at some remove from actual non-Jews, manifesting itself, for instance, in emulation of German Jews (often called simply Germans) or as imitation of literary models of modernity. The association of a minority culture with "diasporism; rootless cosmopolitanism; a penchant for transgression, border-crossing, and being proudly, defiantly different" hardly registers the "thickness" of the Jewish worlds in which Hebrew and Yiddish literature emerged. It is within this rich cultural context that the stigmatization of Jewish difference shows its other face as the *wielding* of

Jewish distinctiveness. Even *The Travels of Benjamin the Third*, which ridicules the "lovebirds" Senderl the Woman and his bosom friend Benjamin in their differences from proper European masculinity, ultimately also redirects its satire against the soldiers in the czar's army, showing how absurd army life appears from any reasonable Jewish perspective.

Nor should we overlook the thickness of the Jewish context in which twentieth-century Jewish modernism emerged. Rabbi Joseph Silverman of New York's Temple Emanu-El, who lodged the 1923 obscenity complaint against the Broadway production *God of Vengeance*, may well have conformed to the colonial model of self-consciousness about Jewish sexual difference in the face of genteel (and Gentile) norms; but the unscandalized theatergoers who for decades sold out Yiddish performances of the play on the Lower East Side were no doubt closer to the perspective embodied in the play. Such majoritarian freedoms are also visible in the production of English-speaking Jews who published or performed in places like New York or Hollywood, and only the persistence of *Leidensgeschichte*—the "lachrymose" view of Jewish history—invites the regular recourse to a discourse of marginalization in critical descriptions of their work.

Finally, my reading is majoritarian in the sense that the rich Jewish subculture that developed among "countercultural, leftist, and queer American Jews" has now fully entered the American mainstream (and beyond).[17] The broadest claim I make in this book is that the Jewish counter-discourse to the sex religion that I have been tracing, even if it has roots in a cultural formation that includes self-criticism over the "backwardness" and impropriety of its sexual habits in relation to European norms, has by now become the dominant discourse around sex in the West. At least in this regard, either Jews are not a minority or marginality is a much broader and more powerful condition than generally recognized.

In distinguishing my argument from postcolonialist minoritarian readings of Ashkenazic culture, I also reject the moralistic evaluation of assimilation as cultural capitulation (and its corollary, that the embrace of Jewish tradition counts as defiant counterculturalism). Secular Jewish culture developed as distinctively Jewish even in its (always partial and ambivalent) embrace of European cultural models. The persistence of Jewish sexual difference in modernity is the major path I travel in this book, and I believe it applies—always roughly and dialectically—to American Jewish culture not only at its radical and queer margins but also more generally. Much of what counts as the Jewish (radical, queer, feminist) margin not only describes much of mainstream American Judaism but has fully spread to mainstream American culture. As just one example, the overthrow of bourgeois models of femininity and bourgeois distributions of marital labor that represents second-wave feminism, and by now characterizes American (or Western) culture writ large, commenced with the activism of a small group of women among whom Jewish women (and, more particularly, Jewish women of Eastern European descent) were significantly overrepresented. Such a socio-logical phenomenon undoubtedly has a range of explanations, but among them might be counted the persistent skepticism about bourgeois models of femininity traceable in Jewish literature and culture from *The Love of Zion* until our own day; despite and within Americanization and suburbaniza-tion, Jewish women retained some sense of women as capable breadwinners and in consequence wore more lightly the role of "the angel in the house." What I see as the Jewish "heresies" at work in feminism may have been mar-ginal cultural streams when Betty Friedan published *The Feminine Mystique* in 1963, but they have hardly remained so. The Jewish counter-discourse to bourgeois discourses on love, gender, and marriage, I should repeat, is not a direct expression of traditional Jewish approaches to sex and marriage, al-though such essentialist arguments are by now part of the popular discourse on Jews and sex. Contemporary Jewish counter-discourses about sex repre-sent the partial persistence, dialectical transmutation, and universalization of traditional tropes, practices, or assumptions. In their hybrid secular form, they may not only express a range of "native" Jewish approaches to sexual-ity but also incorporate belated readings and misreadings of Jewish sexual characteristics by both insiders and outsiders.

Far less visible than the contributions of feminist and queer Jews to American culture, but perhaps more profound, is the role of Jewish sexual heresies in the contemporary desublimation of romantic love. The sex re-ligion Watt describes, with its ideology of perfect union between comple-mentary heterosexual lovers and friends, is a religion in precipitous decline, with the chivalric inheritance of Christian Europe clamoring to be heard against the much louder interjections of such Jewish skeptics and heretics as Freud, Lenny Bruce, Philip Roth, and Erica Jong. The notion that Jews take a more level-headed and natural (if not coarse or vulgar) approach to love is not necessarily an ungenerous misreading of Jewish culture by out-siders who cannot comprehend its internal logic, even if such a reading neglects other strands of this culture—the extravagantly sensual metaphorics of Jewish mysticism, the love songs of the Bible and Yiddish folklore, the passionate lyricism of Hebrew poetry of many ages and contexts. Moshe Leib Lilienblum, surely no outsider, claimed that the Jewish embrace of the romantic norms of European bourgeois culture and literature could never be complete, given that Jews lacked the religious prehistory that Christians had translated and secularized first as courtly love and then as bourgeois marriage.[18] The modern sex religion in its bourgeois European form builds on Christian approaches to celibacy and the adoration of the Virgin Mary that lend both "purity" and exaltation to sexual relations and raise romantic love to the heights of supreme, sublime, and quasi-religious experience (that this legacy also links courtly romance with the exaltation of virility as violence is something more recent scholarship has stressed). Jews, however, adopted the sex religion without the religious substructure that could fuel and undergird the secular adoration of women; in the Jewish scheme of things, other kinds of family love were at least as important as the heterosexual variety. The naturalism of Jewish culture and halakhah, which evaded sublimation and was skeptical of asceticism, set sexuality alongside other bodily functions to be regulated and viewed marital love within the larger context of extended family and ultimately of community.

The construction of a Jewish counter-discourse to the romantic sublime is a product not only of these traditional Jewish assumptions about sex but also of the structural and temporal features of Jewish modernization. As latecomers to the European romantic scene, famously poor specimens of its gender ideals, and minority participants in a crowded cultural field, Jews also produced satiric or transparently fictional varieties of the romance, deflating European romance as romantic ideals deflated them. Jews were not alone in seeing through the illusions of the romantic imagination—the modern novel, in *Don Quixote*, begins from this very deconstruction—but Jews played an important role in the production of heretical counter-discourses that challenged the sex religion. Among the most famous of these discourses is that of Tevye the Dairyman, whose Jewish audacity in challenging God is exceeded only by Sholem Aleichem's audacity in challenging the religion of romance by insisting that the perspective of the parents be included in the narrative of young love. In *Fiddler on the Roof*, this challenge continues to reverberate, as perhaps the strongest emotional brake on the ideology of romantic choice that European (and American) culture was to produce.

I do not mean to suggest that the modern counter-discourse to the bourgeois romantic sublime is either solely expressed by Jews or essentially Jewish. Challenges came from many directions, and the twentieth century saw a sexual revolution that followed on the more sentimental and restrained romantic revolution that was far broader than its Jewish dimension. Shachar Pinsker specifically locates the impetus to write sexually transgressive Hebrew prose outside the narrow republic of Hebrew letters:

> The very notion of romantic love underwent a major reevaluation in fin de siècle European culture. After Schopenhauer, Nietzsche, and Solovyov, early modernist European writers began to foreground sexual urges, the determinism of sexual attraction, and nothing less than the illusionary nature of romantic love.[19]

Nevertheless, I think it is no accident that Jews are so well represented among the writers and thinkers who contributed to this revolution along with and after Schopenhauer, Nietzsche, and Solovyov. It was psychoanalysis, above all, that exposed the more carnal and transgressive appetites obscured by spiritual and mystifying approaches to romance and sex. Freud counters the romantic emphasis on "sentiment" when he writes that "to ensure a fully normal attitude in love, two currents of feeling have to unite— we may describe them as the tender, affectionate feelings and the sensual feelings."[20] In asserting that "the greatest intensity of sensual passion will bring with it the highest mental estimation of the object (the normal overestimation of the sexual object characteristic of men)," Freud echoes in a universal key what Lilienblum asserts as Jewish difference—that the adoration of women is an illusion brought on by passion (or by reading about passion) rather than an accurate evaluation of reality.[21] Psychoanalysis, in such casual deflations of the sex religion, already acts as the "corrective" to romantic "overestimation," the overestimation of beautiful women that both Lilienblum and Freud believe to be native to Western culture. From this perspective, Freud's notion that a "fully normal attitude in love" unites the duality of "tender" and "sensual," romantic and sexual, sublime and physical, might also function to describe the project of Jewish cultural syncretism, social integration and sexual "normalization."

That psychoanalysis is a countercultural discourse is openly declared in Freud's writings, in opposition to ordinary conceptions of sexuality and the European romantic literary tradition. Freud's "Contributions to the Psychology of Love" thus begins with the assertion that his contributions must be distinguished from those of literature, which has thus far been uniquely charged with describing love: "Hitherto we have left it to poets and imaginative writers to depict for us the 'conditions of love' under which men and women make their choice of an object, and the way in which they reconcile the demands expressed in their phantasy with the exigencies of real life."[22] Novelists cannot be expected to explain the origins of desire, since "they have to evoke intellectual and aesthetic pleasure as well as certain effects on the emotions. For this reason they cannot reproduce reality unchanged; they have to isolate portions of it, detach them from their connection with disturbing elements, fill up gaps and soften the whole." Literature is thus allied with "phantasy," however diligently it strives to reconcile romantic fantasy with the realities of object choice. Only the scientific approach—psychoanalysis—can explain love, since it "betokens the most complete renunciation of the pleasure principle of which our minds are capable."[23] Psychoanalysis, then, represents an approach to sexuality that resists literature's softening effects on the subject, allowing for the open expression of carnal as well as real aspects of love rather than restricting descriptions to its spiritual aspect. As we have seen, though, literary descriptions of love take a wider variety of forms than Freud allows. Such writers as Y. L. Peretz provided readers not only with the enticements of romantic fantasy but also with the (no doubt often sexually aggressive) pleasures that accompany its deflation: The poem *Monish* would hardly be worth reading without the interplay of the hero's sublime love for Maria ("My life, soul, oy, my treasure!") and the narrator's complaints about ostensible incapacity of Yiddish to express "love and "feeling" ("It has no spirit, it has no salt—And it smells of goose *shmaltz*!").[24] That is, Freud and Peretz, "scientist" and poet, may nevertheless be playing the same (Jewish) game.

There may be yet another aspect of traditional Jewish approaches to sexuality that informs psychoanalytic thought: the involvement of family in romantic love and heterosexual choice. Although Freud focuses on the nuclear rather than extended family, and regularly bestows on this family not Jewish but Greek names, it is nevertheless true that for psychoanalysis, the natal family is the locus and wellspring of sexual desire. Jewish tradition, as we have seen, similarly connects the attachment between parents and children with those that drive young people to forge romantic and marital unions.[25] Yahil Zaban's reading of Mapu's use of the names Amnon and Tamar in *The Love of Zion* applies Freudian insights to modern Jewish literature, but it makes just as much sense to reverse the direction of analysis, suggesting that Freud brings the childhood family into the scene of European heterosexual romance as yet another iteration of a long Jewish literary tradition.[26] For Mapu, Tamar falls in love with Amnon because her grandfather had already encountered him in a dream and because her father had already promised her to him; just so, for Freud, do we fall in love as adults because the objects of our desire embody erotic patterns formed within the lap of family.

We might read Philip Roth's citation of Freud's essay "The Most Prevalent Form of Degradation in Psychic Life," in the context of a novel-cum-psychoanalytic session, in similar fashion: *Portnoy's Complaint* suggests that Portnoy's condition should be traced to his mother's treatment of him in childhood as "an erotic plaything"; his attraction to non-Jewish women and his need to degrade them are explained, perhaps even seriously, as elaborate displacements and concealments of incestuous impulses. Rather than allow Freud to diagnose Portnoy (by seeing incestuous desire behind his attraction to Monkey), we might use Portnoy to diagnose Freud (by asserting that it is the power of Jewish familial attachments over even the most ostensibly exogamous desire that is disguised, sexualized, and universalized in Freud's family romance). Roth's citation of these psychoanalytic texts in *Portnoy's Complaint* thus suggests alternative Jewish genealogies to Freud's construction of the family romance via Oedipus and Electra. While Freud claimed that novelists were not to be expected to recognize either where love came from or what it truly was, Roth took the bold step of producing a novel that told both these "truths" and exposed them as particularly Jewish.

If Freud and Roth might mutually illuminate each other, Lennie Bruce sheds further light on the relationship between sex and other bodily functions within the Jewish counter-romantic discourse. Attempting to account for the association of Jews with obscenity, Bruce argued that smut has different meanings for Jews and non-Jews:

> To a Jew, f-u-c-k and s-h-i-t have the same value on the dirty-word graph. A Jew has no concept that f-u-c-k is worth 90 points, and s-h-i-t, 10. And the reason for that is that—well, see, rabbis and priests both s-h-i-t but one f-u-c-k-s. You see, in the Jewish culture, there's no merit badge for not doing that. . . . And since the leaders of my tribe, rabbis, are *shtuppers*, perhaps that's why words come freer to me.[27]

Performing the dirty words he also analyzes, Bruce suggests—as Lilienblum and I do—that Jewish culture, even long after secularization, is shaped by a rejection of the possibility or value of celibacy, which reverberates, in Bruce's estimation, in the Jewish failure to elevate sex above other equally universal functions of the body. That Bruce inserts a "coarse" Yiddish (or Yinglish) term to describe Jewish sex points as well to the role Jewish languages and discourses have come to play in the sexual desublimation of American culture.[28] The connections between traditional Jewish attitudes and their modern and postmodern expressions are not, of course, as direct as Bruce implies. Alongside the traditional Jewish failure to develop a rhetoric of the romantic sublime must be ranged both the evident modern successes in forging just such a rhetoric (Mapu's *Love of Zion* can serve as example here) and the equally traditional Jewish norms that dictate sexual modesty in speech and act—norms that Bruce flagrantly transgresses. Indeed, where Bruce uses a Yiddish word to signal the Jewish character of the sexual attitudes he is describing, traditional Jewish culture would more typically have inserted a *Hebrew* (or *loshn-koydesh*) term to euphemistically describe, and modestly obscure, a sexual act or bodily function.[29] Jewish culture, that is, can be legitimately characterized as both particularly direct about sexual matters and extraordinarily modest in this regard.

In a recent book on Jews and obscenity, Josh Lambert works through this puzzle, acknowledging both the twentieth-century associations between Jews and obscenity and the sexual modesty also central to Jewish culture, finally resisting the urge to generalize about any particular connection between Jews and obscenity.[30] Lambert does, however, speak of the power and value that could accrue to Jews who trafficked in obscenity, carving out a space for themselves in a modernist scene in which they were cultural outsiders, exposing the hypocritical "gentility" of Gentiles, and presenting themselves as truth tellers in the face of a culture that shrank from confronting sexual truths. Lest one be tempted to view such writers as Henry Roth, Philip Roth, Erica Jong, and Lenny Bruce as courageous free-speech advocates or martyrs, Lambert shows that obscenity worked well for many Jews, however unwelcome they were in midcentury American country clubs. Henry Roth managed to parlay memories of his sibling incest—through the cultural capital of obscenity—into a nice literary career. Reading Roth's late fictionalized autobiography, Lambert writes that "the particular attraction of literary modernism for Ira [the fictional stand-in for Roth] is that its alchemy has been demonstrated to be particularly effective in transforming into valued commodities precisely the elements of his own social marginalization: Jewishness, poverty, and sexual abnormality."[31] Such magic could work for others, too. Legal funds used to defend publishers of obscenity sometimes turned "Jewish family fortunes" into "a very precious form of cultural capital . . . that some American Jews from wealthy families wanted and needed very much, as they were being denied access to prestige through more traditional channels."[32]

Lambert moves beyond the clichés of Jewish marginalization to an analysis of Jewish power, discovering in obscene speech the ability to arouse attention and confer status. Deviance, Lambert shows us, can also be a source of prestige and status. The persistence of traditional sexual tropes and practices in modern Jewish culture is thus not merely an unconscious mobilization of deep ethnographic memories (much less an ethnic "trait"). More to the point, it can be described as the mobilization by a minority group of alternative cultural options in a competitive and asymmetrical field of production. Modern Jewish culture used what it had not because the past dictates the present but because the present remembers and constructs the past that it needs. So it may not finally matter whether those who see a connection between traditional Jewish attitudes toward sex and such contemporary Jewish expressions as Lenny Bruce and Erica Jong are accurately reading either traditional or post-traditional Jewish culture. Whether these are sensitive readings or gross misreadings of the Jewish past or Jewish distinctiveness, they are by now fully part of what makes secular Jewish culture Jewish.

The persistence of Jewish tradition, and its modern and postmodern recovery, invention, and mobilization, took many forms besides the ones described here. Alongside the desublimation of romance, Jewish writers also mobilized—rather than were merely stigmatized by—alternative gender structures available within a minority culture. Europeanization meant, among other things, the imperative of abandoning traditional Jewish gender roles for the European ideals of masculinity and femininity, but it also opened a space for alternative gender configurations. These have typically been read as a source of stigma, but a case can be made that these gender differences sometimes functioned as a form of cultural power as well, leading to open resistance rather than the defensive universalization that scholars often see in Freud's "translations" of Jewish gender trouble into sexual difference writ large.[33] Such forms of cultural production and resistance, which in accordance with collectivist Eastern European Jewish models might be distinguished from those expressed by a psychosexual individual, include the celebration of Molly Picon's cross-dressing by Yiddish filmgoers and the contributions of Jewish women to second-wave American feminism. Erica Jong's "zipless fuck," whatever its status as an artifact of feminist fiction, represents a confluence of both trends—the ability of Jewish writers to think about sex outside models of romantic courtship and the willingness of Jewish women to break bourgeois taboos against "indelicate" feminine expression. These are just a few legacies of Jewish sexual modernization, which refracted traditional Jewish practices, roles, and structures in various forms and multiple ways—as religious "return," as the rejection of bourgeois gender roles and sexual structures, as queer Jewish identification, and as the construction of a (heterosexual) Jewish counter-discourse to the romantic sublime. There are no doubt others, including the simple adherence to normative traditional or bourgeois sexual and marital structures.

The general arc I have been tracing in this book is touching down. Jewish sexual modernization began with Europeanization and ended with the world becoming (sexually) Jewish. The ways we think about sex today can hardly be imagined without Freud or Lenny Bruce, Philip Roth, Woody Allen, Betty Friedan, Erica Jong, Tony Kushner, and Sarah Silverman. I imagine that this claim is too self-evident to require a learned footnote. What I have done in this book, instead, is to tell the story of how this came to be.

Notes

Introduction

1. Jacob Katz, *Tradition and Crisis: Jewish Society at the End of the Middle Ages*, trans. Bernard Dov Cooperman (New York: New York University Press, 1993), 231. As Katz writes, "virtually overnight, arranged marriages ceased to be acceptable."

2. Pauline Wengeroff, *Memoirs of a Grandmother: Scenes from the Cultural History of the Jews of Russia in the Nineteenth Century, Volume One*, ed. and trans. Shulamit S. Magnus (Stanford, CA: Stanford University Press, 2010), 209. For the German, see Pauline Wengeroff, *Memoiren einer Grossmutter: Bilder aus der Kulturgeschichte der Judens Russland in 19. Jahrhundert, Band I* (Berlin: Poppelauer, 1919), 171.

3. Wengeroff, *Memoirs*, 1:218.

4. Pauline Wengeroff, *Memoirs of a Grandmother: Scenes from the Cultural History of the Jews of Russia in the Nineteenth Century, Volume Two*, ed. and trans. Shulamit S. Magnus (Stanford, CA: Stanford University Press, 2014), 49. For the German, see *Memoiren einer Grossmutter: Bilder aus der Kulturgeschichte der Judens Russland in 19. Jahrhundert, Band II* (Berlin: Poppelauer, 1919), 40.

5. These reform efforts are generally associated with Nicholas I's minister of national enlightenment, Count Sergei S. Uvarov, who took a particular interest in Jewish education. See Michael Stanislawski, *Tsar Nicholas I and the Jews: The Transformation of Jewish Society in Russia, 1825–1855* (Philadelphia: Jewish Publication Society, 1983), 62–69.

6. The translation of the term "Haskalah" as "Jewish Enlightenment" has recently been contested by Olga Litvak in *Haskalah: The Romantic Movement in Judaism* (New Brunswick, NJ: Rutgers University Press, 2012), who argues that the Jewish movement known as the Haskalah overlapped in time, place, and thematic concerns with European Romanticism rather than with the Enlightenment, which was centered farther to the west and preceded the Russian Haskalah by a century. I find Litvak's argument quite persuasive, and my interest in Jewish romance brings my use of the term closer to the literary term "Romanticism" than to the philosophical currents of Enlightenment. My shorthand here is designed to reflect current usage rather than intended as an argument with Litvak.

7. Wengeroff, *Memoirs*, 2:110.

8. Ibid., 44.

9. For this passage in the German, see Wengeroff, *Memoiren einer Grossmutter*, 2:40.

10. Wengeroff, *Memoirs*, 2:43.

11. Talal Asad, *Formations of the Secular: Christianity, Islam, Modernity* (Stanford, CA: Stanford University Press, 2003), 13–14.

12. Peter L. Berger, *The Sacred Canopy: Elements of a Sociological Theory of Religion* (New York: Anchor, 1991), 107, 112–13.

13. Peter L. Berger, *The Desecularization of the World: Resurgent Religion and World Politics* (Grand Rapids, MI: Eerdsman, 1999).

14. Max Weber, *The Protestant Ethic and the Rise of Capitalism*, trans. Talcott Parsons (New York: Penguin, 2002).

15. Shmuel Feiner, *The Origins of Jewish Secularization in Eighteenth-Century Europe*, trans. Chaya Naor (Philadelphia: University of Pennsylvania Press, 2011), xiv.

16. Jacob Katz, *Out of the Ghetto: The Social Background of Jewish Emancipation, 1770–1870* (New York: Schocken, 1978), 32.

17. Homi Bhabha, *The Location of Culture* (London: Routledge, 1994), 4.

18. Asad, *Formations of the Secular*, 17, 95.

19. Wengeroff, *Memoirs*, 2:43.

20. See Naomi Seidman, "Religion/Secularity," in *The Routledge Handbook of Contemporary Jewish Cultures*, ed. Laurence Roth and Nadia Valman (London: Routledge, 2015), 157.

21. Among the studies that trace this genealogy is Michael Gluzman, *The Zionist Body: Nationalism, Gender and Sexuality in the New Hebrew Literature* [Ha-guf ha-tsiyoni: Le'umiyut, migdar u-miniyut ba-sifrut ha-Yisre'elit ha-hadashah] (Tel Aviv: Ha-Kibuts ha-me'uhad, 2007).

22. The term "homosocial" is helpfully clarified in Eve Kosofsky Sedgwick, *Between Men: English Literature and Male Homosocial Desire* (New York: Columbia University Press), 1–4. My own use of the term differs from hers, however, in its characterization of the larger social structures in which homosocial desire takes shape. Where both Sedgwick and I recognize the ways that male homosocial desire is intricately woven around and shot through with compulsory heterosexuality, in the traditional Ashkenazic culture studied in this book this combination is generally free of the homophobia that Sedgwick sees in many of the English literary formations she analyzes.

23. Jeffrey Eugenides, *The Marriage Plot: A Novel* (New York: Picador, 2011), 22–23.

24. Ian Watt, *The Rise of the Novel: Studies in Defoe, Richardson and Fielding* (Berkeley: University of California Press, 1957), 135–73.

25. Eugenides, *Marriage Plot*, 23.

26. For some of these queer studies and postcolonial studies, see Sander Gilman, *Freud, Race, and Gender* (Princeton, NJ: Princeton University Press, 1993); Daniel Boyarin, *Unheroic Conduct: The Rise of Heterosexuality and the Invention of the Jewish*

Man (Berkeley: University of California Press, 1997); Ann Pellegrini, *Performance Anxieties: Staging Psychoanalysis, Staging Race* (New York: Routledge, 1997); and Jay Geller, *On Freud's Jewish Body: Mitigating Circumcisions* (New York: Fordham University Press, 2007).

27. See Naomi Seidman, "Reading 'Queer' Ashkenaz: This Time from East to West," *TDR (The Drama Review): The Journal of Performance Studies* 55, no. 3 (Fall 2011): 50–57.

28. Sander Gilman, *The Jew's Body* (New York: Routledge, 1991), 126.

29. Ann Pellegrini, "Whiteface Performances: 'Race,' Gender, and Jewish Bodies," in *Jews and Other Differences: The New Jewish Cultural Studies*, ed. Jonathan Boyarin and Daniel Boyarin (Minneapolis: University of Minnesota Press, 1997), 109.

30. Boyarin, *Unheroic Conduct*, xvii–xviii.

31. Ibid., xvii.

Chapter 1

1. Moshe Leib Lilienblum, *Sins of Youth* [Hat'ot ne'urim], *Autobiographical Writings*, ed. Shlomo Breiman (Jerusalem: Mosad Bialik, 1970), 1:191. The title is a rabbinic euphemism for masturbation. Translations are my own unless otherwise indicated.

2. For more on these translations, see Joseph Klausner, *History of the New Hebrew Literature* [Historyah shel ha-sifrut ha-'Ivrit ha-hadashah] (Jerusalem: Ahiasaf, 1952), 297. For a more recent survey, particularly into Yiddish, see Shmuel Werses, "The Yiddish Translations of Abraham Mapu's *The Love of Zion*" [Ha-targumim le-Yidish shel Ahavat Tsiyon le-Avraham Mapu] (Jerusalem: Akademon, 1989).

3. Klausner, *History*, 295.

4. Wengeroff, , 2:116–17.

5. Yehudah Leib Katzenelson (Buki ben Yogli), *What My Eyes Saw and My Ears Heard: Remembrances of My Life* [Ma shera'u eynay ve-sham'u oznay: Zikhronot mini hayai] (Jerusalem: Mosad Bialik, 1917), 64.

6. S. An-sky, "Sins of Youth," in *The Dybbuk and Other Writings, ed. David Roskies, trans. Golda Werman* (New Haven, CT: Yale University Press, 2002), 71.

7. Ya'akov Fichman, *Men of Tidings* [Anshe besorah] (Tel Aviv: Dvir, 1937–38), 152.

8. Sholem Aleichem, *From the Fair: The Autobiography of Sholem Aleichem*, ed. and trans. Curt Leviant (New York: Viking Penguin, 1985), 146. In the Yiddish original, the space between these passages is marked by two lines of dashes. See Sholem Aleichem, *Funm Yarid: Lebensbeshreibungen* (New York: Varheit, 1917), 2:142–43.

9. Sholem Aleichem, *From the Fair*, 147.

10. Eliezer Ben Yehuda, *A Dream Come True, ed. George Mandel*, trans. T. Muraoka (Boulder, CO: Westview, 1993), 34.

11. Reuven Brainin, *Abraham Mapu: His Life and Works* [Avraham Mapu: Hayav u-sefarav] (Piotrków, Poland: Tushiyah, 1900), 48.

12. Klausner, *History*, 295.

13. The pamphlet was signed by "The Committee Vindicating the Many" (or, as we might say, "the Moral Majority") and published in Vilna in 1870. See Klausner, *History*, 296n165; and Dan Miron, *From Romance to the Novel: Studies in the Emergence of the Hebrew and Yiddish Novel in the Nineteenth Century* [Ben hazon le-emet: Nitsane ha-roman ha-'ivri veha-yidi ba-me'ah ha-tesha'-'esreh] (Jerusalem: Mosad Bialik, 1979), 9.

14. Klausner, *History*, 296n165.

15. S. Y. Abramovitsh, *Learn to Do Well, Which Is a Love Story* [Limdu hetev, hu sipur ahavim], ed. Dan Miron (New York: YIVO, 1969), 31.

16. Avraham Mapu, *The Hypocrite* ['Ayit tsavu'a], in *The Complete Works of Abraham Mapu* [Kol kitve Avraham Mapu] (Tel Aviv: Dvir, 1947), 252.

17. See David Patterson, *The Hebrew Novel in Czarist* Russia (Lanham, MD: Rowman & Littlefield, 1999), 222.

18. Avraham Mapu, *The Love of Zion*, in *The Complete Works of Abraham Mapu*, 37. I quote the Jewish Publication Society (JPS) *TANAKH* here and throughout, except where otherwise noted.

19. Ibid., 37–38.

20. The JPS has, less familiarly or poetically, "He shall reconcile parents with children and children with their parents."

21. ChaeRan Y. Freeze, *Jewish Marriage and Divorce in Late Imperial Russia* (Waltham, MA: Brandeis University Press, 2002), 190–91. Freeze's citations are from William B. Wanger, *Marriage, Property and the Struggle for Legality in Late Imperial Russia* (Oxford: Oxford University Press, 1994), 84. Tova Cohen and Shmuel Feiner, writing about women's participation in the literature of the Haskalah in Eastern Europe, similarly note a sea change in social attitudes among those who wrote and read this literature:

> Young women in Eastern Europe, "girls of a new generation," found jobs in stores, in workshops or in the houses of merchants, saved money, and searched for a mate without the participation of their families. The romantic ethos continued to capture a place for itself among the young people of this generation, and brought with it not only relatively later marriages of choice but also religious laxity among working girls of the lower classes and female students of the middle and upper classes, among whom there were relatively high numbers of gymnasium and university students.

In Tova Cohen and Shmuel Feiner, *"The Voice of a Hebrew Maiden": Women's Writings of the Nineteenth-Century Haskalah* [Kol 'almah 'Ivriyah: Kitve nashim maskilot ba-me'ah ha-tesha'-'esreh] (Tel Aviv: Ha-kibuts ha-me'uhad, 2006), 27.

22. David Biale, *Eros and the Jews: From Biblical Israel to Contemporary America* (New York: Basic, 1992), 165.

23. Katz, *Tradition and Crisis*, 116–17.

24. Lilienblum, *Sins of Youth*, 1:104.

25. "We have before us a society based on strict class division, but which lacked adequate barriers between one class and another. Precisely because Judaism ruled that 'all families are presumed to be fit' and might intermarry with one another—

and in exceptional cases did so—society could not permit the choice of a spouse on the basis of a chance encounter. But this was certainly not the only reason. The objection to marriage by personal choice in this society was bound up with its entire conception of the role of love and sex. As we have seen, the temptations of the flesh were clearly recognized and frankly admitted. On the other hand, there was no deliberate cultivation of the erotic life, in which the individual might find an emotional outlet or even room for self-expression." Katz, *Tradition and Crisis*, 143–44.

26. Ibid., 118–19.

27. Ibid., 231. In this regard, as in so many others, Moses Mendelssohn functions as a pioneering exemplar: Katz points to Mendelssohn's pride at having courted his bride "in the modern fashion," without the aid of parents or matchmakers; Mendelssohn downplayed the fact that the bride and groom met through the matchmaking exertions of mutual friends and tried "to emphasize that everything connected with the marriage had been his own personal decision." Katz takes a somewhat different tone here than Alexander Altmann, who says that the acquaintance with Fromet, although suggested by others, was a matter of real, passionate love and that "it was rather unusual in Jewish society for a marriage to be arranged without the services of professional matchmakers, but convention was ignored in this instance." Alexander Altmann, *Moses Mendelssohn: A Biographical Study* (Philadelphia: Jewish Publication Society, 1973), 93.

28. I owe this insight to Bourdieu's formulation in *The Logic of Practice*, which provides a close reading of marriage strategies in 1950s Algeria that aims to complicate the notion that agents act according to social "rules" in contracting marriages rather than employ flexible strategies to maximize beneficial outcomes within a set of shifting constraints, taking into consideration "the quality of the hand—the strength of the cards that have been dealt." See Pierre Bourdieu, *The Logic of Practice*, trans. Richard Nice (Stanford, CA: Stanford University Press, 1992), 148.

29. See Immanuel Etkes, "Marriage and Torah Study among the *Lomdim*," in *The Jewish Family: Metaphor and Memory*, ed. David Kraemer (Oxford: Oxford University Press, 1989), 156.

30. Biale, *Eros and the Jews*, 163.

31. Shaul Stampfer, *Families, Rabbis and Education: Traditional Jewish Society in Nineteenth-Century Eastern Europe* (Oxford: Littman Library of Jewish Civilization, 2010), 13–14, 19.

32. Stephanie Coontz, *Marriage, a History: How Love Conquered Marriage* (New York: Penguin, 2006), 145–215; and Edward Shorter, *The Making of the Modern Family* (New York: Basic, 1976), 79–167.

33. See Shachar Pinsker, *Literary Passports: The Making of Modernist Hebrew Fiction in Europe* (Stanford, CA: Stanford University Press, 2011), 147–64. Against this periodization, however, we might mention the work of Yahil Zaban and Olga Litvak, who have separately drawn attention to the powerful and transgressive sexual currents that underlie the apparently "sentimental" attachments in *The Love of Zion*. Yahil Zaban, *Choicest Meal: Food and Sexuality in Jewish Enlightenment Literature*

[Ve-nafsho ma'akhal ta'avah: Mazon u-meniyut be-sifrut ha-haskalah] (Tel Aviv: Ha-kibuts ha-me'uhad, 2014), 31–57; and Litvak, *Haskalah*, 131–56.

34. Marion Kaplan, *The Making of the Jewish Middle Class: Women, Family, and Identity in Imperial Germany* (Oxford: Oxford University Press, 1991), 109.

35. Freeze, *Jewish Marriage and Divorce*, 24.

36. Nathan Hurvitz, "Courtship and Arranged Marriages among Eastern European Jews prior to World War I as Depicted in a Briefenshteller," *Journal of Marriage and Family* 37, no. 2 (1975): 427.

37. Biale, *Eros and the Jews*, 169.

38. Miron, *From Romance to the Novel*, 270. Miron argues that Abramovitsh was so discouraged by his failure to produce a convincing love story in his first attempts that "even in *Fishke the Lame*, Abramovitsh's 'prototypical' love story, the model of the 'romance' (if we can so describe this love between a cripple and hunchback) remains literarily unresolved."

39. Tova Cohen, *"One Beloved, the Other Hated": Between Fiction and Reality in Haskalah Depictions of Women* ["Ha-ahat ahuvah veha-ahat senu'ah": Ben metsi'ut le-vidyon be-te'ure ha-ishah be-sifrut ha-Haskalah] (Jerusalem: Magnes, 2002), 36.

40. For a discussion, see Miron, *From Romance to the Novel*, 320.

41. Mapu, *Love of Zion*, 10.

42. Miron, *From Romance to the Novel*, 24–25; Yahil Zaban, "A Place for Love: Literature of the Enlightenment and the 'Pleasant Place,'" in *A Garden East of Eden: Traditions of Paradise* [Gan be-'Eden mi-kedem: Mesorot Gan 'Eden be-Yisra'el uva-'amim], ed. Rachel Elior (Jerusalem: Scholion, 2010), 339–58.

43. René Girard, *Deceit, Desire and the Novel: Self and Other in Literary Structure*, trans. Yvonne Freccero (Baltimore: Johns Hopkins University Press, 1965), 18, 30.

44. Wolfgang Iser, *The Fictive and the Imaginary: Charting Literary Anthropology* (Baltimore: Johns Hopkins University Press, 1993), 1–2, xi.

45. Ibid., xv.

46. Ibid., 24, 78, 226.

47. Klausner, *History*, 295.

48. Iser, *Fictive and the Imaginary*, 299–300.

49. See Moshe Pelli, *Kinds of Genre in Haskalah Literature: Types and Topics* [Sugot ve-sugyot ba-sifrut ha-haskalah ha-'Ivrit] (Tel Aviv: Ha-kibuts ha-me'uhad, 1999). See also Moshe Pelli, *In Search of Genre: Hebrew Enlightenment and Modernity* (Lanham, MD: University Press of America, 2005).

50. See Dan Miron, introduction to Abramovitsh, *Learn to Do Well*, 7.

51. Altmann, *Moses Mendelssohn*, 298. For a discussion of Mendelssohn's attitudes toward "pleasure reading," see Amos Bitzan, "The Problem of Pleasure: Disciplining the German Jewish Reading Revolution, 1770–1870" (PhD diss., University of California, Berkeley, 2011), 29–30.

52. Quoted in Miron, *From Romance to the Novel*, 235–36.

53. Eliezer Tzvi Zweifel, *Stringed Instruments and Organ* [Minim ye-'ugav] (Vilna, Lithuania: Romm, 1858), 44.

54. Ibid., 52.

55. Miron, *From Romance to the Novel*, 236–37; Zaban, *Choicest Meal*, 31–57.

56. David Patterson discusses at least fifteen novels written in the years 1853–99, a good portion of which might be termed love stories. See Patterson, *Hebrew Novel*.

57. On the connections between the novel and the construction of a national collective, see Benedict Anderson, *Imagined Communities: Reflections on the Origins and Spread of Nationalism* (London: Verso, 1983), especially 37–46.

58. Sholem Aleichem edited as well as contributed to *Di Yidishe folksbibliothek*, and the letters from Abramovitsh quoted in his dedication primarily concerned Abramovitsh's contribution to this same inaugural issue.

59. Sholem Aleichem, "Dedication" ("To My Dearly Beloved Grandfather"), in *Stempenyu: A Jewish Romance*, trans. Hannah Berman (Hoboken, NJ: Melville House, 2007), xi. I have revised Berman's translation throughout this book where necessary to more closely reflect the Yiddish. For the Yiddish, see Sholem Aleichem, *Stempenyu, a yidisher roman*, in *Di Yidishe folksbibliothek* (Kiev: Y. Sheftel, 1888): 1:v.

60. Letter of June 28, 1888, reprinted in *Dos Mendele-bukh*, ed. Nachman Mayzel (New York: Ikuf, 1959), 157. Sholem Aleichem's tendentious reading of Abramovitsh's letter might have been helped by his editing of the full comment on the state of the Yiddish novel. As Abramovitsh continues, "In general, all Yiddish romances are worthless. They nauseate me."

61. Ken Frieden, *Classic Jewish Fiction: Abramovitsh, Sholem Aleichem, and Peretz* (Albany: SUNY Press, 1995), 136.

62. Sholem Aleichem, *Stempenyu*, xi–xii. In Yiddish, see *Stempenyu*, in *Di Yidishe folksbibliothek*, 1:v.

63. I. L. Peretz, *Monish (Balade)*, in *Di Yidishe folksbibliothek*, 1:155. Peretz revised and abbreviated this poem numerous times, and this passage is missing in some later versions.

64. Biale, *Eros and the Jews*, 161.

65. Dan Miron, *A Traveler Disguised: The Rise of Modern Yiddish Fiction in the Nineteenth Century* (Syracuse, NY: Syracuse University Press, 1996), 34–66.

66. Ilana Pardes, *Agnon's Moonstruck Lovers: The Song of Songs in Israeli Culture* (Seattle: University of Washington Press, 2013).

67. The quote is from Roger Boase, *The Origin and Meaning of Courtly Love: A Critical Study of European Scholarship* (Manchester, UK: Manchester University Press, 1977), 126. Leonard Benson, in *The Family Bond: Marriage, Love and Sex in America* (New York: Random House, 1971), characterizes the literary expression of this courtly or chivalric love, which reached a peak in the twelfth century, thus:

> Unselfish service to a noble lady—a married woman of the ruling class—became the duty of the young knight. . . . The knight had the right to go with his lady to the bedchamber, to help her disrobe, even to put her to bed. Occasionally he would sleep with her, but tenderness alone was allowed, not "carnal knowledge." The knight could have symbolic unity with his beloved by tying her veil to his armor, or perhaps she would wear his blood-stained tunic. (113)

68. Cited in Iris Parush, *Reading Jewish Women: Marginality and Moderniza-tion in Nineteenth-Century Eastern European Jewish Society*, trans. Saadya Sternberg (Waltham, MA: Brandeis University Press, 2004), 166.

69. Moshe Leib Lilienblum, "Words of Song" [Divrei zemer], in *The Complete Works of Moshe Leib Lilienblum* (Odessa, Ukraine: Tsitlin Press, 1912–13), 3:181. It may be significant that Lilienblum's origins were in Lithuania, the one area where Hasidism did not make many inroads and where elite Jewish culture hewed more closely to the traditional study of rabbinic texts and directed its innovating energies to ethics in the Musar movement. I thank Dan Miron for this suggestion (personal communication).

70. Ibid., 183.

71. Ibid., 185.

72. Ibid., 187.

73. Sholem Aleichem, "The Judgment of Shomer," trans. Justin Daniel Cammy, in *Arguing the Modern Jewish Canon: Essays in Honor of Ruth R. Wisse*, ed. Justin Daniel Cammy, Dara Horn, Alyssa Quint, and Rachel Rubinstein (Cambridge, MA: Harvard University Press, 2008), 147.

74. David Patterson, *The Hebrew Novel in Czarist Russia: A Portrait of Jewish Life in the Nineteenth Century* (Lanham, MD: Rowman & Littlefield, 1999), 220.

75. Watt, *Rise of the Novel*, 167.

76. Sholem Aleichem, *Stempenyu*, 158–59. This interpolation does not appear in the 1888 version but is among the expansions of the novel in the 1903 version. See Sholem Aleichem, *Stempenyu*, in *The Complete Works of Sholem Aleichem* [Ale verk fun Sholem Aleichem] (Podgórsze, Krakow, Poland: S. L. Deutscher, 1903), 4:103.

77. Justin Cammy cites Henry James's 1879 biographical study of Nathaniel Hawthorne in his "Judging the Judgment of Shomer: Jewish Literature versus Jew-ish Reading," in *Arguing the Modern Jewish Canon: Essays on Literature and Culture in Honor of Ruth Wisse*, ed. Justin Cammy, Dara Horn, Alyssa Quint, and Rachel Rubinstein (Cambridge, MA: Harvard University Press, 2008), 99.

78. Charlotte Brontë, *Shirley* (1849; repr., Hertfordshire, UK: Wordsworth Edi-tions, 1993), 3. The term "anti-literary manifesto" is from George Levine, *The Re-alistic Imagination: English Fiction from Frankenstein to Lady Chatterley* (Chicago: University of Chicago Press, 1983), 15.

79. Mendele Mokher Seforim (Sholem Yankev Abramovitsh), *Of Bygone Days*, in *A Shtetl and Other Yiddish Novellas*, ed. Ruth R. Wisse, trans. Raymond P. Sheindlin (Detroit, MI: Wayne State University Press, 1986), 272.

80. These exceptions include his first Hebrew novels, in the Haskalah style, the 1862 *Learn to Do Well* (later reworked as *Fathers and Sons*) and the 1869 Yiddish novel *Fishke the Lame* (later reworked in Hebrew as *The Book of Beggars*). Not co-incidentally, the love affair in *Fishke the Lame* takes place between beggars, as if ro-mantic love were possible only outside the Jewish middle classes and learned elites.

81. These Christian experiences are of both romantic love and—as Monastery Road and Monish's Maria suggest—the virginity esteemed in Christian and post-Christian ideologies but less exalted in Jewish sensibility.

82. Sholem Aleichem, *Tevye the Dairyman and The Railroad Stories*, trans. Hillel Halkin (New York: Schocken, 1987), 72.

83. Vera Lee, *Love and Strategy in the Eighteenth-Century French Novel* (Cambridge, MA: Schenkman, 1986), 3.

84. Northrop Frye makes a similar point about Quixote and, more generally, the relationship between parodies of romance and displacement/belatedness, arguing that "the tradition of parody can be traced all through the history of the novel, up to and beyond *Ulysses*, and extends to many novelists who had been thought to be still too close to romance. Thus Fielding's *Joseph Andrews* began as a parody of *Pamela*, and Jane Austen's *Northanger Abbey* is a parody of Gothic romance." In Northrop Frye, "From *The Secular Scripture: A Study of the Structures of Romance*," in *Theory of the Novel*, ed. Marshall Brown (Cambridge: Cambridge University Press, 2000), 39.

85. Watt, *Rise of the Novel*, 136.

86. Ibid., 138.

87. Ibid., 137.

88. For a summary of feminist critique of the notion of marriage as a "social contract" and a Jewish feminist approach to this issue, see Laura Levitt, *Jews and Feminism: The Ambivalent Search for Home* (New York : Routledge Press, 1997), 63–90.

89. Nancy Armstrong, *Desire and Domestic Fiction: A Political History of the Novel* (Oxford: Oxford University Press, 199), 253.

90. Watt, *Rise of the Novel*, 173.

91. Ibid., 136.

92. Coontz, *Marriage*, 184.

93. Zeev Gries, *The Book in the Jewish World 1700–1900* (Oxford: Littman Library of Jewish Civilization, 2007), 40.

94. For a discussion of the dispersion of these Yiddish works in nineteenth-century Eastern Europe, see Cohen, *"One Beloved, the Other Hated,"* 134–35.

95. Jeffrey Brooks, *When Russia Learned to Read: Literature and Popular Literacy, 1861–1917* (Princeton, NJ: Princeton University Press, 1985), 79–80.

96. Parush, *Reading Jewish Women*, 245.

97. Gershon Henoch Hacohen Leiner, *Ways of Life* [Orkhot Hayim] (Warsaw: Meir Yehiel Halter, 1890), 12–13. Cited in Parush, *Reading Jewish Women*, 46.

98. Parush, *Reading Jewish Women*, 166. Such effects are by no means a feature only of the distant past. Pearl Abraham's 1995 novel about leaving the contemporary ultra-Orthodox world suggests that reading romance novels primed her for this escape. See Pearl Abraham, *The Romance Reader* (New York: Berkley, 1995).

99. David Patterson describes "the influence of the French romantic novelists, particularly Eugène Sue and Alexander Dumas," on the nineteenth-century Hebrew novel, through the indirect agency of Mapu's borrowings as well as the widespread popularity of Schulman's Hebrew translation of *Mystères de Paris*. See *Hebrew Novel*, 223.

100. Lilienblum, "Words of Song," 182.

101. Israel Abrahams, *Jewish Life in the Middle Ages* (New York: Atheneum, 1981), 169.

102. Boyarin, *Unheroic Conduct*, 55, 63.

103. Ibid., viii.

104. Israel Bartal, "Virility and Impotence: From Traditional Society to the Haskalah," in *Brother Keepers: New Perspectives on Jewish Masculinity*, ed. Harry Brod and Rabbi Shawn Israel Zevit (Harriman, TN: Men's Studies, 2010), 79. The town or suburb Bartal refers to is Śnipiszki in Polish and today Šnipiškęs in Lithuanian.

105. Alan Mintz, *"Banished from Their Father's Table": Loss of Faith and Hebrew Autobiography* (Bloomington: University of Indiana Press, 1989), 90.

Chapter 2

1. Biale, *Eros and the Jews*, 153.

2. Salomon Maimon, *Lebensgeschichte: Vom ihm selbst geschrieben und herausgegeben von Karl Phillip Moritz* (1792–93; repr., Frankfurt am Main: Jüdischer Verlag, 1995), 48–72. For an abridged English translation, see *Solomon Maimon: An Autobiography*, ed. Moses Hadas, trans. J. Clarke Murray (New York: Schocken, 1947), 20–34. Autobiographies that also follow the Rousseauian-Maimonian model include Mordechai Aaron Günzburg's *Aviezer*, finished in 1828 and published in 1863, and Moshe Leib Lilienblum's *Sins of Youth*, the first volume of which appeared in 1876. For more on nineteenth-century Hebrew autobiography, see Shmuel Werses, "Directions in Autobiography in the Haskalah Period," *Gilyonot* 17 (1945): 175–83; Mintz, *"Banished from Their Father's Table"*; Michael Stanislawski, *Autobiographical Jews: Essays in Jewish Self-Fashioning* (Seattle: University of Washington Press, 2004); and Marcus Moseley, *Being for Myself Alone: Origins of Jewish Autobiography* (Stanford, CA: Stanford University Press, 2005).

3. Pauline Wengeroff also describes the examination to which her bridegroom (who was considerably older) was subjected by her father. While her mother was concerned about the financial arrangements of the engagement contract, her father cut off the discussion with these words: "If only the young man's knowledge of Talmud is solid, everything else will work out." *Memoirs of a Grandmother*, 2:26.

4. Jacob Katz, "Family, Kinship, and Marriage among Ashkenazim in Sixteenth to Eighteenth Centuries," *Jewish Journal of Sociology* 1, no. 1 (1959): 12.

5. Etkes, "Marriage and Torah Study among the *Lomdim*," 153–78.

6. Mordecai Aaron Günzburg, *Aviezer* (Vilna, Lithuania: Fuenn Press, 1864), 34–35.

7. Mintz, *"Banished from Their Father's Table*," 27.

8. Günzburg, *Aviezer*, 49.

9. Ibid., 95–103. For an abridged translation of this section, see "Early Marriage and Sexuality: The Memoirs of Mordechai Aaron Guenzburg," in *Everyday Jewish Life in Imperial Russia, Select Documents [1772–1914]*, ed. ChaeRan Y. Freeze and Jay M. Harris (Waltham, MA: Brandeis University Press, 2013), 305–16.

10. Lilienblum, *Sins of Youth*, 1:88.

11. Ibid., 106.

12. For a fascinating analysis of the overlaps between religious rituals of circumcision and marriage and of the significance of this overlap, see Yemima Chovav, *Maidens Love Thee: The Religious and Spiritual Lives of Jewish Ashkenazic Women in the Early Modern Period* ['Alamot ahevukha: Ḥaye ha-dat yeha-ruaḥ shel nashim ba-ḥevrah ha-Ashkenazit be-reshit ha-'et ha-ḥadashah] (Jerusalem: Carmel Press, 2009), 125–26.

13. Cohen, *"One Beloved, the Other Hated,"* 2.

14. Ibid., 184.

15. For a discussion of this feature of the Haskalah novel, see ibid. For the rise of marital age among Eastern European Jews, see Stampfer, "The Social Implications of Very Early Marriage," in *Families, Rabbis, and Education*, 7–25.

16. On this abandonment and on modern Jewish wife abandonment more generally, see Bluma Goldstein, *Enforced Marginalities: Jewish Narratives on Abandoned Wives* (Berkeley: University of California Press, 2007), 10–48. For a discussion of the animus toward mothers-in-law, and more generally to the parents of the bride who supported the young couple, see Biale on "the persistent 'splitting' in these works between the 'good parents' and the cruel outsiders," in *Eros and the Jews*, 153.

17. Twersky's fascinating confession in a long letter to the Yiddish writer Jacob Dineson is translated and introduced in David Assaf, "'My Tiny, Ugly World': The Confession of Rabbi Yitzhak Nahum Twersky of Shpikov," *Contemporary Jewry* 26 (2006): 1–34. The description of his marriage as a forced entry into a harem is on 24.

18. Lilienblum acknowledged the male character of Hebrew literature, writing to Miriam Markel-Mozessohn that he had quoted traditional sources without fear of their vulgarity: "Know and remember that you are the only woman who reads my books, who would require me to watch my speech and my writing in the holy tongue (which is not foreign to such expressions, in the spirit of antiquity), in a book that no refined woman will read besides you?!" Lilienblum (letter of November 18, 1870), Shvadron Collection (National Library, Jerusalem). Quoted in Parush, *Reading Jewish Women*, 235–36.

19. Lilienblum, "Words of Song," 181.

20. Mapu, *Love of Zion*, 20.

21. Yehudah Leib Gordon, *Kotso shel Yud* [The tip of the yud], trans. Stanley Nash, *CCAR: A Reform Jewish Quarterly* 53, no. 3 (2006): 119.

22. Gordon's *Tip of the Yud* is an interesting exception to this rule, since the lovers are thwarted from marrying by the failure of the rabbinical court to uphold Bat-Shua's divorce document, and the story ends in tragedy rather than marriage. Yahil Zaban suggests one ideological motivation for choice: Bat-Shua may not marry Feibush in Gordon's poem because she is a divorcée and thus not a virgin; in "The Birth of the Jewish Tragedy from the Spirit of Enlightenment: Judah Leib Gordon's Poem 'The Tip of the Letter Yod,'" unpublished paper (2013).

23. Peter Brooks, *Reading for the Plot: Design and Intention in Narrative* (New York: Vintage, 1984), 37.

24. Olga Litvak makes an argument for reading political teleology alongside romantic plot developments in such novels as the Russian *In the Heat of Time*, in which the maskilic author, Lev Levanda, "juxtaposes the evolution of [Jewish women's] erotic aspirations and their romance with Poland against the political education of [his hero] Sarin." See Olga Litvak, *Haskalah: The Romantic Movement in Judaism* (New Brunswick, NJ: Rutgers University Press, 2012), 134.

25. The blind beggar woman in Abramovitsh's *Fishke the Lame* (1869; revised and expanded in 1888) is a rare example of a disabled bride, though she is "redeemed" by her beauty and goodness.

26. Women are occasionally, but less frequently, juxtaposed to each other in Hebrew and Yiddish novels: Reuven Braudes's 1888 novel, *Two Extremes*, presents a husband torn between a sophisticated urban beauty and his traditional wife that he has left back in his hometown. Nevertheless, at the end of the novel, he returns to his wife after she has learned to render herself more attractive to her husband by shedding her wig and wearing modern clothing. The two women are both worthy, even if one has to be "educated" toward this value.

27. Such sages or mentors include Sitri in *The Love of Zion*, David Handler in Ettinger's *Serkele*, the German merchant in Aksenfeld's *The Headkerchief*, and Elisheva's "enlightened" grandfather Ovadiah in Mapu's *The Hypocrite*.

28. Mapu, *Love of Zion*, 19–20.

29. Avraham Mapu, *The Hypocrite* [Ayit tsavua], in *The Complete Works of Avraham Mapu* (Tel Aviv: Dvir, 1947), 247.

30. Mapu, *Hypocrite*, 248.

31. Gordon, *Tip of the Yud*, 119.

32. Miron, *From Romance to the Novel*, 25.

33. Ibid.

34. Litvak, *Haskalah*, 139.

35. Zaban, *Choicest Meal*, 42.

36. Sigmund Freud, "Family Romances," in *The Standard Edition of the Complete Psychological Works of Sigmund Freud*, vol. 9 (1906–8), *Jensen's "Gradiva" and Other Works*, trans. James Strachey (London: Hogarth Press and Institute of Psychoanalysis, 1959), 240.

37. Marthe Robert, "The Novel as Displacement," in *Theory of the Novel*, ed. Marshall Brown (Cambridge: Cambridge University Press, 2000), 168. The essay is excerpted from Marthe Robert, *The Origins of the Novel*, trans. Sacha Rabinovitch (London: Harvester, 1980), 3–36.

38. Litvak, *Haskalah*, 140.

39. Zaban, *Choicest Meal*, 42–43. The emphasis in these readings on incestuous desires stands in some contrast with the more prevalent view that allowing young people to choose their own mates will lead to exogamy or intermarriage. As discussed in the Introduction, the moderate maskil Eliezer Tzvi Zweifel excoriated the Jewish novel (according to Miron, with Mapu in mind) through the sexual allegory of the alluring foreign woman, a clear reference to the influences of non-Jewish

romantic literature on the genre and an allusion to a long textual tradition that figures the non-Jewish woman as primary sexual threat to the Jewish collective. That incest is also a lurking fantasy in the move to the bourgeois family is the argument developed here.

40. Mapu, *Love of Zion*, 8.

41. Ibid., 9.

42. Ibid., 10.

43. Mapu's ambivalent embrace of arranged marriage haunts *The Hypocrite* as well, where the mystical element of arrangement is provided not by the older generation (who are in fact enemies) but by the young couple themselves, who promise themselves to one another in their youth. Elisheva and Na'aman represent an unusually mature erotic pair, whose marriage is delayed long enough for both hero and heroine to travel and acquire a far-ranging education, but this union of "consenting adults" also harbors within itself the mystic seed from which it sprang, making it a kind of child marriage, thus finding literary redemption for what is often described—as in Lilienblum's description of his prospective bride as a toddler!—as the identifying feature of traditional marriage.

44. Gordon, *Tip of the Yud*, 118. In the Hebrew, the phrase "found her a husband" (*hekhin la alufah*) might equally, and more disturbingly, be translated as "prepared her master for her."

45. Puah Rakovsky, *My Life as a Radical Jewish Woman: Memoirs of a Zionist Feminist in Poland*, ed. Paula E. Hyman, trans. Barbara Harshav (Bloomington: Indiana University Press, 2002), 28.

46. S. An-sky, *The Dybbuk, or Between Two Worlds*, ed. David G. Roskies, trans. Golda Werman, in *The Dybbuk and Other Writings* (New York: Schocken, 1992), 29. For the Yiddish, see *The Complete Works of S. An-sky*, vol. 2, *Dramas* (Vilna, Lithuania: An-sky Press, 1928), 61.

47. Biale, *Eros and the Jews*, 146. David of Maków, a student of the Vilna Gaon (leader of the anti-Hasidic movement), writes that "they all gather together at night sleeping in one room and who knows what ugly deeds transpire." The still unpublished book by David of Maków, *Shever Poshim* (The downfall of sinners), is reproduced in part in Mordechai Wilensky, *Hasidism and Mitnagnism: The History of the Polemic between Hasidim and Their Opponents* [Hasidim u-mitnagdim: Le-toldot ha-pulmus she-benehem ba-shanim 532–535] (Jerusalem: Mosad Bialik, 1970), 2:41; page 74a of Maków's text.

48. Shaun Jacob Halper, "Coming out of the Hasidic Closet: Jiří Mordechai Langer (1894–1943) and the Fashioning of Homosexual-Jewish Identity," *Jewish Quarterly Review* 101, no. 2 (Spring 2011): 207.

49. Jiří Mordechai Langer, *Die Erotik der Kabbala* (Prague: Josef Flesch, 1923), 108–9, cited in Halper, "Coming out of the Hasidic Closet," 206–7. I have slightly modified Halper's translation.

50. While An-sky's play has Khonen singing "The Song of Songs" to Leah, the 1937 film version begins with Nissen singing a "love song," "The Song of Songs,"

to Sender at his friend's request, thus inviting a more homoerotic reading of their relationship than An-sky had provided.

51. An-sky, *Dybbuk*, 41–42; for the Yiddish, see An-sky, *Complete Works*, 2:89.

52. An-sky, *Dybbuk*, 43.

53. See also Naomi Seidman, "The Ghosts of Queer Loves Past: S. Y. Ansky and the Sexual Transformation of Ashkenaz," in *Queer Studies and the Jewish Question*, ed. Daniel Boyarin, Daniel Itzkowitz, and Ann Pellegrini (New York: Columbia University Press, 2003), 228–45.

54. Gabriella Safran, *Wandering Soul: The Dybbuk's Creator, S. An-sky* (Cambridge, MA: Harvard University Press, 2010), 215–16.

55. Ibid., 216.

56. Ibid.

57. Sharon Green suggests that the story of a love sanctioned by the mystical power of a vow constitutes a Jewish variation on the Cinderella tale; she connects this variation with the distinctive tendency of Jewish romances to cast parents as obstacles, while nevertheless finding cross-generational sanction for forbidden love. Sharon Green, *Not a Simple Story: Love and Politics in a Modern Hebrew Novel* (Lanham, MD: Lexington, 2001), 29–30n15.

58. Rashi describes an apparently well-known but now-lost midrashic tale about a weasel and a well (*hulda u-vor*): "This ancient Jewish love story tells of a young couple who meet by seeming chance, and who make a vow of love that is witnessed by no one but a weasel and a well (sometimes translated as pit or cistern). The vow is later broken, and the boy and girl are then separately visited by a series of misfortunes which do not end until their original vow is honored, and they are finally wed." Rashi's commentary on *Babylonian Talmud Ta'anit 8a*, ed. and trans. Henry Malter (Philadelphia: Jewish Publication Society, 1978), 104–7. For a literary analysis of the tale in its basic iterations, see Ben-Ami Feingold, "The Development of the Motif of the Double Match," *Jerusalem Studies in Jewish Folklore* 7 (1984): 22–27; for a bibliographical listing of the tale in all its appearances from the Talmud through modern Hebrew literature and a more folkloristic interpretation, see Naomi Zohar, "The Story of the Weasel and the Pit in the Literature of the Haskalah," *Criticism and Interpretation* 30 (1994): 121–56; the bibliography appears on 123–36.

59. Feingold, "Double Match," 22.

60. Zohar, "Weasel and the Pit," 139.

61. Ibid., 140.

62. Ibid., 144.

63. Vincent P. Pecora, *Secularization and Cultural Criticism: Religion, Nation, & Modernity* (Chicago: University of Chicago Press, 2006), 19.

64. Ibid., 17.

65. Ibid., 18–19, 22.

66. Alain de Botton, *On Love* (New York: Atlantic, 1993), 10.

67. Niklas Luhmann, *Liebe als Passion: Zur Codierung von Intimität* (Frankfurt: Surhkamp Wissenschaft, 1982), 181.

68. I borrow this term from Walter Benjamin's famous essay on Kafka, which argues that Kafka was far from the first to recognize that "the consistency of truth has been lost." While other writers accommodated themselves to this "sickness of tradition" by "clinging to truth or whatever they happened to regard as truth and, with a more or less heavy heart, forgoing its transmissibility," Kafka "tried something entirely new: he sacrificed truth for the sake of clinging to its transmissibility, its haggadic element. . . . [Kafka's 'haggadic' parables] do not modestly lie at the feet of the doctrine, as the Haggadah lies at the feet of the Halakhah. Though apparently reduced to submission, they unexpectedly raise a mighty paw against it." See Walter Benjamin, "Some Reflections on Kafka," in *Illuminations*, ed. Hannah Arendt, trans. Harry Zohn (New York: Schocken, 1978), 143–44. Benjamin's comments are excerpted from a letter to Gershom Scholem dated June 12, 1938.

69. Safran, *Wandering Soul*, 214.

70. An-sky, *Dybbuk*, 16.

71. Asad, *Formations of the Secular*, 13.

72. Sholem Aleichem, *Menachem Mendl* (Buenos Aires: Yosef Lifshitz/YIVO, 1963), 171.

73. S. Y. Agnon, A *Simple Story*, trans. Hillel Halkin (New York: Schocken, 1985), 36–37.

74. Katz, *Tradition and Crisis*, 231–32.

75. Günzburg, *Aviezer*, 34.

76. Avraham-Ber Gottlober, *Memoirs and Essays* [Zikhronot u-masa'ot], ed. Reuven Goldberg (Jerusalem: Mosad Bialik, 1976), 1:86. Gottlober's account re-creates a romantic scene by omitting that these are names of girls in a notebook rather than actual girls at, say, a dance.

77. Abrahams, *Jewish Life in the Middle Ages*, 170, 174.

78. Gottlober, *Memoirs and Essays*, 1:86.

79. Sigmund Freud, "The Most Prevalent Form of Degradation in Erotic Life," trans. Joan Riviere, in *Sexuality and the Psychology of Love*, ed. Philip Rieff (New York: Collier, 1966), 61.

80. Kaplan, *Making of the Jewish Middle Class*, 108–12.

81. Julian Levinson, *Exiles on Main Street: Jewish American Writers and American Literary Culture* (Bloomington: Indiana University Press, 2008), 173.

82. It is an odd literary coincidence (assuming that Malamud was unaware of the book) that the beginning of Malamud's story closely echoes the opening passage of the first modern Yiddish novel, Aksenfeld's *The Headkerchief* [Dos shterntikhl], written more than a hundred years earlier. Like Leo Finkle, Aksenfeld's Mikhl Gravestone requires a wife for purely professional reasons because he wishes to open his own school and such a promotion depends on his being married. It is only in the course of the novel, and the short story, that the prospective groom discovers the erotic motivations beyond the practical reasons to marry.

83. Bernard Malamud, "The Magic Barrel," in *Jewish American Stories*, ed. Irving Howe (New York: New American Library, 1977), 248.

84. Bernard Malamud, *Talking Horse: Bernard Malamud on Life and Work*, ed. Alan Cheuse and Nicholas Delblanco (New York: Columbia University Press, 1996), 80.

85. S. Lillian Kremer, "Reflections on Transmogrified Yiddish Archetypes in Fiction by Bernard Malamud," in *The Magic Worlds of Bernard Malamud*, ed. Evelyn Avery (Albany: SUNY Press, 2001), 123.

86. Ibid., 124.

87. Malamud, *Talking Horse*, 82.

88. Ibid., 80.

89. Ibid., 81. For the six anecdotes, see Immanuel Olsvanger, *Röyte Pomerantsen: Jewish Folk Humor Gathered and Edited* (New York: Schocken, 1947), tales 12–17 on 9–12. Two others (tales 22–23 on 15–16) also involve matchmaking, but it is not clear that Malamud read them.

90. Malamud, *Talking Horse*, 81–82; Olsvanger, *Röyte Pomerantsen*, 9–10.

91. Malamud counts only six of these tales, and I count eight. He may have missed the last two, which are presented out of order. On the other hand, Malamud might in fact have read them, since it is precisely tale 23 that conforms most closely to Malamud's own.

92. Olsvanger, *Röyte Pomerantsen*, 16–17 (ellipses in the original).

93. Robert Alter, "A Theological Fantasy," in *Critical Essays on Bernard Malamud*, ed. Joel Salzberg (Boston: Twayne, 1987), 67.

94. Malamud, "Magic Barrel," 251.

95. Malamud, *Talking Horse*, 81.

96. Robert Solotaroff, *Bernard Malamud: A Study of the Short Fiction* (Boston: Twayne, 1989), 36.

97. Olsvanger, introduction to *Röyte Pomerantsen*, vii.

Chapter 3

1. Werner Sollors, *Beyond Ethnicity: Consent and Descent in American Culture* (Oxford: Oxford University Press, 1986), 111.

2. Günzburg, *Aviezer*, 40.

3. Mintz, *"Banished from Their Father's Table,"* 116.

4. Gottlober, *Memoirs and Essays*, 1:81.

5. Günzburg, *Aviezer*, 40.

6. Lilienblum, *Sins of Youth*, 1:205–6.

7. Mapu, *Love of Zion*, 20.

8. Ibid.

9. Ibid., 144.

10. Shloyme Ettinger, *Serkele, or, In Mourning for a Brother: An Entirely New Theatrical Piece in Five Acts*, in *Landmark Yiddish Plays: A Critical Anthology*, ed. and trans. Joel Berkowitz and Jeremy Dauber (Albany: SUNY Press, 2006), 120. For the Yiddish, see Shloyme Ettinger, *Serkele*, in *Selected Works of Shloyme Ettinger*, ed. Shmuel Roszanski (Buenos Aires: YIVO, 1965), 126.

11. Shmuel Feiner, "The Pseudo-Enlightenment and the Question of Jewish Mod-

ernization," in *Enlightenment and Diaspora: The Armenian and Jewish Cases*, ed. Richard A. Hovannisian and David N. Myers (Atlanta: Scholars Press, 1999), 181–208.

12. S. Y. Abramovitsh, *The Wishing Ring* [Dos vinshfingerl], trans. Michael Wex (Syracuse, NY: Syracuse University Press, 2003), 116. The Yiddish is in *Collected Works of Mendele Moykher Sforim* (New York: Hebrew Publishing, 1920), 4:11.

13. Katz, *Tradition and Crisis*, 142.

14. Mark Zborowski and Elizabeth Herzog, *Life Is with People: The Culture of the Shtetl*, foreword by Margaret Mead, with a new introduction by Barbara Kirshenblatt-Gimblett (New York: Schocken, 1995), 76–77.

15. Ibid., 76–78.

16. Glenn Dynner, *Men of Silk: The Hasidic Conquest of Polish Jewish Society* (Oxford: Oxford University Press, 1996), 122.

17. Mordechai Zalkin, "The Maskilic Family and Its Place in the Development of the Eastern European Jewish Enlightenment," in *Sexuality and the Family in Jewish History* [Eros erusin ve-isurim: Miniyut u-mishpahah ba-historyah], ed. Israel Bartal and Isaiah Gafni (Jerusalem: Zalman Shazar, 1998), 234–52.

18. Günzburg, *Aviezer*, 40–41.

19. Stampfer, *Families, Rabbis and Education*, 165.

20. Ibid., 165–66.

21. Claude Lévi-Strauss, *The Elementary Structures of Kinship*, ed. Rodney Needham, trans. James Harle Bell and John Richard von Sturmer (Boston: Beacon, 1969), 116.

22. Zborowski and Herzog, *Life Is with People*, 273.

23. The notion of women as "empty signifiers" that enable men to forge marital connections is worked out in Gayle Rubin's critique of *The Elementary Structures of Kinship*, in "The Traffic in Women: Notes on the 'Political Economy' of Sex," in *The Second Wave: A Reader in Feminist Theory*, ed. Linda Nicholson (New York: Routledge, 1997), 27–62.

24. See Etkes, "Marriage and Torah Study," 156.

25. Freeze, *Jewish Marriage and Divorce*, 71.

26. Joel Berkowitz and Jeremy Dauber, introduction to *Landmark Yiddish Plays* (Albany: SUNY Press, 1996), 32.

27. Zehavit Stern, "Look Back in Pride: Parental Authority and Ancestral Reassurance in Haskalah Literature" (unpublished paper, 2005).

28. Ibid., 12.

29. Ibid., 14.

30. Miron, *A Traveler Disguised*, 30.

31. Immanuel Etkes, introduction to Isaac Ber Lebensohn, *A Testimony in Israel* [Te'udah be-Yisra'el], ed. Immanuel Etkes (Jerusalem: Zalman Shazar, 1977), 12.

32. Ibid., 13.

33. Ibid., 15. Etkes parses the social ramifications of Lebensohn's identification with medieval Jewish rationalists; drawing on elite philosophies allowed him to explain the failure of the masses to embrace these philosophical truths.

34. Mapu, *Love of Zion*, 3.

35. It may be relevant to note here that Mapu and Lilienblum came from pious and traditional families that could claim no major ancestral distinction: Mapu, like a number of other maskilim, was the son of a poor teacher and acquired a good education in traditional Jewish sources despite possessing neither family wealth nor distinction (his brother, a self-made businessman, supported him for years).

36. Katz, *Tradition and Crisis*, 118. Avoiding unintentional incest was apparently another purpose of genealogical memory.

37. Yosef Hayim Yerushalmi, *Zakhor: Jewish History and Jewish Memory* (Seattle: University of Washington Press, 1982), 101.

38. Mintz, *"Banished from Their Father's Table,"* 8.

39. Jonathan Boyarin, *Jewish Families* (New Brunswick, NJ: Rutgers University Press, 2013), 29.

40. See Malka Magentsa-Shaked, "Singer and the Family Saga Novel in Jewish Literature," *Prooftexts* 9 (1989): 27–42.

41. Lilienblum, *Sins of Youth*, 1:81.

42. See Shmuel Feiner, *Haskalah and History: The Emergence of a Modern Jewish Historical Consciousness*, trans. Chaya Naor and Sondra Silverton (Portland, OR: Littman Library, 2002). On the Haskalah interest in folklore, see Dan Miron, "Folklore and Anti-folklore in the Yiddish Fiction of the Haskala," in *The Image of the Shtetl and Other Studies of Modern Jewish Literary Imagination* (Syracuse, NY: Syracuse University Press, 2000), 49–80.

43. Walter Benjamin, "Theses on the Philosophy of History," in *Illuminations*, trans. Harry Zohn (New York: Schocken, 1969), 256.

44. Günzburg, *Aviezer*, 50.

45. Ibid., 51.

46. Ibid., 51–52.

47. Donald Harman Akenson, *Some Family: The Mormons and How Humanity Keeps Track of Itself* (Montreal: McGill-Queens University Press, 2007), 281.

48. Ibid., 80.

49. Harold Bloom, *The Anxiety of Influence: A Theory of Poetry* (New York: Oxford University Press, 1973), 9.

50. Ilana Pardes, "Yocheved Bat-Miriam: The Poetic Strength of a Matronym," in *Gender and Text in Modern Hebrew and Yiddish Literature*, ed. Naomi Sokoloff, Anne Lapidus, and Anita Norich (New York: Jewish Theological Seminary Press, 1992), 42.

51. Ibid., 59.

52. Kadya Molodowsky, "Women Songs," in *Paper Bridges: Selected Poems of Kadya Molodowsky*, trans. Kathryn Hellerstein (Detroit, MI: Wayne State University, 1999), 68–69.

53. Ibid., 68.

54. Ibid., 68–69.

55. Kathryn Hellerstein, introduction to *Paper Bridges*, 23.

56. Zohar Weiman-Kelman, "What to Expect When You're Not Expecting: Queer Histories of Jewish Women's Writings" (PhD diss., University of California, Berkeley, 2012), 5. In a recently published analysis of Yiddish women's poetry, Hellerstein points to the "string of Hebraic words" in this poem, which "makes the speaker's life a part of the written Hebraic tradition of sexuality that binds women's desires and dreams (*khaloymes*). The speaker's life, composed from the words of the sacred text, has been ripped from its binding, and its first line is *farrisn*—smudged or torn—making the page ritually impure. This damaged page of a woman's life calls for a new book and a new binding—the Yiddish poetry that Molodowsky writes." Kathryn Hellerstein, *A Question of Tradition: Women Poets in Yiddish, 1586–1987* (Stanford, CA: Stanford University Press, 2014), 124.

57. Dvora Baron, *The First Day and Other Stories*, ed. Chana Kronfeld and Naomi Seidman, trans. Naomi Seidman (Berkeley: University of California Press, 1997), 66.

58. Baron, "Family," 66. The modern Hebrew term for "aunt," significantly, also means in biblical usage "beloved."

59. Ibid., 75–76.

60. See Sollors, *Beyond Ethnicity*, on the workings of "consent" and "descent" in American culture.

61. Baron, "Family," 83.

62. See Lévi-Strauss, *Elementary Structures of Kinship*, 116, 485.

63. Baron, "Family," 86–87.

64. For a comparison of the breakdown in Jewish law in Gordon and Baron, see Zilla Jane Goodman, "Traced in Ink: Women's Lives in 'Qotzo shel Yud' by Yalag and 'Mishpachah'" by D. Baron," in *Gender and Judaism: The Transformation of Tradition*, ed. Tamar Rudavsky (New York: New York University Press, 1995), 191–207.

65. Baron, "Family," 87–88.

66. For a recent biographical description of Sholem Aleichem's courtship of Olga Loyeff, see Jeremy Dauber, *The Worlds of Sholem Aleichem: The Remarkable Life and Afterlife of the Man Who Created Tevye* (New York: Schocken, 2013), 31–36.

67. Lilienblum, "Words of Song," 181.

68. Katz, *Tradition and Crisis*, 118.

69. Stampfer, *Families, Rabbis and Education*, 155–66.

70. Sholem Aleichem, *Tevye the Dairyman*, 49. Tsatskeleh means something like a "little ornament" and may be translated as "Rabbi Fancypants."

71. Ibid., 52.

72. Sollors, *Beyond Ethnicity*, 112.

73. Ibid., 74.

74. Ibid., 72.

75. Israel Zangwill, *The Melting-Pot* (New York: Macmillan, 1909), 198–99.

76. Andrea Most, *Theatrical Liberalism: Jews and Popular Entertainment in America* (New York: New York University Press, 2013), 39–40.

77. Ibid., 77.

78. Ibid., 232.

79. Tony Kushner, *Angels in America, A Gay Fantasia on National Themes, Part One: Millennium Approaches* (New York: Theatre Communications Group, 1992), 5.

80. The character note is from Kushner, *Millennium Approaches*, 3. Jonathan Friedman, *Rainbow Jews: Jewish and Gay Identity in the Performing Arts* (New York: Lexington, 2007), 110.

81. Tony Kushner, *Angels in America: A Gay Fantasia on National Themes, Part Two: Perestroika* (New York: Theatre Communications Group, 1996), 146.

82. Kushner, *Millennium Approaches*, 10.

83. Kushner, *Perestroika*, 123.

84. Ibid., 51.

85. Ibid., 86.

Chapter 4

1. Moses Mendelssohn, *Gesammelte Schriften Jubiläumausgabe* (Berlin, 1929–38), vol. 16, May 15, 1761, letter 103, 205; quoted in Biale, *Eros and the Jews*, 153. Alexander Altmann devotes considerable attention to Mendelssohn's betrothal and marriage, also viewing these as evidence of transformations of Jewish marital practice. See Altmann, *Moses Mendelssohn*, 92–100.

2. Biale, *Eros and the Jews*, 153.

3. See, for instance, a love-letter manual that appeared in sixteenth-century Italy: Samuel Archivolti, *Well of Gardens* (Venice: Aloise Bragadin Print, 1553); quoted in Roni Weinstein, *Marriage Rituals Italian Style: A Historical Anthropological Perspective on Early Modern Italian Jews*, trans. Batya Stein (Leiden, Netherlands: Brill Academic Publishers, 2004), 295. Introducing the section on love letters, Archivolti writes:

> Women will gather courage and learn how to answer sensibly the ardors of their wooers, to love a lover and hate an enemy. . . . A lover writing to his beloved will beg for her favors saying, "it is love or death." You should understand the intense passion of these sayings. Responding to the lover, the gazelle will stoke the flames of his love for her, ensnare him in the net of her words, beguile him with glibness and lure him with her smooth tongue.

4. Watt, *Rise of the Novel*, 136.

5. Rakovsky, *My Life*, 28.

6. Brooks, *Reading for the Plot*, 38–40.

7. Ibid., 39.

8. Stephen Kern, *The Culture of Love: Victorians to Moderns* (Cambridge, MA: Harvard University Press, 1992), 11. Kern describes Miss Havisham in Charles Dickens's *Great Expectations* (1861) as a "bitter parody of the bride to be," who "shows how passive, helpless waiting can turn passionate love into venomous hate" (13).

9. Walter Benjamin, "Theses on the Philosophy of History," in *Illuminations*, ed. Hannah Arendt, trans. Harry Zohn (New York: Schocken, 1969), 261.

10. Stampfer, *Family, Rabbis and Education*, 7–25.

11. Gottlober, *Memoirs and Essays*, 1:85–86.

12. Weinstein, *Marriage Rituals*, 64.

13. Ibid., 69.

14. Sholem Yankev Abramovitsh, "A Fallen Leaf: What Shall We Do?," *Hamelitz* 1 (1878): 1–6; quoted in Gluzman, *Zionist Body*, 106.

15. Günzburg, *Aviezer*, 148. The Hebrew wordplay connects *ish* (man) and *ishah* (women).

16. See Stampfer, *Family, Rabbis and Education*, 7–25. His discussion of the decline of early marriage in the course of the nineteenth century appears on 21.

17. Katz, *Tradition and Crisis*, 115.

18. For an exploration of how the novel constructed modern ideologies of youth, see Franco Moretti, *The Way of the World: The Bildungsroman in European Culture* (London: Verso, 2000), 4.

19. M. M. Bakhtin, *The Dialogic Imagination: Four Essays*, ed. Michael Holquist, trans. Caryl Emerson and Michael Holquist (Austin: University of Texas Press, 1981), 90–91.

20. Mapu, *Love of Zion*, 8–9.

21. Ibid., 9.

22. Ibid., 38.

23. Ibid.

24. Sholem Aleichem's 1888 novella *Stempenyu* is an interesting exception. The final chapter focuses on the handsome hero's scrutiny of himself in the mirror and lament over his own aging (Rokhele, of course, is also growing older, but having given up the joys of flirtation, her aging is less lamentable).

25. Mapu, *Love of Zion*, 60.

26. Ibid., 67.

27. Cohen, *"One Beloved, the Other Hated,"* 140.

28. On the microcosmic and macrocosmic dimensions of the Haskalah romance, see ibid., 168.

29. Watt, *Rise of the Novel*, 162–63.

30. Ibid., 160–61.

31. Samuel Johnson, *Thraliana* I, 172; quoted in Watt, *Rise of the Novel*, 162. The carnality and sexual appetite that earlier ideological formations had assigned to women were now relegated to the male sphere, which meant, Watt argues, that marriage had a dramatically different meaning for men and for women.

32. Watt, *Rise of the Novel*, 162.

33. A very partial list of the most interesting of these sources includes David Biale, "Eros and Enlightenment," in *Eros and the Jews: From Biblical Israel to Contemporary America*, by David Biale (New York: Basic, 1992), 149–75; Paula E. Hyman, *Gender and Assimilation in Modern Jewish History* (Seattle: University of Washington Press, 1995); Daniel Boyarin, *Unheroic Conduct: The Rise of Heterosexuality and the Invention of the Jewish Man* (Berkeley: University of California Press, 1997); and Shmuel Feiner, "The Modern Jewish Woman: A Case Study in the Relationship between the Haskalah and Modernity," in *Sexuality and the Family*

in History [Eros erusin ve-isurim: Miniyut u-mishpahah ba-historyah], ed. Israel Bartal and Isaiah Gafni (Jerusalem: Zalman Shazar, 1998), 225–33.

34. Bartal, "Virility and Impotence," 79.

35. Cohen, *"One Beloved, the Other Hated,"* 33.

36. Of course, this ideal was limited to the class of the *Lomdim*. See Etkes, "Marriage and Torah Study," 153–78.

37. Günzburg, *Kiryat Sefer*, 79; quoted in Cohen, *"One Beloved, the Other Hated,"* 34.

38. I borrow the term "interpellation" from Louis Althusser, "Ideology and Ideological State Apparatuses," in *Critical Theory since 1965*, ed. Hazard Adams and Leroy Searle (Tallahassee: Florida State University Press, 1986), 244–49.

39. Hurvitz quotes a letter from a matchmaker to a father acknowledging that the bride he is proposing "is certainly not an exceptional beauty." Hurvitz, "Courtship and Arranged Marriages," 426.

40. Sholem Aleichem, *Stempenyu*, 30.

41. Boyarin, *Unheroic Conduct*, 333–35.

42. Ibid., 68–69.

43. Feiner, "Modern Jewish Woman," 264.

44. Gordon, *Tip of the Yud*, 113.

45. This distinction has something in common with Moses Mendelssohn's defense of Jewish law as less coercive than the Pauline theology that aimed to liberate humans from "the burden of the law," precisely on the grounds that a religious culture that legislated actions but not beliefs is preferable to one that makes claims on people's minds. See Moses Mendelssohn, *Jerusalem, or On Religious Power and Judaism*, trans. Allan Arkush (Hanover, NH: Brandeis University and University Press of New England, 1983), 90.

46. Günzburg, *Aviezer*, 41.

47. Sholem Yankev Abramovitsh, *Fishke der krumer*, in *Complete Works of Mendele Moykher Sforim* (New York: Hebrew Publishing, 1920), 7:24.

48. Abramovitsh, *Fishke*, 25.

49. Lévi-Strauss, *Elementary Structures of Kinship*, 116, 485.

50. Maimon, *Autobiography*, 33.

51. Günzburg, *Aviezer*, 135–36.

52. As Israel Bartal has shown, Günzburg's description of his father's (traditional) marriage is remarkably close to that of a well-known Hebrew-German textbook for young people by the maskil Naphtali Herz Homberg, *Imre Shefer* (Vienna: Hrashanski Press, 1802), on modern marriage, speaking of the harmonious blend of "the husband's reason and the wife's sense," mutual love, and domestic harmony. See Bartal, "Virility and Impotence," 82–83.

53. Wengeroff, *Memoirs*, 1:215; for the German, see *Memoiren einer Grossmutter*, 1:180.

54. Yekhezkel Kotik, *Journey to a Nineteenth-Century Shtetl: The Memoirs of Yekhezkel Kotik*, ed. and trans. David Assaf (Detroit, MI: Wayne State University

Press, 2002), 358–59. Assaf's note on this passage traces the custom to a seventeenth-century mystical Hebrew source, Avraham Azulay's *Hesed le-Avraham*; this may have been the source Maimon refers to in his own description of the custom.

55. Leo Tolstoy, *Anna Karenina,* trans. Richard Pevear and Larissa Volokhonsky (New York: Penguin, 2004), 456.

56. Asad, *Formations of the Secular*, 13.

57. This improper gender performance is overdetermined in Bat-Shua's case, since as an abandoned woman, "she is a mother—but also a father to her children." Gordon, *Tip of the Yud*, 130.

58. Ibid., 168.

59. Bartal, "Virility and Impotence," 85.

60. Israel Bartal, "Haskalah Literature: Portrayal of Women," Jewish Women's Archive, http://jwa.org/encyclopedia/article/haskalah-literature-portrayal-of-women (accessed October 20, 2014).

61. Gordon, *Tip of the Yud*, 114.

62. Yahil Zaban, "'Folded White Napkins for Wiping One's Hands': The Etiquette Discourse in Haskalah Literature" (unpublished paper, 2010).

63. Ibid. The quotation is from Yehudah Leib Gordon, *The End of Joy Is Sorrow* [Aharit simha tuga], in *Collected Writings of Yehudah Leib Gordon* (Tel Aviv: Dvir, 1960), 44.

64. Katz, *Tradition and Crisis*, 232.

65. BT Shabbat 33a (London: Soncino Press, 1935–48). Moses Maimonides, *Guide for the Perplexed*, 3:8, trans. M. Friedländer (New York: Dover, 1904), 413–14.

66. Stampfer, *Families, Rabbis and Education*, 43.

67. For more on the religious atmosphere imposed on traditional weddings of a slightly earlier period (sometimes in the face of popular impulses toward levity), see Chovav, *Maidens Love Thee*, 126–27.

68. Mapu, *Love of Zion*, 10.

69. Miron, *From the Romance to the Novel*, 25.

70. Biale, *Eros and the Jews*, 165.

71. Iser, *Fictive and the Imaginary*, 34.

72. Taking Richardson's *Pamela* as a primary text for the construction of a new ideology of masculinity as well as femininity, Watt writes that, for men,

> the best that could be hoped for was a social disciplining of the unregenerate Adam within by making marriage the only permitted means of sexual expression: Pamela and her sex, however, with the exception of a few wholly abandoned females, were reserved for higher things; the new ideology granted them a total immunity from sexual feelings, and if they married it was not because they had any need of *medicina libidinis*, but because the pieties of marriage and the family were safe only in their hands. . . . One can only surmise that, by a devious process not unknown to the psychologist, the very difficulties in the situation of women at this time brought about a new concept of the feminine role which masked their actual dependence on sexual attractiveness to the male much more completely than before, and strengthened their tactical position in courtship

by making their acceptance of a suitor a matter, not of joint personal satisfaction, but of *noblesse oblige*. (*Rise of the Novel*, 162)

73. Mapu, *Love of Zion*, 11. This is another occasion in which Mapu activates the biblical intertext that renders Tamar and Amnon brother and sister, at the very moment of the sexualized violence of the encounter with a lion.

74. See, for instance, Litvak, *Haskalah*, 139–40.

75. Kern describes the shift from the nineteenth to the twentieth century in novelistic descriptions of (especially women's) faces and hair to their arms, bodies, flesh, and smells. Kern, *Culture of Love*, 61–88.

76. Gordon, *Tip of the Yud*, 166.

77. Watt, *Rise of the Novel*, 139–40.

78. Sollors, *Beyond Ethnicity*, 106.

79. Watt, *Rise of the Novel*, 160–61.

80. Bhabha, *Location of Culture*, 126.

81. See Feiner, "The Pseudo-Enlightenment," 181–208.

82. Serkele's signal verbal tic, *mayne koykhes*, loosely means "I feel faint" (as in, "I feel my powers weakening"), which is how Joel Berkowitz and Jeremy Dauber translate it. But the phrase more literally means "my powers," tacitly acknowledging through wordplay that she *is* a powerful woman—much along the lines of powerful women in traditional society.

83. Ettinger, *Serkele*, 156.

84. Judith Butler, in *Gender Trouble: Feminism and the Subversion of Identity* (New York: Routledge, 1990), famously spells out the logic of how gender masquerade serves to denaturalize gender performance in its "correct" as well as "drag" expressions. See especially 128–41.

85. Mapu, *Love of Zion*, 10.

86. Ibid.

87. Cohen, "*One Beloved, the Other Hated*," 230.

88. Ibid.

89. Mapu, *Love of Zion*, 22.

90. "Letter from Dvora Daughter of Rabbi Menahem Haefrati to Avraham Mapu," *Hamagid* 3, no. 7 (1856): 46; quoted in Parush, *Reading Jewish Women*, 216. This letter is also discussed in Carole B. Balin, *To Reveal Our Hearts: Jewish Women Writers in Tsarist Russia* (Cincinnati, OH: Hebrew Union College Press, 2000), 19.

91. The novella was first published in Yiddish in 1878 but was later reworked and expanded in both Yiddish and Hebrew. The first Hebrew version appeared in 1896. For more on this complex publication history and for an analysis of the differences between the Hebrew and Yiddish versions, see Menahem Perry, "Analogy and Its Place in the Novelistic Structure of Mendele Moykher Sforim," *Ha-sifrut* 1, no. 1 (1968): 65–100.

92. See Dan Miron and Anita Norich, "The Politics of Benjamin III: Intellectual Significance and Its Formal Correlatives in Sh. Y. Abramovitsh's *Masoes Benyomin Hashlishi*," in *The Field of Yiddish: Studies in Language, Folklore, and Literature*, ed.

Marvin I. Herzog, Barbara Kirschenblatt-Gimblett, Dan Miron, and Ruth Wisse (Philadelphia: Institute for the Study of Human Issues, 1980), 4:1–115.

93. Gluzman, *Zionist Body*, 116.

94. On the connection between *The Travels* and *Don Quixote*, see Leah Garrett, "The Jewish Don Quixote," *Cervantes: Bulletin of the Cervantes Society of America* 17, no. 2 (1997): 94–105.

95. Gluzman, *Zionist Body*, 103.

96. S. Y. Abramovitsh, *The Travels of Benjamin the Third* [Masoes Binyomin ha-shlishi], in *The Complete Works of Mendele Mokher Sforim* (S. Y. Abramovitsh) (New York: Hebrew Publishing Company, 1920), 20. For an English translation that scrubs these romantic associations, see Mendele Mocher Seforim, *The Travels and Adventures of Benjamin the Third*, trans. Moshe Spiegel (New York: Schocken, 1968), 40.

97. Abramovitsh, *The Travels*, 21.

98. Ibid., 25.

99. Gluzman, *Zionist Body*, 116.

100. Abramovitsh, *The Travels*, 85.

101. Ibid., 85, 90.

102. Reuven Asher Braudes, *The Two Extremes* [Shete ha-ketsavot], ed. Ben-Ami Feingold (Jerusalem: Mosad Bialik, 1989), 373.

103. Warren Hoffman, *The Passing Game: Queering Jewish American Culture* (Syracuse, NY: Syracuse University Press, 2009), 71. Hoffman notes that Picon's crossdressing was limited to her Yiddish work on the stage and screen, while English audiences saw her (later in her career) in female garb.

104. Ibid., 70.

105. Alisa Solomon, *Re-dressing the Canon: Essays on Theater and Gender* (London: Routledge, 1997), 97.

106. Woody Allen, *Love and Death* (A Jack Rollins & Charles H. Joffe Production, 1975), 35 mm slides, filmstrip, 85 min.

107. Ibid.

108. Ibid.

109. Ibid.

110. Erica Jong, *Fear of Flying* (New York: Signet, 2003), 11.

111. For a book-length analysis of the reception of *Fear of Flying* and other of Jong's novels, see Charlotte Templin, *Feminism and the Politics of Literary Reputation: The Example of Erica Jong* (Lawrence: University Press of Kansas, 1995); for a broader exploration of Jong's books in the context of other novels of the period, see Lisa Maria Hogeland, "Sexuality in the Consciousness-Raising Novel of the 1970s," *Journal of the History of Sexuality* 5, no. 4 (1995): 601–32.

112. Alice Echols, *Daring to Be BAD: Radical Feminism in America, 1967–1975* (Minneapolis: University of Minnesota Press, 1979), 43; and Ann Snitow, Christine Stansell, and Sharon Thompson, eds., *Powers of Desire: The Politics of Sexuality* (New York: New Feminist Library, 1983), 20.

113. The New Left tensions over sex and feminism were sometimes internecine disputes, pitting Jewish men against Jewish women in a more heated and narrower version of the challenges that Americanization posed to the relationships between Jewish men and women. As Riv-Ellen Prell argues in her analysis of American Jewish gender relations, "gender has served to symbolize Jews' relationship to nation, family, and work because both Americanization and mobility place specific yet different demands on men and women." The demands of Americanization and mobility, felt separately by Jewish men and women, gave rise to, among other effects, the stereotyping of Jewish women as devouring mothers and materialist wives. Prell, *Fighting to Become Americans: Assimilation and the Trouble between Jewish Women and Jewish Men* (Boston: Beacon Press, 1999), 4.

114. Hyman, *Gender and Assimilation*, 75.

115. Hogeland, "Sexuality in the Novel," 626.

116. Biale, *Eros and the Jews*, 225.

117. Jong, *Fear of Flying*, 11.

118. For a discussion of this aspect of traditional Jewish modesty, see Josh Lambert, *Unclean Lips: Obscenity, Jews and American Culture* (New York: New York University Press, 2013), 141–74.

119. John Murray Cuddihy, *The Ordeal of Civility: Freud, Marx, Lévi-Strauss and the Jewish Struggle with Modernity* (Boston: Beacon Press, 1987), 70.

120. Boyarin, *Unheroic Conduct*, 48.

121. On these laws, see Katz, *Tradition and Crisis*, 121; and Boyarin, *Unheroic Conduct*, 48.

122. Watt, *Rise of the Novel*, 162–63.

123. Patterson, *Hebrew Novel*, 220; Mintz, "Banished from Their Father's Table," 90.

Chapter 5

1. Robert Alter, "Literary Refractions of the Jewish Family," in *The Jewish Family: Metaphor and Memory*, ed. David Kraemer (New York: Oxford University Press, 1985), 237.

2. Saul Bellow, "Cousins," in *Him with His Foot in His Mouth and Other Stories* (New York: Harper and Row, 1984), 246. Brodsky's remarks echo those of nineteenth-century writers who praised the Jewish family for its strength and commitment. "Nowhere is family sentiment more profound than among the Jews," claimed the *Archives Israélites* in 1846. "There, conjugal love and parental love still exist in all their strength." Quoted in Jonathan Boyarin, *Jewish Families*, 186.

3. See David Kertzer and Mario Barbagli, eds., "Introduction," in *The History of the European Family*, vol. 2, *Family Life in the Long Nineteenth Century, 1789–1913* (New Haven, CT: Yale University Press, 2001). The introduction provides a useful overview of some of the changes described in Watt as they characterize broader regions in Europe than Watt considers.

4. Bellow, "Cousins," 246.

5. Watt, *Rise of the Novel*, 139.

6. See Andrejs Plakans, "Agrarian Reform and the Family in Eastern Europe," in Kertzer and Barbagli, *History of the European Family*, 2:73–108. As compared to the situation in Western, Central, and Southern Europe, Plakans writes, "low marriage ages, nearly universal marriage, high proportions and considerable variety of household complexity were the *expected* feature of family life in the east in the early nineteenth century" (2:78; emphasis in original).

7. Coontz, *Marriage*, 6.

8. Ibid., 41.

9. Ibid.

10. Beatrice Silverman Weinreich, *Kinship Terminology in a Modern Fusion Language*, Working Papers in Yiddish and East European Jewish Studies 11 (New York: YIVO, 1956), 16–17.

11. Ibid. Weinreich quotes Zborowski and Herzog, *Life Is with People*, 306.

12. Israel Abrahams makes such a case for the development of the institution of the matchmaker, arguing that the matchmaker served the function of community memory, uniting families of distinction while helping avoid consanguineous unions. Abrahams, *Jewish Life in the Middle Ages*, 170.

13. Katz, *Tradition and Crisis*, 127.

14. Wengeroff, "Four Years in My In-Laws' House," in *Memoirs*, 2:73–86.

15. Etkes, "Marriage and Torah Study," 156.

16. Ibid., 159

17. Maimon, *Autobiography*, 31–32.

18. Biale, *Eros and the Jews*, 153.

19. Günzburg, *Aviezer*, 153.

20. Dan Ben Amos and Jerome Mintz, eds. and trans., *In Praise of the Baal Shem Tov: The Earliest Collection of Legends about the Founder of Hasidism* (Northvale, NJ: Jason Aronson, 1993), 20. Daniel Boyarin discusses this chapter of *In Praise of the Baal Shem Tov* in detail in *Unheroic Conduct*, 55–68.

21. The same point is made in Abramovitsh's 1868 novel, *Fathers and Sons*, in which the father of the heroine declares that he likes Peretz, the man he has picked out for his daughter, saying, "he's a boy after my own heart [*bahur ke-levavi*]." For a discussion, see Cohen, *"One Beloved, the Other Hated,"* 117. I thank Zehavit Stern for pointing this out to me.

22. Gordon, *Tip of the Yud*, 133–34.

23. Sholem Aleichem, *Stempenyu*, 176; in Yiddish, *Stempenyu*, in *Di Yidishe folksbibliothek*, 1:80.

24. Sholem Aleichem, *Stempenyu*, 176–77; in Yiddish, *Stempenyu*, in *Di Yidishe folksbibliothek*, 1:81.

25. This untranslated line appears in the Yiddish, Sholem Aleichem, *Stempenyu*, in *Di Yidishe folksbibliothek*, 1:83.

26. Abrahams, *Jewish Life in the Middle Ages*, 170.

27. Sholem Aleichem, *Tevye the Dairyman*, 60; in Yiddish, Sholem Aleichem, *Complete Tevye*, 106.

28. Sholem Aleichem, *Tevye the Dairyman*, 56; Sholem Aleichem, *Complete Tevye*, 100.

29. Kaplan, *Making of the Jewish Middle Class*, 109.

30. Sholem Aleichem, *Tevye the Dairyman*, 55–56.

31. Ibid., 105.

32. Katz, *Tradition and Crisis*, 126.

33. Grace Paley, "Goodbye and Good Luck," in *The Collected Stories* (New York: Farrar, Straus and Giroux, 1995). "Goodbye and Good Luck" was not, according to Paley, the first story she wrote as an adult (that was "The Contest"), but it was the first story accepted for publication, in 1956, in *Accent: A Quarterly* (Urbana, IL). See "Chronology," in *Conversations with Grace Paley*, ed. Gerhard Bach and Blaine Hall (Jackson: University Press of Mississippi, 1997), xvii.

34. Levinson, *Exiles on Main Street*, 144.

35. Paley, "Two Ears, Three Lucks," in *The Collected Stories*, x.

36. Ilya Kaminsky and Katherine Towler, "An Interview with Poet and Fiction Writer Grace Paley," *Poets & Writers*, March 17, 2008, http://www.pw.org/content/interview_poet_and_fiction_writer_grace_paley?article_page=2.

37. Harvey Swados, "Good and Short," *Hudson Review* 12, no. 3 (1959): 458.

38. As Riv-Ellen Prell argues, "Gender has served to symbolize Jews' relationship to nation, family, and work because both Americanization and mobility place specific yet different demands on men and women." *Fighting to Become Americans*, 4.

39. See, for instance, the feminist analysis of Jacqueline Taylor, *Grace Paley: Illuminating the Dark Lives* (Austin: University of Texas Press, 1990).

40. Leonard Michaels and Grace Paley, "Conversation with Grace Paley," *Threepenny Review* 3 (1980): 6.

41. Paley, "Goodbye and Good Luck," 1.

42. Ibid., 6.

43. Ibid.

44. Ibid., 8.

45. Ibid., 10.

46. Ibid.

47. Ibid., 13.

48. Ibid., 6, 8–9.

49. Bakhtin refers to this feature of narrative prose as "the problem of the double-voice, internally dialogized voice," writing that "for the novelist working in prose, the object is always entangled in someone else's discourse about it, it is already present with qualifications, an object of dispute that is conceptualized and evaluated variously, inseparable from the heteroglot social apperception of it." *Dialogic Imagination*, 330.

50. Viktor Shklovskii, *Theory of Prose*, trans. Benjamin Sher (Normal, IL: Dalkey Archive Press, 1990), 190.

51. Bloom, *Anxiety of Influence*.

52. Sandra Gilbert and Susan Gubar, *The Madwoman in the Attic: The Woman Writer and the Nineteenth-Century Literary Imagination* (New Haven, CT: Yale University Press, 1979), 45–92.

53. As Kronfeld writes, the "uncle-nephew" model of literary transmission, "while still a productive conceptual paradigm, needs to be revised to allow for a less mechanistic—and nonsexist—approach to the literary system. Instead, we may want to talk about hierarchies of context-dependent specific types and degrees of centrality or marginality, and about aunts and nieces and a variety of other family members." Chana Kronfeld, *On the Margins of Modernism: Decentering Literary Dynamics* (Berkeley: University of California Press, 1996), 34.

54. Michael Baxandall, *Patterns of Intention: On the Historical Explanation of Pictures* (New Haven, CT: Yale University Press), 58–59.

55. Eve Kosofsky Sedgwick, *Tendencies* (Durham, NC: Duke University Press, 1994), 41.

56. See my discussion of Molodowsky's *Women Songs* as a literary attempt to construct a matrilineage in Chapter 3.

57. For a critical bilingual (Yiddish-Hebrew) edition, see *Glikl: Zikhronot, 1691–1719*, ed. and trans. Chava Turniansky (Jerusalem: Zalman Shazar, 2006). For a discussion of the relationship between Bertha Pappenheim and her ancestor, see Boyarin, *Unheroic Conduct*, 346–52.

58. Sander L. Gilman, "Sigmund Freud and the Sexologists: A Second Reading," in *Reading Freud's Reading*, ed. Sander L. Gilman, Jutta Birmele, and Jay Geller (New York: New York University Press, 1995), 56.

59. Freud struggled with his own diagonal heritage, writing about a traumatic childhood experience involving his uncle Josef Freud and recounting a significant dream featuring this uncle. In a footnote to the interpretation of this dream, Freud nevertheless writes of Josef, "I have known five of my uncles and I have loved and honored one of them." Freud, *Interpretation of Dreams*, trans. James Strachey (New York: Basic Books, 2010), 129n1.

60. See Peter J. Swales, "Freud, Minna Bernays, and the Conquest of Rome: New Light on the Origins of Psychoanalysis," *New American Review* 1 (Spring–Summer 1982): 1–23.

61. Kadya Molodovsky, "Invitation" [Onbot], trans. Irving Feldman, in *The Penguin Book of Modern Yiddish Poetry*, ed. Irving Howe, Ruth R. Wisse, and Khone Shmeruk (New York: Penguin, 1987), 326–27.

62. Paley, "Goodbye and Good Luck," 3, 7.

63. Hana Wirth-Nesher, *Call It English: The Languages of Jewish American Literature* (Princeton, NJ: Princeton University Press, 2006), 9.

64. Leonard Q. Ross [Leo Rosten], *The Education of H*Y*M*A*N K*A*P*L*A*N* (New York: Harcourt Brace, 1937); Henry Roth, *Call It Sleep* (New York: Picador, 2005).

65. Paley, "Goodbye and Good Luck," 8, 13.

66. Ibid., 9–10.

67. Joan Lidoff, "Clearing Her Throat: An Interview with Grace Paley (1981), in Bach and Hall, *Conversations with Grace Paley*, 73.

68. Martha Satz, "Looking at Disparities: An Interview with Grace Paley (1986), in Bach and Hall, *Conversations with Grace Paley*, 194–95.

69. Grace Paley, "Other Mothers," *Feminist Studies* 4, no. 2 (1978): 168.

70. Ibid.

71. Ibid., 166.

72. Gilbert and Gubar, *Madwoman in the Attic*, 51.

73. Paley, "Two Ears," x–xi.

74. The one essay in the 2003 *Queer Theory and the Jewish Question* that discusses family and kinship structures does so in the service of juxtaposing the Victorian bourgeois family with the Jewish pseudo-family of Fagin's gang in *Oliver Twist*: The Jew's "family," writes David A. H. Hirsch, "is composed of the most radicalized of individuals—children separated from their birth families—trained as thieves and prostitutes by Fagin . . . a perverse parody of the middle-class capitalist." See David A. H. Hirsh, "Dickens' Queer 'Jew' and Anglo-Christian Identity Politics: The Contradictions of Victorian Family Values," in *Queer Theory and the Jewish Question*, ed. Daniel Boyarin, Daniel Itzkovitz, and Ann Pellegrini (New York: Columbia University Press, 2003), 316.

75. Sigmund Freud, *Totem and Taboo: Resemblances between the Psychic Life of Savages and Neurotics*, trans. A. A. Brill (New York: Vintage, 1946), 17–24.

Chapter 6

1. Maimon, *Autobiography*, 33.

2. Cohen, *"One Beloved, the Other Hated,"* 28.

3. Stampfer, *Families, Rabbis and Education*, 43.

4. Kotik, *Journey to a Nineteenth-Century Shtetl*, 257–58.

5. Wengeroff, *Memoirs*, 2:36–37.

6. Isaac Euchel, "Igrot meshulam ben Oriah ha'ashtemu'i," ed. I. Friedlander, *Prakim besatira ha'ivrit beshalhei hame'ah ha18th begermaniya* [Chapters in the Hebrew satire in late-eighteenth-century Germany] (Tel Aviv, 1979), 54–55; cited in Cohen and Feiner, *Voice of a Hebrew Maiden*, 23.

7. Lilienblum (letter of 29 Elul 1870), *Ketuvim*, 3–4; quoted in Parush, *Reading Jewish Women*, 235–36.

8. Parush, *Reading Jewish Women*, 58.

9. Parush discusses "the benefits of marginality" in ibid., 62–70.

10. Gordon, *Tip of the Yud*, 114.

11. Hillel, in Gordon, *Tip of the Yud*,133, 136; Fabi and Bat-Shua, in Gordon, *Tip of the Yud*, 166.

12. Gordon, *Tip of the Yud*, 113.

13. Cohen, *"One Beloved, the Other Hated,"* 28.

14. Sholem Yankev Abramovitsh, *In Those Days* [Bayamim ha-hem], in *Complete Works of Mendele Mokher Seforim*, ed. Jacob Fichman (Tel Aviv: Dvir, 1958), 259.

15. Mintz, *"Banished from Their Father's Table,"* 90.

16. Y. Y. Trunk, *Poland: Memories and Scenes* [Poyln: Zikhroynes un bilder], trans. Ezra Fleischer (Merhavia, Israel: Sifriyat Poalim, 1962), 151; quoted in Parush, *Reading Jewish Women*, 75.

17. Shmuel Feiner, "Haskalah Attitudes toward Women," in *Jewish Women: A Comprehensive Historical Encyclopedia* (Jewish Women's Archive, 2009), http://jwa.org/encyclopedia/article/haskalah-attitudes-toward-women.

18. For more on Baron's acquisition of a Hebrew education in her father's sexually segregated study hall and the role it played in shaping her literary production, see my earlier study, *A Marriage Made in Heaven: The Sexual Politics of Hebrew and Yiddish* (Berkeley: University of California Press, 1997), 67–101.

19. Dvora Baron, "Genizah," in *The First Half: Dvora Baron, Her Life and Work (1902–1921)* [Ha-Mahatsit ha-rishonah: Devorah Baron -hayyeha vi-yetsiratah], by Nurit Govrin (Jerusalem: Mosad Bialik, 1988), 420.

20. Amalia Kahana-Carmon, "Song of the Bats in Flight," in *Gender and Text in Modern Hebrew and Yiddish Literature*, ed. Naomi B. Sokoloff, Anne Lapidus Lerner, and Anita Norich (New York: Jewish Theological Seminary Press, 1992), 237. Originally published as "Shirat ha-atalefim be-me'ofam," *Moznayim* 64 (1989): 3–7.

21. See Ricky Shapira-Rosenberg, *Excluded, for God's Sake: Gender Segregation in Public Space in Israel*, trans. Shaul Vardi (Jerusalem: Israel Religious Action Center, 2010), http://www.irac.org/userfiles/Excluded,%20For%20God's%20Sake%20-%20Report%20on%20Gender%20Segregation%20in%20the%20Public%20Sphere%20in%20Israel(1).pdf.; and Elana Maryles Sztokman, *The War on Women in Israel: How Religious Radicalism Is Smothering the Voice of a Nation* (Naperville, IL: Sourcebooks, 2014).

22. For a discussion of the ways that Yiddish theater in early twentieth-century New York fulfilled the role of the synagogue while "easing the transition for immigrants from a religious to a secular life," see Most, *Theatrical Liberalism*, 21–22. The same undoubtedly holds true for Jewish theater in other languages and locations.

23. On this notion of fiction as a counterimage, see Iser, *Fictive and the Imaginary*, 78.

24. According to Howard Eilberg-Schwartz, the exclusion of women from participation in religious ritual and symbolism might be understood precisely as an attempt to forestall the relationship that might "naturally" develop between female mortals and a "bachelor" masculine deity; Israelite monotheism, wedded with heteronormativity, had to exclude women from religious life insofar as it otherwise opened the door much wider for such relations than the ones that connected the male collective and its male deity. Howard Eilberg-Schwartz, *God's Phallus: And Other Problems for Men and Monotheism* (Boston: Beacon Press, 1995).

25. Pardes, *Agnon's Moonstruck Lovers*.

26. Safran, *Wandering Soul*, 214.

27. Most Jewish sources agree that there is no prohibition against women (or menstruants) touching the Torah. A major exception to this rule is the medieval

Beraita de-Nidah. For a critical edition, see Evyatar Marienberg, *La Baraita de-Niddah: Un texte juif pseudo-talmudique sur les lois religieuses relatives à la menstruation* [*The Baraita de-Niddah*: A pseudo-Talmudic Jewish text about the religious laws concerning menstruation] (Turnhout, Belgium: Brepols Press, 2012).

28. Michel Foucault, *History of Sexuality*, vol. 1, *An Introduction*, trans. Robert Hurley (New York: Random House, 1980), 23.

29. See Biale, *Eros and the Jews*, 161 passim; Boyarin, *Unheroic Conduct*, xvii–xviii passim; Paula Hyman, *Gender and Assimilation in Modern Jewish History* (Seattle: University of Washington Press, 1995), 26–27 passim.

30. For an analysis and critique of "voluntary" sex segregation, see David S. Cohen, "Keeping Men 'Men' and Women Down: Sex Segregation, Anti-essentialism, and Masculinity," *Harvard Journal of Law and Gender* 33 (2010): 509–53.

31. Foucault, *History of Sexuality*, 1:23.

32. Naomi Seidman, "On the Margins and Other Impossible Spaces," *Journal of Jewish Identities* 7, no. 1 (January 2014): 18–19.

33. Walter Benjamin, "Some Reflections on Kafka," in *Illuminations*, ed. Hannah Arendt, trans. Harry Zohn (New York: Schocken, 1978), 143–44.

34. Franz Kafka, "The Animal in the Synagogue" [Das Tier in der Synagoge], in *Parabolen and Paradoxe*, ed. Nahum Glatzer, trans. Ernst Kaiser and Eithne Wilkins (1946; repr., New York: Schocken, 1961), 51.

35. Ibid., 50–51.

36. S. Y. Agnon, "The Tale of the Scribe," in *Twenty-One Stories*, ed. Nahum Glatzer (New York: Schocken, 1970), 15–16.

37. Ibid., 12–13.

38. Ibid., 143.

39. Ibid. While there is no precise image that conforms to this one, doves or turtledoves, as a symbol for love (because legend has it that they mate for life), are mentioned numerous times in the Song of Songs, including to describe the beloved woman's eyes behind her veil in 4:1; as in this passage, the object ostensibly intended to separate women from the male gaze (the veil, the lattice of the women's section) functions instead as an ornamental frame for the beautiful image.

40. As Pardes points out throughout her exploration of Agnon's use of the Song of Songs, the question of what constitutes the religious and what the secular mobilization of the text is not so easily settled. Zionist writers took an ostensibly natural reading of the Song of Songs as warrant for a nationalist image of the Land of Israel in which Jews were redeemed in quasi-religious fashion from their diasporic distance from the land and nature. See Pardes, *Agnon's Moonstruck Lovers*, 30–65.

41. Agnon, "Tale of the Scribe," 23. The Hebrew original appears in *Elu ve-elu* [These and these] (Jerusalem: Schocken, 1966), 142.

42. Agnon, "Tale of the Scribe," 23–24. The Hebrew original appears in *Elu ve-elu*, 143.

43. See Pardes, *Agnon's Moonlit Lovers*.

44. Agnon, "Tale of the Scribe," 24.

45. Ibid., 25.

46. For earlier discussions of these ideas, see Naomi Seidman, "The Erotics of Sexual Segregation," in *The Passionate Torah: Sex and Judaism*, ed. Danya Ruttenberg (New York: New York University Press, 2009), 107–15; and "Love in the Women's Section," in *Keep Your Wives Away from Them: Orthodox Women, Unorthodox Desires, An Anthology*, ed. Miryam Kabakov (Berkeley: North Atlantic Press, 2010), 30–35.

47. Joseph Perl, *Revealer of Secrets: The First Hebrew Novel*, trans. Dov Taylor (New York: Westview Press, 1997), 21.

48. Ibid., 26–27. For the Hebrew, see Joseph Perl, *Megaleh temirin: Keshmo ken hu* [Revealer of secrets: As it is called, so is it] (Lemberg [Lviv], Ukraine: Poremba Press, 1864), 8.

49. Footnote 5 of *Megaleh Temirin* (which appears on page 6 of the Hebrew and page 26 of the Dov Taylor translation) cites *Selected Writings of Rabbi Nahman* [Kitzur likutei ha-mora'n] (Vilna: M. Alter, 1800), 43b.

50. On Hasidic eroticism, see Biale, *Eros and the Jews*, 121–48.

51. For an earlier version of this analysis, see Naomi Seidman, "Staging Tradition: Piety and Scandal in *God of Vengeance*," in *Sholem Asch Reconsidered*, ed. Nanette Stahl (New Haven, CT: Beineke Rare Book and Manuscript Library, 2004), 51–62.

52. Rudolph Schildkraut, as cited in Benjamin Weiner, "Judging Vengeance: How the Cops, the Courts, and a Reform Rabbi Tried to Keep a Yiddish Play off the English Stage," *Pakn-Treger* 23 (1996): 15.

53. Sholem Asch, "God of Vengeance," in *Three Great Jewish Plays*, ed. Joseph Landis (New York: Applause Press, 1986), 84.

54. According to Weiner, the judge said that Jews resented the depiction of a Torah scroll, "which is as important to them as the Host to members of the Catholic Church." "Judging Vengeance," 15.

55. For earlier historical evidence of such premarital sex play, see Biale on "bundling" in *Eros and the Jews*, 71.

56. Asch, *God of Vengeance*, 98–99.

57. For instance, Warren Hoffman, "Reel Ritual: Religion, Memory, and Spectatorship in Yiddish Silent Films" (unpublished paper, 2000).

58. For an extended discussion of this topic, see Naomi Seidman, "Gender and the Disintegration of the Shtetl in Modern Hebrew and Yiddish Literature," in *The Shtetl: New Evaluations*, ed. Steven T. Katz (New York: New York University Press, 2007), 193–210.

59. See Goldstein, *Enforced Marginalities*.

60. Miron, *Image of the Shtetl*, 3.

61. Lamentations Rabbah 3:21, in David Stern, *Parables in Midrash: Narrative and Exegesis in Rabbinic Literature* (Cambridge, MA: Harvard University Press, 1991), 57. I have slightly revised Stern's translation to render more evident its intertextual connections with Baron's story.

62. Dvora Baron, "Fedka," in *The First Day and Other Stories*, ed. Chana Kron-

feld and Naomi Seidman, trans. Naomi Seidman with Chana Kronfeld (Berkeley: University of California Press, 2001), 186.

63. Stern, *Parables in Midrash*, 62.

64. Pepi Littman (1874–1930) performed to rapturous crowds in Hasidic drag in the late nineteenth and early twentieth centuries in vaudeville shows traveling around Eastern Europe and was characterized as "a Jewish *chanteuse* in Hasidic trousers." See Zalmen Zylbercweig, *Lexicon of the Yiddish Theater* (New York: Elisheva Press, 1931), 3:1055.

65. Chris Straayer, "Redressing the 'Natural': The Temporary Transvestite Film," in *Film Genre Reader II*, ed. Barry Keith Grant (Austin: University of Texas Press, 1995), 403.

66. Hoffman, *Passing Game*, 70.

67. See J. Hoberman, *Bridge of Light: Yiddish Film between Two Worlds* (New York: Museum of Modern Art and Schocken, 1991), 238.

68. Erving Goffman, *The Presentation of Self in Everyday Life* (New York: Doubleday, 1959). As Goffman writes, "There seems to be no society in which members of the two sexes, however closely related, do not sustain some appearances before each other" (130).

69. Biale, *Eros and the Jews*, 224.

70. Nancy Berkowitz Bate, "Judaism, Genius, or Gender: Women in the Fiction of Isaac Bashevis Singer," in *Critical Essays on Isaac Bashevis Singer*, ed. Grace Farrell (New York: G. K. Hall, 1996), 212.

71. Marjorie Garber, *Vested Interests: Cross-Dressing and Cultural Anxiety* (New York: Routledge Press, 1992), 79.

72. Ibid., 80.

73. Ibid., 227.

74. Boyarin, *Unheroic Conduct*, 143.

75. Garber, *Vested Interests*, 78.

76. Isaac Bashevis Singer, "Yentl the Yeshiva Boy," trans. Marion Magid and Elizabeth Pollett, in *The Collected Stories* (New York: Farrar, Straus and Giroux, 1983), 150. The Yiddish story "Yentl der Yeshiva Bokher" appeared in *Di goldene keyt* 46 (1963): 92.

77. Eve Kosofsky Sedgwick, *Epistemology of the Closet* (Berkeley: University of California Press, 1990), 1–2.

78. James D. Steakley, *The Homosexual Emancipation Movement in Germany* (New York: Arno Press, 1975), 54.

79. Sedgwick, *Epistemology of the Closet*, 87.

80. Ibid., 90.

81. Singer, "Yentl the Yeshiva Boy," 165. In the Yiddish, 106. The Yiddish is more radical than the English translation in referring to "Anshel" through the male pronoun.

82. Coontz, *Marriage*, 184.

Afterword

1. Quoted in Sholem Aleichem, dedication to *Stempenyu*, v.

2. David Hollinger, *Science, Jews, and Secular Culture: Studies in Mid-Twentieth-Century American Intellectual History* (Princeton, NJ: Princeton University Press, 1996), 13.

3. Malamud, *Talking Horse*, 81.

4. For more on these incidents, see Shapira-Rosenberg, *Excluded, for God's Sake*, as well as Sztokman, *War on Women in Israel*.

5. Debra Kaufman, "Engendering Orthodoxy: Newly Orthodox Women and Hasidism," in *New World Hasidism: Ethnographic Studies of Hasidic Jews in America*, ed. Janet S. Belcove-Shlain (Albany: SUNY Press, 1995), 151.

6. Ibid., 152.

7. The example for the political production of sexual "orientation" that Lisa Maria Hogeland provides is Ti-Grace Atkinson's turn to lesbianism in 1970, which Hogeland describes as a "specifically political rather than sexual lesbianism." See Hogeland, *Feminism and Its Fictions: The Consciousness-Raising Novel and the Women's Liberation Movement*" (Philadelphia: University of Pennsylvania Press, 1998), 67. She quotes Atkinson: "It is this commitment, by choice, full-time, of one woman to others of her class, that is called lesbianism. It is this commitment, against any and all personal considerations, if necessary, that constitutes the political significance of lesbianism." Ti-Grace Atkinson, "Lesbianism and Feminism: Justice for Women as 'Unnatural,'" in *Amazon Odyssey*, by Ti-Grace Atkinson (New York: Putnam, 1974), 132.

8. Halper, "Coming out of the Hasidic Closet," 207.

9. Jeffrey Shandler defines this phenomenon as the production by artists, performers, and writers, working mostly independently of one another and in a range of genres, on "works that juxtapose queerness and Yiddish in some way and do so as a means of opposing some cultural status quo." See Jeffrey Shandler, "Queer Yiddishkeit: Practice and Theory," in *Shofar: An Interdisciplinary Journal of Jewish Studies* 25, no. 1 (Fall 2006): 90–113, quote on 92.

10. Jeffrey Shandler, "Notes on Klez/Camp," *Davka* 1, no. 3 (Winter 1997): 29–31.

11. Shandler, "Queer Yiddishkeit," 111.

12. Ibid., 112.

13. I borrow Eve Kosofsky Sedgwick's distinction between a view of homosexuality as "an issue of active importance primarily for a small, distinct, relatively fixed homosexual minority" in contrast to the "universalizing view" that sees the homo/heterosexual binary "as an issue of continuing, determinative importance in the lives of people across the spectrum of sexualities." Sedgwick, *Epistemology of the Closet*, 1.

14. Sedgwick contrasts "minoritarian" instead with "universalizing," which goes too far for what I mean here.

15. Gershon David Hundert, *Jews in Poland-Lithuania in the Eighteenth Century: A Genealogy of Modernity* (Berkeley: University of California Press, 2004), 22.

16. Benjamin Harshav, *The Meaning of Yiddish* (Stanford, CA: Stanford University Press, 1999), 21–22.

17. Alisa Solomon, *Redressing the Canon: Essays on Theater and Gender* (London: Routledge, 1997), 119. Solomon is referring to the crest of the "wave of renewed interest in Yiddish language and culture."

18. Lilienblum, "Words of Song," 182.

19. Pinsker, *Literary Passports*, 162.

20. Freud, *Sexuality and the Psychology of Love*, 59.

21. Ibid., 60–61.

22. Ibid., 49.

23. Ibid., 60–61.

24. Peretz, *Monish* (Balade), 155.

25. Lilienblum, "Words of Song," 182–83.

26. Zaban, *Choicest Meal*, 31–58.

27. Lenny Bruce, *The Essential Lenny Bruce*, ed. John Cohen (New York: Random House, 1967), 32–33.

28. For more on this, see Naomi Seidman, "Talking Sex: The Distinctive Speech of Modern Jews," in "Spoken Word, Written Word: Rethinking the Representation of Speech in Literature," ed. Vered Karti Shemtov, Anat Weisman, and Amir Eshel, special issue, *Dibur Literary Journal* 1 (2015), http://arcade.stanford.edu/dibur_issue/spoken-word-written-word-rethinking-representation-speech-literature-0.

29. One example discussed in this book is the title of Lilienblum's *Sins of Youth*, which uses a Hebrew term that obscures the sin involved—masturbation. Another example is *mikreh laylah* (nighttime incident), a rabbinic term for a nocturnal emission.

30. Lambert, *Unclean Lips*, 141–74 passim. See also my review of *Unclean Lips*, "Jews Talking Dirty," *Chronicle of Higher Education: Review* 60, no. 29 (March 31, 2014), B16.

31. Ibid., 75.

32. Ibid., 69.

33. See, for instance, the analysis of Freud's "universalizing" translation of Jewish masculine anxieties about circumcision into (alleged) female mourning about castration in Jay Geller, "The Godfather of Psychoanalysis: Circumcision, Antisemitism, Homosexuality, and Freud's 'Fighting Jew,'" *Journal of the American Academy of Religion* 67, no. 2 (1999): 355–85.

Index

STANFORD STUDIES IN JEWISH HISTORY AND CULTURE

Edited by David Biale and Sarah Abrevaya Stein

This series features novel approaches to examining the Jewish past in the form of innovative work that brings the field into productive dialogue with the newest scholarly concepts and methods. Open to a range of disiplinary and interdisciplinary approaches from history to cultural studies, this series publishes exceptional scholarship balanced by an accessible tone that illustrates histories of difference and addresses issues of current urgency. Books in this list push the boundaries of Jewish Studies and speak compellingly to a wide audience of scholars and students.

Ivan Jablonka, *A History of the Grandparents I Never Had*
2016

For a complete listing of titles in this series, visit the Stanford University Press website, www.sup.org.